TRANSITIONAL JUSTICE AND EDUCATION

This volume is the seventh in the *Advancing Transitional Justice Series*, a joint project of the International Center for Transitional Justice and the Social Science Research Council. Other volumes include:

Clara Ramírez-Barat, ed., *Transitional Justice, Culture, and Society: Beyond Outreach*

Roger Duthie, ed., *Transitional Justice and Displacement*

Ana Cutter Patel, Pablo de Greiff, and Lars Waldorf, eds., *Disarming the Past: Transitional Justice and Ex-combatants*

Pablo de Greiff and Roger Duthie, eds., *Transitional Justice and Development: Making Connections*

Alexander Mayer-Rieckh and Pablo de Greiff, eds., *Justice as Prevention: Vetting Public Employees in Transitional Societies*

Ruth Rubio-Marín, ed., *What Happened to the Women? Gender and Reparations for Human Rights Violations*

ADVANCING TRANSITIONAL JUSTICE SERIES

TRANSITIONAL JUSTICE AND EDUCATION: LEARNING PEACE

EDITED BY CLARA RAMÍREZ-BARAT AND ROGER DUTHIE
INTERNATIONAL CENTER FOR TRANSITIONAL JUSTICE
UNICEF

SOCIAL SCIENCE RESEARCH COUNCIL · NEW YORK · 2017

INTERNATIONAL CENTER FOR TRANSITIONAL JUSTICE

The International Center for Transitional Justice (ICTJ) assists societies confronting massive human rights abuses to promote accountability, pursue truth, provide reparations, and build trustworthy institutions. Committed to the vindication of victims' rights and the promotion of gender justice, we provide expert technical advice, policy analysis, and comparative research on transitional justice approaches, including criminal prosecutions, reparations initiatives, truth seeking and memory, and institutional reform. For more information, visit www.ictj.org.

UNICEF AND LEARNING FOR PEACE

UNICEF is a leading humanitarian and development agency working globally for the rights and well-being of every child. Child rights begin with safe shelter, nutrition, and protection from disaster and conflict, and they traverse the life cycle: prenatal care for healthy births, clean water and sanitation, health care, and education. Learning for Peace is a four-year partnership between UNICEF, the Government of the Netherlands, the national governments of fourteen participating countries, and other key supporters. It is an innovative, cross-sectoral program focusing on education and peacebuilding. The goal of the program is to strengthen resilience, social cohesion, and human security in conflict-affected contexts, including countries at risk of—or experiencing and recovering from—conflict. For more information, visit learningforpeace.unicef.org.

SOCIAL SCIENCE RESEARCH COUNCIL

The Social Science Research Council is an independent, international, nonprofit organization founded in 1923. Governed by a board of directors, it fosters innovative research, nurtures new generations of social scientists, deepens how inquiry is practiced within and across disciplines, and mobilizes necessary knowledge on important public issues.

The views expressed by the contributors to this volume are their own, and do not necessarily reflect the views of UNICEF or the International Center for Transitional Justice.

Published by the Social Science Research Council

Printed in the United States of America

Series design by Julie Fry

Cover and typesetting by Michael Baron Shaw

Cover photograph by Roger Lemoyne: *Young Afghan Girl Attends a Community UNICEF-Supported School*, Nangarhar, Afghanistan, April 24, 2008

Library of Congress Cataloging-in-Publication Data

Names: Ramirez-Barat, Clara, editor. | Duthie, Roger, editor.
Title: Transitional justice and education : learning peace / edited by Clara Ramirez-Barat and Roger Duthie, International Center for Transitional Justice, United Nations Children's Fund.
Description: New York : Social Science Research Council, 2017. | Series: Advancing transitional justice series ; 7 | Includes bibliographical references.
Identifiers: LCCN 2016020130| ISBN 9780911400038 (pbk. : alk. paper) | ISBN 0911400036 (pbk. : alk. paper)
Subjects: LCSH: Transitional justice. | Education--Political aspects--Developing countries. | Democracy and education--Developing countries. | Developing countries--Politics and government.
Classification: LCC JC571 .T69934 2017 | DDC 370.11/5091724--dc23
LC record available at https://lccn.loc.gov/2016020130

CONTENTS

INTRODUCTION

Clara Ramírez-Barat and Roger Duthie

In the past two decades, researchers, policymakers, and practitioners working in the fields of education, child protection, and peacebuilding have paid increasing attention to the relationship between education and conflict. They have considered this relationship in two directions: first, the impact of conflict on education, and, second, the ways in which education can both trigger conflict and contribute to establishing peace.[1] Most work on education reconstruction after periods of conflict and authoritarianism has primarily adopted a development or peacebuilding perspective; this is understandable, given the clear role education can play in promoting socioeconomic development and preventing a return to armed violence.

Often missing from this analysis, however, is a connection to the specific legacies of repressive policies and human rights violations in the political and social culture of a country—legacies that are particularly relevant where education has been used to divide and discriminate against people and serve ideological purposes, or where conflict has resulted in significant loss of education opportunities for children and youth. From this perspective, the contribution education can make to peace depends not only on the physical reconstruction of schools, the reincorporation of young people into the education system, and the promotion of universal values of tolerance and social cohesion through school curricula, but also on the sensitivity of reforms and programs to the legacies of past injustices in both the education sector and the public culture of a country.

Transitional justice, understood as a set of judicial and nonjudicial measures to promote accountability and redress for massive violations of human rights, is increasingly recognized as fundamental to peacebuilding efforts.[2] Combined with other sets of policies, and to the extent that it provides recognition to victims of human rights abuses and helps restore civic trust in state institutions and among citizens, the pursuit of transitional justice can strengthen the democratic rule of law and prevent the recurrence of violations.[3] In contrast, societies that choose to leave unaddressed past human rights abuses or other forms of severe trauma—as well as their root causes and consequent grievances—risk the sustainability of their efforts of socioeconomic reconstruction and their transition to a more democratic or peaceful future.

In addition to being valuable for its own sake and not only for its instrumental benefits, education has at least two important goals in coming to terms with an abusive past. As in any society, it should develop children's abilities and skills for participating in a country's productive and sociopolitical realms. But, as Susana Frisancho and Félix Reátegui state, education in a post-conflict society is also "charged with the task of enhancing the capacity of citizens, especially— but not only—adolescents and children, to think critically about the present and the past, so they can foresee and construct a better future."[4] While some in both the fields of education and transitional justice have called attention to the need for a more systematic consideration of the relationship between the two,[5] to date neither education reform nor the teaching of the recent past has been treated with the seriousness it deserves within the scope of transitional justice.

Given a shared interest in responding to this knowledge gap, in 2013 the International Center for Transitional Justice (ICTJ) and the United Nations Children's Fund (UNICEF) collaborated on a research project to help articulate the links between transitional justice and education in peacebuilding. Through this research, we wanted to gain a better understanding of the role education can play in post-conflict situations, specifically as part of a broad response to the legacies of human rights abuses. We also had a practical interest: we hoped the research would advance proposals for exploring how approaching education from a transitional justice perspective might contribute to peacebuilding.

The research project sought to answer two main questions. First, how can transitional justice shape the reform of education systems and facilitate the reintegration of children and youth into those systems as a means of contributing to building peace? And, second, how can education expand its outreach agenda to engage younger generations and help transform a culture of impunity into one of human rights and democracy? An important part of approaching these questions was to look for ways in which transitional justice and education could reinforce each other in peacebuilding contexts; but we also wanted to consider the tensions, challenges, and obstacles possibly entailed by any attempt to coordinate education initiatives and transitional justice processes and goals. Given the importance in any society of an institution such as the education system and the fundamental transformative potential of education itself, resistance to changing the status quo for what new generations learn is to be expected, and it must be taken into account in developing realistic strategies to ensure, even if gradually, a positive contribution by education to the long-term process of building more democratic and peaceful societies.

The research was organized into three thematic clusters that involved the commissioning of seventeen papers representing a wide variety of experiences and places. The authors of the papers in the first cluster, on post-conflict education reconstruction and transitional justice, looked at the ways in which different countries have used transitional justice as a framework to promote reforms in the education system, including in the areas of curriculum, school governance and culture, and teacher training, among others. The authors working in the second cluster, on reparations and education, examined the opportunities for and challenges to designing and implementing reparation programs that provide education benefits to victims of human rights violations, including the specific function of such benefits in rehabilitation and reintegration processes. Finally, studies in the third cluster, on outreach, education, and sustainability, considered how education forums and activities can be used to engage children and youth in transitional justice, and how community or locally based outreach activities and informal education initiatives can play a role in addressing the past.

The development of the seventeen studies involved the organization of two authors' meetings, one in Bogotá, Colombia, in February 2014, and the second in New York in April 2014, at which the direction of the research was discussed and refined and progress on it was reported. Finally, in October 2014, a two-day workshop was organized in New York in which the authors discussed their findings with a group of experts in education, transitional justice, child protection, and peacebuilding. Drawing on these studies and the discussions held in Bogotá and New York, ICTJ published in September 2015 a report entitled *Education and Transitional Justice: Opportunities and Challenges for Peacebuilding*, presenting the main findings and policy recommendations of the project.[6] A selection of the commissioned papers is included in this edited volume, while two thematic papers are available online on the ICTJ website.[7]

CONFLICT, EDUCATION, AND PEACEBUILDING: A TRANSITIONAL JUSTICE APPROACH

As a social institution, education is fundamental to the functioning of any society. Education transmits established knowledge and shared culture and can play an important role in forming productive and politically engaged citizens and promoting social cohesion.[8] In the aftermath of conflict, efforts to rebuild an education system can synchronize with the aims of peacebuilding and prevention of recurrence by making younger generations sensitive to the values, attitudes, and skills necessary for peace and tolerance. What, then, does a transitional justice approach bring to the relationship between education and peacebuilding?

During violent conflict and repression, human rights violations are often linked to the provision of education. Rather than representing merely the indirect impact of conflict, these violations are often part of an intentional and systematic attempt to deprive children and youth of schooling and to manipulate and distort teachers and textbooks to legitimize repression and reproduce patterns of violence.[9] The closing and destruction of schools, for example, has been often been used "as a weapon of war to erode civilian support processes and punish insurgents in ways that will compromise irremediably the future of their families and ethnic groups"[10] or "as a weapon of cultural repression of minorities, denying them access to education, or using education to suppress their language, traditions, art forms, religious practices and cultural values."[11] In Peru, the overcrowding of and economic pressure on the education system in the second half of the twentieth century severely diminished the quality of education, especially in the rural and poorest areas, contributing to the prevalence of rote learning and authoritarian teaching methods. As Shining Path's presence in the country gained hold, schools became fundamental to the spread of the subversive group's ideology. The political mobilization of teachers through their unions made them strong supporters of the group but, for the same reason, also key targets of the state's repression.[12]

Beyond the direct impact of conflict on education, repressive political systems have often used education policies to shape or reinforce social divisions, intolerance, and inequality, or to eliminate opportunities for development of a critical citizenship. In South Africa, for example, for decades after the Bantu Education Act passed in 1954, education was used as a means of preserving the apartheid system, not only through provision of better education to white students, but also through the use of curricula to support the ideology of white supremacy and legitimize the unjust status quo. In Chile, the military regime directly affected both the functioning of the education system (and, therefore, the experiences of students, teachers, and parents) and its general social role. Through a series of measures that led to the suppression of the competences of the Ministry of Education and the dismantling of the public education system, the dictatorship put an end to citizen participation.[13]

Because of the important social role played by education, legacies of conflict and repression in the education system can have significant and long-lasting impacts on individuals and societies. The effects on individuals can be psychological, importantly related to developing capacities such as empowerment and resilience; economic, including reduced employment opportunities; and political, considering that "many children leave school with a profound distrust of the institutions of the state in which they live." Furthermore, "because of the poor quality of the education they have received, they are particularly susceptible to the machinations of ethnic mobilizers."[14] Abuses linked to education can also have important social repercussions: since attacks on schools and manipulation of education for political purposes affect not only individuals but also the communities and societies in which they live, legacies of abuse related to the development of a culture of violence and impunity can have long-term impacts on social patterns of transmission of memory. As Gail Weldon has argued, the legacies of conflict not only influence the way in which the new social order is conceived but also the ways in which "traumatic knowledge is passed on from one generation to the next,"[15] thereby potentially fostering recurring cycles of hatred and violence.

Once the conflict or repression comes to an end, however, education can be an important vehicle for remembering the past, facilitating the transmission of memory, and promoting peace and democracy. Because of its formative potential, it can help shape new norms, mediate between contending narratives of the past, and nurture a culture of democratic citizenship across generations. Fundamental in this respect is that

> education as a sector is also uniquely positioned to make a substantive contribution to the repair, reconstruction, and redress of inequalities, divisions, and, in the spirit of transitional justice, political repression and human rights violations. While many transitional justice measures are temporary and focus on the first generation emerging from conflict, education is the only sector that simultaneously reaches both that generation and the subsequent ones, who become increasingly responsible for nurturing and protecting civil society and, in some cases, democracy and democratic institutions.[16]

But education, as an investment in the future, also has a transformative potential and can therefore make a particular contribution, first, to redressing the legacies of conflict and repression, which are often reflected in the education system in terms of inequality, political discrimination, and social division; and, second, to addressing some of the root causes of the previous abuses. Education can play a significant role in empowering individuals emotionally, economically, and sociopolitically and facilitating their process of rehabilitation and overall reintegration into society.[17] Likewise, at the social level, education policies can contribute to reconstructing the public sphere by providing knowledge about the past and creating opportunities for political interaction among citizens, while more broadly contributing to the establishment of a culture of human rights and peace.

Given the effects of conflict and repression on the education system, however, as well as their broader social legacies, that system will usually retain many of the unjust traits that characterized it before the transition or the peace process. Left unaddressed, these legacies will pose important challenges to the system's capacity to fulfill properly a number of its fundamental functions in a democratic society, including serving as a vehicle to build a culture of respect for human rights and democratic citizenship and to foster the inclusion of citizens, especially those most affected by previous patterns of abuse, in the new political project. These challenges may thus limit the overall contribution of education to fostering civic trust and social cohesion.[18]

If understood as part of a societal response to the legacies of past abuses, however, education can be aligned with the aims of transitional justice. It can engage society, especially the younger generations, in a dialogue on the reasons for and importance of dealing with the past. When addressing the impact of violations on education, and accordingly reforming the education system from a human rights and democracy-building perspective, education itself can be part of a transitional justice approach, especially one committed to guarantees that the violations will not recur.

Indeed, as a normally contested area, comprehensive education reform can be an important indicator of the new government's commitment to recognizing the past and ensuring it will not be repeated. However imperfect, transitional justice signals a commitment to learning from mistakes and demonstrating that some form of justice is possible. Education reform that includes teaching about the recent past from a human rights and democratic perspective (among other elements to be discussed below) represents the state's commitment to institutionalizing the gains from transitional justice processes and thereby becomes an important form of acknowledgment and redress.

Because of the way in which it addresses the legacies of the past from a human rights perspective, a transitional justice framework, for its part, can play an important role in identifying deficits in education related to the previous repressive or conflictive logic and help inform the reconstruction of the education sector in post-conflict societies under new or renewed democratic values. In this way, transitional justice can contribute to contextualizing within a particular history of abuses the aims of education reconstruction after conflict and repression, with an eye to strengthening its potential to prevent their recurrence. As Lynn Davies argues,

Justice-sensitive approaches to education reform require open acknowledgment of the role that education itself may have played in the previous conflict and patterns of abuse. . . . Grievances that led to conflict
may have included those about educational access or about cultural or
linguistic exclusion. Attempting to redress these will open some space
to the reduction of education's role in conflict, even if the major sources
of grievance lie outside the education system. In any reconstruction, it
is a question of helping to avoid some of the mistakes made in simply
recreating education as it was.[19]

At the same time, acknowledging the educational impact of human rights
violations on the lives of individuals and communities, engaging the education sector in transitional justice processes, providing education as a form of
reparation, fostering social and political reintegration through education, and
incorporating lessons from transitional justice processes into curricula may, in
the long term, contribute to promoting peace.

STRUCTURE OF THE BOOK

The book is organized into four sections. In the first, three chapters explore a
series of questions about what it means to take a transitional justice approach
to post-conflict education reconstruction. The first chapter, by Ana María
Rodino, is grounded in the experience of Argentina and incorporates insights
from different education approaches. In it, the author comprehensively and
thoroughly examines the elements of the education reform process and how
they might be viewed differently from a transitional justice perspective. After
identifying the goals and scope of education transformations in societies in
transition, Rodino analyzes the roles played by norms and institutions, curricula (including contents and teaching methods), didactic tools (including
materials), and the training of educators in addressing the past.

In the second chapter, Karen Murphy uses the cases of Bosnia-Herzegovina
and Northern Ireland—which she describes as "ambivalent transitions"—
to reflect on the negative consequences of putting education aside in any
social reconstruction process. Her contribution illustrates how, particularly
after identity conflicts, the segregation of schools along identity lines often
remains a key obstacle to justice efforts—one that, importantly, can reach
across generations—as well as how it can be perpetuated in the absence of
transitional justice.

Finally, Gustavo Palma Murga analyzes the teaching of the past in Guatemala, which was recommended in the final report of the country's truth commission. He explores the way the past is characterized in current textbooks according to a vague notion of a "culture of violence" and highlights the gap between what students learn in classrooms and the reality they face outside school.

The second section of the book focuses on education as a form of reparation for victims of human rights abuses and their descendants, emphasizing the capacity of such measures to help reintegrate children affected by the conflict into the school system and, hence, the social system. The first of the three chapters in this section, written by Cristián Correa, provides an overview of countries where education measures have been part of reconstruction and reparation programs, often featuring in the recommendations of truth commissions. He considers how education can function as part of a response both to broad marginalization, exclusion, and destruction and to the consequences of violations against specific victims. He argues that reparations in the form of education should have concrete goals, such as removing obstacles faced by victims and their children in attaining it, but that actual implementation of such efforts remains the critical challenge.

Then, in the next chapter, Lorena Escalona González examines the education benefits awarded in Chile as part of the reparation program that was established for victims of human rights violations in the country during its transition from dictatorship to democracy. Along with providing an overview of the education element of the program, she argues that some of the education reform measures implemented in the country since the beginning of the democratic regime should be seen as part of the social reparation process because of the role they can play in reconstructing the public sphere the dictatorship had destroyed.

Teboho Moja's chapter looks at South Africa, where measures to increase access to education and improve its quality, while not part of a reparation program, were conceived as a form of redress for past injustice. This was because the legacy of apartheid in the country's education system was in part structural; this could be relevant for other countries, such as the United States, where access to education and its segregation are very much related to the past.

The third section focuses on how transitional justice outreach programs can use education as a means to engage children and youth in the issues of memory, history, and justice. A key theme throughout the four chapters in this section is the capacity of the education sector not only to extend the reach of outreach programs, but also to help ensure the work and processes of temporary justice bodies will be sustained. In her chapter, Zoé Dugal analyzes the case of Sierra Leone, where, in part because of the toll of the country's civil war on younger generations, children were for the first time actively involved in a transitional justice process. She explores the different activities developed and materials produced by the outreach programs of both the Special Court for Sierra Leone and the truth and reconciliation commission, raising the issue of legacy and highlighting the significant challenges to connecting such measures with a war-devastated education sector.

In the next chapter, on the youth outreach program of the International Criminal Tribunal for the former Yugoslavia (ICTY), Nerma Jelacic examines a different type of challenge often faced when conducting outreach work with young people: community opposition toward the court itself and, hence, the reluctance of local governments to support the engagement of schools with its outreach program. She describes the effort to overcome these challenges, with differing levels of success across the region, and to transfer ownership of activities to local nongovernmental organizations (NGOs) and teachers.

The third and fourth chapters in this section look at the outreach work of two related types of institutions that might not be considered traditional transitional justice bodies. Mofidul Hoque recounts the outreach efforts of the Bangladesh Liberation War Museum (LWM), which, like memory museums all over the world, has strongly invested in educational programming. Since its inception, the LWM has actively engaged younger generations with the legacy of the 1971 war and human rights violations. Its education program includes a "mobile museum" that visits schools and universities throughout the country and an oral history project conducted in collaboration with schools.

The section ends with Alexander Karn's chapter on historical commissions in Europe that have used outreach programming to engage children and youth. Unlike truth commissions, some historical commissions have actually developed textbooks, the dissemination of which has become fundamental to achieving these bodies' education goals. Karn also weighs the advantages and disadvantages of traditional models of dissemination, like the distribution of textbooks, against more creative means to engage children and youth.

The final section of the book moves to civil society activities aimed at addressing past injustice in different informal education settings, in some cases potentially providing catalysts for similar efforts in the formal education system. Dylan Wray first introduces the Facing the Past program, established in South Africa to provide training for teachers who were asked to teach about the violent past and the transition process as part of the official curriculum. Filling a gap in the Ministry of Education's work, the program not only provides technical assistance and knowledge to teachers, but also emphasizes the emotional element of such work for those who have lived through and had different experiences under apartheid.

Virginie Ladisch and Joanna Rice then describe an ICTJ-UNICEF project in Côte d'Ivoire that began with the intention of working with the national truth commission and the education system but, when its success appeared unlikely, shifted to youth leaders, who created a network of youth-led organizations and an audio report about the role of youth in the past. Highlighting the challenges of working with the education sector in the aftermath of conflict, Ladisch and Rice also demonstrate possible alternative paths to helping young people develop their own capacity to engage in justice issues.

Finally, Lynn Maalouf and Christalla Yakinthou tell the story of Badna Naaref (We Want to Know), an intergenerational oral history project conducted by youth in Lebanon between 2010 and 2012. In a place with no transitional justice and the potential to return to conflict, this initiative reveals how oral history can create an opportunity for youth to learn about the past and reflect on their own realities. As in the former Yugoslavia, the chapter also points to the difficulty in Lebanon of ensuring the support of schools for such efforts in a difficult and still divided environment.

Together, the thirteen chapters that comprise this book are about what it means to address the legacies of the past from an education perspective and how this relates to a broader peacebuilding agenda. Our hope is to raise awareness and foster critical reflection on the importance of the relationship between transitional justice and education among both transitional justice practitioners and educators working in peacebuilding and the prevention of mass atrocities, and to encourage sustained collaboration. We also hope to contribute to a wider debate on how the injustices of the past affect the lives of children and young people in post-conflict and transitional societies, and the role they can play in building the peaceful futures of their countries.

ACKNOWLEDGMENTS

Numerous people and institutions have, in different ways, helped make this project possible. On behalf of ICTJ, we would like to express our most sincere gratitude to UNICEF, not only for its generous financial support, but also for the partnership established through the project's implementation. At UNICEF, we are extremely grateful to Friedrich Affolter, Christian Salazar, and Saudamini Siegrist for their continued collaboration, support, and advice and to Anna Azaryeva, Brenda Haiplik, Pierette James, John Lewis, and Carolin Waldchen. Kind support from Jane M. Stanfield and Nancy Vega should also be recognized here. Special thanks go to the authors of the chapters that make up this book, and more broadly to all the participants in the project, including Rosa Lía Chauca, Elizabeth A. Cole, Cristián Correa, Lynn Davies, Zoé Dugal, Lorena Escalona González, Mofidul Hoque, Nerma Jelacic, Alexander Karn, André Keet, Virginie Ladisch, Lynn Maalouf, Teboho Moja, Karen Murphy, Gustavo Palma Murga, Joanna Rice, Ana María Rodino, Felisa Tibbitts, Dylan Wray, and Christalla Yakinthou.

We also want to thank for vivid and insightful discussions the experts who participated in the meeting ICTJ organized in Bogotá in February 2014—including Claudia Camacho, Juanita Goebertus, Iris Marín, Andrés Pedraza, Luis Eduardo Pérez, María Andrea Rocha, Synthia Rubio, Esther Ruiz, Ricardo Sánchez, Saudamini Siegrist, Fred Spilberg, and María Emma Willis Obregon—and our ICTJ colleagues, Maria Camila Moreno and Gustavo Salazar; as well as those who participated in the two-day education and transitional justice roundtable organized in New York in October 2014, including Ibtihel Abdellatif, Michele Bellino, Tibi Galis, Roy Hellenberg, Mieke Lopes Cardozo, Thein Lwin, Kate Moriarty, Munini Mutuku, Ereshnee Naidu, Diya Nijhowne, María Andrea Rocha, Amra Sabic-El-Rayess, Martina Schulze, Susan Shepler, Alan Smith, Aleesha Taylor, Gail Weldon, Marie Wilson, and Stephanie Zuilkowski.

While ICTJ must be acknowledged as a whole, we would like to express our very special appreciation to Pablo de Greiff and Paul Seils for their guiding roles at different stages of the project and to Cristián Correa, Rachel Goodman, and Virginie Ladisch for their input and unconditional support through the implementation of the project. Thanks are also due to Anthony DiRosa, whose help was instrumental throughout the project, and interns Andrea Brody-Barre, Irina Karic, and Ryan Morgan. At the Social Science Research Council (SSRC), the authors would like to thank Alyson Metzger, Lisa Ferraro Parmelee, and Michael Simon for their invaluable and careful editorial support.

New York, August 2015

NOTES

1   See Kenneth D. Bush and Diana Saltarelli, *The Two Faces of Education in Ethnic Conflict: Towards a Peacebuilding Education for Children* (Florence: UNICEF Innocenti Research Center, 2002); Alan Smith and Tony Vaux, *Education, Conflict and International Development* (London: DFID, 2003); Lynn Davies, *Education and Conflict: Complexity and Chaos* (London: Routledge, 2003); Sobhi Tawil and Alexandra Harley, eds., *Education, Conflict and Social Cohesion* (Geneva: International Bureau of Education-UNESCO, 2004); and Peter Buckland, *Reshaping the Future: Education and Post-Conflict Reconstruction* (Washington, DC: World Bank, 2004).

2   See, for example, OECD-DAC, *Guidance on Evaluating Conflict Prevention and Peacebuilding Activities*, working draft, 2008, http://www.oecd.org/dac/evaluation/dcdndep/39774573.pdf. The *Guidance* expanded the "Utstein Palette" to include transitional justice under its pillar of building a "Culture of Truth, Justice and Reconciliation." See also United Nations, *Guidance Note of the Secretary-General: United Nations Approach to Transitional Justice*, 2010, 3, http://www.unrol.org/doc.aspx?d=2957. This document states that by "striving to address the spectrum of violations in an integrated and interdependent manner, transitional justice can contribute to . . . prevention of further conflict, peacebuilding and reconciliation"; and Camino Kavanagh and Bruce Jones, *Shaky Foundations: An Assessment of the UN's Rule of Law Support Agenda* (New York: New York University, Center on International Cooperation, 2011), 13, who consider transitional justice a relevant crosscutting issue in post-conflict settings.

3   Pablo de Greiff, "Theorizing Transitional Justice," in *NOMOS LI: Transitional Justice*, ed. Melissa Williams, Rosemary Nagy, and Jon Elster (New York: New York University Press, 2012).

4   Susana Frisancho and Félix Reátegui, "Moral Education and Post-War Societies: The Peruvian Case," *Journal of Moral Education* 38, no. 4 (2009): 422.

5   While in the practical realm this approach has been clearly adopted in the international work of the nongovernmental organization Facing History and Ourselves for years, important scholarly contributions have included Eric Stover and Harvey M. Weinstein, eds., *My Neighbor, My Enemy: Justice and Community in the Aftermath of Mass Atrocity* (Cambridge: Cambridge University Press, 2004); Elizabeth A. Cole, ed., *Facing the Violent Past: History Education and Reconciliation* (New York: Rowman & Littlefield Publishers, 2007); and Julia Paulson, ed., *Education and Reconciliation: Exploring Conflict and Post-Conflict Situations* (London: Continuum, 2011).

6   Some of the material in this introduction also appears in Clara Ramírez-Barat and Roger Duthie, *Education and Transitional Justice: Opportunities and Challenges for Peacebuilding* (New York: ICTJ-UNICEF, 2015).

7   See https://www.ictj.org/our-work/research/education-peacebuilding.

8   Education is among the different "social institutions that sustain the relationships that contribute towards social cohesion." Smith and Vaux, *Education, Conflict and International Development*, 46.

9   Here it is fundamental to highlight the significance this specific type of violence against schools has acquired in recent years under the International Humanitarian Law framework, starting with Graça Machel's seminal study, *The Impact of Conflict on Children* (A/51/302, August 26, 1996), and UN Security Council Resolution 1612 (S/RES/1612, July 26, 2005), which established the Monitoring Reporting Mechanism and included "attacks on schools" among the six grave violations against children. It is also important to note that, from a transitional justice perspective, accountability for such violations should include criminal prosecutions. See more about this at the Global Coalition to Protect Education from Attack website, http://www.protectingeducation.org/.

10   Bush and Saltarelli, *The Two Faces of Education*, 11.

11   Smith and Vaux, *Education, Conflict and International Development*, 18.

12   Comisión de la Verdad y la Reconciliación, "El sistema educativo y el magisterio," in *Final Report*, ed. Comisión de la Verdad y la Reconciliación, vol. 3 (Lima: 2003), 551–602.

13   Lorena Escalona González, "Education as a Form of Reparation in Chile," in this volume.

14   Bush and Saltarelli, *The Two Faces of Education*, 16.

15   Gail Weldon, "Conflict, Identity and Intergenerational Transmission of Memory" (paper presented at ICTJ's Transitional Justice and Education Roundtable, New York, October 2014), 2.

16   Karen Murphy, "Education Reform through a Transitional Justice Lens: The Ambivalent Transitions of Bosnia and Northern Ireland," in this volume.

17   Alan Smith, "Children, Education and Reconciliation" (Innocenti Working Paper, UNICEF Innocenti Research Centre, June 2010), 13. The term "reintegration" can be problematic because it implies that (1) a person was integrated once before, which may not necessarily be the case, and (2) that person is necessarily now "outside" of society. Nevertheless, the term is useful because it suggests an improvement in an individual's relationship with his or her community and public institutions, which may have been damaged by the occurrence of massive human rights violations; which has social, economic, and political elements (among others); and which is at least partially based on trust. This last means that reconciliation, if understood to be based on trust, can play an important role in reintegration. The term "reintegration" is commonly used as part of the discourse on displaced persons and former combatants.

18   The importance of the legacy of the past in education and peacebuilding recently was highlighted and included as one dimension under the concept of reconciliation in the 4R's (recognition, redistribution, representation, and reconciliation) developed by Mario Novelli, Mieke Lopes Cardozo, and Alan Smith. See their report, *A Theoretical Framework for Analysing the Contribution of Education to Sustainable Peacebuilding: 4Rs in Conflict-Affected Contexts* (Amsterdam: University of Amsterdam, 2015).

19   Lynn Davies, "Postconflict Education Reconstruction and Transitional Justice," ICTJ, New York, 2016.

PART I

Post-Conflict Education Reconstruction and Transitional Justice

Teaching about the Recent Past and Citizenship Education during Democratic Transitions

Ana María Rodino

The task of teaching about the recent past in societies that have experienced violent internal conflicts and are undergoing processes of democratic transition requires us to identify and discuss the most effective approaches and pedagogical guidelines for doing so.[1] In this chapter, I consider this problem not solely with reference to the teaching and learning of history, but rather as a process of human rights education for the active exercise of democratic citizenship.

The chapter begins by making explicit the sources I draw upon to conduct this reflection exercise, especially regarding the specific experiences I use as primary examples, indicating where they come from and the reasons for choosing them.

Next come two issues that should be taken into account with relation to the theoretical frameworks for teaching about the recent past. The first is the recognition of the existence of diverse disciplines for addressing the subject. The second is the society's relationship with the past in general, and in particular in the Latin American contexts, as studied through two discrete but related paradigms: that of history and that of social or collective memory.

Third, based on these contributions, the chapter turns to the field of education to analyze the changes that should be produced in the education system during periods of democratic transition, the conceptual and methodological approaches that should be used, and the lessons that can be derived from previous experiences. The text presents and discusses the suggested changes and guidelines with relation to the different components of the education system, which include norms and institutions; curriculum (course contents and teaching methods); didactic or pedagogical tools (materials and memory supports); and teacher training.

The chapter concludes with some strategic considerations that should be taken into account for transformations in the education system during processes of democratic transition.

SOURCES AND GEOGRAPHICAL FOCUS

The discussion in this chapter is based on sources from several lines of inquiry:

- Transitional justice and education in different parts of the world
- Human rights and citizenship education
- The teaching of recent history and the pedagogy of collective memory
- The analysis of specific experiences in dealing with the recent past in South America, particularly in Argentina, based on interviews with representatives of institutions and experts working in the field and a review of didactic materials

South America experienced numerous violent conflicts during the second half of the twentieth century that were unprecedented in terms of the scale and nature of the human rights violations committed. Most took place in the Southern Cone during the 1970s and '80s. With some variations, Argentina, Bolivia, Brazil, Chile, Paraguay, and Uruguay all suffered from harsh military dictatorships and brutal internal repression, by their own armies and police forces, of broad sectors of civil society, who were pursued as enemies of the state because of their political and ideological positions. These "dirty wars" were a direct consequence of Cold War politics, in which the tactics of oppression and torture were justified and supported in the Western Hemisphere under the doctrine of national security. The military strategies were combined with political support for neoliberal reforms to the economy and the productive system. The case of Argentina is paradigmatic for both negative and positive reasons. While the dictatorship committed horrific and vicious crimes, civil society took innovative and effective action to resist and denounce these acts and later continued opposing them extensively in the political, legal, educational, and cultural spheres.

The last dictatorship in Argentina (1976–83) was different from the previous ones both quantitatively—that is, in terms of the scope of the violations—and qualitatively, because it established "the historical experience of a state-led systematic form of detention, torture, and extermination of a certain category of citizens."[2] The extreme violence and impunity that characterized this period exemplify what Hannah Arendt has called "administrative massacres,"[3] and they are part of the history of serious crimes against humanity, such as the Holocaust. The experiences of the transition in the aftermath of these violations were also significant and had a multiplying effect that spread beyond the national borders. During the more than thirty years of democratic rule, awareness and understanding of the conflict have grown, along with consistent efforts to combat its legacy. The recent past has remained entrenched in the democratic agenda in Argentina, contrary to what has happened in Spain and Chile, where efforts to deal with the past have not been consistent over time.[4]

Several factors contribute to the paradigmatic nature of the aspects of the Argentinean transition that concern us here:

- The innovative action and impact of the first civilian commission to investigate the fate of the victims (the National Commission on the Disappearance of Persons, CONADEP in Spanish), convened in 1983.[5] This and subsequent commissions of the sort would later be known as "truth commissions."
- The organization and mobilization of civil society under the banners of *memory, truth,* and *justice,* including human rights organizations and the families of victims, accompanied by activists from churches, trade unions, universities, culture workers, and regional organizations, among others.[6] This coming together produced a wealth of information, analysis, social debate, and recommendations for action regarding the legacy of the past.
- Periods of evident political will, during which the state took action to establish the truth and bring the perpetrators of human rights violations to justice. This political will was not constant, however, and there were moments of progress and backtracking. A qualitative leap was made in 2003 with the arrival of an administration that assumed the banners of truth and justice as government policy and stood behind them until they became state policy.
- The wealth of academic and cultural production about the conflict that addressed what happened before, during, and after the dictatorship, from different sectors and with different perspectives. This raised awareness and allowed for broad debate.
- The recovery and creation of education spaces that were defended and maintained during the periods when the state relapsed. While many hosted learning of a nonformal or informal nature (in other words, extracurricular teaching and learning),[7] during moments of greater political will some access to the formal education curricula was achieved. After the qualitative political leap in 2003, education venues and experiences increased notably, as did pedagogical developments.

The case of Argentina is thus very illustrative in the field of education, in terms of proposals made, actions undertaken, and lessons learned.

EDUCATING IN POST-CONFLICT SOCIETIES: FRAMEWORKS

A leading specialist in the field of education and transitional justice noted in 2007 that little or marginal attention had been paid to curriculum reform, teaching methods, and other aspects of the education system in post-conflict societies, either with regard to system reform or the teaching of recent history.[8] While I do not completely agree with this claim, it is true that much of the work addressing these topics in the different fields, both theoretically and in practice, is done in parallel—that is, different areas of education research that share some interests do not necessarily communicate with each other. Moreover, transitional justice practitioners have grossly overlooked the relevant discussions and literature.

Even within the legalistic approach that prevails in the field, different transitional justice mechanisms—including the truth commissions established in several Latin American countries and the bodies of the inter-American system of human rights protection (the Commission and the Court)—have increasingly considered the importance of the educative measures that should accompany the legal actions taken during a democratic transition. This concern is explicitly stated in the final reports of CONADEP (Argentina, 1984); the National Commission for Truth and Reconciliation (Chile, 1991); the Commission for Historical Clarification (Guatemala, 1999); the Truth and Reconciliation Commission (Peru, 2003); the Truth and Justice Commission (Paraguay, 2008); and the Truth Commission on the Palace of Justice (Colombia, 2010). The reports and resolutions on proven human rights violations issued by the Inter-American Commission and Court have, for many years, included specific recommendations for responsible countries to undertake human rights training, both for public servants (in particular those directly involved in the violations in each case: military and police forces and penitentiary and/or justice personnel) and the general public, with the purpose of raising awareness and educating to guarantee the violations do not recur. The Inter-American Court has incorporated these recommendations into the reparations granted in its judgments.[9]

Many related reflections and experiences in education are underpinned by a variety of disciplines, with distinct origins, names, and trajectories but similar research subjects. If we bring together the analyses and recommendations from human rights education, education for peace or for a culture of peace, education for democracy or citizenship education, teaching about recent history, or pedagogy of memory, we will find significant coincidences and complementarities regarding how to address education challenges after serious internal conflicts. These approaches have increased in the past two decades but with apparently little collaboration; their research and theoretical frameworks, their experts, the experiences they promote, and their academic and didactic products tend to differ. This is at least the case in Latin America.

The challenges to transitional justice today are the result not of having ignored the education reform dimension, but rather of the lack of an in-depth and interdisciplinary approach, with theoretical and methodological responses to existing concerns on how to address the necessary education transformations in post-conflict societies. In my view, the challenge ahead is to document good practices and lessons learned to apply the experience acquired to different situations, while remaining flexible enough to adapt to the specific realities and urgent needs of each context. That is, we need to study the literature produced by the different fields of pedagogy and articulate common proposals that may serve as guides in situations of transitional justice.

The efforts in Latin America to educate people to review critically and learn from the experiences of conflict in recent history are positioned between two paradigms that address society's relationship with the past: history as a field of knowledge and professional discipline; and the field of memory studies, which encompasses the recollection and understanding of the past by the general public.[10] These are discrete but related approaches. The first has been a part of traditional curricula in formal education systems, while the second is more contemporary.

The notion of collective memory refers to how members of a group reconstruct the past based on their current interests and frames of reference.[11] It is understood as a social activity because it is shared by a community; because the processes of social exchange of memories influence how they are constructed and preserved; and because collective memory, among other functions, contributes to social cohesion and the preservation of social identity.[12] Given the social nature of memory, the events evoked do not generally converge into one single memory but into a multiplicity of memories, often conflicting and frequently in opposition.[13]

From 1980, the importance of collective memory has become strongly embedded in the public discourse in Argentina and, gradually, in other South American countries that experienced state terrorism.[14] In these cases, as in the Holocaust in Europe or apartheid in South Africa, what today is called the "duty" or work of memory does not refer to keeping alive the memory of the glorious deeds of the past[15]—which was the traditional approach to the history of, for example, the wars of independence of the countries on the American continents. Rather, the collective memory in these countries is understood as the memory of egregious crimes that should never again (*"nunca más"*) be repeated. It is a memory not centered on heroes but on victims.[16]

The relationships—and the tensions—between teaching about the recent past and the duty of memory have been extensively studied in the Spanish-speaking world.[17] Here I only wish to emphasize that the two approaches—history and memory—are complementary, and that they should both be considered when reflecting on education in post-conflict societies. Other specialized contributions should be taken into consideration, especially human rights education, which addresses both the historical-critical and the ethical-political aspects that can guide citizenship education.

GOALS AND SCOPE OF EDUCATION REFORM IN SOCIETIES IN TRANSITION

Sandra Raggio has clearly expressed the ultimate goal of democratic transition processes: "All societies that have experienced devastating violence, wars, genocide, massacres, have worked to restore the idea of community that will give meaning back to communal living."[18] As I understand it, the pursuit of this goal restores the basic objective of education: to construct the meaning of communal living—that is, of living together. The discipline fields mentioned above (history of the recent past, works of memory, and human rights, democracy, citizenship, and peace education) all make essential contributions on how to move toward this goal in the aftermath of events that have profoundly disrupted the sense of community. They motivate reflection on the immediate objectives of "why?" and "for what?" the past should be revisited, which is the basis for proposing how to do so.

Every society that has experienced traumatic conflicts should examine the legacy of authoritarian rule and the effects and consequences that need to be revealed and dismantled to restore communal life. This is the starting point for education reforms. In Argentina (and most other Latin American states), this legacy includes the following:

· Systematic violations of human rights, many of which are today recognized as crimes against humanity (murder, the "disappearing" of people, the kidnapping of children, torture, forms of slavery, inhumane treatment, and different forms of abuses, from physical and psychological to economic)

- Concealment of information about the events that occurred (circumstances, victims, and perpetrators)
- Long periods of impunity, where justice is denied (no prosecution, or even amnesty for material perpetrators or intellectual authors)
- Inconceivable individual and family traumas, going as far as the unprecedented crime of robbing children of their true identities (children of disappeared victims who were kidnapped by military or police officers)
- Divided, incomplete, or schematic narratives and interpretations of the past, which make its analysis more difficult
- Continuity of authoritarian practices and difficulty in eradicating them from both institutions and everyday life[19]

The mobilization of civil society to combat these crimes in Argentina can be summed up by the demands for memory, truth, and justice made by human rights organizations since the dictatorship. The title of the CONADEP report, *Never Again*, clearly reflected the shared expectations about the future, which is why it was later adopted as a motto by the truth commissions of other countries until it became emblematic. The violent past is examined, remembered, and transmitted to prevent it from repeating itself—hence, the similar motto of the publications of the Provincial Memory Commission, Province of Buenos Aires, Argentina, in 2000: "If we all remember, it will not happen again."

SUGGESTED CHANGES, GUIDELINES, AND APPROACHES

I turn now to addressing some key issues on the basis of combined knowledge on teaching about recent history, the work of memory, transitional justice, and human rights education, as well as specific experiences. I seek to answer the following questions:

- What changes should be made to the formal education system in processes of democratic transition?
- What conceptual and methodological approaches are suitable for talking in schools about conflict in the recent past?
- What lessons have we learned from these experiences?

From a variety of sources, I take the recommendations I believe are the most significant and generalizable, organizing them according to the specific components of the education system involved. In this way I seek to demonstrate that education reform efforts should not be one-off or unidirectional. They should move in different directions simultaneously to affect several areas or components of the education system, which is necessary to change a large and complex structure containing many parts that are interrelated but at the same time unique.[20]

Below I group together the recommended changes and guidelines for the four main components of the education system that have a direct impact on what takes place in the classrooms: norms and institutions; curriculum, including course contents and teaching methods; pedagogical tools; and teacher training.

In studies of how to transform education, one of the first recommendations coming from theory and research is that to do so effectively, one must think and act upon it for what it is: a vast, massive, and complex system, with multiple interacting and complementary components.[21] This does not mean all the changes should (or can) occur together or at the same time after the end of a conflict, because each education system is conditioned by the particular context in which it exists—whether the conflict is ongoing or has recently concluded; whether it has caused extensive material and personal damage and the country is too poor to address all the pressing needs; whether no true education system exists, or it is so disarticulated that it becomes inoperative. Each case is different, and some will have serious limitations in implementing the recommendations for education reform.

Beyond specific cases, however, the recommendations presented here represent valuable goals that should be kept in mind, even if they can be achieved only gradually according to the possibilities of each transitional context. They provide a model or guide for leading education reform processes in post-conflict situations, which could later be further broken down in a matrix of indicators to serve as a checklist.

It is important to clarify from the beginning, as Jeff Spinner-Halev keenly observed, that in teaching effectively about the traumatic past in transitional or post-conflict societies, it is easier to proscribe than to prescribe.[22] That the legacy of totalitarianism should be abolished is usually evident, and thus relatively easy to accept, because it is perverse and harmful to social life and the development of new generations. What to change, however, is more controversial, because any novel proposal implies an ideological position and a coherent narrative, which may be difficult to agree on.[23]

EDUCATION NORMS AND INSTITUTIONS

The following recommendations provide possibilities for entrenching within the school system a coherent and sustainable pedagogy of history and memory. As normative changes, they do not constitute a teaching method, but they define values and principles for what will be taught in schools and how it will be taught. In other words, they are an enabling framework for future pedagogical reforms. Three proposals are described below.

1. *Comprehensively review education norms to remove from the school system all vestiges of authoritarianism and oppression stemming from the recent conflict.*
The review and change of norms should be the logical first step for reforming education in processes of transition; otherwise, the previous norms will not only continue to harm the system and the education agents, but will also obstruct or contradict the new measures to be implemented. Such reform of norms does not always occur, however. In Chile, for example, after two decades of democratic rule, some regulations set by the Augusto Pinochet dictatorship are still in force. Students have been protesting for the removal of these laws, and President Michelle Bachelet has pledged to reform them during her second term (2014–18).[24] For example, in 2014 her government repealed the decree law that prohibited organized participation in institutions of higher education.

The legacy of authoritarianism tends to become entrenched at many points of the structure and management of the education system, either explicitly or indirectly. This is why it is so important to undertake a complete assessment of the system to identify precisely what needs to be eliminated, replaced, or reformed. The efforts of diagnosis and the recommended reforms should somehow allow for the participation of all education agents, including administrators, school principals, teachers, students, and parents.

2. *Incorporate the mandate of teaching and memory of the recent conflict into the education legislation.*
Introducing recent history and examination of collective memory into the school curriculum is not something that occurs spontaneously or as a result of the actions of a group of education experts or teachers. It occurs as a result of a social mandate. This is why it must be established as public policy and, ideally, as state policy, not just government or party policy. State policies are the product of broad societal consensus, which is why they do not shift with successive administrations that may have different political-ideological positions. To ensure that the teaching of the recent past becomes a state policy,

that mandate should be incorporated explicitly into the laws that govern the national education system.

Is this a realistic expectation? It may not occur or may occur only timidly at the beginning of a process of democratic transition, given the tensions or imbalance of power among the sectors that continue to clash in the aftermath of massive human rights violations (as in Argentina in the 1980s), or it may occur in an incomplete or biased manner (as in Argentina during the '90s). However, that is the goal to be set, to ensure teaching about the past becomes mandatory and systematic. In Argentina, this was finally achieved with the enactment of the 2006 General Education Law.[25]

Considering legal changes take time and are subject to the balance of power of the antagonistic forces in each specific situation, the question arises as to whether it is possible to teach about the recent past without a legally established policy. The answer is yes, and everything that can be done is helpful. The efforts to critique and raise awareness about the past usually begin under the leadership of civil society organizations (including human rights and victims' families organizations, churches, trade unions, and so on), which influences state actions. Without refuting the importance of these efforts, however, they will hardly achieve the same degree of legitimacy or scope or be as systematic as actions taken through public institutions. Post-conflict education reforms should aim for the latter.

3. Create bodies within public education institutions that will be responsible for planning and implementing policy regarding the teaching and memory of the recent conflict, allocating the resources and providing the necessary specialized operational staff.
With regard to implementing reform policy, it is important to take into account both the institutions in charge of formal education (ministries of education and, in federal countries, national and provincial or state ministries) and other institutions with nonformal education functions (for example, ombudsmen's offices, human rights commissions, or education or culture offices of other ministries or at the municipal level, among others).

Both the formal and nonformal education systems provide opportunities for promoting the teaching of recent history and memory. Each has its own advantages and limitations, which are important to understand if they are to be used effectively. Usually, it is easier to begin with working in the nonformal education realm, as it is removed from the bureaucratic requirements of the school system. However, in the longer run, reforming the formal education system will make it easier to reach the next generations throughout the national territory on a mass scale. The possibility of having access to formal education does not, however, mean nonformal venues should be discarded.

Nonformal education has great potential for teaching, is very flexible, reaches or adapts easily to different audiences and situations, and offers greater creative freedom to its designers, facilitators, and participants than formal education.

In addition, human, technical, and financial resources in support of the responsible institutions are needed. Without at least limited access to these resources, any policy for education reform will remain in the realm of wishful thinking.[26]

CURRICULUM: COURSE CONTENTS AND TEACHING METHODS

The curriculum component of the education process is as crucial as it is complex. Education theory allows us to break down the concept and reflect on its complexity, demonstrating that it has various manifestations.

The most visible of these manifestations is the so-called explicit curriculum, which covers the main pedagogical objectives and contents stated in study plans and programs. As such, it represents a social consensus on what topics should be taught in a country, signaling the value society places on them as part of its education process.

Another manifestation of these values would be the null curriculum, which refers to the contents or topics that for some reason have not been included in the official curriculum and, therefore, are not recognized by the school system. These contents represent the gaps or silences that must be revealed, unmasked, and corrected.

A third and last type is the hidden curriculum, which includes implicit messages that derive from the school culture and the relationships it promotes among education agents—authorities, faculty, students, and families. The hidden curriculum is not evident in the stated objectives and contents, but it has a huge impact because it represents the force of the customary education practices, which often teach even more than the explicit messages.[27]

With regard to the explicit curriculum, we must also distinguish between the contents of the official documents and what is effectively taught in the classrooms. Sometimes these do not coincide, as will be explained below. Teaching about the recent past and memory requires critical consideration and intervention in all these distinct manifestations of the curriculum. Accordingly, the following are recommendations pertaining to course contents and teaching methods.

1. Comprehensively review all manifestations—explicit, null, and hidden—of the curricula for different subjects to determine what changes will be necessary to include the study of the recent past and memory (including deletions and additions, amendments, and reformulations).

Comprehensive review of the curriculum is not always undertaken because the urgent need for action in the field of education frequently precipitates political decisions not underpinned by situational analyses. It should not be ignored, however, because taking action without a diagnosis could lead to trial and error, which consumes more time and resources.

As happens with other taboo or socially divisive topics, in societies emerging from periods of repression or conflict, the recent past as a teaching topic remains in the null curriculum—those things that are not named or discussed.[28] In other cases, the inclusion of the recent past in the explicit curriculum is limited, schematic, or superficial, as we have observed with the human rights education provided in the Latin American school systems.[29] Or it might also happen that, although the inclusion is historically, conceptually, and educationally rigorous and thus satisfactory, the contents remain "on paper" and are not really addressed in the classroom. Rafael Valls, for example, found a high percentage of the Spanish students he interviewed had never studied the Civil War or Francoism in their history courses because, as they explained, the programs were very long, with insufficient time to cover recent history.[30] This was repeated by most of the teachers Valls also interviewed. In my experience, this type of elusive justification related to teaching about the recent past has been a constant in Latin America.[31] In short, good diagnoses are needed to identify hidden or subtle gaps in the curriculum.

2. Decide where in the curriculum to incorporate teaching about recent history and collective memory and how to insert it.
Courses in which recent history will be taught either already exist or will need to be created. The options chosen will reflect the position assumed by each society in each particular moment, based on how it wishes to deal with its conflictive past and the education of future citizens, or how it can do so in light of the prevailing political conditions. The options follow two main tracks: either history (whether it is called history, history and geography, social sciences, or something similar) or civic education (citizenship education, ethics, human rights, or something similar). Ideally, both subjects should be covered.[32]

Although history is a well-established subject within the formal school curriculum, in transitional contexts, teaching about the recent past is not automatically incorporated or prioritized. The topic, closely linked with the legitimacy of the state, is very political, reflecting balances of power between different social sectors and ideologies. This makes the recent past a sensitive subject, disputed and difficult to address in the classroom. As Elizabeth Cole argues, it is frequently necessary for some time to pass before recent history can be included in the curriculum. The time frame for this to happen, how-ever, can only be established depending on the particular situation.[33]

In addition, the history of the recent past generally has been taught in high school—or in the final year of elementary school, at the earliest—that is, to students about twelve years of age and older. A high percentage of young peo-ple in many developing countries are unable to attend high school or unable to finish it—a problem common in Latin America.[34]

For these reasons, introducing changes in the curriculum through civic edu-cation courses instead of history is often considered faster and easier. For exam-ple, this is what happened in Argentina in the 1980s and in Chile. The subjects covered by these courses (primarily democracy, rule of law, human rights, con-flict resolution, diversity and nondiscrimination, and the culture of peace) have the advantage that they can generally be taught to younger children in the lower primary grades and even preschool. The risk is that the topic will be broached in a generic, abstract, and superficial manner, with the content only weakly based on history, especially the history of the country. As Elizabeth Oglesby noted, in Guatemalan classrooms, the recent conflict was being attributed to an unspeci-fied "culture of violence," a tautological and vague cause that diminishes and obscures rather than clarifies the conflict.[35] From this it follows that addressing history and civic education simultaneously, combining the specific perspec-tives of each discipline, would be a much more complete and robust approach.

Human rights education offers some insight into how to incorporate new contents into the explicit curriculum. It proposes, in principle, two modalities: disciplinary and crosscutting. The disciplinary modality consists of incorporat-ing the desired contents and approaches into a single course, as discussed above. The crosscutting modality, on the other hand, distributes them across different disciplines, using a variety of formats (interdisciplinary workshops, research projects, artistic expression, and case analyses, among others). Up until around 2004–6, human rights education experts considered these two modalities opposing and exclusive; but then a very positive approach was developed in the field, and they began to be considered complementary and mutually reinforc-ing.[36] For our purpose here, taking this approach would allow human rights and the recent conflict to be studied in a course as a specific area of knowledge, under the guidance of specialized educators, while at the same time addressing all of their inter- and transdisciplinary facets and implications across other courses.

Finally, although the political authorities are the ultimate decision mak-ers with regard to curricular contents, spaces, and modalities, any substantive changes should require consultation with other national and local actors. Such a consultation process could be controversial as well as difficult to implement.

Cole recommends involving "all parties to the past conflict" in developing the sensitive aspects of the curriculum and textbooks.[37] I believe this is possible in some cases, such as in ethnic conflicts, but improbable and even undesirable in others, like the military dictatorships in Latin America, because it would mean the participation of the armed and security forces in the development of curriculum and texts. I would, rather, prioritize consultation with education agents, including school administrators, teachers, students, parents, and relevant civil society organizations, to take advantage of their experience in the schools and involve them responsibly in the transformations being promoted. This can be done by establishing mechanisms for their participation in discussion of the reforms through teachers unions or professional organizations, education conferences, calls for participation, and specific sector consultations, among other avenues.

3. Inquire about the effects of the authoritarian past on the day-to-day life of the schools and communities to identify these effects and propose objectives and strategies for transforming their adverse consequences for social life.

To enforce their political agendas, authoritarian regimes seek to entrench themselves in intensely hierarchical relationships within society that are based on conformity and unquestioning obedience. The school is no stranger to this phenomenon, promoting obedience as necessary to maintaining the discipline needed for learning.[38] The authoritarian model of school discipline is often so strong it survives repressive regimes. Education agents, particularly teachers, tend to assume it is a natural part of the school institution itself. The culture of obedience is part of the powerful hidden curriculum.

Education change in democratic transitions should aim to reveal and criticize the legacy or consequences of the authoritarian rule embedded in the interpersonal relationships within the education institution, the families, and the community. These include, for example, the despotism of the administrative and academic authorities, arbitrary behaviors, imposed silences (due to censure or self-censure), lack of solidarity, fear, distrust, resentment, and everyday discrimination and violence, either evident or disguised. It should also encourage the education agents to propose changes to the system and to their own behavior and to assume the responsibility for producing them.

Constructive strategies to promote reflection on this issue can include extracurricular activities to motivate group participation (for example, student government and peaceful coexistence or conflict resolution committees) and discussions within the classrooms about the teaching and learning methods used. None of these activities is carried out during dictatorships.

4. Critically analyze and make changes to the teaching method in schools.
Analyzing and changing the teaching method in schools is vital. Some experts believe it is the most important post-conflict transformation to promote and focus on, even more so than the course contents.[39] Ideally, it should be done as changes are being made to the contents; but if these changes are delayed, transformation of the teaching method must begin through teacher training. Teaching methods are part of the hidden curriculum, and they often have more impact on the learning process than the contents to be taught.

Methods for teaching about the recent past and memory should not be based on memorization and the repetition of events dogmatically dictated as truths, because they promote intellectual passivity, a worldview with rigid categories, and the submissive acceptance of the ideas of "authority" figures in the schools and society. Rather, they should promote methodological approaches that build capacities that include the following:

- Critical thinking
- Inquiry and research
- The ability to consider multiple points of view
- The understanding of complex ideas, including conflicts, ambiguity, and uncertainty
- The willingness to question explanations and simplistic models
- An open and curious attitude and willingness to understand the world and the people in it
- Group work and collaboration
- The ability to empathize and show solidarity with others
- Ethical judgment and personal commitment to ethical principles
- Participation and sense of agency
- The capacity to discuss interpretations of the past and their implications for the present with other people and dissent from each other's views without resorting to violence

Expressed in the language of pedagogical theory, encyclopedic conceptions that support the mere accumulation of information are unanimously rejected by experts in the field, as are behaviorist conceptions that seek the mechanical transformation of conduct through stimulus–response conditioning and reward–punishment logic. Rather, contemporary approaches to social and cognitive psychology (or constructivism, as it is generically known in the Spanish-speaking world), which focus on understanding the human process of constructing history, culture, and knowledge, should be embraced. It is precisely cognitive or constructivist psychology that promotes the development of the capacities listed above.

In other words, the proposed reforms to the method for teaching history imply a departure from the traditional approach to a shift toward others:

- From an exclusive interest in the actions of the military and political elites to an interest in other sociocultural sectors that are not part of the elite and in the lives of the common citizen
- From focusing solely on the nation as a geopolitical unit to broader visions that include the local as well as the regional and international spheres
- From the chronology of events to an understanding of processes
- From the dogmatism of absolute truths and sole causality to multi-causal information and analyses[40]
- From conceiving history as "given facts" to a concern for how historical knowledge itself is constructed. The idea is to expose students to the tools of historians and the sources of evidence with which to interpret events, to enable them to understand how there can be different interpretations of the same event.[41]

One can argue that implementing these new methodological approaches is risky. They could, for example, promote relativism in judgments about the past. Educators must be aware of these challenges and learn to handle them. This is why it is so important to focus not on teaching a predetermined set of events, but instead on teaching the skills necessary to question and think about events—to seek and analyze evidence, to view issues as problems to be solved, to reason, and to justify, among others. While this is a complex and challenging process, it is much more educational from the ethical, intellectual, and civic perspectives than dogmatic indoctrination or uncritical repetition.

The proposed teaching strategies to address specifically the most complex and controversial issues of the traumatic past also tend to coincide. Among them, in the Latin American context, the following are often recommended:

- *Reconstruct the historical context with all of its complexity and nuances, using a variety of sources.* Mario Carretero and Marcello Borrelli recommend explaining historical transformations and conflicts not only in terms of the intentions and objectives of the human agents, but also by analyzing the social structure and linking human acts with social conditions, as well as avoiding simple reductionism (good versus bad, innocent victims versus villains) and purely "present-istic" analyses that do not account for the differences in beliefs or goals that can exist between the societies of the past and those of the present.[42]

- *Recognize the role of conflict in history.* Do not conceal or reduce the conflict to generalities to avoid possible disputes. Rather, "propose a perception of the concept of conflict in history as an initiator of changes and a source of creation, removing the negative connotation linking it to chaos and turmoil."[43] Do not refuse to deal with the problems of the past, no matter how sensitive or controversial they may be.

- *Adopt a pedagogical approach that addresses the conflict from an educational perspective.* Open and conduct the debate among the students as an educational exchange within a safe environment, paying special attention to the role of the teacher in guiding and facilitating the discussion. A number of well-designed conceptual and applied proposals for taking this approach exist.[44]

- *Use case studies from other places to help students look critically at their own history and imagine how individual actions could have changed its course and prevented injustice and suffering.* By studying other conflicts, students will learn that having to confront violence and injustice is not a problem in just one country but, sadly, is widespread around the world. Cole suggests using cases from abroad, especially when the recent conflict in the country is very sensitive and politically difficult to discuss in the classrooms.[45] One paradigmatic case studied around the world is the Holocaust.[46]

- *Connect the past that is being taught with the present of those who have to make sense of it, and keep it open to the future so it has relevance, currency, and validity for new generations.* While it is not necessary to justify the importance of transmitting the traumatic past to new generations, we should note such transmission is not something that happens naturally or automatically; and for that reason each society needs to have a conceptual and methodological discussion about the matter. Moreover, because the past does not remain unchanged over time, every society has to reinterpret it over and over again. The challenges thus differ depending on the historical moment in which the past is being taught. In the immediate aftermath of conflict, the challenge is how to tackle in a sensitive and fair manner issues that, because they are extremely contentious, tend to divide not only the society but also its educators. When the past is more distant, and the generations that lived it have already grown up, the challenge is to avoid the mechanical transmission of what happened and to leave the reinterpretation of the past to the younger generations so they can make sense of it.[47] One way reinterpretation of the past can bring meaning to the present is by considering whether and how the rights that were previously violated are currently being recognized and exercised.[48]

In addition to these recommendations from Latin American authors, Cole considers that teaching about the traumatic past should not be a protracted exercise of pure negativism, a succession of crimes and horror. While at the beginning of the transition it will be important to keep vivid the memory of the past crimes to ensure the protection of key values and human rights, such as the rights to truth (to know what happened) and justice (by sanctioning those responsible for crimes and providing recognition and reparation to victims and their families), as times passes by, mere negativity may not be the most effective education method for engaging new generations with the memories of the past and an active commitment to nonrecurrence for the purpose of proposing models for action and future behavior. Cole vindicates Robert Fullinwinder's concept of a "usable past" that can be used by young people to discover values and projects for building the future.[49]

5. Design strategies for working with the memory of the recent past, distinct from but complementary to the changes in the curriculum, that promote collaboration between the school and other social actors in education activities.

The "duty of memory" means to ensure transmission of the history of violent conflicts that damaged the social fabric.[50] Principally, it implies denouncing the crimes that were committed and demanding justice to punish those responsible and repair the harm done. It also requires working to ensure the horror experienced is not diminished by the passage of time or indifference, and that the past is remembered as a lesson to prevent its recurrence. This is an ambitious education task that goes beyond the school setting.

When talking about memory we refer to forms of representation and preservation, of the collective experience lived. It is not something recorded spontaneously; rather, it is constructed through social practice. In this sense, Hugo Vezzetti argues, memory requires tools and material frameworks (to use another word, supports) that make it possible to reveal significant events and issues from the past to the social actors of today and, more importantly, to allow them to establish a relationship and a dialogue with this past. Social memory resides less in the mind of each individual than it does in material and public artifacts: ceremonies, books, films, monuments, anniversaries, sites, and so on. For this reason, to Vezzetti the expression "works of memory" is not a metaphor but is instead something very concrete, in the sense that agents, initiatives, efforts, time, and resources are required to ensure these supports are strong and long lasting.[51]

Each society, located in a specific time and place, must consider what these "works of memory" should be and how they shall be conducted and should plan and design strategies for their implementation and monitoring. This topic exceeds the scope of this chapter, which focuses on the formal education system. I would like to emphasize, however, that it is important to consider how the school system can participate in these broader social memory works, which go beyond the system but also include it.

One recommendation in this respect is that education initiatives in post-conflict societies should not be restricted to the physical space or the curricular function of the school but should instead link the school to community life. Different strategies can be designed to involve education actors in socially valuable extracurricular activities complementary to curricular goals (related either to knowledge, values, and attitudes or to skills for taking action). A good example is community-based action or research projects, conducted with the immediate community of the school or with others (domestic or even foreign) who are concerned with reflecting on their recent pasts and committed to building a democratic and just future.[52]

There are many different possibilities if we use our creativity and think contextually. The important thing is to develop and promote such initiatives as part of public policy on education because they will rarely arise spontaneously within the schools, which traditionally tend to focus inward and become even more encapsulated in periods of conflict.

DIDACTIC TOOLS: TEACHING MATERIALS AND MEMORY SUPPORTS

Didactic tools are just as crucial to teaching about the recent past as the teaching method. They generally are more than the aids or means for the educator to implement a methodological model: they comprise the model that is adopted and implemented by the educator. The wide variety of such tools ranges from classic didactic resources (printed textbooks and audiovisual media for classroom teaching) to tools and supports that channel the works of memory through material means to recover the past (memory sites, monuments, museums, artifacts, installations, and celebrations, among others).[53] The discussion below elaborates on two recommendations regarding didactic tools.

1. Select and develop didactic tools for teaching history and memory in formal and nonformal processes, keeping different age groups in mind.

What tools should be chosen or created to teach about complex, difficult, and sensitive issues, such as the recent past? Which will work best? Under what circumstances? These are all very pertinent questions. Although responding to them would go beyond the scope of this chapter, they should be asked before undertaking any education process, and I offer some basic considerations that might be helpful in this regard, taken from the literature and my work in this area.[54]

Practically speaking, each type of tool has its own particular characteristics (advantages and disadvantages, possibilities and limitations), and each contributes in specific ways to the education process that will be undertaken. For this reason, it is more useful and effective to choose groups or sets of distinct tools that complement each other than to select or develop a single tool.

TEXTBOOKS

School textbooks are the first resource used to develop curricula under ordinary conditions and for established topics. However, they are not necessarily the most appropriate starting point when introducing the history of the recent past in the classroom, for several important reasons—logistical, political, academic, and pedagogical. Developing, publishing, and distributing a textbook is both time consuming and costly. It must be based on solid data and first-rate research (which takes time to produce in post-conflict situations) and requires constructing a message that is shared by the majority of the population, as well as the corresponding methodology.

According to Cole, at the international level many valuable research projects with the participation of multiethnic or politically diverse teams of educators and historians have been successful in terms of the products developed, but not with respect to reaching the classrooms, either because the books were not published or were not officially endorsed and, in the best of cases, were left to be used as supplementary materials or distributed to the general public.[55] That is why she recommends new history or civic education books not be produced too soon after a conflict has ended. Instead, efforts should focus, first, on purging the existing textbooks of distorted and hateful messages and, second, on using complementary materials, such as brochures, student notebooks, teacher guides, and document folders, that are easier to agree on and prepare.

LANGUAGES AND VISUAL AND AUDIOVISUAL MEDIA

An interesting possibility is the use of visual and audiovisual resources that can bring the past into the classroom. One of these is photography. For John

Berger, "Photographs are relics of the past, evidence of what has come to pass" that with their representations expose us to uncomfortable situations and unimaginable horrors while at the same time helping us reflect on the difficulties of representation, memory, and understanding.[56] They are both a support and a challenge to teachers because "they make it necessary to educate the students on how to see, because looking is not the same as seeing and seeing does not necessarily imply an understanding of what the image represents or narrates about the past."[57]

Another important resource is audiovisual aids, in a wide variety of formats and combinations of image, sound, and text. They have the great advantage of being familiar to young people and facilitating motivation, empathy, collective dialogue, and a disposition toward complex learning processes. Their use also contributes to the development of important cognitive and social skills, such as audiovisual literacy and the critical analysis of omnipresent audiovisual messages, like those of the mass media. The audiovisual messages to be used in classrooms can be produced ad hoc for teaching and memory processes, or they can be selected from among sources available in society, such as television programs, YouTube videos, and commercial films, among others.

ORAL HISTORIES AND TESTIMONIES

Oral histories and testimonies are highly recommended for their capacity to bring the experiences of the past closer by recovering the voices of the protagonists.[58]

Testimonies are an effective resource within the category of tools that do not explain, but rather "show," a personal story without pretending to constitute a theory or model. Several voices are usually present in a testimony (the victim, who narrates, or, in the victim's absence, a witness who assumes his or her voice; a witness who gives testimony; the person who interviews and collects the testimony; and, when it is used for education purposes, the teachers who read and analyze the testimony). It is important to recognize all the voices and not mix or overlap them, so that none substitutes for another.[59]

As mentioned above, each type of tool has its own possibilities and limitations, as well as risks. Testimonies are no exception, and they should be used carefully and with judgment. Julia Rosemberg and Verónica Kovacic suggest two basic precautions: first, identify the situation and moment in which the testimony was produced; and, second, "remember that these first person voices cannot and should not be considered neutral discourses that replace the explanations about what happened, but are rather one more resource that allows us to learn more about the past."[60]

MEMORY SUPPORTS: MEMORY SITES AND COMMEMORATIONS

The "patriotic" memory supports of the distant past (commemorating, in Latin America, the wars of independence against colonial powers) were the state monuments dedicated to fallen heroes, which Inés Dussel and Ana Pereyra fittingly labeled "petrified forms of memory."[61] Since the recent past is of a different nature, other media are used today to bring us closer to the experiences, illusions, and pain of the victims. Based on the Argentinean experience, Raggio notes, "An important component of the memory policies that have been implemented in the last few years has been the establishment of memory sites in the recovery of spaces that were the setting of horrific acts and that reveal the magnitude of state terrorism in our country."[62] These include sites of detention, concentration camps, and places where crimes were committed, among others, and they are spaces for remembrance and commemoration that sometimes provide proofs for the justice courts and always provide lessons for the new generations.

While these are generally real sites, it is also possible—and necessary—to resort to reconstructed or recreated sites. Think, for example, about some of the supports used in different museums to provide a sensorial and emotional connection to the experiences of the victims of the Nazi regime, such as a pile of shoes and other pieces of clothing and a display of railroad boxcars used to transport detainees (in the Holocaust Museum in Washington, DC) or the replication of some sites (the reproduction of the home of Anne Frank in Buenos Aires) and the recreation of others (the "Daniel's Story" exhibit in the Washington Holocaust Museum, a child-appropriate display that recreates a series of rooms used by a Jewish boy in Germany to demonstrate how his life changed from before the onset of Nazism to the time of the concentration camps).

Another preferred memory support is provided by the ephemerides and parallel commemorations organized in remembrance of past events.[63] Days of commemoration always mark events in an effort to link them to the shared identity of a community and its continuity in time. When they are included in the national calendar (like the March 24 and April 2 holidays in Argentina),[64] they reach the entire population of a country and also make possible special educational activities in schools. This option goes beyond merely remembering events of the past; examining the events in the classroom through documents, sources, and well-designed activities allows students to rethink, analyze, and discuss them in the present and from their own particular reality.

Many disciplines make conceptual and technical contributions to the creation of didactic tools: artistic, educational, mass media, museum, architectural, urban design, and informatics production, among others. This is a task that undoubtedly requires interdisciplinary efforts.

2. *Design strategies for use of the didactic tools and plan for their broad distribution or dissemination.*

The selection or preparation of training tools must include establishing expectations for their use by educators. While education transformations in post-conflict situations must incorporate new resources as well as new study contents, they are insufficient if not accompanied by methodological guidelines. It is not logical to assume teachers know (or will spontaneously grasp) how to use the new tools in a manner consistent with the approach that inspired them or with the recommended methodological criteria for addressing the recent past. Frequently, their efforts will be impeded by unfamiliarity, inexperience, or resistance to working on this topic.

In Argentina, the institutions in charge of formal education or spaces that combine formal and nonformal education produce guidelines for teachers and students on how to use the tools already available and, needless to say, incorporate methodological guidelines into the tools of their own design. The latter emphasize pedagogical objectives without neglecting the conceptual framework.[65]

TRAINING OF EDUCATORS

The following recommendation should guide the training of educators:

Train teachers on how to teach recent history and memory, particularly teachers of history, civic education, human rights, and other subjects in which it has been decided the topic will be mainstreamed.

All components of the education system discussed here play an important role in the citizenship education process after violent conflict, and none can be ignored without affecting the whole. Theory and specific experiences have consistently shown, however, that the factor with the highest impact on the results of the process is educators and the way they educate. Curricula carefully crafted with ethical and democratic contents, constructivist and participatory methodological models, and materials with plural, critical, and antiauthoritarian messages are all of little use in the hands of teachers who are poorly prepared, fearful, indifferent, authoritarian, ultranationalist, or racist (or characterized by any other trait that represents the most negative aspects of the past conflict).

Similarly, in post-conflict societies, and especially in cases of very recent conflict, most practicing teachers will have experienced the conflict from the perspective of one or another of the parties (perpetrators, victims, or witnesses).

This experience, and the consequences it has had over their lives, will affect their capacity to teach about the past. This is crucial because, again, it is the educator who ultimately mediates between the system and its beneficiaries.

While there is broad consensus among experts that educators are the most influential factor in the education process, it is also broadly agreed that, in practice, this is the educative component that is most lacking and the hardest to change. Quantitatively, educators are an extensive group, dispersed around the country; qualitatively, they are very heterogeneous in their opinions and personal histories, and many have direct links with the past, either as actors or witnesses, with certain ideological and political orientations. In addition, they are allowed great flexibility in the use of the curriculum, methodology, and materials within their classrooms, each of which is a sort of "black box" hidden from the external observer.[66] Furthermore, the new historical narratives and methods for teaching them are complex to apply, can be politically risky, and may differ from the ideological or pedagogical positions of some teachers.

The Argentinean experience shows that "the past also affects the school," and resistance, inconformity, or conflict in dealing with it always exists. As Raggio observes, "The silence, the opposing positions of teachers about the past, some fears about dealing with certain issues all still remain and . . . are also transmitted."[67] The same can be said regarding Chile.[68] These attitudes may have to do with the personal opinions or pedagogical limitations of some teachers; but, according to Raggio, the main difficulty is the reluctance of the school system itself to deal with conflictive or controversial issues. Its traditional position was to transmit certainties and avoid intellectual or social conflicts, and the teachers bear its uncertainties and contradictions as well as their own. This is why Federico Lorenz warns that, "in schools, the difference in opinions about the past is a reality that must be dealt with and not just a methodological safeguard."[69]

While acknowledging the difficulties, training educators is an unavoidable priority. It should be framed within the comprehensive approach of human rights and democratic citizenship education and must encompass several objectives: a cognitive objective, concerned with the knowledge and analysis of the recent past; an ethical objective, oriented toward human rights and democratic values and attitudes; and a technical objective, focused on the methodological skills necessary for teaching.

At the beginning of the transition, training teachers tends to be a civil society initiative with limited scope. The nongovernmental organizations (NGOs) that are most committed to the change, on occasion with the support of international agencies, organize voluntary training workshops for in-service educators, formal and nonformal. These activities are carried out in the most accessible regions of the country, usually urban areas, in the form of specific and brief actions, such as workshops, seminars, short courses, and meetings. Over time—depending on each situation and the extent to which teaching and memory about the recent past come to be part of public policies on education—NGOs will be joined by state institutions at national, provincial, and local levels, and the training of teachers will become more extensive, far reaching, and robust.

The final goal should be to ensure this training becomes large in scale, universal, and systematic. This will only be possible when the history of the human rights violations is incorporated into teachers' initial training programs as part of a serious approach to human rights and democratic citizenship education.[70] It is a long-term process that requires the transformations produced during the transition process to be established as public policy.

Based on the experience in Latin America, one variable that makes the inclusion of a human rights education perspective into initial teachers' training more difficult is the type of institutions in charge of this job in each country. Incorporation of this perspective is easier when it depends on the national education administration (tertiary-level institutions under the ministry of education) because these institutions must comply with the related public policies; the process is slower and less certain when it depends on universities, because they are autonomous institutions.

CONCLUSIONS AND SOME STRATEGIC CONSIDERATIONS

This chapter presented the main pedagogical guidelines, derived from the literature from different lines of thought and my own experience, with respect to the transformations in education that should happen in a post-conflict society undergoing a process of democratic transition. It proposed and examined several profound changes that should be made to the different components of the school system, as follows:

In education norms and institutions:
- Comprehensively review education norms to remove from the school system all vestiges of authoritarianism and denial of rights resulting from the recent conflict.
- Incorporate the mandate of teaching and memory of the recent conflict into the education legislation.
- Create bodies within public education institutions that will be responsible for planning and implementing policy regarding the teaching and

memory of recent conflict, allocating the resources and providing the specialized staff necessary to operate them.

In the curriculum (course content and teaching method):
- Comprehensively review all manifestations—explicit, null, and hidden—of the curricula for different subjects to determine what changes will be necessary to include the study of the recent past and memory (including deletions and additions, amendments, and reformulations).
- Decide where in the curriculum to incorporate teaching about recent history and how to insert it.
- Inquire about the effects of the authoritarian past on the day-to-day life of the schools and communities to identify these and propose objectives and strategies for transforming their adverse consequences for social life.
- Critically analyze and make changes to the teaching method in schools.
- Design strategies for working with the memory of the recent past, distinct from but complementary to the changes in the curriculum, that promote collaboration between the school and other social actors in education activities.

In didactic tools (teaching materials and memory supports):
- Select and develop didactic tools for teaching history and memory in formal and nonformal processes, keeping different age groups in mind.
- Design strategies for use of the didactic tools and plan for their broad distribution or dissemination.

In training of educators:
- Train teachers on how to teach recent history and memory, particularly teachers of history, civic education, human rights, and other subjects in which it has been decided the topic will be mainstreamed.

While these proposals are clearly necessary, their implementation will not be simple, fast, or uniform. For this reason, I conclude by briefly pointing out some strategic conditions that should be kept in mind when making post-conflict transformations in education. Such transformations should be addressed:

- In a comprehensive and integral manner, placing them conceptually within the broader human rights and democracy education approach, and changing each component of the education system and its key variables, as I have attempted to illustrate in this chapter.[71]

- In a contextualized manner, basing the changes on situational diagnoses of the reality where the intervention will be made (examining, for example, the balance of social forces; opportunities and difficulties in the transformations; allies and opponents; perceptions and interpretations of education agents; influences external to the school; and so on).
- In their evolution over time, planning actions for change that are desirable and possible to implement in the short, medium, and long terms to sustain and further the transformations.

Together, all of the recommendations offered in this chapter approach post-conflict transformations in the education system not just as problems to be solved solely with reference to historical teaching and learning, but rather as a process of human rights education for the active exercise of democratic citizenship.

APPENDIX 1.1. EDUCATION AND MEMORY PROGRAM

National Ministry of Education, Buenos Aires, Argentina
Argentina's Education and Memory Program[72] was born in 2004 and consolidated in 2006, after the approval of the new General Law on Education, which sought to reassert the guiding role of the state in education while at the same time respecting the federalist system of the country.

Although the federalist system in Argentina leaves the responsibility of developing curriculum and managing their schools in the hands of the provinces, the National Ministry intervenes in curriculum development through the establishment of a Nucleus of Priority Learning, which all are required to observe. These are the normative frameworks that constitute the national educative policy.

The program includes four broad topics and several actions related to ephemerides and historical dates. The topics are the following:

1. State Terrorism: Memories of the Dictatorship
2. The Malvinas War: Memory, Sovereignty, and Democracy
3. Teaching the Holocaust and Other Genocides of the Twentieth Century
4. The Post-Dictatorship and the Following Decades of Democratic Life (included in 2013)

At the same time, the program intervenes in four complementary areas of work:

1. Curriculum introduction
2. Preschool and continuous teacher training
3. Material production, delivered in teacher training programs
4. Establishment of a national focal network in memory and education

The approach is one adopted by human rights organizations, focusing on memory, truth, and justice, which in 2003 became a national policy. (Previously, the only initiatives were carried out by individuals and human rights institutions.)

The program develops the pedagogy of memory. It considers that teaching about the recent dictatorship is different from teaching about some events of the distant past, such as the independence wars against Spanish colonialism, for several reasons:

• It is closer in time to students and teachers.
• It tackles issues that are still socially controversial.
• It implies a more problematic intergenerational relationship.
• It is an area in which the school constructs a moral judgment (on an emotive level), but in which building explanations is more difficult (on a cognitive level).

Among the main objectives of the program are to come to a minimal agreement regarding the past military dictatorship—that is, a condemnation of state terrorism—without limiting the analysis, and to open questioning about the local level—that is, to begin with the question, "What happened in my community?"

APPENDIX 1.2. "YOUTH AND MEMORY: WE REMEMBER FOR THE FUTURE" PROGRAM

Comisión Provincial de la Memoria, Provincia de Buenos Aires, Argentina
The Youth and Memory Program has been in operation in the province of Buenos Aires since 2001.[73] The program invites teams composed of teachers and students to undertake research during one school year about local stories related to authoritarianism and their impact in the community, using primary

sources. As a result of the research, the teams produce short films, books, journals, murals, urban interventions, and websites, among other outputs. When the year is over, the different teams meet in the recreation center of the provincial government, at which they present to the other teams the results of their work. In 2002, 35 teams participated in the meeting; in 2012, there were 850.

The program's pedagogical approach is based on two considerations: first, the students themselves have to develop their own questions; and, second, they can choose the way in which they want to express or show the results of their research.

Under a rather broad thematic framework proposed by the program—Authoritarianism and Democracy—the students can choose more specific topics to focus on. The aims are as follows:

- *Compare the past and present.* While there is currently much awareness and sensibility about the recent past in Argentina, there is not that much or very little about present problems. The program aims to include reflection about the present situation when thinking on the legacies of the past.
- *Build the link between past and future.* The program considers that knowing about the past will not automatically make someone more sensitive and understanding about the present. This understanding is something that has to be built.
- *Consider youth as subjects with rights and as political subjects.* The problems of the past are renewed in today's reality (for example, young people may ask, "Why do I live in such a bad neighborhood? When did this neighborhood become a bad place to live in?"). By rediscovering the origins of the past in their neighborhoods, young people open the possibility for building a different future.
- *Think about the dictatorship beyond the tragedy of forced disappearances.* While forced disappearances are the best-known representation of the Argentinean dictatorship, authoritarianism manifests itself in many different ways. This is important because memory about the dictatorship becomes also a way of reflecting about what democracy is.
- *Break the individualist ideal that holds we are authors of our own destinies.*
- *Discover the happiness of being with others.*
- *Make clear that the transmission of the past is not the same as the teaching of history.* There are many different ways of transmitting the past in a society besides the teaching of history.

As it has grown, the program has become an experience highly valued by both students and their teachers. For students, it can trigger both conflict and reflection; for teachers, it allows them to reconnect with their students, recover their interest in teaching, and acquire self-esteem. Moreover, the event at the end of the year constitutes a very valuable opportunity for and experience of meeting and living with people from different neighborhoods, towns, and social groups within the province of Buenos Aires. In this way, democracy is learned as a "method"—it is not a goal, but a process.

NOTES

1   This chapter was translated into English by Carolina Carter. For the sake of brevity, I use the expressions "recent past" and "recent history," commonly found in the literature, with the stipulations, first, that they refer to series of events that vary, depending on geographical location, although they always involve violent authoritarian regimes, mass violations of human rights, and traumatic effects on society; second, that the timelines are somewhat vague, since these are more or less recent events, depending on each case; and, third, that they constitute an ongoing area of study. For further considerations, see Mario Carretero and Marcelo Borelli, "Memorias recientes y pasados en conflicto: ¿Cómo enseñar historia reciente en la escuela?" *Cultura y educación* 20, no. 2 (2008): 203.

2   Hugo Vezzetti, "El territorio de la memoria social: Un mapa por trazar," *Revista Puentes* 1, no. 1 (2000): 23. *Translator's Note*: In literal quotes, the page number corresponds to the original text in Spanish.

3   Ibid., 22. See also Hannah Arendt, *Eichmann in Jerusalem: A Report on the Banality of Evil* (New York: Penguin Books, 1963).

4   Carretero and Borelli, "Memorias recientes y pasados en conflicto."

5   Chronologically speaking, the first truth commission in Latin America was the National Commission for the Investigation of Forced Disappearances in Bolivia, which was established in 1982 to investigate the military dictatorships between 1964 and 1982. Since this commission was closed before concluding its investigations, however, it was unable to deliver a final report, and the whereabouts of the documents and papers it collected are currently unknown.

6   It is important to note that civil society in Argentina never adopted, and on the contrary rejected and continues to firmly reject, the banner of "reconciliation," as other societies did after their recent conflicts. It understood this proposal was being offered in lieu of seeking justice for the crimes committed during the dictatorships. This had been clear in the case of Chile and previously in Spain.

7   The differentiation among "formal," "nonformal," and "informal" education is common in the field. According to Kenneth D. Bush and Diana Saltarelli, formal education refers to "formal structures of schooling (a teacher who teaches and a student who learns," whereas informal and nonformal learning take place outside of official educational institutions: "Informal education is learning that occurs without being specifically planned and structured. Examples might be socialization, learning how to behave in a family or learning a trade from a parent. Nonformal education is planned and organized, offering specific learning environments and opportunities. These are usually more flexible and open than the formal education typified by schooling." Kenneth D. Bush and Diana Saltarelli, eds., *The Two Faces of Education in Ethnic Conflict: Towards a Peacebuilding Education for Children* (Florence, Italy: United Nations Children's Fund Innocenti Research Centre, 2000), ix, https://www.unicef-irc.org/publications/pdf/insight4.pdf.

8   Elizabeth A. Cole, "Transitional Justice and the Reform of History Education," *International Journal of Transitional Justice* 1 (2007): 115–37.

9   A few examples serve to illustrate this point. In the case of Myrna Mack Chang v. Guatemala (Inter-American Court of Human Rights, judgment of November 25, 2003, http://www.worldcourts.com/iacthr/eng/decisions/2003.11.25_Mack_Chang_v_Guatemala.pdf), the court ordered the Guatemalan state to "educate and train all members of its armed forces, the police and its security agencies regarding the principles and rules for protection of human rights, even under state of emergency" and "include education on human rights and on International Humanitarian Law in its training programs for the members of the armed forces, of the police and of its security agencies" (para. 282). In Tibi v. Ecuador (Inter-American Court of Human Rights, judgment of September 7, 2004, http://www.worldcourts.com/iacthr/eng/decisions/2004.09.07_Tibi_v_Ecuador.pdf), the court stipulated that the Ecuadorean state "must establish a training and education program for the staff of the judiciary, of the public prosecutor's office, of the police and of the penitentiary system, including the physicians, psychiatrists and psychologists, on the principles and provisions regarding detention of individuals, their legal rights and guarantees, the right to have an attorney, to receive visits, and for the indictees and the convicts to be lodged in different facilities" (para. 263). Subsequent rulings have made education-related recommendations on other topics, depending on the characteristics of the violations being tried—for example, on the need to identify and combat gender stereotypes and provide training for public officials and the general public in this area. See, for instance, Gonzalez et al. ("Cotton Field") v. Mexico (Inter-American Court

of Human Rights, judgment of November 16, 2009, http://www.worldcourts.com/iac-thr/eng/decisions/2009.11.16_Gonzalez_v_Mexico.pdf) and Atala Riffo and Daughters v. Chile (Inter-American Court of Human Rights, judgment of February 24, 2012, http:// www.worldcourts.com/iacthr/eng/decisions/2012.02.24_Riffo_v_Chile.pdf).

10   Peter Seixas, "What Is Historical Consciousness?" in *To the Past: History Education, Public Memory, and Citizenship in Canada*, ed. Ruth W. Sandwell (Toronto: University of Toronto Press, 2006), 1–22.

11   Maurice Halbwachs, *On Collective Memory* (Chicago: University of Chicago Press, 1992).

12   Jorge Manzi, "La memoria colectiva del golpe de Estado en Chile," in *Enseñanza de la historia y memoria colectiva*, ed. Mario Carretero, Alberto Rosa, and María Fernanda González (Buenos Aires: Paidós Educador, 2006), 297–322.

13   See ibid.; Elizabeth Jelín, *Los trabajos de la memoria* (Buenos Aires: Siglo XXI Editores, 2001), and Vezzetti, "El territorio de la memoria social."

14   Federico Lorenz, "El pasado reciente en la Argentina: Las difíciles relaciones entre trans-misión, educación y memoria," in Carretero et al., *Enseñanza de la historia*, 267–86.

15   Jelín, *Los trabajos de la memoria*.

16   See Vezzetti, "El territorio de la memoria social," and Sandra Raggio, "¿Historia o memoria en las aulas?" in *Efemérides en la memoria. 24 de marzo, 2 de abril, 16 de septiem-bre. Propuestas para trabajar en el aula*, ed. Sandra Raggio and Samanta Salvatori (Rosario: Homo Sapiens Ediciones, 2012), 13–30.

17   See Carretero et al., *Enseñanza de la historia*; Carretero and Borelli, "Memorias recientes y pasados en conflicto"; and Jelín, *Los trabajos de la memoria*.

18   Raggio, "¿Historia o memoria en las aulas?" 15.

19   We could add another violent conflict that had traumatic consequences for Argentinean society: the 1982 Malvinas War (in English, the Falklands War). While of a different nature and involving other agents, it was linked to the military dictatorship in power at that time. The war is today a part of the public policy of memory, and it was incorporated into the formal education curriculum by mandate of the 2006 National Education Law.

20   For example, any formal education system comprises the legislation it is governed by, the specific education policies of any administration, and the institutions at several lev-els (the national level; the provincial or state level in countries with federal systems of government; the municipal or district level; and the level of each education center or school). It also includes infrastructure; different agents with distinct functions (authori-ties, technical staff, supervisors, school principals, teachers, students, and parents); the course curricula; the teaching/learning materials; the evaluation subsystem; and the training and selection of educators, to cite some of the more visible components.

21   See Inter-American Institute of Human Rights, *Inter-American Report on Human Rights Education*, 10 vols. (San José: Inter-American Institute of Human Rights, 2002–13), and Ana María Rodino, "La institucionalización de la educación en derechos humanos en

los sistemas educativos de América Latina entre 1990 y 2012: Avances, limitaciones y desafíos," in *Cultura e educação em direitos humanos na América Latina*, ed. Ana María Rodino, Giuseppe Tosi, Maria de Nazaré T. Zenaide, and Mónica Beatriz Fernandez (Paraíba: Editora Universitária da UFPB, 2014), 61–82.

22 Jeff Spinner-Halev, "Education, Reconciliation and Nested Identities," *Theory and Research in Education* 1, no. 1 (2003): 51–72.

23 Some points difficult to agree on in most cases refer to, for example, the responsibilities of different sectors involved in the recent conflict, the events that triggered it, the perception of the role of each individual actor or group during it, and how to specifically attribute "guilt" or "innocence."

24 The main issue raised by the student body and broad sectors of the faculty and civil society in Chile is the privatized and profit-driven nature of the current education system, which restricts access to education. In 2015, a law was passed prohibiting profitmaking within the public school system. The government pledged to change the financing mechanism of schools and to create a new law on higher education, aiming to eliminate the 1990 Constitutional Organic Law on Education (LOCE, in Spanish) which, passed by Pinochet's government, still regulates some aspects of the current education system.

25 Argentina, National Education Law No. 26.206, underpinned by the Five-Year Compulsory Education and Teacher Training Plan (Res. 188/2012 of the Federal Education Council). See articles 3 (general objectives of education) and 92 (specific contents) of the law, which read as follows:

Article 3: Education is a national priority and constitutes a state policy to build a just society, reaffirm sovereignty and national identity, deepen the exercise of democratic citizenship and respect for human rights and fundamental freedoms, and strengthen the social-economic development of the nation.

Article 92: The following are contents of the curricula that are common to all jurisdictions:

a) Strengthening the regional perspective in Latin America, particularly in the MERCOSUR region, in the context of building a national identity that is open and respectful of diversity.

b) The goal of recovering our Malvinas, Georgias del Sur, and Sandwich del Sur Islands, in accordance with the stipulations of the First Transitory Provision of the National Constitution.

c) The exercise and construction of collective memory about the historical and political processes that disrupted the constitutional order and established state terrorism in order to foster reflection and democratic sentiments, defense of the rule of law and full realization of human rights among the students, in accordance with the provisions of Law No. 25.633 (Ley 25.633, se instituye el 24 de marzo como Día Nacional de la Memoria por la Verdad y la Justicia [De Agosto 2002]).

d) Knowledge of the rights of children and young people established by the Convention on the Rights of the Child and by Law No. 26.061 (Ley No. 26.061 de Protección Integral de los Derechos de Niños, Niñas y Adolescentes [De Octubre 2005]).

e) Knowledge of cultural diversity and the rights of indigenous peoples, in accordance with Article 54 of this law.

f) The content and approaches that contribute to establishing relationships based on equality, solidarity, and respect between the sexes, in accordance with the Convention on the Elimination of All Forms of Discrimination against Women, on the same level as the constitution, and laws no. 24.632 (Ley No. 24.632. Aprueba la Convención Interamericana para Prevenir, Sancionar y Erradicar la Violencia contra la Mujer "Convención de Belem do Para," suscripta en Belem do Para, Brasil, el 9 de junio de 1994 [de Abril 1996]) and 26.171 (Ley No. 26.171. Aprobación del Protocolo Facultativo de la Convención sobre la Eliminación de todas las Formas de Discriminación contra la Mujer, adoptado por la Asamblea General de la ONU el 6 de octubre de 1990 [de Diciembre 2006]).

26   Inter-American Institute of Human Rights, *Inter-American Report on Human Rights Education*.

27   Ana María Rodino, "La educación en derechos humanos: Un aporte a la construcción de una convivencia escolar democrática y solidaria. Programa Interamericano sobre Educación en Valores y Prácticas Democráticas," *Serie política en breve sobre educación y democracia*, vol. 2 (Washington DC: Oficina de Educación y Cultura, OEA, 2012).

28   For example, this happened in El Salvador and South Africa, where for different reasons the history courses were suspended after the end of the conflicts.

29   See ibid., issues 7, 8, and 10 (2008, 2009, and 2013); see also Rodino, "La institucionalización de la educación en derechos humanos."

30   Rafael Valls, "La guerra civil española y la dictadura franquista: Las dificultades del tratamiento escolar de un tema potencialmente conflictivo," *Enseñanza de las Ciencias Sociales* 6 (2007): 65 (quoted in Carretero and Borelli, "Memorias recientes y pasados en conflicto," 210).

31   The discrepancies between the recognized explicit curriculum and the curriculum effectively followed by the teachers in their classrooms are hard to detect and even harder to correct. They are only detected through rigorous investigations that include direct observation of classes and/or surveys of students, and they are (somewhat) corrected through oversight mechanisms that have been established by the system—for example, the observation of classes by course supervisors or school principals. Improving teacher training can also help prevent these discrepancies.

32   These two options are the most relevant in formal education for addressing recent history within the explicit curriculum. Without a doubt, the topic could also be addressed in such courses as literature, art, or religion, which commonly occurs when an

education system opts for the modality of crosscutting incorporation ("going across" different courses). While this is a good practice, it should not replace the disciplinary approach of the history and/or civic education courses. Other courses can provide additional opportunities to discuss the topic, but they should never be substitutes.

33 Elizabeth A. Cole, "Ourselves, Others and the Past that Binds Us: Teaching History for Peace and Citizenship," in *Education for Global Citizenship*, ed. Margaret Sinclair (Doha: Education Above All, 2012), 229–44. During the first decade of democratic rule in Argentina, schools taught about the national constitution and human rights as part of civic education, not history. The emphasis was on the education of citizens for democracy-building, grounded in human rights as the basis for creating a new future and breaking and stepping away from the recent dictatorship. Raggio, "¿Historia o memoria en las aulas?" Schools timidly began addressing the past in the 1990s and expanded their teaching about it around 2004–6. The estrangement from the discipline of history (which continues even today) was even more notable in Chile because the democratic transition was negotiated with the armed forces. The conciliatory approach the parties agreed on minimized the authoritarianism and actions of the Pinochet dictatorship, to the extent that official textbooks do not even contain terms like "coup d'état" or "dictatorship." Carretero and Borelli, "Memorias recientes y pasados en conflicto," 212.

34 Cole, "Ourselves, Others and the Past that Binds Us."

35 Elizabeth Oglesby, "Historical Memory and the Limits of Peace Education: Examining Guatemala's 'Memory of Silence' and the Politics of Curriculum Design" (New York: Carnegie Council on Ethics and International Affairs, June 2004), 28.

36 Rodino, "La institucionalización de la educación en derechos humanos."

37 Cole, "Ourselves, Others and the Past that Binds Us," 243.

38 Inés Dussel and Ana Pereyra, "Notas sobre la transmisión escolar del pasado reciente de la Argentina," in Carretero et al., *Enseñanza de la historia y memoria colectiva*, 243–66.

39 Cole, "Ourselves, Others and the Past that Binds Us"; Harvey M. Weinstein, Sarah W. Freedman, and Holly Hughson, "School Voices: Challenges Facing Education Systems after Identity-Based Conflicts," *Education, Citizenship and Social Justice* 2, no. 1 (2007): 41–71; Monique Eckmann, "Education in the Context of 'Divided' Memories—How Can a 'Pedagogy of Conflict Elaboration' Contribute?" EWC Statement Series 4 (Stockholm: European Wergeland Centre, March 2014); and Carretero and Borelli, "Memorias recientes y pasados en conflicto."

40 Carretero and Borelli, "Memorias recientes y pasados en conflicto."

41 Cole, "Ourselves, Others and the Past that Binds Us."

42 Carretero and Borelli, "Memorias recientes y pasados en conflicto," 206.

43 Ibid., 205.

44 See Elizabeth A. Cole and Judy Barsalou, "Unite or Divide? The Challenges of Teaching History in Societies Emerging from Violent Conflict" (Washington, DC: USIP, 2006);

Cole, "Transitional Justice and the Reform of History Education"; Cole, "Ourselves, Others and the Past that Binds Us"; Carretero and Borelli, "Memorias recientes y pasados en conflicto"; and Eckmann, "Education in the Context of 'Divided' Memories."

45 Cole, "Ourselves, Others and the Past that Binds Us."

46 For recent experiences, see the work of the US nongovernmental organization Facing History and Ourselves in the United States; of Gail Weldon in South Africa, especially her article "Thinking Each Other's History: Can Facing the Past Contribute to Education for Human Rights and Democracy?" *International Journal of Historical Learning, Teaching and Research* 5 (2005), http://centres.exeter.ac.uk/historyresource/journal9/9contents.htm; and in Argentina, the Ministry of Education's program Education and Memory (see appendix 1.1), and the activities of the Anne Frank House museum.

47 Jelín, *Los trabajos de la memoria.*

48 Lorenz, "El pasado reciente en la Argentina."

49 Cole, "Ourselves, Others and the Past that Binds Us," 241.

50 Jelín, *Los trabajos de la memoria.*

51 Vezzetti, "El territorio de la memoria social," 19.

52 Along this line, a relevant participatory and formative experience in Argentina is the program Youth and Memory: We Remember for the Future (see appendix 1.2).

53 The following are general considerations, but I sometimes refer specifically to a tool or type of tool to draw attention to the distinct situations in which they may be used. I mention just a few and only briefly, since many theoretical contributions and concrete tools have been produced for specific experiences. For more information, I recommend consulting the websites of governmental and nongovernmental education institutions that work on these issues, including those consulted during the research for this chapter. Specifically with reference to Argentina, see http://www.comisionporlamemoria.org/jovenesymemoria/el-programa.htm and http://www.me.gov.ar/educacionymemoria; and http://www.espaciomemoria.ar.

54 Rodino, "La institucionalización de la educación en derechos humanos."

55 Cole, "Ourselves, Others and the Past that Binds Us."

56 John Berger, "Usos de la Fotografía," *Elementos* 7, no. 37 (2000): 51, cited by Julia Rosemberg and Verónica Kovacic, *Educación, memoria y derechos humanos. Orientaciones pedagógicas y recomendaciones para su enseñanza Ministerio de Educación de la Nación Argentina y Organización de Estados Americanos* (Buenos Aires: Ministerio de Educación de la Nación, 2010), 20.

57 Rosemberg and Kovacic, *Educación, memoria y derechos humanos,* 27.

58 Raggio, "¿Historia o memoria en las aulas?"; Rosemberg and Kovacic, *Educación, memoria y derechos humanos*; and Carretero and Borelli, "Memorias recientes y pasados en conflicto."

59 Salvatori, "En el aula, ¿cómo enseñamos el pasado reciente?" in Raggio and Salvatori,

Efemérides en la memoria, 31–38.

60   Rosemberg and Kovacic, *Educación, memoria y derechos humanos*, 29.

61   Dussel and Pereyra, "Notas sobre la transmisión escolar del pasado reciente de la Argentina," 274.

62   Raggio, "¿Historia o memoria en las aulas?" 8.

63   Ephemerides are notable events that are remembered on their anniversaries.

64   March 24, the date of the military coup of 1976, is commemorated as the National Day of Memory for Truth and Justice, and April 2, the date the Malvinas War began in 1982, is commemorated as the Day of the Veteran and of the Deceased in the Malvinas War (see Raggio and Salvatori, *Efemérides en la memoria*).

65   See Raggio and Salvatori, *Efemérides en la memoria*; Rosemberg and Kovacic, *Educación, memoria y derechos humanos*; and the extensive collection of materials with their respective user guides in the cited websites (journals, document files, journalistic and literary texts, posters, photographs, sound and audiovisual recordings, and films).

66   Cole, "Ourselves, Others and the Past that Binds Us."

67   Raggio, "¿Historia o memoria en las aulas?" 22.

68   Abraham Magendzo and María I. Toledo, "Moral Dilemmas in Teaching Recent History Related to the Violation of Human Rights in Chile," *Journal of Moral Education* 38, no. 4 (2009): 445–65.

69   Lorenz, "El pasado reciente en la Argentina," 282.

70   Rodino, "La institucionalización de la educación en derechos humanos."

71   One example of integration is provided by the program Education and Memory, of the Ministry of Education of Argentina. Its most important lines of action are described in appendix 1.1.

72   This program description is based on an interview with Cecilia Flachsland and Mariano Harracá, members of the Education and Memory program, National Ministry of Education, Buenos Aires, October 10, 2013. More information can be found at http://www.me.gov.ar/educacionymemoria.

73   This program description is based on an interview with Sandra Raggio, research and education coordinator, Provincial Memory Commission, La Plata, October 11, 2013. See also www.comisionporlamemoria.org/jovenesymemoria.

CHAPTER 2

Education Reform through a Transitional Justice Lens: The Ambivalent Transitions of Bosnia and Northern Ireland

Karen Murphy

This chapter explores the role of institutional reforms within the education sector after conflict and the opportunities such reforms could provide for advancing transitional justice efforts, focusing on the question of education segregation in divided societies with identity-based conflicts. Through the case studies of Northern Ireland and Bosnia and Herzegovina (BiH), the chapter looks at reforms that have been made, as well as those that have been neglected or put aside because of the challenges faced by both of these divided societies, including growing sectarianism. While attention to the role of education in societies emerging from mass violence has grown,[1] examples of comprehensive reforms of the education sector that are well integrated into wider transitional justice frameworks are few. The neglect of education reforms is particularly glaring, as the sector often plays a critical role with respect to conflict—in perpetuating and reproducing social inequalities and divisions, for example, as well as by acting as a medium for propaganda, dissemination of myth, and misinformation.

Education as a sector is also uniquely positioned to make a substantive contribution to the repair, reconstruction, and redress of inequalities, divisions, and, in the spirit of transitional justice, political repression and human rights violations. While many transitional justice measures are temporary and focus on the first generation emerging from conflict, education is the only sector that simultaneously reaches both that generation and the subsequent ones, who become increasingly responsible for nurturing and protecting civil society and, in some cases, democracy and democratic institutions. These subsequent generations are responsible for upholding the new norms and protections put into place during the country's transition, and/or for continuing to appropriately acknowledge and redress past abuses and their effects on individuals, communities, and society as a whole. In many ways, the education sector is the most appropriate medium for reaching young adult citizens and introducing them both to the violent past and its varied legacies and to the transitional justice measures used to redress and record them. It is also the

most appropriate medium for embodying and passing on the skills, dispositions, and behaviors that must be learned to nurture and protect democratic
citizenship and human rights.

The chapter begins by discussing reform efforts carried out in South Africa
and the United States, presented here as examples of two societies that have
had to address past and present racial segregation in their education systems.
The next section examines the challenges faced by education reform in what I
describe as "ambivalent transitions" in BiH and Northern Ireland, respectively.
In both cases, education reform has been hindered by the absence of a broader
transitional justice framework, while the persistence of segregated schools
has, in turn, effectively undone progress made by other efforts to create parity,
repair society, and promote reconciliation. The experiences of these countries
demonstrate the difficulty of achieving such goals in societies that lack commitment both to reforming education and to addressing the past.

EDUCATION REFORM AND THE CRITICAL ISSUE OF SEGREGATION

Education reforms in the aftermath of conflict or repression often include policy changes, such as the introduction of new norms (rights and responsibilities
in line with a new constitution or bill of rights, for instance) and the removal
of policies of the former regime. A particularly important area of consideration for structural reforms in education with reference to transitional justice is segregation by identity group.[2] In many divided societies, schools are
segregated, reflecting the sociopolitical norms at work more widely. Some of
these divisions—as in South Africa during apartheid and the southern United
States during the Jim Crow era—reflect legal policies that are focused on the
separation of citizens to advance a particular sociopolitical-economic agenda
and the intentional unequal distribution of resources to privilege one group
over others.

In terms of education, this meant that in both these cases, the lion's share
of resources (such as books, school facilities, provision for extracurricular
activities, and investment in teacher training programs) was allocated to white
schools. Schools for black children in both South Africa and affected areas
of the southern United States suffered from a fundamental lack of resources.
Moreover, rather than introducing rigorous curricula through which students
could be taught to think or excel with college or university in mind, these
schools instead "trained" them in vocational skills, with second-class citizenship as the assumed goal.

Particularly in light of the education reforms they both implemented focused on segregation, the United States and South Africa provide instructive examples for considering BiH and Northern Ireland, both divided societies with identity-based conflicts and violent struggles in the recent past.

While not a perfect model, South Africa provides some important lessons. Policymakers there began transforming the education landscape before the formal democratic transition of 1992. Soon after the transition, the nineteen separate departments of education were closed down and replaced by a single, newly created nonracial department; formerly white schools were opened to students of other backgrounds; textbooks were revised; curricular reforms were initiated; and new norms were created to address gross inequalities in the distribution of resources across schools.[3] In no way is education reform complete or evenly implemented across provinces and schools today, but South Africa's efforts, in comparison to those (not) made by other countries, stand out. Its new history curriculum, in particular, is rare among divided societies and countries in transition.

The first curriculum after apartheid was considered problematic because it was challenging to implement, focused on a new way of teaching and learning (outcomes-based as opposed to content- and performance-based education), and largely devoid of content; among other things, history was omitted from the syllabus.[4] Subsequent revisions made over the past ten years, however, have resulted in a new national history curriculum, which requires an exploration of the violent past and the human behavior that animated it from the perspective of human rights. The curriculum asks students to study the transition itself and some of the transitional justice efforts, such as the South African Truth and Reconciliation Commission (TRC), which operated in the country in the first years after the democratic elections of 1994. Teachers are also asked to teach differently than they did before—to become curriculum developers, not rote deliverers, and to facilitate dialogue and discussion while teaching their learners how to think historically.

These approaches have prompted both teachers and learners to think and to develop the skills, dispositions, and behaviors necessary to protect and preserve democracy, human rights, and civic participation. Importantly, these reforms in its education system were consistent with South Africa's transitional justice interventions and the dominant message of the country's leaders after the end of apartheid. The interventions, such as the Constitution of 1996 and the TRC, were inclusive and framed within a national identity narrative— as opposed to a group- or tribe-based one—that was first and foremost South African. The national history curriculum became informed by the content and spirit of these broader changes, and, in this way, teachers and schools were not asked to act in isolation from the dominant norms being established in other areas. They were, instead, supported by a foundation and framework that upheld national values.

Despite these efforts, many challenges remain today in South Africa's education system. While technically all state schools are now open to all learners, the geographical and socioeconomic legacies of apartheid, as a matter of fact, left most schools segregated. While it is true that, over the past twenty years, they have become more diverse, particularly in the more desirable, often formerly white, areas, access is mediated by socioeconomic considerations. Moreover, parents and learners themselves are responsible for navigating the education landscape; neither road maps nor guides are available to help them choose schools that offer better opportunities and enjoy more resources, including networks that lead to future opportunities. Middle- and upper-middle-class parents, who are primarily white, have the benefit of having attended these schools themselves or knowing others who have, making navigation and selection of the best schools easier. This means people with the most resources and information (an asset of privilege), who remain disproportionately white even with the emergence of a black middle class, are able to take greater advantage of the system. From this perspective, South Africa has a great deal of work to do and few effective models to follow.

The United States, which also has a history (although different) of racial separation, oppression, and inequality, as well as a commitment to democracy and social justice, has a spotty record in terms of education reforms that meaningfully address this history. Racial segregation legally ended in 1954 with *Brown v. Board of Education*, the US Supreme Court decision that invoked the transformative Fourteenth Amendment—itself an example of legislative redress and repair efforts made to rebuild the country and create some semblance of justice in the wake of the Civil War and slavery. The court left it to local governments, however, to interpret their time frames for and approaches to implementation.[5] Most states dragged their feet well into the 1970s, when the Supreme Court upheld the use of busing to bring children from one community to another in the hope of integrating schools. This process was met with protest and, in some places, such as Boston, with anger and violence.[6] Over time, it also did not stick. Today, many cities in the United States still have schools divided by race and socioeconomic status. Those in Chicago, Dallas, New York City, and Philadelphia are some of the most segregated in the country; in New York City, more than half the schools are over 90 percent black and Hispanic, with no substantive plans on the horizon to address the problem.[7]

Sheldon Berman, interim superintendent of Andover Public Schools in Massachusetts, who was superintendent of Jefferson County Public Schools in Louisville, Kentucky, during a period when integration was the central battle, sees this issue as fundamentally tied to the health of American democracy. "If our nation is to thrive," he says,

> we must revive a national conversation about the growing racial and ethnic segregation in our schools. We need to engender support from key community leaders, including local government and faith-based organizations, for an approach to student assignment that fosters and sustains school diversity. These leaders can broadly frame the diversity dialogue around such advantages as revitalizing the community, enhancing economic opportunity, strengthening educational opportunity and preparing students to participate in a democracy.[8]

While the strategy Berman articulates here is for repositioning the value of diversity for US schools, his points are also relevant from a transitional justice perspective. Diversity within schools is not an abstract ideal, but one that is tied to fundamental values of justice and equality under the law and to a philosophy that separation is fundamentally bad for a society with a history of inequality and division based on identity groups.

In these circumstances, school integration can function as an act of redress and reconciliation. It would represent a legal intervention aimed at bringing, in this case, Americans together across identity groups. But it would necessarily be done with reference to a divided American past and the inequalities that resulted from the divisions themselves and the unequal distribution of resources. Diversity, in a formerly segregated society, could be viewed as a just goal, aimed not only at bringing people together across communities but also at providing more equal opportunities and access to resources across communities.

In fact, however, recent jurisprudence, including the 2007 Supreme Court decision *Parents Involved in Community Schools v. Seattle School District 1* (discussed below),[9] is threatening efforts to integrate schools. According to Berman, "At the height of the nation's desegregation efforts in 1988, nearly half of African Americans in the South attended integrated schools. Since then, schools have resegregated to levels that existed in 1970."[10] Berman's experience as superintendent of Louisville Public Schools is illustrative of this process. He faced an uphill battle against resegregation, including the *Parents Involved* case and, ultimately, lack of federal support from the US Department of Education, which once stood behind integration/desegregation. He also faced state and local battles with parents and community members.

The *Parents Involved* decision itself reflects the challenges confronted by those who would frame integration as a transitional justice issue. In it, the Supreme Court effectively says a student's race cannot explicitly be used to achieve integration. Chief Justice John Roberts writes that "the way to stop discrimination on the basis of race is to stop discriminating on the basis of race"[11]—an argument that does not take into account the significant role played by race, racism, and racial discrimination in American history or the continued and varied legacies of that history.[12]

In an opposing effort to highlight the importance of integration and the dangers of segregation and the need to be explicit about the role of race, scholars such as Susan Eaton from the Charles Hamilton Houston Institute for Race and Justice and Harvard University and Gary Orfield from the Civil Rights Project at the University of California, Los Angeles (UCLA), have conducted extensive research and published several reports on the benefits of diversity, which include "reduced neighborhood, college and workplace segregation, higher levels of social cohesion and a reduced likelihood for racial prejudice."[13] Other research conducted by the Charles Hamilton Houston Institute has found students from more racially and economically diverse schools more likely to be academically successful, to graduate from high school, to attend integrated colleges and universities, and to graduate from college.[14] They also enjoy significantly more opportunities for career and educational advancement and are more likely to work in diverse settings. Furthermore, adults who have attended diverse schools

> will exhibit greater workforce readiness for occupations that require interacting with customers and coworkers from all racial backgrounds, and functioning in an increasingly global economy. . . . They are less likely to be involved with the criminal justice system and there is some evidence that they will earn more income than those who attend segregated schools. Adults who attended diverse schools are more likely to have cross-racial friendships and exhibit mutual trust, respect, and acceptance of those who are racially, ethnically, and socioeconomically different from themselves.[15]

A study of nonminority students demonstrates that

> diverse schools are linked to a host of positive learning outcomes for white students. These include more robust classroom discussions, the

promotion of critical thinking and problem-solving skills and higher academic achievement. The presence of different racial and ethnic backgrounds in a classroom is closely connected to heightened dialogue and debate. . . . In other words, diverse perspectives provide multiple lenses through which to view and understand problems and events. The complex, more flexible thinking that white students develop from these exchanges is an essential academic benefit flowing from diverse classrooms.[16]

These are skills, dispositions, and behaviors that are essential for civic participation in a diverse democracy, and they should be cultivated in citizens who are inheriting the legacies of a violent, divided past. From a transitional justice perspective, they are essential both for navigating a state emerging from mass violence and for making that state more secure and stable and protecting values that respect and promote human rights and democracy for subsequent generations.

Importantly, racially segregated schools have negative effects on students' academic achievement, which

often lags behind that of their peers at more diverse schools. Racially isolated schools often have fewer effective teachers, higher teacher turnover rates, less rigorous curricular resources (e.g., college preparatory courses), and inferior facilities and other educational resources.[17]

Students in these schools also have fewer networks to draw upon for educational, career, and other life opportunities. In societies emerging from mass violence with histories of division based on identity, segregated schools reinforce these divisions and exacerbate tensions between and among people. In other words, segregated schools can effectively undo other efforts to create parity, repair society, and promote reconciliation.

THE CASE STUDIES OF BOSNIA AND HERZEGOVINA AND NORTHERN IRELAND

Two countries that have emerged relatively recently from mass violence and, it could be argued, are still in a transitional phase are Bosnia and Herzegovina (BiH) and Northern Ireland. While the two cases differ in many ways, the countries do have a great deal in common, particularly when viewed through the lens of education and transition.

The way a country's conflict ends profoundly shapes and informs its transition. Those in BiH and Northern Ireland were both ended by negotiated settlements, the Dayton Accords (1995) and the Belfast Agreement (1998), respectively. Both largely neglected education reforms and ignored key factors at the root of the conflicts, such as interpretations of the past and its legacies and the connections between political and cultural power and identity. Moreover, the agreements themselves legitimated segregation based on an honoring of cultural, linguistic, religious, and political identity. The fear of a group's identity being threatened or subsumed by another permeates both agreements and provides a window into some of the challenges both countries face, particularly within the education arena.

Finally, in both BiH and Northern Ireland, reforms were proposed and then either partially implemented or abandoned. Without the implementation of wider, more comprehensive transitional justice frameworks, it is difficult to imagine substantive education reforms—which have the best chance of making a positive difference when they are consistent with a wider set of policies and norms—sticking in either country. By the same token, while leaving education out of these processes risks undoing them, focusing on education alone often translates into little change at the macro level and places teachers, administrators, and, most importantly, students potentially in harm's way as they tackle challenges the wider society has neglected or abandoned.

BOSNIA AND HERZEGOVINA

The violence of BiH's conflict took place primarily between April 1992 and December 1995 and followed on the heels of the breakup of the former Yugoslavia. For more than three and a half years, violence took place between and among the three major identity groups of the Republic of Bosnia: the Catholic Croats, the Orthodox Serbs, and the majority Muslim Bosniaks. The war was characterized by the establishment of concentration camps, mass rape, ethnic cleansing, and genocide. According to *The Bosnian Book of the Dead*, 95,940 people were killed; Reuters reported that "roughly half the dead were civilians, while 82 percent of those were Bosnian Muslims. . . . Some 10,000 women were killed, again the majority Bosniaks. Of 24,000 Serb dead, 20,000 were soldiers."[18] The International Criminal Tribunal for the former Yugoslavia (ICTY), established in 1993, issued verdicts and indictments against both Croat and Serb forces for ethnic cleansing and determined that a massacre of Bosnian men by Serb forces in Srebenica in 1995 was an act of genocide.[19]

Before the breakup of the former Yugoslavia, the Republic of Bosnia was known as a multiethnic society, where religious and cultural tolerance was common and intermarriage not atypical. A shared Yugoslav identity was shaped by a commitment to a larger, socialist identity as imposed by Josip Broz Tito, who emphasized "Brotherhood and Unity," and by particular narratives related to the role the country played in World War II against Nazi Germany. Importantly, within the former Yugoslavia, citizens were also united by a shared language, Serbo-Croatian.[20]

Of course, the Yugoslavian "national" project was both mythic and incomplete. While Harvey Weinstein and Eric Stover show that many in BiH have nostalgic memories of the former Yugoslavia, suggesting changes happened overnight, heightened nationalism and ethnocentrism emerged, in fact, over time. Differing interpretations of the past, historical grudges, and complaints of discrimination, among other markers of conflict, increased over years.[21]

The war and postwar periods in BiH were characterized by the widespread involvement of the international community, including the United Nations and its major agencies, numerous nongovernmental organizations (NGOs), both small and large, specific countries (such as Britain, France, Germany, Russia, and the United States), and international institutions, including the International Monetary Fund (IMF), the Organization for Security and Co-operation in Europe (OSCE), and the North Atlantic Treaty Organization (NATO), to name a few. After the war, the international community was—and it remained—actively engaged in efforts to rebuild and reconstruct BiH. The international actors who supported Bosnia's transition, however, were particularly reluctant to make education a substantive part of their early efforts. According to Valery Perry, who was deputy director of the Education Department of the OSCE Mission to Bosnia and Herzegovina in the mid-2000s,

> The primary focus was initially on reforms and basic services that were vitally needed in the shattered country, such as reconstruction, separation of the military forces in BiH, refugee return, and basic infrastructure development. There was also an emphasis on elections, which the IC [international community] viewed as a critical part of an early exit strategy. . . . The IC's mandate primarily focused on implementation of the peace agreement, in which education is not a top priority. This is evidenced by the fact that no organization, international or domestic, was given a clear mandate to ensure educational reform.[22]

At one point in the reconstruction process, the role of education was highlighted, according to Perry, as something that must be substantively addressed. She relates that at a January 2002 conference on education reform sponsored by the Office of the High Representative (OHR),[23] Principal Deputy High Representative Donald Hays acknowledged, "We are late in tackling this issue, one that should have been viewed as a core issue for BiH post-war recovery and an issue that will definitely influence the success or failure of all our efforts to create a free, democratic and stable BiH."[24]

Furthermore, while some actors clearly approached reforms in Bosnia with transitional justice in mind, it has not been the primary perspective from which reforms have been made in the country. In contrast to South Africa, for example, which highlighted repair, reconstruction, and reconciliation, Bosnia's reforms in the realm of education have been primarily technical, with a general reluctance to place value on or make judgments about the actions taken by individuals and groups in the past. Significantly, South Africa's major reforms were also internal and national, rather than developed and reinforced by external actors.

The Dayton Peace Accords of 1995 created the political foundation for the end of the conflict at the same time they reinforced both separation by ethnic group in schools and the messy, unnavigable bureaucratic structure of the overall education system. According to Clare Magill, Dayton created a weak state with a complex bureaucracy, one often crippled by local and communal—and therefore ethnic—politics. She also argues that the peace agreement shaped education in two fundamental ways tied to language, which had the effects of ensuring segregation:

> First, the GFA [General Framework Agreement, or Dayton Agreement] recognized and protected the Bosnian, Croatian, and Serbian languages. Second, the new BiH Constitution included the texts of various international human rights conventions and treaties, among them the European Convention on the Rights of the Child, which guarantees the right of all children to be educated in their own language. Together, these two outcomes of the Dayton Agreement meant that each of the three major ethnic groups could justify the continuation of separate, segregated education, in spite of the fact that Bosnian, Serbian, and Croatian are mutually intelligible. This paved the way for the use of linguistic arguments to support political motivations by those arguing for separate schooling.[25]

Thus, language became a way to politicize education, and its protection a primary strategy for separating children along ethnic lines in postwar BiH. The accords also contributed to what would become known as the "two-schools-under-one-roof" phenomenon, where students from different ethnic groups attend the same school but are physically separated, are taught in their specific languages (Croatian, Serbian, or Bosnian), and participate in their specific ethnic curricula.

Against this backdrop, the OSCE, largely inspired by efforts to bring BiH into alignment with other European countries in preparation for its entry into the European Union, began around 2002 to take on education reform as part of its purview, and the international community started putting more pressure on BiH to promote integration and reconciliation among youth and through education reforms. As Azra Hromadžic, who has researched this issue extensively, writes:

> Under the plan, 54 ethnically divided "two schools under one roof" were to be reunified. To date, however, only in Vares, Zepce, and Mostar (the Mostar Gymnasium) have the two schools merged officially to become one legal body with two components; in all the other cases, the two schools have retained their separate legal identities. However, even the "integrated" schools maintained separate ethnic curricula for the students of the three majority ethnic groups, thus preserving ethnic segregation. What this means in practice is that ethnically divided youth share the same school buildings and administrative services but follow different curricula and attend classes in separate classrooms.[26]

Similar outcomes have occurred across BiH. Perry offers an example of a new school in Stolac for whose development the World Bank had contributed funds. Bosnian Croat children were enjoying the new site and resources while "Bosniak children were forced to be schooled out of private homes in sub-standard conditions."[27] Learning of this, the OHR said the Bosniak children should also be able to enjoy the new school if there was space for them. According to Perry, while the OHR's intentions were good, it

> underestimated the divisions in Stolac and the nationalist politics that drive the hardline city in Herzegovina. Rather than integrating the Bosniak children into the school, the school was essentially divided into Bosnian Croat and Bosniak sections, separating students by floor, with piles of chairs and desks serving as barriers in the corridors and with

separate entrances for each group. Other similar cases occurred in BiH as nationalists sought to ensure the minimal level of compliance and to continue homogenous education to the maximum extent possible.[28]

By some estimates, more than fifty schools in BiH are still divided in these ways.[29]

Despite a recent court decision in Mostar to desegregate schools in the towns of Stolac and Capljina, where Bosniak and Croat children attend school separately in the same institution, no meaningful plan appears to be in place for integration of Bosnia's schools in the near future.[30] Some argue the "two-schools-under-one-roof" idea was originally an interim measure to bring students of different ethnicities together in the same physical space, particularly as former refugees and internally displaced people returned home. It quickly became another impediment to creating a shared society after the war, however, and has persisted over the years.[31]

A significant source of tension related to integration is the way in which the concept is perceived and interpreted by BiH's major identity groups. Hromadžic's research is particularly useful here. She writes,

> The local notion of integration is best captured by the phrase *biti zajedno* (to be together), which essentially means joint classrooms and curricula. This is seen in contrast to *biti razdvojen* (to be separated). For the majority of people, especially the Croats and the Serbs in B&H, integration is understood as either the return to the prewar Yugoslav ethnic relations or as an assimilation into a larger, dominant group and a related loss of ethnocultural identity. Both are seen as dangerous to the survival of the ethnically defined communities.[32]

According to Hromadžic, an essential conflict exists between the international community's conception of integrated education and the realities in BiH. In her case study on the attempts to integrate the Mostar Gymnasium, she describes the fundamental threat to their identity felt by Croatian people from these efforts, and the way they strategically used the Dayton Accords, particularly with respect to the use of language, as a way to maintain their separateness. She quotes a former principal of the school:

> The problem [of integration] becomes most obvious when we talk about language. Our local languages are similar in some ways, but they are mostly different. And *narod* [a people] without language is not *narod*

at all. Which language would students listen to at school? Parents fear that the Croat language will be destroyed.... This is bigger than politics; it's about society and about culture.[33]

In addition to the fact that most students are being educated in separate spaces, they are also learning distinct curricula and having their distinctness from each other reinforced by the language of instruction. The separate curricula extend to history and politics, where ethnic and national perspectives inform what is taught. Scholar Janine Clark considers these two aspects of the education system—the approach to history education and segregation—"fundamental obstacle[s] to reconciliation." She argues that

education is a primary vehicle through which these rehumanizing and trust-building processes can take place. An education system that keeps young people divided, however, thus helping to fuel prejudice and stereotypes, is a fundamental obstacle to reconciliation. Hence, the central contention of this article—which is premised on the so-called "contact hypothesis"—is that unless and until the education system in BiH undergoes a major overhaul, so that segregation and exclusion are replaced with integration and inclusion, the prospects for genuine reconciliation remain somewhat remote.[34]

Clark also points to the detrimental effects of the OHR's March 2002 Interim Agreement on Accommodation of Specific Needs and Rights of Returnee Children, which gave parents the right to send their children to the schools of their choice in postwar BiH.[35] This led many parents to base their decisions on the curricula (in turn based on ethnic or national group), reinforcing both the physical and the social, intellectual, historical, and political segregation of their children.

Where changes in education have occurred and are occurring in BiH, most appear guided by large external organizations, such as the United Nations Children's Fund (UNICEF), the Council of Europe (CoE), the World Bank, and OSCE. In 2003, for example, a series of curricular reforms were introduced in Bosnia, many of which appear to have been facilitated by OSCE. They included "six pledges" relating to accessibility and nondiscrimination in education; modernization and improvement of the quality of preschool, primary, and general secondary education; modernization and improvement of the quality of vocational education; modernization and improvement of the quality of higher education; financing and management in education; and legislation in education.[36] The implementation of these reforms, however, has been inconsistent and has suffered from precisely the issues previously highlighted by Magill and Perry: a weak federal state, an unnavigable bureaucracy, and a highly politicized environment animated by ethnic divisions and fears of losing one's ethnic identity or having it subsumed by another.

An aspect of this reform that made some progress was the proposal for a common core curriculum and the inclusion of special needs children into mainstream education. These changes, however, were not met with new professional development requirements or opportunities for teachers. According to Adila Pašalić-Kreso and others,

> These changes have not been accompanied by a significant change in the system of the professional training of teachers or by the intensified training and preparation of teachers to face these challenges. The reason for this can be sought in the fact that the changes were mainly instigated by the international community, and that they were realised at the legislative level, without any real change in the contexts in which the change would take place and without adequate preparations in practice.[37]

The common core curriculum was specifically intended to create more continuity across BiH. Given the number of people forced into other communities, the movement of children from school to school has been a challenge since the war ended; by honoring their right to education, common core could facilitate this movement. The common core addressed most of the curriculum, apart from those subjects—politics, history, and religion—that are particularly divisive. Not one curriculum but, rather, a series of required elements, it was adopted by education ministers in 2003 and supposed to have been introduced in the 2003–4 school year.

Although implementation appears minimal, a new Agency for Pre-Primary, Primary and Secondary Education (APOSO) was created in 2009 to monitor the quality of education in BiH, including the common core.[38] APOSO is responsible for a holistic curriculum revision within the new syllabus of standards and competencies. With regard to history education, a board with members representing all identity groups developed new learning standards for grades 6, 7, and 9 that were to have been implemented in all of BiH in 2014, along with teacher trainings on how to deal with competencies in teaching. Whether all the education ministries would accept these reforms and implement them remained questionable, however.[39]

Also agreed in 2002 was that after that year, cantons would not use text-books from neighboring countries (Croatia and Serbia) to promote their particular ethnic or national perspectives. Although a textbook commission worked to ensure the removal of "inappropriate" content from them, the use of these supporting texts from neighboring countries continued into (at least) 2006. To gain insight into the challenges regarding textbook oversight and curricular content, consider this note from the US Department of State:

> Textbooks in Bosnian Croat–majority areas refer to Croatia as the homeland of all Croat people, while texts in the RS [Republika Srpska] instill a sense of patriotism towards Serbia and Montenegro. During the year the Interentity Textbook Review Commission drafted guidelines for authors of new textbooks that emphasized multiple points of view, including those of women and national minorities. Despite their earlier commitment to the commission, five Bosnian Croat cantonal ministers of education and RS Minister of Education Milovan Pecelj refused to sign the guidelines.[40]

Significantly, history education was not included among these early reforms, nor were pedagogical strategies that would have moved teachers from an authoritarian position in the classroom to one that modeled democratic values and norms. While attempts have been made to develop a shared vision and address the most controversial aspects of the past, eighteen years after the war students still learn distinct, often competing, narratives and speak in languages they consider "their own" and fundamentally different from their neighbors'. The head of the OSCE mission reflected on this reality in 2006:

> When I hear that certain well-regarded local authors are taught in, say, Mostar in one curriculum as foreign writers simply because they are not of the same ethnicity as those studying under that particular cur-riculum, I grow distressed. If Bosnia and Herzegovina is to succeed as a community—as a commonwealth of citizens, even if composed of different cultures, religious beliefs, and languages—then this will hardly do. After all, how will you grow up feeling that you are a citizen of the State of Bosnia and Herzegovina if you are taught that your capital is actually Zagreb or Belgrade, if you are taught that the only possible ori-entation for your community and your country is Islamic, or if you are taught that everyone who does not speak or worship exactly like you does not belong with you?[41]

OSCE, in particular, has tried to remain on top of this issue. Among other things, the agency developed "Guidelines for Textbook Writing and Evaluation of History Textbooks for Primary and Secondary Schools in BiH," which were adopted by all ministries of education,[42] and, together with the CoE, a *Teacher Manual on Contemporary History Teaching in Schools.*[43] OSCE is now implementing the project History for the Future—Towards Reconciliation through Education, "which seeks to establish common principles, outcomes and standards for teaching history for the whole country to ensure a common base of knowledge, culture and values for all students."[44] Given the challenges above, however, including nationalism and decentralization, as well as weak policies for training teachers and continuing their professional development, it is unclear how widespread or deep these efforts have been, although OSCE and the CoE have both offered ongoing training for teachers.

Another intervention aimed at addressing the teaching of history in the country is being led by the Georg Eckert Institute (GEI), in cooperation with the German Foreign Ministry.[45] The education resources created by GEI focus on everyday life during the war period and avoid particularly controversial events and issues, such as the concentration camps and the genocide in Srebenica. Because everyday life was relatively the "same" across ethnic communities, GEI argues that it is touching on something they shared. GEI also supported a four-week teacher institute with historians to develop teaching materials and, with OSCE and the CoE, offered in-service teacher training on history methods and the teaching of sensitive subjects. Unfortunately, few teachers are using the materials created by GEI due to a combination of factors, including lack of support from the Ministry of Education, the psychological barriers involved in confronting the material, and the absence of requirements from the curriculum.[46]

An important exception in both history education and integration is Brčko, an international district with a special school system. Here all three of the major identity groups attend class, including history class, together, and they "are using books from 3 parts of the country." Katarina Batarilo-Henschen from GEI referred to this as a "forced, but very effective situation of multi-perspectivity in history education."[47]

Euroclio, a European education NGO, has also focused on history education reforms in BiH. Its efforts include the development of resources and the "modernization" of teacher training and methods. According to Euroclio, as of 2009 it had sixty-two members participating in its BiH organization and a growing network of education organizations and educators. Its work began in 2003 and manifested in the History that Connects program which, it says, aims to improve history education in all the countries of Former Yugoslavia as well as the wider Western Balkans in a way that furthers peace, democracy, tolerance and critical thinking. Educators in the region work together towards developing inclusive and multi-perspective materials on the sensitive history of the region. The development of the material can be understood as an intense competencies-building course and be used as [the] basis for an alternative approach for national curricula.[48]

Reportedly, however, while the teachers using the materials and methods are excited by them, their use is limited because it has not been supported—and has perhaps been deterred—by the pedagogical institutes.[49]

Efforts are also underway to make teacher education more diverse, both in terms of ethnic participation and what teachers are learning. One such effort is led by a group of teachers who are seeking to bypass the cumbersome bureaucracy to provide professional development opportunities to other teachers. The Tuzla English Teachers' Association (TETA) seeks to provide teachers with the ability to work together across boundaries and to learn and practice new skills. This effort breaks down barriers by ethnicity and provides essential professional development—professional development being another area that is far too murky in Bosnia, where teachers are primarily lecturers, imparting technical knowledge to their students. Several scholars have raised concerns about this approach, highlighting students' lack of skills and dispositions (critical thinking, among them) to support the country's young democracy. Teachers remain married to more formal, authoritarian, and technical approaches to teaching.

Coupled with dated and divisive curricula, authoritarianism in teaching presents troubling signs for an already fragile society. It is also a legacy of the past: before the war, education prioritized the learning of facts over the development of analytical skills. According to Astrid Fischer,

Education in the Yugoslav period was devised in accordance with the ideology and principles of the Tito regime. Curricula and teaching methods were guided by socialist values, stressing collective solidarity and political loyalty over critical thinking. The official ideology was particularly demonstrated in the teaching of 20th century history. The Second World War was portrayed as a heroic fight against fascism. Atrocities and crimes among Yugoslavs were overlooked in favour of an all-inclusive partisan perspective. This dependence on a "fragmented memory" that selects historic events and claims that there was only one "true" history is still apparent in textbooks across the entire post-Yugoslav region. It has been recycled now from a nationalist perspective.[50]

Another legacy of the past is the dynamic between central or federal policies and the republics. Today, this plays out within the context of BiH's canton structure. With education policies pushed down to the canton and local authorities, ethnic politics prevails and divisions multiply. This approach is also reflected in the sites where teachers are trained—the pedagogic institutes specific to their locales, which tend not to share information or collaborate.

NORTHERN IRELAND

Northern Ireland's thirty-year violent conflict is commonly referred to as "the Troubles." The protagonists of this low-level, multidecade war have often been characterized in religious terms, as Protestants versus Catholics. In many ways, this is shorthand for a political and cultural conflict that brewed throughout the twentieth century. Traditionally, Protestants are affiliated with Loyalism and Unionism, which favors connection to Great Britain, while Catholics are affiliated with Republicanism and Nationalism, which locates a future with the Republic of Ireland and identifies the current arrangement as part of a long history of imperialism.

When Ireland was partitioned in 1920, creating the Republic of Ireland (to the South) and the six counties of Northern Ireland, the Protestant majority ruled the North as a Protestant state, with a Catholic minority firmly placed as second-class citizens. Over the years, Catholics gained a greater foothold in society and, inspired in part by the US civil rights movement, began to claim equal rights, particularly in employment and housing. Catholic claims to equality were met by both legislative reforms and violence. On October 5, 1968, a civil rights march in Derry/Londonderry degenerated into violence, with the state police force—the Royal Ulster Constabulary—caught by the media in the act of beating unarmed civilian marchers. This event marks the beginning of the modern Troubles, as 1969 ushered in more rioting between Catholics and Protestants, resulting in the deployment of the British army in Ireland.

The period between 1969 and the ceasefires of 1994 was marked by the development and violent activities of paramilitaries, which included the Irish Republican Army (IRA) on the Nationalist side, and the Ulster Volunteer Force and the Ulster Defense Association, among others, on the Loyalist side. Paramilitary activity included bombings, shootings, beatings, forced removals, and community intimidation.

Community participation in the establishment and maintenance of Northern Ireland's paramilitaries is a sensitive and difficult issue to confront, but the reality, as one teacher said in a professional development seminar organized in 2012 by an international education and professional development NGO called Facing History and Ourselves, is that "we can't say we didn't know who they were. Our communities fed them, housed them, kept their secrets."[51] This was just one way in which civilians were intimately drawn into—and, in some ways, participated in—the conflict. Close to 3,600 people were killed during this period, and tens of thousands were injured. A quarter of those killed or injured were between the ages of eighteen and twenty-three and mostly male. While the number of deaths is low compared to other conflicts, Northern Ireland is a small country, and it has often been said that everyone knows someone who was killed in the Troubles.

As Duncan Morrow has written and lectured, the Northern Irish conflict can be characterized by fundamentally competing views of the past. Both communities identify themselves as victims and see each other as responsible for the violence. In South Africa, it was largely possible to answer two fundamental questions about the conflict: Who was responsible? Who are the victims? In Northern Ireland, the ability to answer these questions remains elusive. Despite many commissions of inquiry and other efforts, no overarching framework has emerged for addressing the past or getting at the roots of the conflict, which include the fact that the state itself is not a source of social cohesion.[52]

Education has long been intertwined in Northern Ireland's conflict, in part because of its perceived (il)legitimacy as a state institution. Schools taught particular historical narratives shaped by the religious and political beliefs of the dominant community. During the Troubles, the conflict was kept out of the schools, as most teachers chose to remain silent to keep their students safe. Their silence, however, was—and is—part of a wider cultural response to the violence and a seemingly intractable conflict.

The 1998 Good Friday Agreement, also known as the Belfast Agreement, provided a political foundation for peace. Although Northern Ireland remained part of the United Kingdom, the agreement included an understanding that its citizens could carry British or Irish passports, and that their respective political and cultural identities should be considered legitimate and honored. The agreement also provided for Northern Ireland to become part of Ireland if that were the "wish" of the majority of the people, and it recognized that "an essential aspect of the reconciliation process is the promotion of a culture of tolerance at every level of society, including initiatives to facilitate and encourage integrated education and mixed housing."[53]

Yet, sixteen years after the Belfast Agreement, Northern Ireland's schools remain largely segregated by religion, with 93 percent of youth attending segregated schools.[54] Importantly, however, unlike in South Africa and the United States, Northern Ireland's main two communities are nearly equal in population, and resources are provided nearly equally across schools. In other words, while we can point to majority black schools in South Africa and the United States and see fewer resources and networks for career and educational opportunities and advancement and more violence and poverty, in Northern Ireland, in reality or as a practical matter, the divisions between Catholics and Protestants show up less than those among social classes. In this case, that means the greatest differences in resources and opportunities exist between elite schools and all others, whether Catholic or Protestant.

In addition to Catholic schools, state schools (Protestant), and mixed schools (Protestant with some Catholics), Northern Ireland has some integrated schools, which constitute the most direct attempt to bring Catholic, Protestant, and nondenominational students together across a deeply divided society.[55] The first integrated school was developed in 1981, with parents driving the effort. Since then, sixty-two such schools have been created (forty-two primary and twenty post-primary), educating just under 22,000 children.[56] Importantly, integrated schools are not always selected by teachers or by parents because of their values. Some parents choose them because they are the best local option, and some teachers choose to teach in them because they offer jobs in a market with few opportunities. Furthermore, many schools, both integrated and segregated, maintain a position of neutrality in dealing with the conflict and its history and legacies, so students at integrated schools are not necessarily better able to face the violent past. They are, however, going to school together each day, which is no small feat.

Discussion about and programming aimed at bringing Northern Ireland's children together across their divided society and the many divisions that animate the education sector have existed for more than thirty years. Since 2007, however, shared education programming (SEP), through which pupils from different schools get together to learn in subject areas required within the curriculum, such as math and science, while building on past programming has become a specific focus of policy, donor support, and disagreement in this area. SEP, which emphasizes the sharing of learning experiences by pupils across communal borders and the sharing of resources by schools, has enjoyed significant funding from external donors, such as the Atlantic Philanthropies and the International Fund for Ireland; it also currently enjoys the political support of the minister of education. It encompasses the Shared Education

Programme, founded by Professor Tony Gallagher, pro-vice chancellor of Queen's University Belfast, where it is based, as well as initiatives developed by the Fermanagh Trust and by the North Eastern Education and Library Board, through its Primary Integrating/Enriching Education Project.[57] According to a recent report of the Ministerial Advisory Group,

> These three programmes have involved 66 partnerships drawing together over 210 schools and 16,000 children and young people across Northern Ireland. Each of these partnerships has involved schools engaging in cross-sectoral collaboration concentrating on substantive, curriculum-based activities.[58]

For Gallagher, SEP means providing ways to offer pupils more subjects, to help schools share resources, and to create a medium for pupils to begin to share each other's schools. Addressing the last issue was in many ways a pragmatic response to the slow pace of developing more integrated schools. As Gallagher said in an interview,

> We thought if you could persuade schools to work together across the divide, but focus on the high-quality core curricular activities, that might be what it would take. . . . If you can make it work educationally, and do your core activity better, then schools have an incentive to keep it going. Rather than beginning with reconciliation, you begin with what is important now and then move towards reconciliation.[59]

Some scholars and community leaders, however, are beginning to wonder aloud if shared education has become a way of abandoning the integrated school movement and giving already ambivalent policymakers a way around committing to a "shared future" through integrated education. A report produced by a United Nations Educational, Scientific and Cultural Organization (UNESCO) team, led by Professor Alan Smith from University of Ulster, reveals some of the tensions behind the support—financial and political—for shared education programming over the promotion of integrated schools:

> Firstly, political and policy discourse has shifted towards the concept of "shared education" despite public support for "integrated education" remaining extremely high. The current discourse on shared education assumes that the vast majority of our children will continue to be educated in separate schools for the foreseeable future. By accepting this

political parties move towards education policies that plan for separate
development rather than structural change and reform of the separate
school system. This shift is now reflected in key education policy documents. For example, the new Education Bill (2012) makes no direct reference to integrated education despite government having a statutory
responsibility to encourage and facilitate. No formal representation for
integrated education is proposed in the establishment of the new Education and Skills Authority (ESA) and there is no reference to integrated
education in the Programme for Government (2011–15). Political mani-
festos and policy initiatives in Northern Ireland do not reflect many of
the preferences expressed by parents and the wider population as represented in survey data. Over the last decade this data consistently reports
that public support for formally integrated schools remains very high
in terms of its contribution to peace and reconciliation, promoting a
shared future, and promoting mutual respect and understanding.[60]

Given growing sectarianism in Northern Ireland and the failure in 2013 of
talks facilitated by US diplomat Richard Haass to produce a deal settling differences among the opposing parties, the shared education approach is consistent with the ambivalence with which Northern Irish policymakers have
led the country. From an ambiguous end-of-conflict agreement (the Belfast
Agreement) to the consistent abandonment of plans around a "shared future,"
the favoring of shared over integrated education is in keeping with the norms
currently governing the society. Thus, according to the Ministerial Advisory
Group, despite recent polling showing greater support for integrated schools,

> The Group does not agree that integrated schools should be viewed
> and actively promoted as the "preferred option" in relation to plans to
> advance shared education. Parents and children have the right to their
> religious, cultural and philosophical beliefs being respected. The vision
> of the Ministerial Advisory Group, as set out above, is therefore predi-
> cated on parental choice.[61]

It is important to note that the polling does not mean those polled would
actually send their children to integrated schools, and that policymakers continue to be elected despite their often extreme and competing points of view.
Nevertheless, such polling results could be the catalyst for bold leadership, in
the spirit of coming to terms with the past and reconciliation, to support integrated education once again as a critical aspect of that vision.

Boldness is needed because, in contrast to South Africa's education reforms, which have largely been consistent with the ethos driving its transition, integrated schooling in Northern Ireland works against the country's dominant values. In many ways, SEP is more aligned with the terrific ambivalence with which the Northern Irish have approached the past and the prospect of a shared future. First, shared education does not mean pupils and/or their teachers confront the past and its legacies together. Most often, in fact, they are sharing resources in subjects far removed from areas of disagreement. Second, while attending each other's schools for required classes does demand intercommunal negotiation and significant efforts at border crossing, these efforts do not fundamentally change the segregated structure of schooling. Rather, they adapt to them.

Regarding the curriculum, a major revision made in 2007 required for the first time an exploration of the past as being relevant to developing the skills and dispositions students need as citizens in the present and for the future. While the Office of the First Minister and Deputy First Minister supported some training of educators and advisors in the new curriculum, however, its implementation has been, at best, uneven. The NGO Facing History and Ourselves played a role in informing the 2007 revision and the history reforms within it, particularly those asking pupils to explore the conflict and its legacies with an eye to decision making and ethics. The reforms include two objectives that ask teachers to explore the causes and consequences of the 1920 partition of Ireland and reflect on the relationship between the history of the conflict and its legacies. Interestingly, "moral character" and ethics are explicitly integrated into the curriculum statement. For example, it suggests that study include and pupils be asked to consider issues such as the behavior of historical figures and whether it was ethical or unethical and to "investigate how history has been selectively interpreted to create stereotypical perceptions and to justify views and actions."[62]

The 2007 revision builds on important work done through the introduction of citizenship education and, before that, through a program called Education through Mutual Understanding (EMU). One of the architects of citizenship education in Northern Ireland, Michael Arlow, spoke in 2012 about the situation that informed its development as well as its reception and, ultimately, its limitations, which is particularly relevant with reference to transitional justice:

When you look back to what happened with EMU was when it was initially introduced with a huge backlash from some particular communities in relation to seeing it as an attempt to undermine people's political and religious identity. Where we wanted to go with it was to build on what had been achieved by EMU in regard to the exploration of identity, to help people understand their own identity better and then how to relate to those with different identities . . . If you're working towards reconciliation or helping people to coexist peacefully, to put it another way, if you don't do that without a dimension of justice then you are potentially just reinforcing the injustices that are already there. So we understood that there had to be another layer of justice related to Human Rights in there. . . . What we did see citizenship as doing was inspiring young people to think that they had a role to play, something to giving them the tools to fulfilling [sic] that role.[63]

Arlow also pointed out that this was a very specific moment in time,

> where the Department of Education. . . . had a say over the education system in Northern Ireland and they could make their own decisions and some of the key officials like Christine Jendoubi, at the time, said they were very conscious of the fact that they now had this opportunity and they wanted to be able to say to future generations, "When we had control over our own affairs, this is what we did."[64]

It was at this moment that Facing History and Ourselves first trained teachers and library board advisors (called curriculum advisors elsewhere) in Northern Ireland, many of whom attended workshops and seminars to begin to consider implementing citizenship education.[65] Their thinking went into the 2007 history curriculum revision, in which citizenship education is interwoven. Not long after the revision, however, the role of the library boards was effectively changed, as was the requirement for continuing professional development. Library board advisors—who played a critical role in Northern Ireland and an obvious role in the articulation and implementation of a new curriculum[66]—lost their positions, and their work was chaotically and unevenly reformed by the government. To complicate matters further, continuing professional development for teachers was also put on what appears to be permanent hold.

Given the impact the 2007 reform could have had, particularly for history and citizenship education, one would think the government would have seized the opportunity to ensure high-quality implementation, which would have included training and follow-up support. This was far from the case. Training for history teachers is absolutely essential where silence, sectarianism, and neutrality are the approaches of choice, and expecting them to fulfill the new requirements successfully without it is absurd. Most teachers, like most adult citizens of Northern Ireland, have been educated in one community, have trained as teachers in one community, and then have taught in one community.[67] Citizenship education as a requirement was also marginalized. It now falls under "Learning for Life and Work," and the subject has not been appropriately professionalized—that is, most of those teaching in the area are not specialists in it.[68] These missed opportunities, again, are consistent with the overall ambivalence that has guided the Northern Irish transition.[69]

In 2010, Corrymeela, a local NGO focused on reconciliation, applied for funding from the International Fund for Ireland to advance the work begun by Facing History and Ourselves. With support from some library board representatives, whose status is currently in limbo, Corrymeela and Facing History began to build upon the work the latter had started in 2003 and the curricular foundation provided by the 2007 revision. The collaboration has resulted in Facing Our History, Shaping the Future, a program that trains teachers, provides resources, and works directly with pupils both in their schools and in cross-communal residential settings.

Many educators who have attended Facing Our History's trainings have expressed their concerns and ambivalence toward teaching about Northern Ireland's past. They feel they do not have sufficient resources, and many feel enormous pressure and frustration for being made responsible for "reconciliation." Because the dominant ethos of the country is not dedicated to facing the past and sharing the future, teachers are positioned in this case to act against the norms of society. It should not be surprising, then, that their approaches to facing the violent past have included silence, sectarianism, and neutrality, none of which supports a transitional justice approach. Again, the failure to embrace reforms fully is consistent with the ambivalence that guides Northern Irish policy.

In his analysis of where Northern Ireland was fifteen years after the Belfast Agreement, Duncan Morrow created a chart of commitments it made, the subsequent failures to put these recommendations into practice, and in some cases the dismantling or setting back of the recommendations. These included making a "priority of integrated and shared education," which, Morrow notes, "has resulted in an impasse on educational reform; shared education declared but not clear; no progress on integrated education."[70] Importantly, this failure to move forward is consistent with the failure to implement efforts to resolve a range of issues, from shared housing to intercommunity work to the desperate need to address the past.

Important elements of education reform are in place, including a revised curriculum, resources for teaching about the past, and strategies for developing integrated schools (as well as polls showing widespread public support for these institutions). But in the way are what appear to be relatively mundane structural and bureaucratic issues—policies that have been adopted over the years that make little sense in any situation but particularly in a postwar one. Classes are thirty-five minutes long, for example—hardly time to engage in substantial discussion and learning. Particularly with the pressure of exams, it is understandable why teachers do not approach topics that require nuance and complex thinking skills and why they resort to authoritarian methods. Northern Ireland's schools also separate pupils by academic ability, which adds another layer of division.

In addition, the absence of effective curricular support means teachers no longer have a partner to help them translate the curriculum. Relying on external organizations, particularly nonprofits, for resources and training prevents the education system from substantively taking responsibility for these essential roles, and having the work dependent on grants means a nonprofit can be actively engaged in a project and then move on to something else when the money runs out.

These "smaller" issues all exist within a wider cultural and political climate in Northern Ireland that has favored elected representatives who lean to the extremes over the center and who speak to their respective communities instead of to the country as a whole. In a moment when sectarianism, dissident violent activity, and rioting have grown, the inability to realize meaningful education reforms is particularly problematic.

CONCLUSION

Both BiH and Northern Ireland suffer not only from a lack of commitment to education reforms, but from a wider lack of commitment to addressing the violent past, redressing human rights violations, and articulating a shared future. These deeply divided societies carry legacies both of their respective conflicts and of the ways their end-of-conflict agreements articulated new political foundations—legacies that have had profound effects on social reconstruction generally and on the education sector specifically. Both countries suffer from an inability to come to terms with the past and to find agreement about what happened. They share a fear on the part of identity groups that their identities have been threatened or will be subsumed by the other(s), and they share an unwillingness to engage in processes that will meaningfully address or remedy these dynamics.

The most effective reforms are part of a wider transitional justice framework. Within education, for example, asking students to take risks that adults around them refuse to take will result in failure and frustration, as will reforms that isolate teachers, classrooms, schools, and the education system as a whole from wider support. South Africa's relative success is tied to the comprehensive and consistent approach, from its leadership through to the reform and transformation of institutions, that the country took to reconstruction, reconciliation, and repair. A vital aspect of South Africa's transition was the way the country dealt with the violent past—it became central, visible, and legitimate.

Importantly in this process, South Africans viewed and still view the state as a site of social cohesion, not conflict. BiH and Northern Ireland—and many other states—share the significant challenge that the state itself is not a point of cohesion for its citizens, but a source of conflict. Unless and until this overriding issue is addressed and integrated into a wider framework, transitional justice measures, including those taken through education, will be limited both in scope and in impact.

NOTES

1   Increasingly, organizations such as the International Center for Transitional Justice, the US Institute of Peace, and the Georg Eckert Institute have included in their work—either explicitly or implicitly—an interest in education reforms as part of a wider effort to address legacies of the past. It is still fairly standard, however, to find transitional justice defined more narrowly, with a focus on tools such as truth commissions, reparations, prosecutions, and reconciliation initiatives. Even historical commissions and other efforts to investigate the violent past do not often automatically come up with recommendations regarding education—and even less often does implementation follow when recommendations are made.

2   While I focus here primarily on issues of segregation and integration, with a broader transitional justice perspective in mind, I would also add curricular reform and professional development to the list of essential reforms within the education sector. What is thought and how it is thought are fundamental questions when considering the capacity of education to portray new systems of values. The interventions both in BiH and Northern Ireland have the potential to alter fundamentally the education system and, indeed, society as a whole.

3   See Linda Chisholm, "Policy and Critique in South African Educational Research," *Transformation* 18 (1992): 149–60; Linda Chisholm and Bruce Fuller, "Remember People's Education? Shifting Alliances, State-Building and South Africa's Narrowing Policy Agenda," *Journal of Education Policy* 11, no. 6 (1996): 693–716; Jonathan D. Jansen, "Understanding Social Transition through the Lens of Curriculum Policy," *Journal of Curriculum Studies* 27, no. 3 (1995): 245–61; and Jonathan D. Jansen, "Curriculum Reform Since Apartheid: Intersections of Policy and Practice in the South African Transition," *Journal of Curriculum Studies* 31, no. 1 (1999): 5–6.

4   Linda Chisholm and Jonathan Jansen have written extensively on the so-called 2005 Curriculum and its revision. See, for example, Linda Chisholm, "The Making of South Africa's National Curriculum Statement," *Journal of Curriculum Studies* 37, no. 2 (2005): 193–208.

5   Brown v. Board of Education of Topeka, 347 U.S. 483 (1954), https://supreme.justia.com/cases/federal/us/347/483.

6   Ronald P. Formisano, *Boston Against Busing: Race, Class, and Ethnicity in the 1960s and 1970s* (Chapel Hill: University of North Carolina Press, 1991).

7   Ford Fessenden, "A Portrait of Segregation in New York City's Schools," *New York Times*, May 11, 2012, http://www.nytimes.com/interactive/2012/05/11/nyregion/segregation-in-new-york-city-public-schools.html. For excellent resources on school segregation and integration in the United States, see the Civil Rights Project at the University of California, Los Angeles, http://civilrightsproject.ucla.edu/research/k-12-education/integration-and-diversity. A recent study from the Civil Rights Project identifies New York as having the most segregated schools in the country, even more so than the South. The report argues, "This is ultimately a discussion about choice. Choice can either increase opportunity and integration, or increase inequality and stratification. In a society where the most disadvantaged children typically get the weakest schools, and the most privileged attend schools that give them even more advantages, the last thing we should do is to stratify children even more. We learned in the South a half-century ago that choice plans without civil rights standards increase stratification of schools and leave almost all the children of color still segregated. Such 'freedom of choice' and 'open enrollment' plans were tried in many hundreds of districts. The record, as the Supreme Court recognized in 1968, was a failure. Only when choice is

linked to key civil rights standards, such as strong public information and outreach, free transportation, serious planning and training for successful diversity, authentic educational options worth choosing, and no admissions screening, can choice be a force for successful integration." John Kucsera and Gary Orfield, "New York State's Extreme School Segregation: Inequality, Inaction and a Damaged Future," the Civil Rights Project, March 26, 2014, http://civilrightsproject.ucla.edu/research/k-12-education/integration-and-diversity/ny-norflet-report-placeholder. See also Gary Orfield and Erica Frankenberg, with Jongyeon Ee and John Kuscera, "Brown at 60: Great Progress, a Long Retreat and an Uncertain Future," the Civil Rights Project, May 15, 2014, http://civilrightsproject.ucla.edu/research/k-12-education/integration-and-diversity/brown-at-60-great-progress-a-long-retreat-and-an-uncertain-future.

8   Sheldon Berman, "The Resegregation of America's Schools," *School Administrator* 11, no. 70 (2013): 14–21.

9   Parents Involved in Community Schools v. Seattle School District No. 1, 551 U.S. 701 (2007).

10 Berman, "The Resegregation of America's Schools," 15.

11 *Parents Involved*, plurality opinion by Chief Justice Roberts, 747–48.

12 Also see Joel K. Goldstein, "Not Hearing History: A Critique of Chief Justice Roberts's Reinterpretation of Brown," *Ohio State Law Journal* 69, no. 5 (2008): 791–846.

13 Susan Eaton and Gina Chirichigno, "The Impact of Racially Diverse Schools in a Democratic Society," National Coalition on School Diversity Research Briefs, no. 3 (Boston: Charles Hamilton Houston Institute for Race and Justice, 2010), http://www.school-diversity.org/pdf/DiversityResearchBriefNo3.pdf.

14 Roslyn Arlin Mickelson, "The Reciprocal Relationship between Housing and School Integration," National Coalition on School Diversity Research Briefs, no. 7 (Boston: Charles Hamilton Houston Institute for Race and Justice, September 2011), http://www.school-diversity.org/pdf/DiversityResearchBriefNo7.pdf.

15 Mickelson, "The Reciprocal Relationship between Housing and School Integration," 3.

16 Genevieve Siegel-Hawley, "How Non-Minority Students Also Benefit from Racially Diverse Schools," National Coalition on School Diversity Research Briefs, no. 8 (Boston: Charles Hamilton Houston Institute for Race and Justice, 2012), http://www.school-diversity.org/pdf/DiversityResearchBriefNo8.pdf.

17 US Department of Education and US Department of Justice, "Guidance on the Voluntary Use of Race to Achieve Diversity and Avoid Racial Isolation in Elementary and Secondary School" (Washington, DC: US Department of Education and US Department of Justice, 2011), 1, http://www2.ed.gov/about/offices/list/ocr/docs/guidance-ese-201111.pdf.

18 Daria Sito-Sucic and Matt Robinson, "After Years of Toil, Book Names Bosnian War Dead," Reuters, February 15, 2013, http://www.reuters.com/article/2013/02/15/

us-bosnia-dead-idUSBRE91E0J220130215.

19   ICTY, Prosecutor v. Radislav Krstic, Case No. IT-98-33-T, Judgement (The Hague, August 2, 2001), http://www.icty.org/case/krstic.

20   This is still true; however, most groups emphasize the distinctiveness of their languages and claim the shared language was manufactured. Language has become a route for ethnic/national politics and has specifically been used to reinforce segregation in schools.

21   See Eric Stover and Harvey Weinstein, eds., My Neighbor, My Enemy: Justice and Community in the Aftermath of Mass Atrocity (Cambridge: Cambridge University Press, 2004), particularly the chapters on BiH.

22   Valery Perry, "Reading, Writing and Reconciliation: Educational Reform in Bosnia and Herzegovina," European Center for Minority Issues, working paper 18 (Flensburg: ECMI, 2003), 2.

23   The Office of the High Representative, created by the Dayton Agreement of 1995, is an international agency responsible for overseeing the implementation of civilian aspects of the peace agreement ending the war in Bosnia and Herzegovina.

24   Office of the High Representative, "PDHR Hays Calls for Urgent Education Reform," press release, January 2002, http://www.ohr.int, quoted in Perry, "Reading, Writing and Reconciliation," 3.

25   Clare Magill, Education and Fragility in Bosnia and Herzegovina (Paris: UNESCO and International Institute for Educational Planning, 2010), 13, http://unesdoc.unesco.org/images/0019/001910/191060e.pdf.

26   Azra Hromadžic, "Discourses of Integration and Practices of Reunification at the Mostar Gymnasium, Bosnia and Herzegovina," Comparative Education Review 52, no. 4 (2008): 544–45.

27   Perry, "Reading, Writing and Reconciliation," 30.

28   Ibid.

29   Denis Dzidic, "Bosnia's Segregated Schools Maintain Educational Divide," Balkan Insight, February 13, 2015, http://www.balkaninsight.com/en/article/bosnia-s-segregated-schools-maintain-educational-divide/1431/52.

30   Institute for War and Peace Reporting, "Bosnian Court Rules Against Segregated Schools," May 15, 2012, http://iwpr.net/report-news/bosnian-court-rules-against-segregated-schools.

31   See, for example, Internal Displacement Monitoring Center, "Bosnia and Herzegovina: Ethno-Political Agendas Still Prolonging Displacement," November 14, 2014, http://www.internal-displacement.org/europe-the-caucasus-and-central-asia/bosnia-and-herzegovina/2014/bosnia-and-herzegovina-ethno-political-agendas-still-prolonging-displacement.

32   Hromadžic, "Discourses of Integration and Practices," 554.

33   Ibid., 556.

34 Janine Natalya Clark, "Education in Bosnia-Hercegovina: The Case for Root-and-Branch Reform," *Journal of Human Rights* 9, no. 3 (2010): 346.

35 Ibid., 347.

36 Adila Pašalić-Kreso, Hasnija Muratovi, Radmila Rangelov-Jusovi, and Dženana Trbi, "Bosnia and Herzegovina," in *The Prospects of Teacher Education in Southeast Europe*, ed. Pavel Zgaga (Ljubljana: University of Ljubljana, 2006), 171.

37 Ibid., 187.

38 See Bosnia and Herzegovina Agency for Pre-Primary, Primary and Secondary Education, "About Agency," 2013, http://www.aposo.gov.ba/en/about-agency.

39 Katarina Batarilo-Henschen, Georg Eckert Institute, email exchange with the author, January 15, 2014.

40 Internal Displacement Monitoring Center, *Bosnia and Herzegovina: Broader and Improved Support for Durable Solutions Required. A Profile of the Internal Displacement Situation*, August 28, 2008, 148, http://www.internal-displacement.org/assets/library/Europe/Bosnia-and-Herzegovina/pdf/Bosnia-and-Herzegovina-August-2008.pdf.

41 Ibid., 149.

42 Commission for the Development of Guidelines for Conceptualizing New History Textbooks in Bosnia and Herzegovina, "Guidelines for Textbook Writing and Evaluation of History Textbooks for Primary and Secondary Schools in Bosnia and Herzegovina," *BIH Official Gazette* (August 2006).

43 Council of Europe and OSCE Mission to BiH, *Teacher Manual on Contemporary History Teaching in Schools* (Sarajevo: OSCE, 2006), http://www.theewc.org/uploads/content/archive/manual%20for%20history%20teachers_2.pdf.

44 OSCE Mission to Bosnia and Herzegovina, "Curricular Reform," OSCE fact sheet, http://www.oscebih.org/Default.aspx?id=31&lang=EN.

45 Georg Eckert Institute for International Textbook Research, "The Institute," http://www.gei.de/en/the-institute.html, and Janine Albrecht, "Shaping Education in Bosnia-Herzegovina," *DW Online* 7 (January 2014), http://www.dw.de/shaping-education-in-bosnia-herzegovina/a-17345653.

46 Batarilo-Henschen, email exchange with the author.

47 Ibid. Using unpublished documents obtained from OSCE (OSCE Mission to Bosnia and Herzegovina, *Lessons from Education Reform in Brčko: A Report Prepared by the OSCE Mission to BiH Education Department*, 2007), Janine Clark also highlights Brčko as an example that might be replicated in other parts of BiH. She writes, "The OSCE Education Officer for Brčko District 'estimates that on average students spend less than 25–30 per cent of their lesson time separated by nationality and that in some cases children spend even more time together.' Although children in Brčko District are still taught separately for some subjects, what is important is that there is far more contact between them than there is between children in other parts of BiH, for example in Central Bosnia Canton.

More significantly, the example of Brčko provides a possible template for reform of the education system in BiH as a whole. In short, what it demonstrates is that 'mono-ethnic schools may not be the only way to arrange things in the country.'" Clark, "Education in Bosnia-Hercegovina," 355.

48 Euroclio-European Association of History Educators, "History that Connects the Western Balkans," http://www.euroclio.eu/new/index.php/work/history-that-connects.

49 This is according to the author's contacts in BiH, who suggest inspectors from the institutes speak negatively about this work. It would be worth asking, on the other hand, whether this is because the inspectors feel challenged by the methods and content used by Euroclio's project.

50 Astrid Fisher, "Integration or Segregation? Reforming the Education Sector," in *Peacebuilding and Civil Society in Bosnia-Herzegovina: Ten Years after Dayton*, ed. Martina Fischer (Münster: Lit-Verlag, 2006), 298–99.

51 From the author's notes from Facing History and Ourselves Seminar, Northern Ireland, June 2012.

52 See Morrow in these presentations: Duncan Morrow, "The Political Context of Transitional Justice in Northern Ireland" (presentation, "The Past, History Education and Transitional Justice: A Learning Space Reflecting on Northern Ireland," Ballycastle, Northern Ireland, March 2014), https://www.youtube.com/watch?v=C7V_6TaSj00; Duncan Morrow, "The Practice, Progress and Failings of Community Relations Work in Northern Ireland Since 1990," YouTube video, 1:03:35, from the IPAC Seminar Series, University of Ulster, United Kingdom, May 2012, posted by IRiSSwatch, May 23, 2012, https://www.youtube.com/watch?v=gaUXiyMYZdo.

53 Government of the United Kingdom of Great Britain, Northern Ireland Office, *The Agreement: Agreement Reached in the Multi-Party Negotiations*, Belfast, April 10, 1998, https://www.gov.uk/government/uploads/system/uploads/attachment_data/file/136652/agreement.pdf.

54 Philip O'Sullivan, "Education in Northern Ireland: Segregation, Division and Sectarianism?" July 2013, http://www.open.edu/openlearn/society/politics-policy-people/sociology/education-northern-ireland-segregation-division-and-sectarianism.

55 This situation may change, as a court in Omagh recently ruled in a groundbreaking case that the Department of Education "was not allowed to stifle the growth of the integrated sector to protect falling numbers in Catholic and controlled schools." The judge, Mr. Justice Treacy, argued that "the department had failed in its legal duty to 'facilitate and encourage' integrated education." See *Belfast Telegraph*, "Blow for John O'Dowd's Education Policy after Court Rules Expansion of Integrated Schools Cannot Be Stifled," May 16, 2014.

56 Northern Ireland Department of Education, "Integrated Schools," https://www.deni.gov.uk/articles/integrated-schools, accessed January 12, 2015.

57 More information about this program can be found at http://www.schoolsworkingto-gether.co.uk.

58 Paul Connolly, Dawn Purvis, and P. J. O'Grady, *Advancing Shared Education*, report of the Ministerial Advisory Group (Belfast, March 2013), 20.

59 Meabh Richie, "A Bridge across the River Foyle," *Times Education Supplement Connect*, July 8, 2011, http://www.atlanticphilanthropies.org/news/bridge-across-river-foyle.

60 Ulf Hansson, Una O'Connor Bones, and John McCord, *Integrated Education: A Review of Policy and Research Evidence 1999–2012*, UNESCO Centre at University of Ulster, January 2013, 4, http://cain.ulster.ac.uk/issues/education/docs/ief_2013_report_unesco.pdf.

61 Connolly et al., *Advancing Shared Education*, 107.

62 Northern Ireland Department of Education, *The Education (Curriculum Minimum Content) Order (Northern Ireland) 2007*, January 2007, http://www.deni.gov.uk/nisr_20070046_en.pdf.

63 Michael Arlow, Memory Bank Narratives transcript of interview by Civic Voices, Belfast, April 27, 2012, 5.

64 Ibid., 6.

65 This was part of a wider set of trainings offered by the Department of Education. According to Arlow, "It was also very convenient because they had some spare cash that they were able to put into teacher training and so on, and we ended up with one of the biggest teacher training programmes for a single subject ever to run in Northern Ireland." Ibid.

66 Leadership is an important aspect of continuing professional development. A review of leadership programs, "Preparing School Principals to Be Effective Leaders," published by the Education and Training Inspectorate (ETI) in March 2013, can be found at http://www.etini.gov.uk/index/surveys-evaluations/surveys-evaluations-post-primary/surveys-evaluations-post-primary-2013/preparing-school-principals-to-be-effective-leaders.pdf.

67 In research the author is currently conducting with Sarah W. Freedman, teachers in Northern Ireland consistently express frustration about the limits of their pupils' knowledge of recent history. Ironically, this sometimes prevents them from teaching about the conflict. They also identify pupil and parental responses as reasons for not entering into particularly sensitive discussions. For example, one teacher made a point of avoiding discussions regarding policing because of the responses of her primarily Loyalist pupils. Pupils lack knowledge of the recent past generally, and the conflict itself is opaque. It is difficult for them to recognize the legacies of the Troubles, to relate history to the present, and to make connections in general. On quantitative surveys, the Northern Irish pupils score consistently lower than South African learners, who have a high sense of civic and historical efficacy.

68 See Arlow's very useful presentation at a conference hosted jointly by Corrymeela

and Facing History and Ourselves on "The Past, History Education and Transitional Justice: A Learning Space Reflecting on Northern Ireland," Corrymeela Ballycastle, March 15–24, 2014, https://www.youtube.com/watch?v=V8-Egg3PEFY. Arlow spoke about "Education for Mutual Understanding" and the design and implementation of the citizenship curriculum, which many viewed with such enormous expectations and sense of possibilities.

69   Alison Kitson's research on history education in Northern Ireland is particularly apt here. Kitson interviewed teachers, professors of education, and others involved in teaching and researching history education. She also studied textbook trends. In a 2004 interview about her work, Kitson said, "History is in a unique position to help pupils understand the origins of the Northern Irish conflict and explore why it has become such an intractable issue. It can play a powerful role in tackling social division and promoting peace by encouraging pupils to understand how different interpretations of the past have come about and how these interpretations have played, and continue to play, such a key role in the conflict. At its best, history teaching actively encourages pupils to consider conflicting viewpoints, to challenge popular misconceptions (including the 'versions' of history encountered outside the classroom) and to make explicit and powerful connections between Ireland's past and the present situation." Science-Blog, "Research Reveals History Teaching in Northern Ireland Is Often Balanced to the Point of Blandness," September 2004, http://www.scienceblog.com/community/older/2004/10/20049583.shtml. See also Kitson's chapter, "History Teaching and Reconciliation in Northern Ireland," in *Teaching the Violent Past: History Education and Reconciliation*, ed. Elizabeth Cole (Plymouth: Rowman & Littlefield, 2007).

70   Duncan Morrow, "Stuck Dancing at the Crossroads," in *15 Years On: Reflecting on the Successes and Failures of the 15 Years since the Belfast/Good Friday Agreement*, February 15, 2013, http://15yearson.wordpress.com/2013/02/15/stuck-dancing-at-the-crossroads/.

CHAPTER 3

History, Memory, and Education: Is It Possible to Consolidate a Culture of Peace in Guatemala?

Gustavo Palma Murga

Guatemala experienced a long and costly internal armed conflict from the 1960s to the mid-1980s.[1] The conflict formally ended in 1996, after a ten-year process of negotiations between the government and the general command of the insurgency groups, with the signing of the Agreement on a Firm and Lasting Peace. Several proposals discussed during this process led to a series of additional agreements that were to become state policy on key elements of the country's economic, political, social, and cultural life. Two are of interest for the purposes of this chapter: the Agreement on the Establishment of the Commission to Clarify Past Human Rights Violations and Acts of Violence That Have Caused the Guatemalan Population to Suffer[2] (which became the Commission for Historical Clarification, Spanish acronym CEH) and the Agreement on Identity and Rights of Indigenous Peoples (Spanish acronym AIDPI).[3] The first is relevant because the CEH produced a voluminous report on the violent acts that occurred during the conflict,[4] in which it recommended that the state directly and widely disseminate knowledge about these acts—especially through the education system—so future generations would learn about and not repeat them. The second is important because it points to the need to eradicate historical discrimination against the indigenous population and proposes education reform that would include this part of the country's recent history in a new curriculum.[5]

In Guatemala, education is considered an important institution that should contribute to the development of the country.[6] The skills acquired through the education process are crucial, as they enable students to learn a set of values and attitudes (basic ethics) for interacting within society throughout their lives. The government's education plans and programs, the political discourse on the issue, the business sector agendas, and the demands of social organizations working for the advancement of education all aim to achieve this end. Similarly, education is symbolically important because it is perceived as the mechanism par excellence to promote a cohesive national identity. This is illustrated in the definition used to guide the postwar education reform process:

Education is a decisive factor for strengthening the cultural identity of each one of our four peoples and affirming national identity. The recognition and appreciation of Guatemala as a pluri-ethnic and multilingual state underscore the need to transform the educational system so that it reflects this cultural diversity and responds to the social needs and demands of its inhabitants.[7]

This chapter will analyze the state initiatives implemented in the past ten years to comply with the CEH recommendations for the incorporation of teaching about the violence of the conflict into the new curriculum, as developed through education reform. The CEH recommendations highlight the need to promote awareness of the recent past to ensure it is not repeated. History plays a key role in this task, providing a setting and perspective to inform but also to encourage reflection so the understanding of what happened can lead to new social behavior. It can also contribute to the creation of shared visions and memory of the past that can serve to strengthen a sense of common identity among the country's inhabitants.

The chapter begins with a description of the education system to which the CEH recommendations are addressed, followed by a brief characterization of the conflictive environment in which they are being implemented. It then offers some reflections on the place assigned to history and memory within the education system, before closing with conclusions.

THE NATIONAL EDUCATION SYSTEM

According to the National Statistics Institute, the estimated population of Guatemala in 2012 was 15,073,375 inhabitants.[8] Of these, 5,606,004 were children or adolescents between the ages of five and nineteen, the range for attending the primary and middle levels of the education system.[9] Official figures on the coverage of education show that in 2011, the national enrollment rate reached 66 percent at the primary level but only 22 percent in the middle-level basic cycle and 17 percent in the diversified cycle.[10] Overall, approximately one-third of the education system's target population is not receiving any regular schooling.

My analysis highlights the extent of the inequalities. First, as table 3.1 shows with data from 2012, the number of enrolled students decreases as they advance in the education system. The total number of children who attend middle level is less than half of those who attend primary level, with the fewest students in the diversified cycle.

Table 3.1. Urban and Rural Students Enrolled in School in Guatemala, 2012

Level	All students	Urban	Rural
Primary	2,556,314	702,608 (27.5%)	1,853,706 (72.5%)
Basic cycle	746,516	451,380 (60.5%)	295,136 (39.5%)
Diversified cycle	393,043	354,768 (90.3%)	38,275 (9.7%)
Totals	3,695,873	1,508,756 (40.8%)	2,187,117 (59.2%)

Source: Created with information from the Guatemala Ministry of Education, database of the *Anuario estadístico 2013* (Guatemala City: Ministry of Education, 2013).

Second, most of the students who attend primary school live in rural areas.[11] This fact can be interpreted in a positive light, as the rural population is apparently being given the opportunity to gain access to the education system, and, indeed, most rural children attend primary level. Table 3.1 shows, however, that the proportion of students who are rural shrinks as they advance through the levels.

Third, only 33.5 percent of enrolled students are indigenous, whereas the total indigenous population is estimated at 39.2 percent.[12] The proportion of students who are indigenous is highest at the primary level and declines at higher levels (see table 3.2).

Table 3.2. Indigenous Students Enrolled in School in Guatemala, 2012

Level	Indigenous students	Percentage of all students
Primary	986,225	38.6
Basic cycle	184,865	24.8
Diversified cycle	65,555	16.7
Totals	1,236,645	33.5

Source: Created with information from the Guatemala Ministry of Education, database of the *Anuario estadístico 2013* (Guatemala City: Ministry of Education, 2013).

Based on these figures, we can say that the state is not adequately or equally providing a basic service—education—to a large portion of the school-age population. One consequence of this is the difficulty of disseminating the new curriculum developed based on the CEH recommendations and the education reform process.

THE CONFLICTIVE ENVIRONMENT FOR REFORM

Among the topics discussed during the peace negotiations were those on which this chapter focuses: history, memory, and education. These are essential issues for any society, as they form the basis for building the bonds crucial to establishing social foundations and forms of collective action. History and memory in Guatemala continue to provoke reaction and contestation, which shows how critical they are to the debate on the national social self-perception. Since the presentation of the reports of the Human Rights Office of the Diocese of Guatemala, *Guatemala: Nunca más*, and the CEH, *Guatemala memoria del silencio*, the media have reported on the deep and frequently heated controversy over the relevance of disseminating these documents. Those who oppose having done so argue how inconvenient it is, in their words, to reopen the wounds of the past and would prefer to "turn the page and move forward." Those who, in contrast, believe it is necessary to address these issues head on contend that the nation cannot move forward without first knowing and discussing the multiple effects of history, especially of the recent conflict, on society. Society must understand the magnitude of what happened and that those responsible for human rights violations should be brought to justice and the victims and their families receive due reparations.[13]

The 2013 criminal trial of General Ríos Montt for genocide and crimes against humanity revived this controversy with force. The media published innumerable opinion pieces reopening the debate, showing how persistent and vital that debate remains today. The controversy reached the point that, on May 13, 2014, the Guatemalan Congress approved a nonbinding resolution stating (in contradiction to one of the CEH conclusions) that genocide had not occurred during the internal armed conflict. This resolution constituted legislative interference in the judicial branch and has been interpreted as one more effort to silence any voices insisting on the institutional responsibility of the army and high military officials for these crimes. In addition, it clearly reflects how far the country remains from reaching even a minimal degree of consensus on its recent history. No possibility appears to be in sight for dialogue on the steps that must be taken to achieve some level of "reconciliation."

Against this background, eighteen years after the signing of the peace agreement, it is important to examine the extent of the country's compliance with the commitments it acquired at that time to establish the foundations for "national reconciliation." The ongoing debate on how to interpret what happened during the armed conflict can be seen in a positive light, because it means the issue is being publicly discussed, with multiple voices continuing to demand justice and reparations. Indeed, it is now impossible to deny what happened. At the same time, however, the debate also demonstrates the increasing and visceral opposition of critics, manifested in systematic attacks and accusations against those making these demands. These groups also have the economic means to ensure their voices are heard and, above all, to shape public opinion. Consequently, instead of facilitating a broad public debate to promote some sort of national reconciliation, the confrontational environment continues to polarize society.[14]

HISTORY AND MEMORY AND THE NATIONAL EDUCATION SYSTEM

This section examines the place the CEH assigned to history and memory within the education system, its recommendations for instituting them, and the measures the system has taken, through curriculum revision and the use of various textbooks, to implement those recommendations as part of a broader national education reform process following the peace agreements.

THE COMMISSION FOR HISTORICAL CLARIFICATION (CEH)

The agreement that created the CEH declares that "the people of Guatemala have a right to know the whole truth concerning [the conflict], clarification of which will help to avoid a repetition of these sad and painful events and strengthen the process of democratization in Guatemala." It goes on to state that one of the commission's purposes will be to recommend "measures to preserve the memory of the victims."[15] This, in fact, became a central point of the work of the CEH, embodied in part II of its recommendations, "Measures to Preserve the Memory of the Victims":

The historical memory, both individual and collective, forms the basis of national identity. Remembrance of the victims is a fundamental aspect of this historical memory and permits the recovery of the values of, and the validity of the struggle for, human dignity.[16]

The CEH also requested that the state, the Guatemalan National Revolutionary Unity (URNG), and Guatemalan society take action to dignify the memory of the victims, through public acknowledgement of responsibility for the human rights violations committed during the conflict, the construction of monuments and public parks, and the commemoration and assigning of names of victims to education centers, buildings, and public highways.[17]

Part IV of the recommendations, "Measures to Foster a Culture of Mutual Respect and Observance of Human Rights," says that the state, "as a moral imperative and as a duty, [must] disseminate the contents of the report by all means possible and also promote an educational campaign to promote a culture of mutual respect and peace . . . aimed at the country's diverse political and social sectors."[18] It recommends that "the curricula of primary, secondary and university level education include instruction on the causes, development, and consequences of the armed confrontation and likewise of the content of the Peace Accords with the depth and method relevant to the particular level,"[19] and that "the Government, by means of the educational reform envisaged by the Peace Accords, foster an environment of tolerance and respect and promote self-awareness and awareness of the other, so that the dividing lines created by the ideological, political, and cultural polarization may be erased."[20]

These are specific recommendations, including precise means and mechanisms for implementation. The memory and knowledge of recent history are identified as important foundations for the new national project. A new social horizon is possible by developing citizens who are capable of adopting a critical, yet positive, perspective on who they are, based on their knowledge of the previous historical processes and the potential to move toward new forms of social relations.

EDUCATION REFORM

The chapter on "Cultural Rights" in the Agreement on Identity and Rights of Indigenous Peoples includes a section on education reform, which emphasizes education as one of the most important vehicles for the transmittal and development of "cultural values and knowledge."[21] Education, the agreement states, should be inclusive to promote recognition of the cultural and linguistic diversity of Guatemala; present throughout the entire country (decentralized and regionalized); bilingual; and participatory (for parents and communities in determining curriculum, for example). The recommendations of the CEH do not, however, explicitly consider education as a transmitter of a renewed historical vision and a promoter of inclusive historical memory. The only thing that stands out in this respect about the proposals for education reform is that it should "include in educational syllabuses programs that strengthen national unity through respect for cultural diversity."[22]

The first step in the implementation of education reform was the creation of a Parity Commission,[23] which formulated the general philosophical principles to guide the process. These are reflected in its document, "Design of the Educational Reform,"[24] which reiterates the importance of education as a means to guarantee a socially harmonious present and future. It refers to the concept of peace as

> a state of awareness, a way of living in harmony with oneself, others, and the universe. It is harmonization with the cosmos, the mind, the spirit, and the heart. That great peace is linked to being, to being well, and feeling well, which requires the satisfaction of people's psycho-bio-social needs, based on solidarity, equity, and justice.[25]

From this perspective, the education strategy seeks to achieve a harmonious future. But the document does not mention memory or history as part of this construction; instead, peace and a culture of peace are the most significant aims of the education process. Its notable objectives are related to the promotion of peaceful and harmonious coexistence among the nation's peoples based on inclusion, tolerance, solidarity, respect, equality, equity, and mutual enrichment; the elimination of all discrimination; political, civic, and citizen education for participation in and the exercise of democracy; and the defense of human rights.[26] The result of this process is expected to be the internalization and practice of these "civic virtues" by the students and, as a result, by future "virtuous citizens."[27]

The education reform process is guided by four axes, outlined in the reform design document,[28] which, in turn, give rise to eight axes that serve as the basis for the actual proposal for the new curriculum.[29] Looking at both the design document and the new curriculum proposal, five topics are particularly important for our purposes: identity, formation of values, human rights, democracy, and a culture of peace. Again, however, no links are made to the promotion of any type of relationship between history and memory, or at least their potential to help develop future citizens.[30] Social peace is

expected to come from the assimilation and practice of a series of civic virtues, but without questioning—from a critical historical perspective—why
their promotion is important. In this view, which puts responsibility mainly
on the social virtues of the individual who looks toward the future, history
loses much of its weight.

THE NEW CURRICULAR FRAMEWORK

The new curricular framework emphasizes the importance of a comprehensive education process that will prepare the student to contribute to democratic life, a culture of peace, and sustainable development.[31] The guiding
statements and principles of these themes are repeated throughout the pri-
mary- and middle-level school texts, with nuances added as the level rises.[32]
The education process is to have its impact on the capacity of young people
to develop respect and appreciation for the historical-cultural diversity of the
Guatemalan nation, as well as their own identities.

The civic education axis of the curriculum reiterates the need to identify,
conceptualize, internalize, and practice the principles and values that under-
pin for students, as young people and future citizens, a way of being and living aimed at strengthening a culture of peace. Components of history included
in the first grade of the primary level will, in the third grade, be inserted into
a timeline that covers colonialism; the initial republican period; the dictatorships of the twentieth century; the popular, revolutionary, and counterrevolutionary movements in Central America; and the "democratic processes,"
including the peace negotiations. In the sixth grade, the relationship between
the Cold War and the internal armed conflict will be established. The recent
history of Guatemala is studied in more detail in the third grade of the middle-
level basic cycle, spanning from the so-called "October Revolution of 1944" to
the age of globalization.

A critical reading of the curriculum proposed for both civic education and
history confirms that the content related to the former is coherent and gives
continuity to the topics that will be discussed in the classroom. The content
for history, however, focuses on providing information and on the chronological order of events. While a substantive change from the prereform curriculum is obvious, a sense remains of the "formative value" of civic education, as
opposed to the "informational" nature of history.[33]

TEXTBOOKS

Although school textbooks play a key role in shaping students' basic beliefs and knowledge in the areas of history and civic education, no common official text exists in Guatemala for these areas of study at the primary or middle levels of school. The Ministry of Education distributes a set of textbooks for public schools at the primary level,[34] while private schools use textbooks produced by private publishers.[35] Thus, no single "interpretation" of the curriculum reaches the students. This could be considered a positive scenario, because the system is not promoting a sole, predominant view of the country's history. It can also constitute a risk, however, because each textbook offers a distinct perspective on Guatemalan history. The absence of a common text also places significant responsibility on teachers, who must provide students with a balanced analysis and point of view, which requires the teachers to have a solid background in these topics. Furthermore, the variation can be interpreted as reflecting a lack of state interest in developing a shared basis for understanding the nation's history.

How are the contents of the main education axes that are examined in this chapter presented in schoolbooks? An analysis of the textbooks issued by the Ministry of Education for the public primary level and three private publisher collections is presented below.[36]

OFFICIAL TEXTBOOKS

The textbooks used by public schools from the first grade through the primary level focus strongly on civic education, which can be divided into three areas: individual and social values; human rights and civic duties; and democracy and peaceful coexistence.[37] Under the "democracy and peaceful coexistence" area, the books explain that democracy is possible through the internalization and practice of the values of and respect for human rights, positing that democracy is for each and every individual. How can democracy be achieved? Through the universalization of rights and opportunities under conditions of equality. Once achieved, this universalization will prevent conflicts and guarantee peace for all. It will be possible to live in liberty, freely express one's opinions, and elect one's leaders.[38]

In the third grade, the history course covers the colonial period through the nineteenth century, while the twentieth century is studied from the revolutionary period onward.[39] The official textbook for this course emphasizes the economic, political, and social changes that took place through the so-called counterrevolutionary period that followed the revolutionary period.

It continues with an overview of the conflicts in Central America in the second half of the century, with details about events in Guatemala. The primary causes of the "internal armed conflict" are listed as poverty, the unequal land tenure system, illiteracy, the vitality of social movements, authoritarianism, and repression. The army and the guerrillas are identified as the visible actors in the conflict, but intellectuals, workers, peasants, political parties, and university and high school students are also said to have been involved. Finally, a large section of the book is dedicated to the democratization process and the peace negotiations. The text concludes by suggesting the country is now embarked on a "new national project."

The sixth grade textbook includes a section called "A Better Future," which talks about memory through the story of a girl who relates the experience of her grandfather during the internal armed conflict. According to the text, "The story of Julia's past is similar to that of many Guatemalan families. The armed conflict in our country pitted Guatemalans against each other for thirty-six years (1960–1996)."[40] The consequences of this conflict, it continues, were disastrous: violence, death, destruction, and the displacement of the population.

The section closes with questions for the students about the origins of the conflict and its protagonists, and the lesson plan that follows (*Habla tiempo, habla . . . Imaginemos un pueblo sin historia . . .*) highlights the importance of history in general, while also suggesting specific ways to remember, through the retention of old objects or the knowledge of elders. The text is accompanied by a reflection on the importance of memory for the indigenous peoples: without roots, they cannot make plans for the future, which is why knowing one's past is essential for individuals and societies. It also suggests the importance of words and the relevance of oral tradition for communities. The latter, it says, is one of the most important sources for constructing history, as it helps to recover the testimonies of those who witnessed or experienced the events.[41]

OTHER TEXTS

Three collections were selected for analysis in consultation with teachers who said the texts are among those most widely used in private education establishments, at least in the urban areas of the capital city, where attendance at this type of school is most common. Two are published by transnational publishing companies and one by a Guatemalan company. They cover the primary level and the first three years of the middle level.[42]

All the texts analyzed offer an overview of events that took place in the country from the middle of the twentieth century, with some variations.[43] From different perspectives, they all identify the revolutionary period

(1944–54) as the starting point of recent historical processes, describing changes in the economy, the social order, and politics. They then posit that 1954 saw the closing of spaces for political participation, the transition to military governments, and the beginning of the conflict. They later explain the return to civilian rule and the process of political negotiations that ended with the signing of the peace accords, marking the beginning of the construction and consolidation of a new society, founded on peace and a set of civic values.

The texts point to global bipolarity—that is, the distribution of most power to two blocs, the United States and the Soviet Union—to explain Guatemala's recent history and, more specifically, the causes of its conflict. They highlight international actors and their influence, in particular the United States and Cuba, as well as the ideological confrontation between East and West during the Cold War. They suggest that communism, embodied by the Soviet Union and Cuba, sought equality more than freedom, while describing its antithesis, capitalism, as a liberal system that favors freedom over equality and promotes democracy and free markets, with the United States as the emblematic example.

The causes of the conflict are addressed and explained from bipolar, circumstantial, and structural perspectives. The first two included the futility of dialogue as a means of resolving the country's problems and the stigmatization of certain forms of political participation. The structural causes included poverty, unequal distribution of wealth, discrimination, and racism. The result of all this was the imposition, development, and consolidation of militarism, authoritarian governments, and, consequently, a militarized state. The texts also consider polarization within society, evidenced by the unarmed groups that formed to support the army (business people and workers) and those supporting the guerrillas (teachers, students, and workers).

After explaining the conflict in some detail, the texts highlight the different names used interchangeably to refer to it: internal armed conflict, internal armed confrontation, internationalized armed conflict, internal war, and civil war. They also list the many traumatic acts and situations that took place during this period: political persecution, forced disappearances, kidnappings, murders, torture, exile, and refuge in neighboring countries. It is important to mention that at least two of the texts say the climax of the violence was genocide, defined as a series of military operations to exterminate the members of a social group—in this case, the indigenous communities.[44] Also described as socially traumatic are the scorched earth policy, which was implemented through more than six hundred massacres during the conflict, and the use of civil self-defense patrols, model villages, and development centers as mechanisms to control the civilian population.

With some nuances, the texts identify the protagonists of the war as the guerrillas (referred to as either the revolutionary movement or the insurgency) and the army. The former is described as a communist-inspired movement that sought to impose a socialist system on the country. Its members, say the texts, were peasants and students, who are blamed for the massacres committed against the population. The army is described as an institution supported by the United States that gradually began to assume governmental functions until it gained control of the state and consolidated itself as an economic group. The army persecuted all forms of political opposition and frequently used the "state of siege" as a social control mechanism.

The common denominator described during this period is the violence, which brought about a climate of social inhibition. Scant reference is made to the participation of other social sectors in the events, giving the impression that the confrontation was between the guerrillas and the army. Mention is made, however, of "paramilitary groups," whose objective was to eliminate the opponents of the regime. They are defined as clandestine groups that executed people and took justice into their own hands.

The texts then discuss the "return to democracy" period, which was characterized by the holding of "free and fair" elections—the main objective of which was to put a political regime and system of government in place that would respect human rights and work for the well-being of the population. This period began in 1985 with the establishment of a National Constituent Assembly, the drafting of a new constitution, and general elections. A new government was elected at the beginning of the following year by universal suffrage, with high voter turnout. Next came the ten-year process of negotiations between the guerrilla organizations and the government, which concluded in December 1996 with the signing of the Agreement for a Firm and Lasting Peace. This is explained as having taken place in Central America more generally, pointing to a similar process that was being undertaken in El Salvador. The texts also highlight the role played by "friendly" countries and, especially, the United Nations, in this process.

The texts suggest that the peace accords provided an opportunity for political dialogue and resolution of the national and regional conflicts, for political inclusion, and for the reorganization of the productive activities that had been affected by the conflict to create jobs and stimulate development. This process, it is said, strengthened civilian power and, consequently, the awareness of the roles individuals should play in a democratic society and state where collective decision making should be the norm. The texts also stress the need to guarantee the rights of indigenous peoples but do not establish any links with the traumatic experiences they suffered during the conflict.

One important result of the peace process highlighted is the CEH final report, which summarizes the most significant aspects of the conflict. The report of the Human Rights Office of the Archdiocese of Guatemala, *Guatemala: Nunca más*, is mentioned in similar terms, and the ongoing exhumations to find and identify the bodies of the victims of the conflict—which the texts consider important for strengthening the justice system, respect for human rights, the reconstruction of history, national reconciliation, and a culture of peace—are also discussed. The historical summary in each text ends with a different version of the statement about the importance of peace as the only way to consolidate a democracy.

HISTORY AND MEMORY: CONCEPTS AND IMPLICATIONS

The particulars of the concepts of history and memory help clarify how they are understood and, hence, pedagogically approached—above all, to determine their potential social and political uses by future generations of citizens. For example, according to the CEH report, "Historical memory, both individual and collective, is the underpinning of national identity. The memory of the victims is a fundamental aspect of historical memory, through which the values and struggles for human dignity are recovered."[45] According to this definition, memory is linked to national identity and to knowing the experiences of those who survived past violence. By placing these experiences in their specific context, they become important for creating solidarities that go beyond the individual victims.

No definition of history is given, but the concept is instead formulated in operative terms. Several parts of the report insist on the importance of the work of the CEH, for example, for "the historical clarification" of human rights violations.[46] This historical clarification process was carried out through the collection of innumerable testimonies from people who experienced abuses or were indirect victims. Rather than proposing a specific definition of history, the CEH highlights the importance of constructing a narrative that can be used to clarify certain acts.

Neither concept—memory nor history—appeared in the initial documents produced on education reform in Guatemala;[47] they emerged only in the proposed new curriculum.[48] One objective of history education in the proposal is for history to "contribute to the systematization of the oral tradition of the nation's cultures, as the basis for building internal capacity for self-development and achievement of positive and beneficial exogenous relationships."[49] Note, however, that this refers to oral tradition rather than history, and beyond it are no basic definitions of either concept in the curriculum.

Moreover, the concept of nation that underpins the entire proposed curriculum is understood as formed through oral tradition, or historical knowledge, but not social memory, although the various textbooks later developed do include several definitions of memory, with different emphases and perspectives. The Ministry of Education's textbook for the sixth grade of the primary level, for example, refers to memory as follows: "We all need to learn about our past and value what we are; [we need to learn about] the subsequent events that have taken place in our collective lives. This is historical memory."[50] This simple definition does not distinguish between memory and history but instead combines them to emphasize the importance of knowing about the past to generate greater individual and social value. The past is understood as an important factor for stimulating individual and social self-esteem. This passage further illustrates how history is defined in some of the textbooks:

> When we talk about your past, we are talking about your history. So, when we talk about the past of humankind, we are talking about its history. The history of humankind comprises significant events. . . . But these grand events were not isolated, they were part of the development processes; in other words, they are linked to prior events (causes) and to subsequent events (consequences). . . . Thus, history is the development of society through time. Also, History, with a capital H, is the science that studies the development of society.[51]

In the everyday language used in this definition, we can identify some conceptual elements of history that are being conveyed to the students. In the first place, although the text recognizes the continuity between historical processes, it reduces them to "grand events," with no information given about what criteria or perspectives are used to select them. Although the notion of process is present, the idea remains about past events. Therefore, history tells what happened in the past, but it is not linked to the present (except for the fact that it is the result of the "significant events" of the past). Another, similar textbook definition focuses on another type of "grand event": "The history of humankind is marked by the violent reactions to the conflicts that occur between individuals, peoples, and countries. Wars, invasions, lynching and more have occurred throughout history, in an attempt to resolve conflicts."[52]

Reading Beatriz Sarlo, one could argue that, according to these proposed conceptual definitions, the function of history is to convey information:

> Non-academic history confronts the past in a manner less dictated by discipline and method. It seeks to satisfy present, intellectual, emotional, moral and political needs. Its principles are simple and are not contrary to common sense. It offers certainties, not hypotheses.[53]

Since history seeks to respond to immediate needs, in other words, it avoids approaches that can help form strong and critical opinions.

Contrary to those who take this approach to historical knowledge are those who posit the writing and reading of history as a political act, which, regardless of its interpretation, is imbued with specific political and social perspectives. Whoever researches and writes history does not do so in the abstract. Their questions—and their proposed responses—have a meaning and orientation that set priorities in the topics they choose to address.

This relationship of causality and motivation is reproduced in the process of teaching history. Underlying the overstated "objectivity" that should, so some say, dictate the teaching of history is a precise intentionality. Conveying information about "grand events" means the elements that do not appear in this reconstruction of history were not "important," are not worthy of being— or should not be—remembered. Subjectivity, and not objectivity, guides the decisions about what and what not to report. According to Mario Carretero and Marcelo Borrelli,

> One of the principal functions of teaching history is the political and cultural role it plays in dealing with the past. From a psychological perspective, this leads to understanding history as a bearer of meanings and symbols. The content of the history taught in schools is the backbone of social-cultural representations.[54]

In other words, these meanings and symbols are important because they integrate individuals among themselves and with their society and their past. Their strength will depend on the type of information that is conveyed—a reflection that gains in relevance when addressing the recent past, especially when it has been traumatic, as in Guatemala. Far from limiting the options to an affirmation/negation duality, Carretero and Borrelli expand the range of potential explanations and their implications:

Among the problems that exist in attempting to transmit these terrible events is proposing simplistic historical explanations, devoid of the conflictive elements that characterized them and that continue to be a topic of debate. Another is providing Manichean explanations that reduce the historical complexity to a confrontation between "good" and "bad." And another is conveying a *present-minded or non-empathetic view of the events that does not allow for* recognizing or comprehending that in the past societies had beliefs, values, and goals that are different from those of today [italics added]. Similarly, historical events are analyzed in terms of moral judgments that prevent the development of *historical thinking.*[55]

The authors insist that the classroom is infused with moral values. What is transmitted there should have "meaning," depending on the students' "place in society." It is as if the students have to be given moral codes that clarify how to understand the past correctly. This cannot be ignored, because the collection of memories children and adolescents build is permeated by these values.

In summary, the conceptual definitions of the concepts of both history and memory in the main documents consulted are scant; this does not mean, however, that they do not portray a specific point of view they seek to convey to students. In the case of memory, they present several analytical approaches, depending on the point of view. The CEH characterizes memory as individual and collective; underpinning the national identity; important for learning about the experiences of victims of the conflict; and a starting point for supporting social values and the struggle for dignity. The Ministry of Education defines it as an important step for preserving knowledge about the histories and traditions of communities, thanks to the collective memory of the community elders.[56]

While these approaches are certainly not worthless, I would question their relevance in terms of the formation of student identity. As Carretero and González reflect along these lines,

In relation to the recent past, it is important to keep in mind how the memory about what happened is conveyed. Attention should be paid to the different policies for transmitting these events and the degree of cultural and pedagological authority with which they are presented. [This is important] above all to detect the nature and contents of the memory that is being built, which becomes an official, homogenizing history, lacking nuances and conflicts; merely a chronological account of history and the past.[57]

The appropriate pedagogical approach to history and memory is thus part of an in-depth and ongoing debate. An important question is how far the education system in Guatemala can go with the definitions of history and memory that are being conveyed, and, even more importantly, the implications of their internalization and use by the students.

CONCLUSION

Several issues from this brief overview should be revisited and approached as problems to be solved relative to the users and beneficiaries of the education system, the proposed curriculum, and the ways history and memory are conceived and addressed in Guatemala, particularly in light of the recommendations on education reform made by the CEH to the Guatemalan state.

To start with, it is important to keep in mind the unequal access to education services in the country. A significant percentage of children and young people do not attend school, a situation that gets worse when children reach adolescence because they have fewer opportunities to receive an education. This unequal access is the result of failed state policies to provide services and of the economic difficulties of many families, and it affects the development of individual capabilities and skills. When they begin their adult lives, young people are burdened with imposed inequalities, which lead to a series of deficiencies related to, for example, the development of processes of abstraction that strengthen the capacity to criticize and analyze their realities.[58]

As for educational content, the textbooks reviewed in this chapter mention a number of causes of the conflict, which contrast to the bipolar approach used to explain how the conflict then played out. The prevailing idea is that the confrontation was only between the army and the guerrillas, and that the population was a passive victim. The different social, political, and economic actors involved are thus rendered invisible, reinforcing the interpretation of the conflict as a "battle between two demons."[59] This view leads students to believe that, while it was a traumatic event, the conflict was resolved between the two contenders.

It is also important to highlight the different approaches to civic education and history. The former has a "formative" orientation, based on normative notions, from the primary level to the final grade in the diversified cycle. The purpose is to form good citizens based on the knowledge, internalization, and practice of a set of virtues and values developed gradually. History, in contrast, is "informative" in nature. While on the whole it is studied from a process perspective, it does not prioritize the development of a critical reading of the past. For example, it provides information about the most important events of the past seventy years without presenting them as problems to be questioned. This is justified by arguing the approach should not be biased but, rather, objective and impartial. As discussed above, this issue is part of the debate about the relevance of remembering or forgetting what happened in the country during the conflict.

The distinction between "forming" and "informing" contains an implicit hierarchy of the objectives and results of the education process in the subjects of history and memory. If education is the fundamental channel for transmitting the knowledge and skills needed by students to discover, understand, and explain themselves and act accordingly in society, then we must not ignore the characteristics of the social setting in which the education process takes place. Students arrive in the classroom influenced by previous socialization processes that shape views and experiences,[60] especially family-related, that are constructed on the basis of the economic, religious, and cultural environments in which they live. This creates a set of values and perceptions about reality.

During the education socialization process, then, the students establish emotional and cognitive bonds with information that is similar to the "formative information" they have received outside the classroom. They may even reject everything that does not coincide with the information provided by their primary social environments. Thus, the "information" provided in history will not necessarily be as relevant as the "formation" offered in civic education, which is more likely to coincide with what students learn at home.

Now, is informing students about how historical narratives develop enough to make them understand the complexity of how they are created? Is there not a risk of trying to make society homogeneous? Is there not a risk of converting history into a series of events that occurred outside the classroom and, therefore, are not relevant to students' lives? Or that are perceived as static or as something entirely in the past? Not taking these aspects into account can lead to favoring the "way things should be" by providing students with information that is current but not necessarily relevant to their everyday lives.

It is evident that the education process does not occur in the abstract. Instead, it is immersed in society's inherent contradictions. Students are exposed to a constant cognitive duality: that of the classroom and that of the "street." The complex social environment in which they live marks their lives in a way completely at odds with what they learn in the classroom. In other words, everyday reality is not where the education process begins. This is why formal education is creating a *cognitive dissonance*[61]—the discomfort experienced by an individual who holds two or more contradictory cognitions—especially in the contradictory implications this has on the social behavior of the students.

In countries with recent traumatic pasts and current high levels of social and economic inequality, the education process faces significant challenges that are not always considered in the proper perspective. Studies on education, which generally center on problems of coverage and quality, should also consider such issues as the type and quality of life of those who have access to these services and, more importantly, of those who do not. The concerns that occupy the lives of many families in post-conflict societies can ultimately impose a particular perception of reality, in which issues and problems different to the ones that matter in the classroom prevail. Thus, it is worth asking: What effects can a sustained process of transmission of values and knowledge about a culture of peace have when the reality in which students live does not guarantee their basic livelihoods? How important is it to learn to live in peace within a society that does not guarantee such peace will become real?

Another consideration is the role of the teacher in this process. As mentioned above, the teacher is responsible for guiding the implementation of and, above all, for contributing to the critical analysis of the curriculum. This requires a review of the type and quality of teachers' training and their own perspectives on or beliefs about the reality in which they live, as well as the way they position themselves in it.[62] While one may argue that this is in the realm of the subjective, one cannot ignore that teachers are political actors who read and interact with reality in specific ways. While the influence they exercise—voluntarily or involuntarily—over the students will not create tensions if their opinions coincide with those the students have already formed as a result of the socialization process within their families, the discussion of complex topics and processes can be a different matter: students may select and appropriate the information they believe is useful and, above all, consistent with the set of values and information they already possess. The challenge faced by the teachers is to achieve an adequate harmony among their discourse, the practices they seek to stimulate, and, especially, the specific contexts in which these education processes occur. Carretero and Borelli refer to this challenge when they posit,

> It is important to keep in mind that when discussing aspects of recent history the students already have information and preconceived ideas about some of these events, which come from their families, the media, the groups to which they belong, other perspectives, etc. This can lead, among other things, to "moral reactions" to certain traumatic historical events. Also, when transmitting information on this type of event, the

teacher's own opinion cannot be avoided, but this opinion should not close the door to discussing and exchanging different perspectives.[63]

Thus, the prospects of the education system's forming and informing current and future generations of students based on consistent cognitions about the recent past are conditioned by these factors. A new curriculum, new textbooks, and new approaches are not enough. The surrounding reality, with its accumulation of information and incessant disputes and differences, should occupy a privileged position, in particular because it gives meaning and potential to newly acquired knowledge.

The signing of the peace accords in Guatemala was considered a starting point for strengthening the rule of law and developing new forms of social coexistence. In the years that followed, several steps were taken in this direction, including the discussed education reform. Little progress was made, however, in eliminating the root causes of the conflict. This is a complex situation in which advances made in certain areas are limited by the lack of progress in others. For example, school enrollment has increased, the new curriculum incorporates the CEH recommendations, and what happened during the conflict is talked about more openly. No significant change has taken place in the levels of poverty and social exclusion, however, which means the reality of the large majority of the population has not changed for the better.

The question is, are greater educational coverage, a new curriculum, and discussion of the recent past sufficient to advance a more inclusive model of society? Education is fundamental for the harmonious consolidation of society, but it cannot achieve this on its own. In the medium to long term, however, it can contribute to the formation of future citizens imbued with new ideas and new perspectives on themselves and society. Consequently, it is crucial not only to support the education system but to subject it to periodic review to ensure it is making a positive contribution.

NOTES

1   This chapter, including material quoted from other sources, was translated into English by Carolina Carter.

2   Signed in Norway on June 23, 1994. In *Acuerdos de paz firmados por el Gobierno de la República de Guatemala y la Unidad Revolucionaria Nacional Guatemalteca (URNG)* (Guatemala City: Universidad Rafael Landívar-Instituto de Investigaciones Económicas y Sociales—Misión de Verificación de las Naciones Unidas en Guatemala [MINUGUA], 1997), 247–51.

3   Signed in Mexico on March 31, 1995. Ibid., 253–74.

4   Commission for Historical Clarification (CEH), *Guatemala memoria del silencio*, 12 vols. (Guatemala City: UNOPS, 1999). The previous year, the Human Rights Office of the Archdiocese of Guatemala had published its report *Guatemala: Nunca más* (Guatemala City: Archdiocese of Guatemala, Office of Human Rights, 1998), which contained information that complemented the CEH's report. Three days after the launch of this publication, Bishop Juan Gerardi Conedera, the driving force behind the report, was murdered.

5   The education reform process took several years. It was conceptually and philosophically based on the Joint Commission on Educational Reform's document, *Diseño de reforma educativa: Runuk´ ik jun k´ak´a tijonïk*, developed by the Joint Commission on Educational Reform (Guatemala City: Joint Commission on Educational Reform, 1998). This was followed by other general policy documents, including the *Marco general de la transformación curricular* (General Framework for Curricular Reform), proposed by the Comisión Consultiva para la Reforma Educativa (Consultative Commission for Educational Reform) in 2003.

6   While the Ministry of Education has a significant budget, a large percentage of its resources is allocated to the salaries of the public officials—bureaucrats and teachers— which leaves little for investing in infrastructure or, most importantly, improving the quality of the education process.

7   Joint Commission on Educational Reform, "Marco filosófico de la reforma educativa," chapter 2 in *Diseño de reforma educativa*, 33.

8   The figures used correspond to the estimates for this year prepared by the National Statistics Institute. See Instituto Nacional de Estadística Guatemala, "Temas/Indicadores," http://www.ine.gob.gt/index.php/estadisticas/tema-indicadores, accessed April 19, 2014.

9   The education system in Guatemala is divided into three levels: primary, middle, and university. The first comprises the first six years of study, while the second has two cycles: basic and diversified. The first, common cycle, lasts three years, while the second is two years long and offers several training options. The final level, university, will not be discussed here.

10   The school enrollment rate is defined as the rate of enrollment with relationship to the

school-age population of the country. Instituto Nacional de Estadística Guatemala, "Caracterización Estadística," 2012, http://www.ine.gob.gt/index.php/estadisticas/caracterizacion-estadistica.

11 The sources consulted do not specify the criteria used to establish these groupings.

12 The Guatemalan population is traditionally divided into indigenous and nonindigenous (also called *"ladina"*). It is important to note that the sources for the enrollment information did not indicate how this identification was made. The percentage of the indigenous population in the country is estimated on the basis of the last general population census conducted in 2002. Instituto Nacional de Estadística Guatemala, "Caracterización Estadística."

13 Berthold Molden offers a fairly complete overview of the debate in Guatemala on what he calls "the politics of history" in *Políticas sobre la historia en Guatemala: Historiografía, justicia de posguerra y resarcimiento (1996–2005)* (Guatemala City: AVANCSO, 2014).

14 One example of this conflictive environment that emerged during the trial against General Ríos Montt was the publication of several pamphlets in the local papers signed by the "Fundacion contra el Terrorismo" (Foundation against Terrorism). These pamphlets, with a Cold War logic, accused individuals, groups, and institutions from different sectors of being terrorists and communists and, above all, responsible for what had happened in the country.

15 In *Acuerdos de paz*, 247.

16 CEH, *Guatemala memoria del silencio, vol. 5, Conclusions and Recommendations*, 61–62.

17 Ibid., 62–63.

18 Ibid., 68–69.

19 Ibid., 69.

20 Ibid., 69–70.

21 Note that these are fairly broad and complex concepts. See "Acuerdo de identidad y derechos de los pueblos indígenas" in *Acuerdos de paz*, 253–74.

22 Ibid., subsection f, 262.

23 The commission was created through Government Agreement No. 262-97 and comprised "representatives of the Government and of the Indigenous Organizations." The agreement did not specify the institutions from which the five indigenous representatives should come.

24 In the process of drafting this document, the commission had access to more than forty proposals prepared by civil society organizations.

25 Joint Commission on Educational Reform, *Diseño de reforma educativa*, 37.

26 Ibid., 3–38

27 The *Marco general de la transformación curricular* proposes a "Vision of the Nation" to guide this process: "Guatemala is a multiethnic, multicultural, and multilingual country that is developing as a fair, democratic, plural, and peaceful nation. It is based on the wealth

of its natural, social, ethnic, cultural, and linguistic diversity and on values for peaceful coexistence and the consolidation of a culture of peace, to ensure the equitable development and individual and collective well-being of all Guatemalans. This is a rule-of-law state that promotes policies and actions to eradicate stereotypes and the cultural practices that have fostered discrimination. For this purpose all potentially discriminatory laws have been repealed. It is a nation in which everyone fully enjoys their human rights and their right to freedom; pluralism is respected and fostered; sustainable development is adequately promoted through science and technology. The conditions of equality favor the well-being of its inhabitants, and education is recognized as one of the fundamental means to achieve these objectives." Comisión Consultiva para la Reforma Educativa, *Marco general de la transformación curricular*, 36.

28 Democratic life and a culture of peace; unity in diversity; sustainable integral development; and science and technology. Joint Commission on Educational Reform, *Diseño de reforma educativa*, 52–55.

29 The main axes of the curriculum are multiculturality and interculturality; gender, ethnic, and social equality; family life; civic engagement; sustainable development; social and environmental security; job training; and technological development. These are disaggregated into components and subcomponents that are organized systematically and sequentially into learning areas. *Marco general de la transformación curricular*, 54.

30 The civic engagement axis contains the components "Human Rights Education and a Culture of Peace" to guide the student in learning about the recognition of, respect for, and promotion of human rights of indigenous peoples and of different specific groups. The "Civic Education" component promotes civic values based on the knowledge, interpretation, and understanding of the rules and laws that govern life in society. The expected result of this approach is a fundamental respect by students for their country and for everything that symbolizes their identity and strengthens their civic values. Guatemala Ministry of Education, *Curriculum Nacional Base: Sexto grado: Nivel primario* (Guatemala City: Ministry of Education, 2008), 31.

31 The "curricular transformation" was defined as "the pedagogical and technical updating and renovation of the educational approaches, schemes, methods, contents, and procedures; of the different ways of providing educational services and the participation of all social stakeholders." Guatemala Ministry of Education, *Curriculum Nacional Base: Sexto grado*, 15.

32 The first three primary-level grades include the "Social and Natural Environment" and "Civic Engagement" areas; in 2012, the name of the former was changed to "Social Sciences." The three years of the middle-level basic cycle and the subsequent two years of high school include only one area, called "Social Sciences and Civic Education."

33 The history curriculum in the previous curricular framework aimed to provide a "political reading" based on a discussion of the presidents from independence onwards. The

new curriculum sought to describe political and, to a certain extent, economic processes. Previously, the civic education area focused on patriotic symbols and a "way things should be," underpinned by civic "virtues" (such as respect, obedience, and responsibility, among others). See AVANCSO, *Imágenes homogéneas en un país de rostros diversos: El sistema educativo formal y la conformación de referentes de identidad nacional entre jóvenes Guatemaltecos* (Guatemala City: AVANCSO, 1998 and 2002).

34 School textbooks are not distributed at the middle level. Private publishers are used instead, depending on the teacher's selection and criteria.

35 A unit formally exists within the Ministry of Education in charge of reviewing the contents of textbooks published by private publishers, but this review is not carried out. No mention is made of this requirement in the textbooks consulted.

36 The selected publishers—Santillana, Norma, and Piedra Santa—all have extensive experience in the publication of textbooks and education material in the country. Their books are also among the most used in private education centers, at least in Guatemala City. These are, however, commercially oriented projects rather than efforts that reflect concern about what contents to present and how to do so. In fact, these texts are recognized by the names of the publishers, not the authors.

37 It is interesting to note that the textbook for the third grade includes a reference to racism, which is defined as "a form of discrimination assumed by people who believe they are superior because of the color of their skin, ethnic origin, culture, gender, or social position." The text continues: "Discrimination between human beings is an obstacle to friendly and peaceful relationships between peoples and disrupts the peace, security, and peaceful coexistence between peoples. Each member of an ethnic group has the right to receive education in their own language, without discrimination." Guatemala Ministry of Public Education, *Medio social y natural: Tercer grado* (Guatemala City: Ministry of Public Education, 2013), 172.

38 It is noteworthy that these texts barely mention topics related to national symbols. As highlighted above, before the education reform, symbols of this nature were an important part of the official programs and textbooks. AVANCSO, *Imágenes homogéneas* (1998), especially chapter 4, 63–67.

39 This period runs between 1944 and 1954.

40 Guatemala Ministry of Education, *Ciencias sociales: Sexto grado*, vol. 1 (Guatemala City: Ministry of Education, 2003), 325–26.

41 Ibid., 335

42 Norma and Santilla are transnational publishing companies, while Piedra Santa is a Guatemalan publishing house.

43 This does not mean the previous periods of Guatemalan history are not addressed, although they are discussed with differing degrees of detail.

44 Andrea Linares Rodríguez, *Manual del educador: Escenarios 3: Ciencias sociales y formación*

ciudadana: Ciclo básico del nivel medio (Guatemala City: Grupo Editorial Norma, 2008), 141. The concept of genocide does not appear in the official textbooks or in the curriculum. The Basic National Curriculum for the third year of the basic cycle, however, refers to the political, economic, and social-cultural situation after the Second World War and mentions "the Genocide and the Holocaust" (49), among other historical events.

45 CEH, *Guatemala memoria del silencio*, vol. 5, 61–62.

46 See, for example, ibid., vol. 1, 51.

47 In other words, in the Joint Commission on Educational Reform's *Diseño de reforma educativa* and the Ministry of Education's *Marco general de la transformación curricular*. The new curriculum was put in place in 2005.

48 The explanation for this difference, among others, is that those who began the process—the technical staff in the ministry—were not the same as those who many years later prepared these curriculum guides.

49 Guatemala Ministry of Education, *Curriculum Nacional Base: Primer grado nivel medio-ciclo básico: Área de ciencias sociales y formación ciudadana* (Guatemala City: Ministry of Education, 2009), 9.

50 Guatemala Ministry of Education, *Ciencias sociales: Sexto grado*, vol. 1, 333.

51 Magda Aragón, *Identidades 6: Serie de ciencias sociales: Manual del educador* (Guatemala City: Grupo Editorial Norma, 2006), 84.

52 Guatemala Ministry of Education, *Ciencias sociales: Quinto grado* (Guatemala City: Ministry of Education, 2005), 331.

53 Beatriz Sarlo, *Tiempo pasado: Cultura de la memoria y primera persona* (Buenos Aires: Siglo XXI Editores Argentina, 2005), 16.

54 Mario Carretero and Marcelo Borrelli, "Memorias recientes y pasados en conflicto: ¿Cómo enseñar historia reciente en la escuela?" *Cultura y educación. Revista de teoría, investigación y práctica* 20, no. 2 (2008): 202.

55 Ibid., 206.

56 Guatemala Ministry of Education, *Ciencias sociales: Sexto grado*, vol. 2 (Guatemala City: Ministry of Education, 2005), 334–39.

57 Mario Carretero, Alberto Rosa, and María Fernanda González, eds., *Enseñanza de la historia y memoria colectiva* (Buenos Aires: Paidós, 2006), 32.

58 Anthony Giddens, *Sociología* (Madrid: Alianza Universidad, 1994), 466. On the other hand, Pierre Bordieu posits that the specific degree of productivity of all pedagogical work that is not carried out by the family depends on the distance between the *habitus* the education system seeks to instill (that is, the personality structure of the individual as it fits into society) and the one that has been instilled by other forms of pedagogical efforts, especially within the family. Pierre Bordieu and Jean Claude Passeron, *La reproducción: Elementos para una teoría del sistema de enseñanza* (Mexico City: Distribución Fontamara, 1996), 114–16.

59   An emblematic example of this perspective is provided by David Stoll, *Entre dos fuegos en los pueblos ixiles de Guatemala* (Quito: Ediciones Abya-Yala, 1999).

60   "The individuals living in different social conditions will acquire distinct dispositions to create certain lifestyles, understood as a set of preferences, beliefs and systematic practices. They will also receive an education linked to a social class. Just as each social group will receive different dispositions that will subconsciously guide them to classify and experience reality in a particular way, each one of them will possess a distinct cultural capital. In other words, a set of intellectual ratings produced either by the school system or transmitted by the family. These acquisitions that compose the habitus will produce effects over the years of school education." AVANCSO, *Imágenes homogéneas* (2002), 28.

61   The analytical category of cognitive dissonance is described by Ignacio Martín Baró, *Acción e ideología* (San Salvador: UCA editores, 1990), 262–65.

62   Last year a serious confrontation began between Ministry of Education officials and the students of middle-level centers that train primary school teachers. The ministry decided to eliminate the teacher training program that was given at the end of the middle level and move it to the university level, based on the poor quality of the training the program was providing. The students argued that this measure would effectively privatize teacher training because access to universities is severely limited for many students for social and economic reasons.

63   Carretero and Borelli, "Memorias recientes y pasados en conflicto," 207.

PART II

Reparations, Redress, and Education

CHAPTER 4

Education for Overcoming Massive Human Rights Violations

Cristián Correa

The right to reparation of victims of armed conflict and gross violations of human rights has been increasingly recognized in international law and the practice of states.[1] With varying degrees of success, victims have, over the past three decades, more frequently demanded and exercised their right to obtain effective remedies, including the truth about the violations committed against them, the prosecution and punishment of those found guilty, institutional reforms to guarantee similar violations will not be committed again, and concrete forms of material and symbolic reparation. One important component of reparation demanded by victims is often education. This can take different forms, such as restitution of the right to education for a person who was prevented from exercising it as a direct result of a violation committed against him or her[2] or as part of a reconstruction effort, where massive violence and destruction or historical forms of marginalization and oppression withheld this important right from entire groups.

Education is a basic right with a strong capacity to affirm the dignity of those who have suffered violations and a potentially powerful transformative effect. It can play a very important role in overcoming the consequences of oppression and violence and setting conditions for peace and justice, particularly for those most vulnerable and especially for children and youth, for whom it can be an important tool of reintegration into communities and society.[3] Education can provide resources and opportunities to victims to improve their lives, to secure sustainable incomes, and to develop and exercise their capabilities. It can create opportunities for those marginalized or discriminated against for gender, ethnic, religious, or political reasons, and even to transform the patterns of discrimination, especially with regard to gender hierarchies. Finally, education can potentially change mindsets about conflict, the use of force, relations between communities, and the implications of respect for human rights among authorities, the civil service, and security and military forces.

Understanding the role of education in post-conflict and post-authoritarian transitions can help us address the challenges faced by many countries confronting past abuses and violence with regard to both reconstruction and reparation. Those challenges include overcoming the consequences of the marginalization and destruction of certain areas, populations, or communities by increasing the coverage and quality of the education available; responding to and helping victims overcome the obstacles imposed by the most serious violations of human rights to gaining access to or completing education; and distinguishing between the need for reconstruction and the need for reparation, while at the same time acknowledging that reparation requires certain levels of reconstruction and guarantees of satisfaction of basic social rights.[4]

This chapter draws on the experiences of Peru, South Africa, and Chile, as well as other cases where education measures have been part of reconstruction and reparation programs or have featured in the recommendations of truth commissions, as in Nepal, Colombia, and Kenya. Some examples are also discussed from the jurisprudence of the Inter-American Court of Human Rights, which has included education measures among the several forms of reparation it has ordered for violations of civil and political rights, both as collective and individual approaches.

In explaining these experiences and drawing lessons from them, I first discuss the nature, characteristics, and challenges of massive programs of reparation and how education measures can be integrated into them. I then present two separate but related forms of measures that have been used to address education deficits in transitional countries and/or to address human rights violations: education as part of the response to marginalization, exclusion, or destruction affecting broad populations; and education as part of the response to the consequences of human rights violations committed against specific categories of victims.

PROVIDING REPARATIONS FOR THE IRREPARABLE

Numerous international instruments and conventions recognize the right of victims of gross human rights violations and severe violations of international human rights law to reparation, and the practice of states and decisions of international tribunals and bodies confirm their recognition.[5] Determining how to provide reparation in such cases, however, is still contested. The nature of extrajudicial killings, forced disappearances, rape, torture, and other atrocities makes difficult the use of the limited, monetary language of compensation, as the incommensurable dimensions of personal loss are difficult to reduce to amounts of money.

The challenge is even greater when violations are massive, and when the passage of time has brought only a sense of abandonment by and denial from state authorities and, in many cases, significant portions of society. This leads us to question a basic assumption of the notion of reparation: that reparations should attempt to restore victims to their status quo ante, to their situation prior to the violations. Even with adequate resources, the conditions in which violations are committed and/or the victims' poverty and lack of education may prevent them from providing the evidence required to make effective claims. As a result, reparations may exclude many of those who need help the most: the poor, those living in rural or marginalized areas, and the uneducated, which in many cases will be women, children, and the elderly.

If reparations cannot be proportional to the harm suffered by each victim, then how can we claim they are fair? How can we define the components of a massive reparation program to guarantee its accessibility? I have argued elsewhere that one way of responding to these questions is to consider rights violations as a message that victims are not human, have no dignity, and are not members of the community. That message is communicated through verbal and (mostly) physical language—the killing, the act of rape, and the disregard of any right that accompanies the act of violence—but also by years of abuse, disregard of the victims' rights, and neglect by the police, the judiciary, or even the media or neighbors, who turn a blind eye and do not fulfill their basic duties in response to a heinous crime.

Reparations should, therefore, be considered as the opposite message, which society and its representatives have to communicate through verbal but (mostly) material language, that victims are human, have dignity, and are members of the community.[6] This does not necessarily mean ruling out proportionality from the definition of reparation, but rather understanding proportionality in a way that guarantees the inclusion of all victims, especially those most vulnerable. It requires looking at the general consequences of the crimes in the current lives of victims, not making an individualized assessment of the conditions that existed when the violations were committed and projecting them through to the present. The notions of inclusion and membership help identify some degree of commonality based on the rest of society's standards of living that can, in turn, help define reparations; the notion of dignity helps determine a minimum threshold for and different components of those measures that at least allow for sustainable living conditions.

This is not easy, however. In societies with large disparities, for example, using the mean family income as the standard for reparations may have no relationship to the standard of living of most victims, or their neighbors, who may be poorer than the average family. A psychosocial support program for victims needs to offer effective services, which may be beyond the capacity of an overburdened and understaffed public health system. Given the disparities in the quality of primary and secondary education in many countries, even if university scholarships look attractive as a form of reparation, only a small portion of victims or their children—most likely those who are wealthy or have already received a better education—would be able to benefit from them. University scholarships for those victims who have the ability to perform academically is a form of reparation the average family in most countries cannot afford to take advantage of.

Such a standard cannot be absolutely rigid, then, but it should offer general guidance for defining how to overcome the obstacles victims face in attempting to live with dignity and in conditions not so different from those of the rest of society. Victims and their advocates would need to consider the living conditions of the rest of society when making their proposals, but the government would not be able to reject them based solely on the claimed absence of resources. A consideration of "the mean family income" forces us to look at reparations beyond the frequently substandard social programs for education or health care available in many communities, without creating expectations that are impossible to meet.

Reparations understood as this kind of message should take into consideration the different consequences of violations on victims in the present, which are often psychosocial, physical, or socioeconomic. For women, violations often have more devastating effects, given their social and economic dependency on husbands and male relatives, or as a result of ostracism, abandonment, or pregnancy related to sexual violence. All of these consequences affect the ability of victims to guarantee a better future for themselves through education—which could mean completing primary or secondary school, receiving skills training, taking literacy courses, or completing a university degree—including the ability to study. Moreover, children of direct victims, affected by poverty and other consequences of the violations suffered by their parents, usually cannot continue their studies. In some cases, the inability to provide for their children's education is what causes the most pain to survivors.[7]

Reparation programs that define benefits by looking at the consequences of violations for victims provide measures such as psychosocial support, medical assistance, economic assistance to overcome poverty, and education to both survivors and their children. The provision of social services as reparation, however, raises important questions. If free health care and education are provided to all people in the country, for example, is that not enough? Can reparations simply function as a mechanism of guaranteeing the social and economic rights the state is obligated to provide anyway?

Understanding reparation as a message of dignity and membership can help answer these questions. Reparations should provide conditions of well-being according to the dignity of the person and that of other members of society. This means they should help remove the specific obstacles victims face in exercising the same social and economic rights afforded any other citizen in the country. In terms of psychosocial support, they should be entitled to services that help them overcome the traumatic consequences of violence and isolation; in terms of financial measures, reparations should help them live future lives that can guarantee a medium level of well-being;[8] in terms of education for them and their children, measures should help victims remove the obstacles they face as result of the violation suffered in getting access to education and completing their studies or training as far as they can according to their capacities.[9] Reparations should add something to the existing services that guarantees the accessibility and pertinence of those services to victims.

To these individual measures focused on those who suffered the most severe forms of violations, other programs should be added, according to the nature of the violence and repression. Collective forms of reparation to communities affected by massive violence might be aimed at helping them achieve living conditions not so different from those of neighboring communities. The consequences of intentional policies of exclusion and marginalization, destruction of infrastructure, and historical deficits in the satisfaction of social and economic rights need to be considered to make reparations effective.

Regardless of their form, reparations need to be accompanied by explicit messages of acknowledgment of the responsibility of the state for the violations committed, and they should take into account the opinions and proposals of victims, guaranteeing their participation as a way of recognizing them as citizens. Approaching reparation as a message of dignity and membership can help define the measures of a reparation program and the number and quality of those measures, as well as the mechanisms for their delivery. It also helps to affirm the relationships among reparation, truth, justice, and guarantees of the violations' not being repeated. This approach helps distinguish reparations derived from responsibility for violations of human rights from humanitarian assistance, which does not derive from such responsibility. The distinction is important because in many cases governments are unwilling to acknowledge their responsibility, thereby equating human rights violations with natural disasters.

Education is a fundamental social and cultural right and an essential factor in the "full development of the human personality."[10] Measures for improving access to education for victims of human rights violations is an important component of most reparation efforts designed or implemented in post-conflict or post-authoritarian situations, as the cases below show. Education is also important to reconstruction and peacebuilding, particularly in guaranteeing stability and that abuses will not be repeated. While providing education for all members of society in a transitional situation can contribute to strengthening social cohesion, overcoming differences, and consolidating peace, however, those who suffered the most serious violations may require additional measures to help them overcome the obstacles those violations impose on their ability to get access to it.

The sections below will discuss two ways in which education policies can be part of the response to past injustice, looking at education first as part of the reconstruction effort targeted at all affected or marginalized communities, and second as being provided to the specific victims of the most serious violations. While the extent to which the former should be considered reparation (rather than the fulfillment of a general state obligation regarding social, economic, and cultural rights) is arguable, these efforts are important to include in a discussion of reparation and transitional justice. Reconstruction and the satisfaction of rights that address previous discrimination or its historical legacies play an important role in establishing the basis of a future polity, helping to draw the line clearly between a former logic of oppression and conflict and a new one of democracy and peace.

Reconstruction can also be essential to the implementation of some forms of reparation that are focused on certain victims; for example, having schools in areas affected by conflict or marginalization is a prerequisite for providing scholarships to victims of certain violations. In many of the cases discussed here, education as part of reconstruction has been recommended by truth commissions tasked with examining past injustice and its causes. In some, elements of reconstruction aimed at increasing access to education are articulated as specific measures of redress, even if not as parts of reparation programs.

EDUCATION AS RECONSTRUCTION AND REPARATION

Armed conflict leaves a legacy of destruction that seriously affects the ability of many people to exercise their right to education. It is not just schools that are destroyed, but also roads, electricity grids, and other infrastructure needed for children and youth to attend school. Often a generation of teachers is missing, as many were killed or fled, while many future teachers were not able to complete their studies. A sense of insecurity, fear, and distrust often affects the ability of teachers to live close to the communities they serve and prevents parents from sending their children to school. The economic consequences of conflict and widespread poverty also affect the ability of children and youth to study, as competing needs force many to use their time in income-generating activities.

Oppressive regimes can also have broad negative effects on education systems. In some cases, political repression combined with socioeconomic marginalization targets entire communities, as in South Africa during apartheid, where education for blacks was kept intentionally substandard compared to that for whites and other ethnic minorities.[11] In Morocco and Tunisia, certain regions labeled as conflictive, or dominated by groups considered to oppose the regime, were denied basic services or received inferior ones.[12]

This form of intentional marginalization constitutes a violation of the obligation to provide social, economic, and cultural rights without discrimination. In both such cases, policies for guaranteeing those rights, including the right to education, are needed, and they should be based on the obligations established by international law. Among those obligations, the provision of universal access to primary education is mandatory, and not subject to a progressive approach.[13] Furthermore, discrimination in the provision of education between boys and girls, or based on ethnic, religious, political, nationality, social origin, or any other status, is prohibited.[14]

Countries trying to overcome the legacies of armed conflict or oppression need to address those legacies that affect their education systems, with particular urgency when the conflict was rooted in inequality or when oppressive regimes intentionally marginalized specific regions or populations. What is the role of transitional justice in these efforts? This is a highly contested issue, as many argue that transitional justice should address violations of socioeconomic rights much like it addresses violations of civil and political rights, through truth seeking, criminal accountability, reparation programs, and guarantees of the violations' not being repeated.[15]

Certainly, I would argue, transitional justice needs to deal to some extent with the legacies of economic and social rights violations; the question, though, is which transitional justice approaches are best suited to deal with them and how to design them to do so. Consider not only that substandard education systems or major differences in the coverage and quality of education provided for certain areas of the country or certain populations affect massive numbers of people, but also that the root causes for the violations lie deep in the history and the power struggles that have characterized those countries.[16] Are these root causes something reparations can and need to address?[17] It is useful here to observe what has, in fact, been done in countries that, emerging from conflicts or repressive regimes, have identified the need to improve the coverage provided by their education systems.

Truth commissions have been useful tools in identifying the need to address forms of marginalization and exclusion and making recommendations, usually in the form of institutional reforms, reconstruction, or development policies. As will be discussed below, however, after initial enthusiasm for overcoming inequality in education, efforts usually fall short. The cases of South Africa, Peru, Timor-Leste, Morocco, and Sierra Leone will be briefly presented to assess the extent to which education policies recommended by truth commissions to overcome legacies of the past have been implemented. The forms of oppression or marginalization suffered by significant parts of the populations in these countries differed, as did the characteristics of the marginalized populations; but all were excluded from education to a great extent.

SOUTH AFRICA

In South Africa's apartheid, the exclusion was about race, in response to which the country's Truth and Reconciliation Commission made clear recommendations about education measures as part of its proposal on "Community Rehabilitation." The recommendations included reforms to address the "appalling" standard of black education, which translated into forms of assistance for the continuation of studies through community colleges, youth centers, and accelerated basic education and training programs; rebuilding schools, particularly in rural and disadvantaged areas; and mainstreaming support services through the education process to address the needs of students, including mature students in search of employment.[18] As Teboho Moja explains, the policies for improving the coverage and quality of education for the poor and black population were considered a form of redress for their exclusion and the substandard education provided them during apartheid. This meant broad reform of the education system, including its content and administration, to guarantee it reached excluded communities.[19] In 2013, 20 percent of the government budget was allocated to education, the equivalent of 6 percent of the country's gross domestic product (GDP),[20] while the public expenditure per student in 2011 was US$1,993—among the highest in sub-Saharan Africa[21]—a clear demonstration of a sustained commitment to improving education.

Almost sixteen years after the TRC report was handed to President Nelson Mandela, this effort shows significant results,[22] but also the challenges that lie ahead. The coverage and the rate of completion of secondary education for

black students have improved substantially, as has attendance in higher education, and the gap between black and white students has diminished consider-
ably. Important differences remain, however, especially between the poor and
the rich and between those living in urban and rural areas or slum areas and
those without slums.[23] The magnitude of exclusion is something that certainly
cannot be solved in one generation; it calls for a sustained effort to identify and
respond to the obstacles faced by those constituencies that, despite the policies
implemented, remain excluded.

PERU

In Peru, the 1980–2000 internal armed conflict was strongly connected to the
education sector and contributed to increasing the marginalization of affected
communities, as explained by Rosa Lía Chauca.[24] The Truth and Reconciliation
Commission (CVR, according to its Spanish acronym) understood this and
recommended improving the quality of education and promoting education
for peace,[25] as well as increasing the presence of the state in areas affected by
the conflict through the provision of social services.[26] These recommended
measures were presented as institutional reforms and not as reparation for
specific violations of human rights. Specific reparation measures involving
educational content were also recommended, but they focused on communities affected by extreme violence and individual victims who, as a result of the
violence, could not continue or pursue their studies, as will be discussed later
in more detail.

Improvements in education since 2000 have been significant, but differences between urban and rural populations remain great, as rural areas are
those historically most affected by marginalization. As a middle-income
country, Peru's education problems are not so much with enrollment, but
with completion and quality for children and youth belonging to indigenous communities of the Andes and the Amazon basin.[27] The fact that the
Ministry of Education records figures on the causes for delay in rural education and, since 2004, has distinguished between coverage for people whose
mother tongue is Spanish and those whose mother tongue is an indigenous
language shows a degree of concern for overcoming marginalization in education. UNESCO (the United Nations Educational, Scientific and Cultural
Organization) reports, however, that Peru is one of the Latin American countries that still have significant "achievement gaps in mathematics and reading between rural and urban students, exceeding 15 percentage points."[28] The
Ministry of Education reports progress in supporting bilingual education for

4,128 schools attended by children who speak indigenous languages, covering 180,000 children. This is a relevant effort and was part of the reforms promoted by the CVR, but it still falls short, considering that the same ministry had identified 18,217 schools with more than 1 million children whose primary language is indigenous.[29]

The public investment in education does not reflect prioritization, either. Resources allocated to the education sector for 2014 were 15.2 percent of the total public budget, which is equivalent to 3 percent of the GDP.[30] A public commitment has been made to increase this to 6 percent of the GDP but at a very gradual pace, to be achieved in twelve years.[31]

TIMOR-LESTE

In Timor-Leste, the Commission for Reception, Truth, and Reconciliation (CAVR, by its acronym in Portuguese) examined human rights violations committed during the internal armed conflict and the twenty-four years of Indonesian military occupation that followed the departure of the Portuguese colonial government. The commission included in its work violations not only of civil and political rights, but of social and economic rights. It stated that the Indonesian occupation used the education system to promote the integration of Timor-Leste into Indonesia, which superseded the goals of providing education that was useful and of good quality or meeting basic learning needs.[32]

In addition, the commission considered the education system implemented by the Portuguese to be substandard.[33] It commended the commitment of the Timorese government to universal education and recommended that "measures [be] undertaken to ensure that the Government policy of universal education is extended in practice to all children, especially orphans, the disabled and those in remote rural communities including to guarantee that all girl children have full and equal access to education, and that more opportunities for vocational training are provided."[34]

In its *National Education Strategic Plan 2011–2030*, the Timor-Leste Ministry of Education analyzed enrollment statistics from 2004 to 2009 and laid out a plan for education and education management reform for 2009–15.[35] The figures showed a considerable increase in coverage[36] in primary education[37] but no progress in secondary education, and the enrollment ratio for the third cycle of basic education and in secondary education was still very poor. Additionally, the 2010 census showed the urban net enrollment ratio for primary education was 80.2 percent, whereas the rural ratio was 67.4 percent; and the difference was even wider in secondary education (30 percent and 9.1

percent, respectively).[38] Among the main problems identified were the high and early dropout rates, as the number of those enrolled in grade 4 was less than half the numbers in grades 1 and 2.[39] Some good news is the significant increase in the literacy rates of people ages fifteen to twenty-four living in rural areas, from 60 percent in 2004 to 81 percent in 2007.[40]

The public effort to improve education is not reflected in its budget allocation. In 2011, education accounted for 8.1 percent of the public budget, equivalent to 3.1 percent of the gross national product,[41] despite the Ministry of Education's 2009 Educational Plan, which proposed increasing its allocation from 13 percent to 20 percent by 2015. The 2014 budget allocated 11.9 percent to education.[42] With an average GDP growth since 2007 of almost 11 percent per year,[43] and an average increase in public expenditure from 2009 to 2014 of 25.5 percent,[44] education does not seem to be a priority.[45]

MOROCCO

The Commission for Equity and Reconciliation in Morocco (IER, by its acronym in French) also tried to address the marginalization of regions and communities most affected by political repression. Those regions, which had been viewed as opposed to the regime or had secret detention centers located in them, suffered from discrimination and lack of social services. The IER made recommendations for collective reparation for them, which included addressing marginalization, mostly through community projects, but also targeting development and social policies there. As a result, the Human Rights Advisory Commission, responsible for implementing the IER recommendations, signed several agreements for improving education in the areas defined by the Community Reparations Program. In addition, the government launched a general policy for improving education coverage and literacy programs, especially among rural populations and women, calling for "a decade for education."[46]

Since then, the World Bank has reported significant progress in improving education coverage in Morocco, which has reached almost full enrollment in primary and upper secondary education.[47] As the report acknowledges, however, this progress has not been able to overcome the legacy of marginalization of rural areas or areas affected by repressive policies and neglect:

Significant gaps remain between rural and urban students and between female and male students beyond the primary level. In lower secondary education, for instance, the net enrollment rate is 79 percent for boys in urban areas but only 26 percent for girls in rural areas [as of 2013]. This gender gap is indicative of the social and cultural norms that continue to place rural girls in particular at a disadvantage.[48]

In terms of the quality of education, Morocco is among the twenty-one countries in which less than half of primary school children learn basic concepts and acquire abilities in mathematics and reading,[49] a result that does not correspond to its being a middle-income country.[50]

In addition to working to improve education for children, Morocco has made a significant effort to improve adult literacy, especially for women.[51] The literacy rate for women increased between 2004 and 2011 from 60.5 percent to 74 percent and, at this writing, was estimated to increase to 75.9 percent by 2015.[52] Despite this effort, though, Morocco is still "very far from the target" of "achieving an adult literacy target of at least 95 percent by 2015."[53]

SIERRA LEONE

The Truth and Reconciliation Commission of Sierra Leone also identified obstacles to guaranteeing the right to education to all Sierra Leoneans and made proposals for responding to them. The commission recognized that, since colonial times, the provision of education had been better for those living in the "colony" (coastal areas dominated by settlers and their descendants) than for those living in the rest of the country (the "protectorate," which comprises the interior areas, inhabited by precolonial settlers).[54] Discrimination also affected women and girls, whose access to education was significantly lower than that of men and boys.[55]

The commission also stressed the difference between spending on the military and spending on education.[56] It described the devastation caused by the war in terms of the ability of the state to provide basic services, particularly education, emphasizing the need for reconstruction and for training and retaining qualified teachers, especially to serve rural schools.[57] It made recommendations for guaranteeing access to free and compulsory primary education for all children, living in all provinces, with equal access for girls and boys; these included the suppression of hidden fees, as well as the creation of incentives to encourage secondary school attendance.[58] These proposed efforts were among the recommendations for community reparations, aimed at the hardest hit communities. The idea was to define the program based on the assessments performed by development institutions, in consultation with the affected communities.[59]

Since the issuance of the commission's report, significant improvements have been observed in the coverage of education, as well as in the reconstruction of education infrastructure.[60] Gender inequality remains high,[61] however, as does the disparity between rich and poor children.[62] Substantial differences also remain between rural and urban education, a feature that has characterized inequality in the country since colonial times and was identified as one of the drivers of the conflict.[63] Public expenditure on education was 3.7 percent of the GDP in 2011, which was equivalent to 13.7 percent of total public expenditure.[64] Along with Morocco, Sierra Leone is among the forty-eight countries that are "very far" from the target of achieving an adult literacy rate of at least 95 percent by 2015.[65]

Consistent with the emphasis placed by the TRC on the training of teachers and the need for accelerated education programs, initiatives supported by international donors have been implemented in Sierra Leone, such as the Complementary Rapid Education for Primary Schools (CREPS) program and the Distance Education Teacher Training program.[66] While the ratio between teachers and students in the country is one to thirty-one, however, the ratio between trained teachers and students is one to sixty-five,[67] making Sierra Leone one of the countries in which the training of existing teachers is a bigger challenge than the recruiting of new ones.[68]

SUMMARY

The five cases above show the existence of important efforts to improve the provision of education to marginalized communities, at least partially in response to the needs identified by truth commissions.[69] Those commissions pointed to structural injustices that were either the result of or among the causes of the conflicts. This is particularly clear with regard to policies targeting specific populations that had suffered discrimination—people of certain ethnicities, those who spoke certain languages, inhabitants of rural areas or certain provinces, girls and women, and so on.

The progress made in education coverage in the countries discussed reveals at least some correlation between the recommendations made by the truth commissions and the priority education policies have received. In South Africa, Peru, and Morocco, truth commissions may have had some impact in making education for marginalized groups a priority. This is less clear in Sierra Leone and Timor-Leste, where the degree of appropriation by the government and the political elite of the work of the commissions seems to be lower, as demonstrated by the limited or lack of implementation of recommendations.

These types of efforts, however, are not enough to address long periods of marginalization, sometimes representing the entire history of a country. The examples show clearly that targeted efforts to respond to the rights of those marginalized frequently last only through the first years of a reconstruction effort, and over the years the rhetoric on addressing historical injustices is sometimes replaced by a less conflictive one about modernization and development, as in the case of South Africa, where the notion of redress, which was prominent in the initial policy design after apartheid, has faded in importance.[70]

Despite general improvement in education coverage and completion rates for the specific groups that were subjected to discrimination, some distinctions can be drawn among the cases. In some, targeted efforts were stronger or produced better results, as in Peru with regard to indigenous and rural inhabitants and in South Africa with regard to the black population. Efforts to overcome gender or rural inequality in Sierra Leone, Morocco, and Timor-Leste, however, have been less successful or have been accorded less priority. While this can be partly explained by socioeconomic differences, at least in Sierra Leone and Timor-Leste, in all five countries more effort could be directed toward improving equality of education for marginalized populations. The education budgets in Sierra Leone, Peru, and Timor-Leste could be increased, particularly considering the high economic growth experienced in the past decade by the last two; and Morocco's stalled effort is not only the result of a lack of economic capacity.

In all five countries, disparities are the result of years of discrimination against and invisibility of a portion of the population, so changing that course requires the conviction and power to change the priorities of the political system. The relative success of Peru and South Africa may be explained by the existence of strong civil society organizations and pressure groups representing marginalized groups that can push for the implementation of truth commission recommendations, as well as by the degree of social involvement in the work of those truth commissions.

Reconstruction efforts that increase the coverage and quality of education for previously marginalized populations could be understood as nothing more than compliance with existing state obligations under the International Covenant on Economic, Social, and Cultural Rights (ICESCR) and other instruments of international law. Acknowledging the deliberate targeting of communities for the provision of substandard services—as in South Africa—as violations of rights might be important, however; and responding to historical marginalization is likely to require a long-term investment of resources and political capital, which cannot be limited to the narrow boundaries and limited time frames of transitional justice policies, even if the former can be initially spearheaded by the latter. Moreover, a frequent emphasis on peace-building and security, without addressing deep inequalities that were important factors in the conflict, makes it difficult to prioritize sufficiently a stronger commitment to improving coverage, quality, and equality in education, as documented in the case of Sierra Leone.

Perhaps the most serious challenge to policies that seek to overcome high degrees of marginalization is dealing with its deep roots. Inequality is the result not of chance or geography, but of the way elites governing those countries in colonial and postcolonial times understood the role of the marginalized populations. If social and economic rights are denied for generations, the denial of political and civil rights during an armed conflict or under a dictatorship is not surprising. Recognizing the latter in the aftermath of conflict is common, but recognizing the former requires a deeper and longer-term commitment that could subvert the socioeconomic privileges of elites. This seems to be an area where transitional justice can make only modest—if important—contributions, by highlighting the injustices. Trying actually to resolve such deep-rooted injustices through a reparation program might end up diluting the effort to redress more specific injustices experienced by victims of the most serious crimes.

EDUCATION AS A RESPONSE TO CONSEQUENCES OF SERIOUS VIOLATIONS OF CIVIL AND POLITICAL RIGHTS

In addition to the experiences of marginalized regions or groups, reconstruction efforts need to take into special consideration the condition of direct victims of serious violations of human rights or international humanitarian law. These victims suffer extraordinary harm, and the consequences to their lives can be devastating. Among their more pressing needs, they frequently include education, particularly education for their children. A recent study on the perception of victims of forced disappearance and torture in Nepal, for example, identified difficulties educating their children as among the most serious types of harms they had suffered, and access to free education as one of their highest priorities.[71] What is particularly relevant for this chapter is that victims identified education as a priority not only in the immediate term, but the long term as well.

If restoring victims to their previous situations is impossible, a reparation policy should seek to remove the obstacles they encounter in exercising their rights as full citizens. For such a policy, education can be a powerful instrument, given its importance for improving living conditions, for generating opportunities for self-development, and for strengthening the ability to exercise rights; and providing victims with opportunities for it can be one way, among others, to try to repair the harm caused. This is why education measures have been included, together with others, in some reparation programs, as well as in court decisions relating to violations of human rights.

Reparations through education measures in such cases are directed to particular victims of certain violations, and not to whole segments of the population. They are not necessarily related to violations of the specific right to education but are used as a form of redress for the consequences of other crimes.[72] They are complementary to measures aimed at overcoming marginalization, but they are different in focus and intensity. Their urgency, however (as the opportunity to reach victims and their children may be brief), does not mean they can be addressed by a single short-term effort, as they are intended as responses to needs that extend over time.

EDUCATION AS REPARATION TO DIRECT VICTIMS OF RIGHTS VIOLATIONS

The frequent inclusion of education among reparations for victims of torture, sexual violence, and forced recruitment, as well as for children of victims of summary executions or forced disappearance, recognizes the impact of those violations on the ability of victims to study and have the same opportunities as those who are not victims. Education measures as part of a reparation program or court decision can take different forms and approaches, which have not been systematized and often respond to the changing realities of specific situations. These differences will be explained through brief descriptions of the experiences of countries that have implemented or at least designed some measures or programs of reparation for victims through education measures.

The first example of such an effort was that of the National Commission on the Disappearance of Persons of Argentina, which recommended the provision of economic assistance to the children or families of the disappeared, including scholarships.[73] Not necessarily in response to the recommendation, several years later the province of Buenos Aires created a scholarship that covered university studies for children of the disappeared as a form of reparation.[74] The national policy recommended has not been implemented, however.

The extent to which education reparations are implemented is sometimes difficult to assess, in part because in some countries measures directed to victims are implemented under different labels, such as assistance, solidarity, or relief, or with ambiguous language that obscures the acknowledgment of state responsibility for the violations. Nevertheless, reparation to victims in the form of education measures has been implemented in Chile, Peru, and, to a lesser degree, Sierra Leone. Measures targeting victims but under the label of relief or assistance have been implemented in Nepal and Colombia, although in Colombia the language is confusing, and sometimes the term reparations is used. Finally, no education measures for victims have been implemented in South Africa and Timor-Leste, but legal provisions are being discussed in the former that eventually could lead to a reparation program that includes them. The experiences will be presented in that order.

CHILE

The National Commission on Truth and Reconciliation of Chile specifically recommended education measures for the children of those killed and "disappeared" during the 1973–90 dictatorship. In its 1991 report, the commission acknowledged the complexities of a reparation policy involving education:

> At first glance it might seem that the educational problems of the immediate relatives of human rights victims have to do with younger children, but that is not the case. Most of the children are adolescents or even adults whose opportunities for attending school or the university can now hardly be recovered. The events that so radically altered people's future plans usually took place years ago. The situation of people who lost their opportunity to receive an education is of special concern to us.
>
> The cases we have examined have shown us how the chances of entering and remaining in the various levels of the educational system were disrupted for children and adolescents who were not especially predisposed to take such a risk. Here again poverty and declining living conditions have aggravated the problem of education for many of these families. In addition such children and young people have had to bear with emotional upheaval and learning problems during their elementary and high school years.[75]

The program, which was later implemented, included scholarships for university and technical education, as well as a monthly stipend. This amount, paid in addition to the compensation payment provided to all the close relatives of the victims, was also given to those enrolled in secondary education. The program covered children of victims until age thirty-five.[76] From 1992 to 2014, it provided 5,251 scholarships.[77]

Through the work of a second truth commission that became aware of the impact of the violations on the children of victims, Chile later expanded its recognition of victims to those who suffered political imprisonment and torture. As a result, it recommended the provision of scholarships for the survivors, as well as for their children.[78] The government excluded the provision of scholarships for the children of victims, however, limiting reparations to direct victims of imprisonment and torture, whose average age when the reparation law was approved was fifty-five years. Only after years of intense pressure was the program expanded to allow survivors to pass on their right to a scholarship to a child or grandchild.[79] This expanded the number of scholarship recipients and the utility and coverage of the reparation measure: 9,717 scholarships were provided to direct victims between 2005 and 2014, and, after the transfer of a scholarship to one child or grandchild was authorized in December 2009, the number of recipients increased by an additional 22,483.[80]

PERU

The reparation program recommended by the Truth and Reconciliation Commission of Peru and later passed into law also included an education component. This program sought to

> assist and provide new or better opportunities for victims and their relatives who, as result of the process of violence, lost the possibility of receiving an adequate education or to finish primary, secondary, high technical or university studies.[81]

The program was originally targeted at the children of victims of summary executions, murder, and forced disappearances and at victims of rape, torture, kidnapping, forced displacement, arbitrary detention, forced recruitment, and violation of due process of law who had to interrupt their studies, as well as their children and individuals under eighteen years of age who belonged to self-defense committees.[82] For the children of victims, the program was later limited to only those whose parents had died or were disappeared.[83]

Reparation through education measures was supposed to add to the comprehensiveness of the reparation program. Of the 72,446 victims who had received a compensation amount as of September 2014, however (a lump sum equivalent to US$3,700 per direct victim, to be distributed among relatives in case of killing or disappearance), only 2,188 received an education benefit. Of these, 1,598 participated in a literacy program; 377 received full university scholarships through the Reparations on Education Program

(REPARED);[84] and 213 were admitted to technical or university programs because of their status as victims.[85] Even if the scholarship and the admission were to be guaranteed, some students from marginal Andean or Amazon regions would find it difficult to adapt to the academic environment without a good support network. Those from marginalized areas or those whose primary language is Quechua or another indigenous language also have faced prejudice and discrimination.

Such obstacles suggest the success of a policy for improving victims' access to university education requires not only the provision of assistance but also an effort to work with schools in confronting racist or cultural prejudices.[86] Although the Ministry of Education established an accompaniment program for those students at risk of dropping out, it directed it not exclusively to victims but to all beneficiaries of scholarships from the National Program for Scholarships and Educational Loans.[87] While the policy responds to the needs of students, it does not include specific components for responding to victims. Its coverage is also minimal relative to the number of victims.

Another obstacle is that reparation programs providing scholarships are usually implemented only decades after the violations occurred. Among the many victims who had their studies interrupted as a result of the violations they suffered, this limits the number of potential beneficiaries to those who are still young enough to benefit fully from tertiary education. In Peru, after intense lobbying, victims obtained government approval in 2016 to transfer the right to receive a scholarship to one child or grandchild.[88] This change has the potential to increase significantly the number of victims or families who can benefit. Questions remain, though, about the willingness and ability to allocate more resources to these scholarships to ensure they benefit all victims who wish to take advantage of them.

SIERRA LEONE

In Sierra Leone, the Truth and Reconciliation Commission reported that schools, training, and education represented the second most common demand (41 percent) made by victims in their statements (behind homes and shelters, at 49 percent).[89] In addition to its recommendations for reconstructing school infrastructure, training and retaining teachers, and guaranteeing primary education to all children, the commission called for education measures for victims of specific human rights violations. These included provision of free senior secondary education to children who were amputees, war wounded, or victims of sexual violence or who had been abducted or forcibly conscripted (unless they receive schooling from a disarmament, demobilization, and reintegration program), as well as to orphans or children of amputees, war wounded, disabled parents, or victims of sexual violence.[90] It also recommended including these children in the advanced learning program already being implemented (CREPS).[91] For this purpose, individuals eighteen years of age or younger by March 1, 2002, were considered children.[92]

Unfortunately, little has been done to implement these recommendations. The government, through the National Commission for Social Action (NaCSA), and with the funding of the UN Peacebuilding Fund (PBF) and the assistance of the International Organization for Migrations (IOM), registered more than 32,000 victims and distributed an interim payment of Le 300,000 (approximately US$100) to each.[93] For adult victims, this was labeled an interim reparation payment, and for child victims, it was labeled reimbursement for education expenses, including school fees and the cost of uniforms and books. No other measure for guaranteeing senior secondary education to these most vulnerable children has been implemented. In addition, CREPS, which the commission recommended be expanded to victims, closed shortly after the TRC delivered its report.[94]

The commission also recommended a skills training and microcredit program for the most vulnerable victims, including children.[95] This could have been a good alternative for youth who had passed their schooling age. Only a few projects have been implemented, however, helping few victims, and they were not necessarily on the list of victims registered by NaCSA with UN Women funds[96] or by the PBF with the assistance of the IOM.[97]

NEPAL

The Interim Relief Program implemented by the Ministry of Peace and Reconstruction in Nepal for what are called "conflict-affected persons" is meant to provide support to the relatives of victims of killings and disappearance as a result of ten years of armed conflict, as well as to other categories of victims,[98] covering a total of 128,424 beneficiaries.[99] The relief measures, which include scholarships for children of those killed and disappeared and for injured students and the children of those injured or arbitrarily detained, if they are 50 percent or more disabled,[100] have benefited more than 8,000 students.[101] The scholarships help pay hidden education fees for children under eighteen years of age who are attending primary or secondary school, with a limit of three children per family.[102] The budget for these scholarships is not guaranteed, however, and on occasion the departments of education of some provinces receive lower amounts than needed, which results in families receiving less than they are supposed to or not receiving the scholarships at all.[103]

Victims value this program. According to a study conducted by the International Center for Transitional Justice,[104] women whose husbands were killed or disappeared ranked the scholarships second in importance to them among the different relief measures, after only the cash payments, and men ranked them sixth. Victims also valued the skills training some received. Nevertheless, they saw the measures as fulfilling immediate needs, not as reparation for violations committed or as a measure of justice. Furthermore, despite the program's positive reception, it was deemed insufficient by victims interviewed, as education is seen as an ongoing need. Particular complaints referred to the three-child limit, the fact that the scholarship does not cover the real costs of sending a child to school, and the age limit, which excludes those who turned eighteen after the program was initiated.[105]

COLOMBIA

The Colombian Law on Victims and Land Restitution includes education among the forms of assistance it provides to victims. It establishes several measures regarding education for vulnerable victims, including assistance for completing primary and secondary education and a fund for credits to get access to technical and university education.[106] From 2012 to 2014, the program allowed almost one million children annually among those registered as victims to attend school (although enrollment at these levels is meant to be free and mandatory for all Colombian children). It also provided adult literacy programs for more than 151,000 victims, mostly those who suffered displacement, between 2010 and 2014.[107]

For higher education, the program offered is based on granting credits under special conditions: if school is completed and other requirements are fulfilled, the loan is forgiven, making the fund practically a scholarship fund. Additionally, the government body responsible for technical education has created courses in different fields that are directed at victims. The implementation of the program for higher education and technical education has been slow and underfunded, however, and the number of scholarships for university studies and the variety of technical courses offered fall short of the large number of victims.[108] The law defines these measures as humanitarian assistance, without a clear commitment in terms of obligation or reparation.[109]

SOUTH AFRICA

In South Africa, the Truth and Reconciliation Commission did not include specific recommendations for the implementation of education programs for victims, but it did consider education needs in its definition of interim reparations and in the reparation grant. Additionally, in 2011, the Department of Justice began discussing regulations for a program of assistance to victims for basic education.[110] The program was limited to victims already registered by the TRC and consisted of cash payments to victims, their direct relatives, or those taking care of them, living in socioeconomically vulnerable conditions. For basic education, it included school fees, boarding, and uniform and transportation allowances, covering grade R,[111] general (primary and secondary), and further education. For higher education and training, the draft regulations included fees and transportation, boarding, and textbook allowances.

The South African Coalition for Transitional Justice submitted comments to the draft regulations, demanding changes in terms of accessibility and expanding the list of potential recipients beyond the closed list of victims registered by the TRC. For more than three years, no further progress was made in approving or implementing this policy,[112] until November 2014, when new regulations were gazetted and presented for debate with civil society for final approval.[113]

TIMOR-LESTE

In Timor-Leste, the recommendations of the truth commission (CAVR, by its Portuguese acronym) included a program for the support of single mothers with the provision of scholarships for their school-age children. As with the rest of the recommendations made by the commission, however, this one has not been taken up by the government. As previously explained, the effort in Timor-Leste has focused exclusively on overcoming the deficit in education throughout the country and dealing with some disparities between girls and boys, but not, in contrast to the implementation of a program for the assistance of veterans, addressing the more specific needs of children who were orphaned or subjected to specific violations.

SUMMARY

The different policies in these countries show how education can function as a form of reparation for human rights violations, even when those entitled to them are not the direct victims of those violations. Victims know the impact violations can have on their ability to educate their children and consider it one of the most serious harms. Nevertheless, the implementation of reparation policies responding to such harms remains difficult. The cases of Chile, Nepal, and, to a lesser degree, Peru and Colombia stand as the few in which this recognition has been translated into concrete, massive policies. In Nepal and Colombia, however, the programs are defined as assistance or relief, not as reparation based on an acknowledgment of the state's responsibility for past violations.

Explanations for the different degrees of implementation differ. Chile, for instance, has been governed by political coalitions that differentiate themselves from the dictatorship,[114] while a strong victims' movement has kept pressure on the government to implement not only reparations but also institutional reforms and criminal investigations. In Peru, the situation is different, as violations were committed during an internal armed conflict and by governments elected under democratic conditions. One post-transition president served his first term during the armed conflict, while the current president is a former military officer. Here, the active involvement of civil society—consisting, in part, of its participation in drafting the recommendations of the truth commission— explains why at least some implementation has taken place, despite the lack of interest from the past two administrations. And in Colombia, very active victims and civil society movements, a high degree of judicial activism from the courts, and the successful political commitment of the administration of Juan Manuel Santos to advancing accountability simultaneously with peace talks explain the degree of implementation, even while the armed conflict remained ongoing.

It is not easy to generalize from these examples. In South Africa, where the post-apartheid governments have certainly differentiated themselves from the previous regime, and where a strong victims' movement has kept the pressure on, implementation of the reparations recommended by the truth commission has nevertheless been partial, and education measures have not been directed to victims. This may be the result of strong support for the African National Congress (ANC), which has led it to pay little attention to internal dissidence, and a general preference for providing benefits to veterans, a community more active and loyal to the ANC than victims.

In Nepal, implementation of the relief program for victims is more a response to international pressure and resources than a government priority. The parties in the internal armed conflict appear to have little interest in acknowledging responsibility for past violations. A relief program funded with international aid that helps victims registered by local political committees and controlled by a government ministry seems to offer the two parties in power benefits without any costs, however.

It should also be noted that while the provision of education as reparation to victims of human rights violations has been part of the recommendations of several truth commissions and reparation policies, it is not a universal trend. Some truth commissions have not included provisions of this type for individual victims, as evidenced, for instance, by Guatemala's 1999 Historical Clarification Commission report, Morocco's 2006 Commission of Equity and Reconciliation report, and Kenya's 2013 Truth, Justice, and Reconciliation Commission report.

EDUCATION AS COLLECTIVE REPARATIONS

The notion of collective reparation is sometimes confusing, as the term is used for different purposes.[115] It can mean broad regional development programs, as in Morocco, or more limited community reparations, focused on repairing harms to community properties or values. The first category is closer to the reconstruction and peacebuilding efforts, institutional reforms, and provision of socioeconomic services for marginalized communities discussed above. The second—specific community reparations—has been implemented in some cases that have included education, either as part of a reparation program or as the result of a court decision. Nonetheless, the nature of education services makes it easy to confuse individual and collective reparation with the protection of social, economic, and cultural rights, which is an obligation of the state, not just to victims, but to the entire population. The frequent overlap between marginalized communities and victims of massacres, disappearances, and torture makes these distinctions even more difficult.

Community reparations have been implemented in very few countries. The broadest program has been in Peru, which, as of June 2013, had implemented projects in 1,892 communities out of 5,697 identified as the most affected by violence,[116] and the government announced it had added 326 more communities for 2014.[117] The program consists of providing each community with an opportunity to define and implement a single investment project costing up to US$37,000, and 13 percent of those implemented by 2010 referred to building or rehabilitating schools or classrooms.[118] These projects, however, are limited to improving infrastructure, not guaranteeing the presence of teachers or the improvement of education. Additionally, even the improvement of education infrastructure may not be prioritized for the community's choice of its one project because of more pressing needs.

A collective reparation program is also being implemented in Colombia. It is an ambitious program targeting more than 833 communities and organizations over ten years, with a total budget of COP 400 billion (approximately US$212 million).[119] The program includes a diagnosis of the harm suffered by each community and the community's participation in defining its own reparation plan, comprising the reconstruction and rehabilitation of infrastructure and services.[120] Several of the policy's pilot projects have included the recognition of obstacles to access to education as a result of damage to education infrastructure or the absence of security or even teachers and the general impoverishment of the community, among the consequences of the conflict and a historically weak presence of the state.[121]

Unlike Peru's policy, Colombia's is not limited to one project per community but responds to different dimensions of harm in each. Implementation of the reparation plans has been slow, however, so concrete results are unclear.[122] One community selected for pilot implementation was a regional university that had been controlled by paramilitary forces and suffered different forms of repression. The project involves labor, administration, historical memory, recovery of victims' dignity, education, and guarantees that violations will not be repeated.[123] It was initiated in 2007, but as of November 2015 it had not been finished, casting doubt on the feasibility of implementing a policy that may be too complex for the limited resources available, the levels of poverty in and marginalization of the affected communities, and the coordination of different actors such an initiative requires.

The challenge is even more complex with regard to reparations involving indigenous and ethnic communities, which have suffered not only from extreme violence, but also from historical marginalization. Marginalization in these cases refers to the lack of access to and quality of education, but also to education that does not adequately value the specific culture of those communities. The collective reparation program involves a carefully drafted process of consultation, which was designed with the involvement of those communities and defined in special regulations so the different dimensions of harm and exclusion could be addressed. In August 2015, the Victims' Unit, responsible for implementing reparations, revealed that of 304 communities and groups identified for collective reparation, 157 representing ethnic groups, 24 had finalized the process of consultation and defined their reparation plans.[124] Whether the effort will translate into concrete measures that can address the different issues identified in the reparation plans defined by each community, however, it is too early to say, as implementation is pending.

The Truth, Justice, and Reconciliation Commission of Kenya (TJRC) received several requests for the building of schools from victims it interviewed.[125] It recommended as part of community reparation socioeconomic measures to be decided by minority or indigenous communities that suffered systematic marginalization, historical land injustices, massacres, or environmental degradation. The program is defined as a second-priority effort, to be implemented after individual reparations for the most vulnerable victims in the form of pensions and psychosocial and health care rehabilitation.

The recommendations for this program mention a fund and a mechanism to be defined by an implementation committee. These are in addition to a set of recommended "government policy measures," which include building and staffing schools. The policies are supposed to be implemented as part of the moral and political obligation to provide reparation, including a symbolic dimension. As the commission described it, "the government needs to acknowledge that it is prioritizing development of marginalized areas . . . because of previous neglect."[126] It is not clear, however, if or how the government of Kenya will implement this program.[127] Furthermore, despite being labeled as reparations by the TJRC, the policy measures recommended fall into the category of targeted development to affected communities, as described above. The recommendations for government policy measures, even if they are characterized as reparations, are clearly meant to address historical injustices or marginalization. What can be more specifically described as collective reparation are the community-based measures. This distinction might help guarantee targeted communities do not need to identify minimal protection of social, economic, and cultural rights, such as access to education, among the community reparation projects, as those rights should be part of the targeted development or government policy measures.

Beyond the countries discussed above, the Inter-American Court of Human Rights has also ordered education measures in its decisions to guarantee effective reparations for communities. In one of its first decisions, involving summary executions of members of an indigenous community in Suriname, the court recognized that the compensation amount, which was supposed to be sufficient for the children of victims to study until a certain age, was not enough to guarantee that objective. Consequently, it ordered the state to reopen the school located in the community where most of the children lived.[128] In decisions involving collective harms, the court has included education among measures for reparation, as well as the provision of basic social services.[129] In cases of indigenous communities, it has ordered states to "supply sufficient bilingual material for appropriate education of the students at the school in the current settlement of the Community."[130] These decisions reveal a different approach to education as reparation,[131] one more focused on effectively helping victims to receive education, through measures in addition to compensation.

In addition to guaranteeing access to education, the court has ordered measures to ensure the provision of education includes content and methodology that address the cultural particularities of indigenous communities, which could be seen as a way of addressing violations of cultural rights, as well as guaranteeing that the members of those communities perceive the education provided to them as relevant. In 2012, in response to a massacre in El Salvador, the court ordered a community development project that involved building a school.[132]

The first of the court cases mentioned reinforces the need for complementarity between education policies for all the areas affected by substandard education and specific measures, such as scholarships for victims. Functional schools should be built for all people in the country, but victims of the most serious violations need special forms of reparations for gaining access to them. Both sides of the equation are needed: people who do not qualify as victims of the most serious crimes will not have access to education if only reparations are provided, while scholarships for victims will be ineffective without functioning schools. The court's decisions regarding the cultural appropriateness of curricula used in schools in indigenous communities offer an important insight about guaranteeing the relevance of the type and quality of education provided and tailoring it to the recognition of the rights and dignity of the affected communities. The massive policies providing education as reparation should not underestimate the importance of these components.

Communities affected by massive human rights violations often include in their demands for collective reparation all their needs in terms of social and economic rights. That victims demand through any means at their disposal the fulfillment of their rights according to their most pressing needs, including education, is not necessarily a problem; it may, in fact, be an opportunity, I would argue, because an approach based on a strict legal understanding of reparation and restitution to the status quo ante may largely ignore those needs.

Moreover, the distinction between human rights violations committed through extensive physical violence and those resulting from years of neglect, discrimination, and the state's inability to ensure the social, economic, and cultural rights of its citizens is artificial in the eyes of many of those who have suffered from both. Physical violence is often used to impose a model of exploitation of natural resources or an economic model based on the exclusion of certain groups, as the apartheid regime in South Africa shows.[133]

For policymakers designing a reparation program, however, it is important to maintain the distinction between reconstruction policies for all areas marginalized or affected by the conflict and reparations for specific communities. The Colombian program described above requires as part of community reparations the existence of certain minimal socioeconomic rights, and it is in this category that the building and staffing of schools might go. Those measures, though, respond to the general obligation of providing education, particularly in areas affected by violence or marginalization. Additional, specific measures aimed at addressing collective harms, including memorialization, strengthening the community social fabric, and guaranteeing culturally sensitive education for indigenous communities, should be distinct from but complementary to scholarships for children directly affected by the most serious crimes. The Kenyan example is also useful in distinguishing between government measures and community reparations.

In both the Colombian and Kenyan cases, however, how the distinction and complementarity will be navigated in practice remains to be seen. Perhaps the most relevant question here will be how to avoid overpromising, particularly in societies that are historically in debt to their poorest and most vulnerable members.

CONCLUSION

Providing access to education can be a very important contribution to reparations for human rights violations. These do not need to be violations specifically of the right to education, as violations of many other rights can have a serious impact on the ability of victims to continue their educations or to provide education to their children. This can be a source of suffering for both adults and children, which is why the impact of violations on the education of victims and their children has been recognized in different administrative reparations and by international court decisions.

Based on the different approaches in the cases discussed here, it is possible to make some distinctions among types of policies and measures. The building and staffing of schools should not be considered reparations, even in cases where schools have been destroyed or communities need them as result of displacement and relocation. Providing primary and secondary education is a basic social, economic, and cultural right, as stated in international law. Universal primary education is also one of the Millennium Development Goals, although the level of achievement of this goal has been low.[134] Since countries emerging from armed conflict thus need to rebuild and staff schools that were destroyed, the provision of schools, teachers, and school libraries should be considered as reconstruction and as the fulfillment of obligations under the ICSECR, as should the provision of bilingual classes or the inclusion of cultural components for indigenous children. These efforts should be aimed at all children, without distinguishing victims from nonvictims. A truth commission or a reconstruction program with a transitional justice focus can identify these as much-needed measures for overcoming the legacies of the conflict, but that does not make them reparations.

In cases where the lack of schools or trained teachers is not just the result of the destruction caused by a war or the displacement of populations but has deeper roots in historical marginalization, the obligation to ensure the social and economic rights of the relevant populations is even more compelling, as discrimination is not tolerable under the notion of progressive realization that characterizes social and economic rights. In these cases, it is more difficult to draw a line. Overcoming historical marginalization imposed by intentional neglect or apartheid policies could be considered as merely fulfilling the obligation to ensure social, economic, and cultural rights without discrimination. At the same time, these measures could be understood as a cessation of such violations. A reparatory component, though, requires the recognition that social, economic, and cultural rights were violated and discrimination was imposed or tolerated, and it is an acknowledgment of responsibility. Thus, these policies might have a mixed nature, as in South Africa, where improving the education system for black children accorded with the notion of redress.

The challenge faced by such policies might be a politically difficult one, however, as devoting resources to addressing historical discrimination is likely to require a long political struggle against an entrenched elite. Such a struggle can be supported through institutional reforms, but it will be part of the political debate in the country, where the notion of rights and obligations could be an important tool, but not the only one. Trying to confront deep injustices through a reparation policy ordered or recommended by a truth commission or in compliance with a reparation law with a limited budget might result in either superficial or no implementation. Acknowledging responsibility and offering an apology could be even more unlikely.

In addition to the reparative component of restituting violated social rights, reparations in education should include measures aimed at achieving concrete goals and addressing specific needs of those victims who suffered the most, both individually and as communities. For individual victims, reparations should try to remove the obstacles faced by victims and their children in getting access to education, with regard either to the education they missed as result of violations or the negative consequences of the violations for their current ability to continue their educations. The first could call for advanced study programs that could help youth receive degrees equivalent to the primary, secondary, or other levels they could not complete due to the violations suffered. It could also mean establishing adult literacy programs or technical or professional training for people who are no longer of school age.

In many cases, a poor widow might not be able to afford sending her older child to school, as she might need his or her help at home or earning money to sustain the rest of the family. If she has to choose which of her children attend school, it is more likely to be the boys than the girls. Cash transfers, conditioned on attendance, could help replace the earning capacity of those children and enable that widow to send all her children to school. School kits, including uniforms and classroom materials, could also help victim families allow their children to attend school. From this perspective, reimbursing education expenses or providing resources for a limited number of years, as do the relief payments in Nepal and Sierra Leone, is not enough. If subsidies and incentives are not available before they are needed, only those with certain means will benefit, as the destitute will not be able to wait for reimbursement.

In cases where it is possible to offer university education to victims, preparatory courses, psychosocial and academic support, and other interventions could effectively help youth complete their degrees, as the experience of Peru shows. Just offering a limited number of scholarships, significantly fewer than the number of victims who could apply for them, as demonstrated by Peru and Colombia, does not seem enough.

For communities affected by violence, education measures should also address the negative consequences of violations on community members' access to education, in addition to complying with the minimum education goals set out by the ICESCR. Reparations should consist of specific forms of assistance that address the obstacles victims face in attending school and completing their educations. This could include programs that address harms suffered by the community in terms of its social cohesion or its ability to perform certain traditional activities or exploit its own resources; child care services for mothers of infants; collective forms of psychosocial support that could help students and their parents trust each other and attend the same schools; or memorialization initiatives. The specific programs should be based on the communities' assessment of the obstacles their children face in attending school and the skills their youth and adults need to find jobs.

The challenge remains of how to implement these policies effectively. Not all such measures can be implemented in every country. The lesson from Colombia is a compelling one: a program may be designed that fulfills the most complex requirements but does not take into account the real capacity of the country to implement it. How can we know what is fair and possible in each country? Perhaps looking at the degree of access to education and the educational achievement of those in the country who did not suffer massive violations or those who did not suffer from historical forms of marginalization can help answer the question. Such standards could approximate what people expect in terms of education for themselves or for their children, which may be as close to fair as a country with limited resources can get.

The effort should go beyond a few "feel good" pilot projects, however. Balancing the complexities and costs of doing something aimed at perfection with the need to cover all the communities and people in most need is important. An overambitious program could mean the exclusion, when the resources or political visibility for reparations diminishes, of many victims and communities who suffered serious violations. Additionally, distinct but complementary reconstruction and reparation can help target international development aid to the reconstruction of those communities, so that national resources are better focused on reparation.

Reparations in the form of education for massive human rights violations, even those recommended by the truth commissions that examined the needs of victims and the capacity of the state, frequently remain unimplemented or under-implemented. Paying more attention to the needs of victims, assessing the level of achievement of the rest of the society to get a sense of what can be expected, and considering a two-pronged approach that includes fulfilling obligations under the ICESCR, as well as reparations to victims, could help respond to this difficult challenge.

NOTES

1   The author wishes to thank Amanda Addison, research intern at the International Center for Transitional Justice, for her valuable assistance.

2   For a comprehensive study about reparations and the right to education, see Frances Capone, Kristin Hausler, Duncan Fairgrieve, and Conor McCarthy, *Education and the Law of Reparations in Insecurity and Armed Conflicts* (London: British Institute of International and Comparative Law, 2014).

3   Cecile Aptel and Virginie Ladisch, *Through a New Lens: A Child-Sensitive Approach to Transitional Justice* (New York: ICTJ, 2011).

4   Another, very important post-conflict role for education is related not to access to it, but to the content of the curricula and the methodologies used. Education can contribute to a country's efforts to learn from past violations or address forms of discrimination or prejudices prevalent in its culture. It can also contribute to the recognition of the dignity of certain marginalized communities by integrating methodologies and content that stress the value of and appreciation for the communities' own cultures and languages.

5   As stated by the Permanent Court of International Justice (PCIJ), the predecessor of the International Court of Justice, "It is a principle of international law, and even a general conception of law, that any breach of an engagement involves an obligation to make reparation." PCIJ, *Chorzów Factory* case (Merits), Germany v. Poland, Judgment No. 17 of September 13, 1928, 29. See also United Nations, International Law Commission, "Responsibility of the States for Internationally Wrongful Acts," *Official Records of the General Assembly, Fifty-Sixth Session, Supplement No. 10* (A/56/10), approved by United Nations General Assembly, Resolution 56/83 of December 12, 2001, and corrected by document A/56/49(Vol. I)/Corr.4. In regard to International Conventional Law, see United Nations General Assembly, Resolution 2200 A (XXI), "International Covenant on Civil and Political Rights," December 16, 1966, art. 2.3, including the interpretation of its provisions by the Human Rights Committee: General Comment No. 31 (80), "The Nature of the General Obligation Imposed on States Parties to the Covenant," adopted on March 29, 2004 (CCPR/C/21/Rev.1/Add.13), para. 16. See also United Nations General Assembly, Resolution 2106/20, "International Convention on the Elimination of All Forms of Racial Discrimination," A/RES/2106/20, December 21, 1965, art. 6; Resolution 39/46, "Convention against Torture and Other Cruel, Inhuman or Degrading Treatment or Punishment," A/RES/39/46, December 10, 1984, art. 14; Resolution 44/25, "Convention on the Rights of the Child," A/RES/44/25, November 20, 1989 (hereafter CRC), art. 39; and Resolution 61/177, "International Convention for the Protection of All Persons from Enforced Disappearance," A/RES/61/177, December 20, 2006, art. 24. Similar obligations are found in the following instruments of international humanitarian law: Hague, "Convention Respecting the Laws and Customs of War on Land," Convention IV, October 18, 1907,

art. 3; Diplomatic Conference on the Reaffirmation and Development of International Humanitarian Law Applicable in Armed Conflicts, "Protocol Additional to the Geneva Conventions of 12 August 1949 and relating to the Protection of Victims of International Armed Conflicts (Protocol I)," 1125 U.N.T.S. 3, June 8, 1977, art. 91; and the Rome Statute of the International Criminal Court, 2187 U.N.T.S. 90, July 17, 1998, arts. 68 and 75. These provisions have been systematized by the United Nations General Assembly, Resolution 60/147, "Basic Principles and Guidelines on the Right to a Remedy and Reparation for Victims of Gross Violations of International Human Rights Law and Serious Violations of International Humanitarian Law," A/RES/60/147, March 21, 2006, which in its preamble establishes that the principles and guidelines contained in the instrument "do not entail new international or domestic legal obligations but identify mechanisms, modalities, procedures and methods for the implementation of existing legal obligations under international human rights law and international humanitarian law."

6   Cristián Correa, "Making Concrete a Message of Inclusion: Reparations for Victims of Massive Crimes," in *Victimological Approaches to International Crimes: Africa*, ed. Rianne Letschert, Roelof Haveman, Anne-Marie Brouwer, and Antony Pemberton (Cambridge/Antwerp/Portland: Intersentia, 2011), 185–233.

7   This is a direct observation made by the author when interviewing survivors of political imprisonment and torture in Chile as part of the work of the Valech Commission, and it has been confirmed by conversations with victims in countries such as Peru, Kenya, Tunisia, Côte d'Ivoire, and Colombia through the author's work at the International Center for Transitional Justice (ICTJ). The report of the South African Truth and Reconciliation Commission made a similar observation regarding victims' perceptions of the ripple effects of human rights violations on families and communities: "A deponent might, for instance, refer to the death of her son, but highlight the consequences for her grandchild's education, her daughter's emotional state, and her own financial situation." Truth and Reconciliation Commission of South Africa, *Truth and Reconciliation Commission of South Africa Report* (Cape Town: Truth and Reconciliation Commission, 1998), 5:126.

8   In Chile, a pension based on the mean family income was implemented for the relatives of those killed and disappeared. In South Africa, the Truth and Reconciliation Commission recommended a series of payments over six years also based on the mean family income, but the government later implemented a single payment of another amount.

9   In defining reparations in education, though, making a strict application of a mean opportunity threshold requires an adjustment to the personal conditions, capacities, and aspirations of victims. Many victims might aspire to reach tertiary or superior education even if the average person can rarely reach that level. Nevertheless, it can be argued that in many societies reaching tertiary education is an aspiration of the average person.

10   United Nations General Assembly, "International Covenant on Economic, Social and Cultural Rights" (hereafter ICESCR), December 16, 1966, art. 13.

11 Teboho Moja, "Education as Redress in South Africa: Opening the Doors of Learning to All," in this volume.

12 For Morocco, see Instance d'Equité et Reconciliation, *Rapport final* (Rabat: Conseil Consultatif des Droits de l'Homme, 2010), 3:54.

13 ICSECR, art. 13.2.a. CRC, art. 28.1.a, recognizes a progressive approach to all social, economic, and cultural rights, including all the measures listed by article 28 with regard to the right to education. It affirms, though, the mandate of equal opportunity.

14 ICSECR, art. 2.2; CRC, art. 2.1.

15 See, for example, Mahmood Mamdani, "The Truth According to the Truth and Reconciliation Commission," in *The Politics of Memory: Truth, Healing and Social Justice*, ed. Ifi Amadiume and Abdullahi An-Naim (New York: Zed Books, 2000), 176–83. In December 2008, the *International Journal for Transitional Justice* (vol. 2, no. 3) contributed to this discussion through a collection of essays by several scholars and practitioners, who challenged a narrow approach to transitional justice limited to violations of civil and political rights, several of which are discussed here. For more recent debate about this issue, see Lisa Laplante, "On the Indivisibility of Rights: Truth Commissions, Reparations, and the Right to Development," *Yale Human Rights and Development Journal* 10, no. 4 (2014): 141–77, and Dustin N. Sharp, ed., *Justice and Economic Violence in Transition* (New York: Springer Science+Business Media, 2014).

16 This point is clearly presented by Roger Duthie, "Transitional Justice, Development and Economic Violence," in Sharp, *Justice and Economic Violence*.

17 I try to address this question in Cristián Correa, "Integrating Development and Reparations for Victims of Massive Crimes," working paper, Center for Civil and Human Rights, University of Notre Dame, 2014, http://humanrights.nd.edu/assets/136618/correareparations2.pdf.

18 Truth and Reconciliation Commission of South Africa, *Report*, vol. 5, ch. 5, paras. 107–12.

19 Moja, "Education as Redress in South Africa."

20 Republic of South Africa, "Millennium Development Goals Country Report 2013," 2013, 37, http://www.gov.za/sites/www.gov.za/files/MDGR_Report_2013.pdf.

21 UNESCO, *EFA Global Monitoring Report 2013/4: Teaching and Learning: Achieving Equality for All* (Paris: UNESCO, 2014), 382.

22 Explained in great detail in Moja, "Education as Redress in South Africa."

23 In 1996, the attendance for primary education was 78 percent, and for secondary it was 91 percent. There were significant differences, however, between white and Asian populations and black and colored ones. The completion rate for secondary education was 14 percent for black students and 61 percent for white ones. Figures of coverage at the different levels of education show a remarkable increase in attendance of the black population in primary education from 1996 to 2007, from 77 percent to 96 percent, and a more modest one in secondary education, from 91 percent to 96 percent. The secondary

completion rate for black students in 2007 was 19 percent, however, and for whites, 47 percent. Only 17 percent of male black students finished secondary education in 2007. The gap in years of education between white and black youth between the ages of seventeen and twenty-two was reduced from 2.76 in 1996 to 1.62 in 2007. See Carola Grün and Kenneth Harttgen, "An Assessment of South Africa's Reform Post-Apartheid for Education and Mobility," paper commissioned for UNESCO's *EFA Global Monitoring Report 2010: Reaching the Marginalized*, September 3, 2009, http://unesdoc.unesco.org/images/0018/001865/186566e.pdf. The difference in access to higher education in 2011 was also high; even if the headcount of black students increased from 53 percent to 69 percent of the student body between 1996 and 2011, the proportion of black youth (ages twenty to twenty-four) enrolled at universities in 2011 was 16 percent, while among white youth it was 56 percent in 2010. Nico Cloete, "A New Look at Demographic Transformation: Comments on Govinder et al. (2013)," *South African Journal of Science* 110, no. 1/2 (2014): 1–4, http://dx.doi.org/10.1590/sajs.2014/a0048.

24   Rosa Lía Chauca, "Reparaciones y educación en Perú" (internal case study, ICTJ research project: Transitional Justice, Education and Peacebuilding, 2015).

25   *Informe de la Comisión de la Verdad y Reconciliación*, 2003, 9:99.

26   Ibid., 87, 89, and 90. The commission understood this effort as part of the state's obligation to respond to social, economic, and cultural rights, in an effort to overcome the historical marginalization of those communities. It was also considered an important component for peace and stability.

27   In 2001 (right after the Alberto Fujimori regime collapsed and was replaced by an interim government), the rate of completing primary education for children ages twelve to thirteen living in urban areas was 78.9 percent, while for those in rural areas it was 48.3 percent. By 2013, urban completion had increased to 87.4 percent and rural to 65.8 percent, which was partly attributable to a decade of economic growth but also to an effort to improve rural education. The completion rate for primary students whose mother tongue is Spanish improved from 75.4 percent in 2004 to 82.8 percent in 2013 and for those whose language is indigenous from 40.6 percent to 62.7 percent. Republic of Peru, Ministry of Education, *Tasa de conclusión primaria, grupo de edades*, 12–13, http://escale.minedu. gob.pe/tendencias?p_auth=XqcTgM4n&p_p_id=TendenciasActualPortlet_ WAR_tendenciasportlet_INSTANCE_90Hs&p_p_lifecycle=1&p_p_state=normal &p_p_mode=view&p_p_col_id=column-1&p_p_col_pos=1&p_p_col_count=2&_ TendenciasActualPortlet_WAR_tendenciasportlet_INSTANCE_90Hs_idCuadro=25. Secondary education completion rates for rural youth (ages seventeen to eighteen) in 2013 were 42.3 percent, after a remarkable improvement from 17.4 percent in 2001, but were still significantly lower than the completion rate of 73.2 percent for urban youth. For youth whose mother tongue is not Spanish, completion improved from 14.5 percent in 2004 to 42.5 percent in 2013. Republic of Peru, Ministry of

Education, *Tasa de conclusión secundaria, grupo de edades,* 17–18, http://escale.minedu.
gob.pe/tendencias?p_auth=tAManB2b&p_p_id=TendenciasActualPortlet_
WAR_tendenciasportlet_INSTANCE_9oHs&p_p_lifecycle=1&p_p_state=
normal&p_p_mode=view&p_p_col_id=column-1&p_p_col_pos=1&p_p_
col_count=2&_TendenciasActualPortlet_WAR_tendenciasportlet_INSTANCE_
9oHs_idCuadro=15. The dropout rate in primary education, which for children living in rural areas was 4.1 percent in 2003 and for those in urban areas 1.1 percent,
was reduced for the former to 2.3 percent in 2009, while for the latter it remained
almost the same. Republic of Peru, Ministry of Education, "No. 4. Causas del atraso
en la culminación de primaria en el área rural (2)," June 8, 2011, http://escale.minedu.
gob.pe/edudatos;jsessionid=ad2f4dd797257ba3cc49b0e85962?p_p_id=115&p_p_
lifecycle=0&p_p_state=normal&p_p_mode=view& 115_struts_action=%2Fblogs_
aggregator%2Fview_entry&_115_urlTitle=n%C2%BA-4-causas-del-atraso-en-la-
culminacion-de-primaria-en-el-area-rural-2.

28   UNESCO, *EFA Global Monitoring Report 2013/4,* 19.

29   Republic of Peru, Ministry of Education, *Ministerio de Educación, Memoria institucional*
2012–2013, 52, http://www.minedu.gob.pe/DeInteres/xtras/minedu_memoria_institu-
cional_2012-2013.pdf. Several organizations have provided assistance to the Peruvian
government in rural reform projects, including the World Bank. Obstacles to improving
the provision of education in rural areas remain, however, among them the difficulty of
coordinating efforts between the Ministry of Education and those responsible in regional
governments and a lack of certainty about sustainability for funding at the regional level.
World Bank, *Implementation Completion and Results Report (IBRD-71760) on a Loan in the
Amount of (US$52.5 million) to the Republic of Peru for a Rural Education Project in Support of the
First Phase of the Rural Education Program,* June 25, 2008, 27, http://www-wds.worldbank.
org/external/default/WDSContentServer/WDSP/IB/2008/08/05/000333037_20080805
013808/Rendered/PDF/ICR00008620ICR1DisclosedoAug0102008.pdf. The evaluation
of another project reached a similar conclusion, stating that high turnover of authorities
and employees, as well as difficulties resulting from a decentralization process because
of a lack of funding and clear priorities, affect the ability to maintain the priority these
policies require. USAID, *Evaluation of USAID/Peru's Education Program: Apprendes and Cett-
Andino,* final report, April 2010, 2–3, http://pdf.usaid.gov/pdf_docs/PDACP962.pdf.

30   Republic of Peru, Ministry of Economy and Finance, *Guía de orientación al ciudadano,
proyecto de presupuesto 2014,* 14.

31   Reflexión Democrática, 2014 *Presupuesto del sector público,* http://www.reflexiondemo-
cratica.org.pe/wp-content/uploads/2013/11/Ley-de-Presupuestos-WEB.pdf.

32   Commission for Reception, Truth and Reconciliation, *Chega! The Report of the Commission for Reception, Truth and Reconciliation in Timor-Leste (CAVR),* executive summary
(Dili: CAVR, 2005), 144–45.

33   Ibid., 166.

34   Ibid., 171–72.

35   The statistics show that enrollment in the first two cycles of primary education (grades 1 to 6) increased from 67 percent in 2005 to 83 percent in 2009 and in the third cycle (grades 7 to 9) from 20 percent to 25 percent; but in secondary education (grades 10 to 12), it decreased from 13 percent to 12 percent. Democratic Republic of Timor-Leste, Ministry of Education, *National Education Strategic Plan 2011–2030*, 2011, 5, 14–35.

36   The measure of coverage is the gross enrollment ratio (GER). These figures represent the number of students enrolled in a given level of education, regardless of age, expressed as a percentage of the official school-age population corresponding to the same level of education. For the tertiary level, the population used is the five-year age group, starting from the official secondary school graduation age. The GER can exceed 100 percent due to the inclusion of students who are overage and underage because of early or late entrances or grade repetition. In this case, additional information is needed for a rigorous interpretation of the GER to assess the extent of repetition, late entrances, and so on. UNESCO, *UIS Glossary*, http://glossary.uis.unesco.org/glossary/en/term/2048/en. In this chapter, I used for some cases the GER as an indicator and for others indicators of the net enrollment ratio (NER)—which refer to the enrollment of children at the respective school ages—according to what was available for each country.

37   It should be noted, though, that the three sources consulted show significant differences in the enrollment rates. The net enrollment ratio in 2007, according to the Ministry of Education report, was 76 percent, while in a United Nations Development Programme report it was 63 percent. UNDP, *Timor-Leste Human Development Report 2011: Managing Natural Resources for Human Development Developing the Non-Oil Economy to Achieve the MDGs*, 2011, 22, http://www.laohamutuk.org/econ/HDI10/TLHDR2011En.pdf. In the 2010 census it was 70.6 percent. National Statistics Directorate (NSD)—United Nations Population Fund (UNFPA), *Population and Housing Census of Timor-Leste, 2010, Volume 3: Social and Economic Characteristics*, 2011, xvii, https://www.mof.gov.tl/wp-content/uploads/2011/06/Publication-3-English-Web.pdf.

38   Statistics Timor-Leste, "Highlights of the 2010 Census Main Results in Timor-Leste," 2010, 2, http://dne.mof.gov.tl/published/2010%20and%202011%20Publications/Census%20Summary%20English/English%20Census%20Summary%202011.pdf.

39   Democratic Republic of Timor-Leste, Ministry of Education, *National Education Strategic Plan 2011–2030*, 2011, 16.

40   UNDP, *The Millennium Development Goals, Timor-Leste* (UNDP, 2009), http://www.tl.undp.org/content/dam/timorleste/docs/library/MDGReport2009Englishv.1.pdf. The 2010 census figure, for the rural literacy rate in Tetum, however, is 65.7 percent. National Statistics Directorate, *Population and Housing Census of Timor-Leste, 2010 Volume 3: Social and Economic Characteristics*, 141.

41   UNESCO, *EFA Global Monitoring Report 2013/4*, 381.

42   Author's calculations based on figures obtained from the Government of Timor-Leste website (US$178.6 million, of a total budget of $1.5 billion). Government of Timor-Leste, "2014 Budget Law Passed by National Parliament," media release, January 28, 2014, http://timor-leste.gov.tl/?p=9655&lang=en.

43   World Bank, "Country at a Glance: Timor-Leste," http://www.worldbank.org/en/country/timor-leste.

44   International Monetary Fund, "IMF Executive Board Concludes 2013 Article IV Consultation with Timor-Leste," press release no. 13/430, November 7, 2013, https://www.imf.org/external/np/sec/pr/2013/pr13430.htm.

45   Actually, another policy for responding to the legacy of the independence struggle consumes an important portion of the government budget—not a policy referring to victims, as reparations have not been implemented, but one establishing a substantial pension program for veterans. World Bank, *Timor-Leste Social Assistance Public Expenditure and Program Performance Report*, report no. 73484-TP, June 24, 2013, http://www-wds.worldbank.org/external/default/WDSContentServer/WDSP/IB/2013/06/27/000442464_20130627152921/Rendered/PDF/734840WP0P126300PER000240June00eng.pdf.

46   World Bank, "Maintaining Momentum on Education Reform in Morocco," news release, September 11, 2013, 1–2, http://www.worldbank.org/en/news/feature/2013/09/11/maintaining-momentum-on-education-reform-in-morocco.

47   "Investments made over the past decade in school infrastructure along with support to the poorest students contributed to increases in national enrollment rates from 52.4 percent to 98.2 percent in primary education, from 17.5 percent to 56.7 percent in lower secondary education, and from 6.1 percent to 32.4 percent in upper secondary education. There has also been clear progress toward equity, with the gap between urban boys and rural girls at the primary education level narrowing to just 3.5 percentage points by the 2012 school year." Ibid.

48   Ibid.

49   UNESCO, *EFA Global Monitoring Report 2013/4*, 29.

50   It is ranked 129th in the Human Development Index for 2014. UNDP, *Human Development Report 2014: Sustaining Human Progress*, http://www.undp.org/content/dam/undp/library/corporate/HDR/2014HDR/HDR-2014-English.pdf, 162.

51   In 2012, the Illiteracy Eradication Directorate of the Ministry of Education received honorable mention for the UNESCO Confucius Prize, recognizing its work in this area between 2005 and 2011, which has benefited over 4.5 million people, 80 percent of them women. UNESCO, *The Winners of the UNESCO International Literacy Prizes 2012: Cultivating Peace*, 14, http://unesdoc.unesco.org/images/0021/002175/217539E.pdf.

52   UNESCO, "Adult and Youth Literacy, National, Regional and Global Trends, 1985–2015," UIS Information Paper, June 2013, 38, http://www.uis.unesco.org/Education/Documents/

literacy-statistics-trends-1985-2015.pdf.

53   UNESCO, *EFA Global Monitoring Report 2013/4*, 75.

54   Truth and Reconciliation Commission of Sierra Leone (TRC-SL), *Witness to Truth: Report of the Sierra Leone Truth and Reconciliation Commission* (Freetown: Graphic Packaging Limited GCL, 2004), vol. 2, ch. 2, para. 46.

55   Based on a 1985 census, the commission stated the illiteracy rate for the female rural population was 89 percent. Ibid., vol. 2, ch. 2, para. 552.

56   Based on the UNDP's *Human Development Report 2003* (http://hdr.undp.org/sites/default/files/reports/264/hdr_2003_en_complete.pdf), the commission stated that between 1999 and 2000, 3.6 percent of the GDP was spent on the military and 1 percent on education. TRC-SL, *Witness to Truth*, vol. 2, ch. 3, para. 250.

57   Quoting World Bank figures, the commission stated that "35 percent of classrooms needed to be reconstructed, while 52 percent needed either to be repaired or rehabilitated." Additionally, it cited the need for training, attracting, and retaining qualified teachers. TRC-SL, *Witness to Truth*, vol. 2, ch. 4, paras. 174–75.

58   Ibid., vol. 2, ch. 3, paras. 384–86, 358–61.

59   Ibid., vol. 2, ch. 3, paras. 497–98, and ch. 4, paras. 206–9.

60   Between 2000 and 2011, the gross enrollment ratio (GER) for primary education increased from 70 percent to 122 percent; for lower secondary education from 27 percent to 62 percent; and for upper secondary education from 21 percent to 32 percent. Although dropout rates are very high in primary education, the GER for the last year of primary education improved from 45 percent in 2000 to 76 percent in 2011. UNESCO, *Sierra Leone EFA Profile*, 2, http://www.unesco.org/new/fileadmin/MULTIMEDIA/FIELD/Dakar/pdf/SierraLeoneprofileEFAoct2012.pdf.

61   Participation in primary education, which increased from eighty-nine for every hundred boys to ninety-three for every hundred between 1999 and 2011, saw little improvement for girls, and only seventy-nine girls for every hundred boys were enrolled in lower secondary education, which was 52 percent of the girls of the corresponding age. UNESCO, *EFA Global Monitoring Report 2013/4*, 352–53, 368. No figures are available for upper secondary education, but the disparity might be high, as in 2006 it was reported that 56 percent of girls were married below the age of eighteen. United Nations Girls' Education Initiative (UNGEI), "Sierra Leone: Key Indicators," http://www.ungei.org/infobycountry/sierraleone.html.

62   The youth literacy rate among poor children is 11 percent and among rich ones 81 percent. UNESCO, *EFA Global Monitoring Report 2013/4*, 209–10.

63   Mario Novelli, "The Role of Education in Peacebuilding: Case Study—Sierra Leone" (New York: UNICEF, 2011), 12–13, 20–22.

64   UNESCO, *EFA Global Monitoring Report 2013/4*, 382. In 2010, public expenditure on primary education per student was US$80, lower than the average among low-income

countries (US$94) and in sub-Saharan Africa (US$131). The adult literacy rate was 43 percent, with a six-to-ten ratio of females to males (Ibid., 382–83, 388).

65 Ibid., 75.

66 Novelli, "The Role of Education in Peacebuilding," 38–40, 54.

67 UNESCO, *EFA Global Monitoring Report 2013/4*, 86.

68 Ibid., 227.

69 Truth commissions are not indispensable for identifying these needs nor are they an essential component of transitional justice policies. They have, however, been useful mechanisms for finding narratives that help countries navigate the challenges of addressing the past and defining a future based on the recognition of the rights of all their inhabitants, even though defining such narratives alone does not guarantee the countries will follow through. Perhaps examining long-term effects of such commissions, thirty or fifty years later, could help determine their importance.

70 Moja, "Education as Redress in South Africa."

71 ICTJ and Environment Health and Population Activities (CREHPA), *"To Walk Freely with a Wide Heart": A Study of the Needs and Aspirations for Reparative Justice of Victims of Conflict* (New York: ICTJ, 2014).

72 Reparations through the provision of opportunities for education in these cases could be understood as a form of social rehabilitation, according to the traditional categorization of reparation as restitution, compensation, rehabilitation, satisfaction, and guarantees of nonrepetition. They might also be understood as a form of satisfaction, based on the symbolic nature of education, or as restitution, when the violation has interrupted the education of a victim. Roger Duthie and Clara Ramírez-Barat discuss this in their essay, "Education as Rehabilitation for Human Rights Violations," in *International Human Rights Law Review* 5, no. 2 (forthcoming 2016). For some victims, however, education could also be a form of restitution, if their right to it was denied as a direct result of the violation. Perhaps in these situations it could even be understood not as reparation, but as the mere cessation of the violation. Finally, in some cases in which the violation committed did not have any impact on the victims' ability to continue their education, its provision could be understood as a form of compensation, with scholarships added to payments in a reparation program as a means for redressing material and moral harm that can never be fully redressed.

73 Maria Jose Guembe, "Economic Reparations for Grave Human Rights Violations: The Argentinian Experience," in *The Handbook of Reparations*, ed. Pablo de Greiff (Oxford: Oxford University Press, 2006), 22.

74 Argentina, Law 11,914 of the Province of Buenos Aires, 1996.

75 Chilean National Commission on Truth and Reconciliation, *Report of the Chilean National Commission on Truth and Reconciliation* (Notre Dame, IN: University of Notre Dame Press, 1993), vol. I/II, foreword, xxi–xxii, 1069.

76 Chile, Law 19,123 of 1992, arts. 29–31.

77 Lorena Escalona González, "Education as a Form of Reparation in Chile," in this volume.

78 Republic of Chile, Ministry of the Interior, National Commission on Political Imprison-
    ment and Torture, *Informe de la Comisión Nacional de Prisión Política y Tortura*, 2004, 525,
    http://www.derechoshumanos.net/paises/America/derechos-humanos-Chile/informes-
    comisiones/Informe-Comision-Valech.pdf.

79 Chile, Law 20,405 of 2009, transitory art. 6.

80 González, "Education as a Form of Reparation in Chile."

81 Peru, Decree 015-2006-JUS, art. 17.

82 Ibid., arts. 18 and 45. Self-defense committees were organizations created by residents to
    defend their communities.

83 Peru, Decree 047-2011-PCM, art. 1.

84 The scholarship includes tuition, housing, a stipend, health insurance, an amount for
    buying a computer, and a course to prepare students for the demands of university-level
    courses.

85 National Coordinator for Human Rights and National Association of Centers, *Reporte de
    avance de reparaciones (económicas)* (Lima: Coordinadora Nacional de Derechos Humanos
    and Asociación Nacional de Centros, 2015).

86 Chauca, "Reparaciones y educación en Perú."

87 Republic of Peru, Ministry of Education, Office of Scholarships and Undergraduate
    Education, "Lineamientos del modelo de intervención para el soporte académico y
    socioafectivo del becario," 2014, approved by Resolución Directorial Ejecutiva No. 079-
    2014 MINEDU-VMGI-OBEC-PRONABEC of March 12, 2014.

88 Supreme Decree 011-2016-JUS.

89 TRC-SL, *Witness to Truth*, vol. 2, ch. 4, para. 30.

90 Ibid., para. 178.

91 Ibid., para. 179.

92 Ibid., para. 97.

93 Mohamed Suma and Cristián Correa, *Report and Proposals for the Implementation of
    Reparations in Sierra Leone* (New York: ICTJ, 2009). After 2009, this program continued
    registering victims and providing interim payments through a series of smaller projects.
    Peace Building Fund, *MPTF Office Final Programme Narrative Report*, reporting period
    January 2011 to December 2012.

94 Novelli, "The Role of Education in Peacebuilding," 39.

95 TRC-SL, *Witness to Truth*, vol. 2, ch. 4, 262–63.

96 The UN Women/NaCSA project targeted 650 survivors of sexual violence through
    a skills training and microfinance program. The total number of such victims regis-
    tered as of this writing is 3,602. Aruna Turay, "In Sierra Leone, NaCSA Certifies Female
    War Victims," *Awareness Times*, May 17, 2011, http://news.sl/drwebsite/exec/view.

cgi?archive=7&num=17525.

97 The PBF/IOM project was directed to support an organization of 350 young amputees. The total number of amputees registered as of this writing is over 1,100. UNDP, Multi-partner Trust Fund Office, project: "PBF/IRF-25 Amputee Support, Sport Development and Advocacy in Sierra Leone," http://mptf.undp.org/factsheet/project/00076881.

98 ICTJ, *From Relief to Reparations: Listening to the Voices of Victims* (Katmandu: ICTJ, 2011), 4.

99 ICTJ and CREHPA, *"To Walk Freely with a Wide Heart,"* 10.

100 Ibid., 7, 17.

101 Ibid., 10.

102 Ibid., 18, 22.

103 Ibid., 24.

104 The study involved the application of different tools, included a total of 410 victims, and was conducted in ten districts of Nepal in July and August 2013. The specific questions about prioritizing different education measures were asked during focused ethnographic studies involving 150 female and 124 male victim-beneficiaries of the Interim Relief Program. See ICTJ and CREHPA, *"To Walk Freely with a Wide Heart."*

105 Ibid., 28–34.

106 Colombia, Law 1,448 of 2011, art. 51.

107 Government of Colombia, First Senate and House Committees, *Informe del gobierno nacional para las Comisiones Primeras de Senado y Cámara* (Bogotá: Government of Colombia, 2014), 99–102.

108 In 2014, the government made three calls for submission of applications for higher education scholarships, receiving more than 27,000 applications, but granting only 2,042. Ibid., 162.

109 For a more complete analysis of the implementation of reparations under this program, see Ana Cristina Portilla and Cristián Correa, *Estudio sobre la implementación del Programa de Reparación Individual en Colombia*, ICTJ, 2015, https://www.ictj.org/sites/default/files/ICTJ-COL-Estudio-reparacion-individual-2015.pdf.

110 The regulations are defined under the concept of assistance. They are understood, however, as the application of the Promotion of Unity and Reconciliation Act of 1995, General Notice 282 of 2011, of the Department of Justice and Constitutional Development (Gazette No. 34279, May 5, 2011).

111 Grade R in South Africa (also called reception or grade 0) is a preschool year for children of four years of age who will turn five before June 30. It is not compulsory.

112 Moreover, during the last year, the Department of Justice moved to another strategy, on community reparations, which initially covered eighteen communities; so it is unlikely these regulations will be approved and the program implemented in the short term.

113 General Notice 852 of 2014 of the Department of Justice and Constitutional Development (Gazette No. 38157, November 3, 2014).

114 In the twenty-five years since democracy was restored in Chile, the country has been governed by six presidents. Five were from the coalition that opposed the dictatorship, and one, Sebastián Piñera (2010–14), was from the coalition that supported the dictatorship but differentiated itself from it and continued the implementation of human rights policies, including not interfering with the prosecution of military personnel for past human rights violations.

115 ICTJ and Moroccan Advisory Council on Human Rights (CCDH), *The Rabat Report: The Concept and Challenges of Collective Reparations* (New York and Rabat: ICTJ and CCDH, 2009).

116 Defensoría del Pueblo, *A diez años de verdad, justicia y reparación: Avances, retrocesos y desafíos de un proceso inconcluso.* Informe defensorial 162 (Lima, 2013), 30.

117 *Serperuano,* "Más de S/.230 millones ha destinado el Gobierno del Perú para resarcir a las víctimas de la violencia armada," July 15, 2014, http://www.serperuano.com/2014/07/mas-de-s-230-millones-ha-destinado-el-gobierno-del-peru-para-resarcir-a-las-victimas-de-la-violencia-armada/.

118 ICTJ and Association for Human Rights (APRODEH), *¿Cuánto se ha reparado a nuestras comunidades? Avances, percepciones y recomendaciones sobre reparaciones colectivas en Perú 2007–2011* (Lima: ICTJ and APRODEH, 2011), 18.

119 National Council for Economic and Social Policy of Colombia, National Planning Department, "Lineamientos, plan de ejecución de metas, presupuesto y mecanismo de seguimiento para el plan nacional de atención y reparación integral a víctimas," Conpes Document 3726, May 30, 2012, 36, 43.

120 Colombia, Decree 4800/2011, art. 229.

121 International Organization for Migration (IOM), *Del daño a la reparación colectiva: La experiencia de siete casos emblemáticos* (Bogota: IOM, 2012), 87–95.

122 After more than three years of implementation of the Victims Law, the government at this writing has identified and started working with 304 collective reparation plans. Of those, 72 have been approved, including the 7 pilot plans developed before the law was passed, and their implementation has been started. Government of Colombia, "Informe anual del Presidente de la República sobre los avances en la ejecución y cumplimiento de la Ley 1448 de 2011" (August 2015): 16.

123 Comisión de Seguimiento de los Organismos de Control, *Segundo informe de seguimiento y monitoreo de la implementación de la Ley de Víctimas y Restitución de Tierras 2012–2013,* 2013, 578, http://www.contraloria.gov.co/documents/155638087/161614507/Informe+final+Victimas+2013.pdf/c82e7c71-2052-4cb8-b38b-57c9ba9af93d?version=1.0.

124 Government of Colombia, "Informe anual del Presidente," 16–17.

125 Truth, Justice and Reconciliation Commission of Kenya, *The Final Report of the TJRC,* 2013, 4:101, http://digitalcommons.law.seattleu.edu/cgi/viewcontent.cgi?article=1006&context=tjrc.

126 Ibid., 4:112.

127 In March 26, 2015, President Uhuru Kenyatta issued an official apology for violations reported by the TJRC and made a commitment to the creation of a reparation fund and a state department responsible for implementing measures in favor of affected or at-risk communities. How those measures will be implemented is not clear, however, nor is whether they will include any of the education measures mentioned by the commission.

128 Inter-American Court of Human Rights, Aloeboetoe et al. v. Suriname, Judgment of September 10, 1993 (Reparations and Costs), series 15, para. 96.

129 Social services have, for example, been provided through the creation of a community development fund to be administered jointly by the community and the government. Inter-American Court of Human Rights, Moiwana Community v. Suriname, Judgment of June 15, 2005 (Preliminary Objections, Merits, Reparations and Costs), series 125, paras. 214–15.

130 Inter-American Court of Human Rights, Yakye Axa Indigenous Community v. Paraguay, Judgment of June 17, 2005 (Merits, Reparations and Costs), series 125, para. 221. Similar orders have been included in Inter-American Court of Human Rights, Sawhoyamaxa Indigenous Community v. Paraguay, Judgment of March 29, 2006 (Merits, Reparations and Costs), series 146, para. 230; and in Inter-American Court of Human Rights, Plan de Sánchez Massacre v. Guatemala, Judgment of November 19, 2004 (Reparations), series 116, para. 110.

131 Most frequently, in cases of individual violations or even massacres, the court has included the harm to victims' ability to continue their educations as part of the harm the compensation amount needed to cover. Only in a few more recent decisions has it included separate measures, such as scholarships, to allow them to continue their educations, based on specific harms to their life plans. In these cases, the measures have been identified as forms of rehabilitation or satisfaction (see, for example, Inter-American Court of Human Rights, Cantoral-Benavides v. Peru, Judgment of December 3, 2001 (Reparations and Costs), series 88, para. 80; The "Juvenile Reeducation Institute" v. Paraguay, Judgment of September 2, 2004 (Preliminary Objections, Merits, Reparations and Costs), series 112, para. 321; Gómez-Palomino v. Peru, Judgment of November 22, 2005 (Merits, Reparations and Costs), series 136, paras. 144–48; Rosendo Cantú et al. v. Mexico, Judgment of August 31, 2010 (Preliminary Objections, Merits, Reparations, and Costs), series 216, para. 257; and Norín Catrimán et al. v. Chile, Judgment of May 29, 2014 (Merits, Reparations, and Costs), series 279, para. 432.

132 Inter-American Court of Human Rights, Massacres of El Mozote and neighboring locations v. El Salvador, Judgment of November 20, 2012 (Merits, Reparations and Costs), series 252, para. 339.

133 On the connections between reparations for violations of civil and political rights and violations of social, economic, and cultural rights, see Ruben Carranza, *Relief,*

Reparations, and the Root Causes of Conflict in Nepal (New York: ICTJ, 2012), as well as his "Plunder and Pain: Should Transitional Justice Engage with Corruption and Economic Crimes?" *International Journal for Transitional Justice* 2 (2008): 310–30; Duthie, "Transitional Justice, Development, and Economic Violence"; and Cristián Correa, "Integrating Development and Reparations."

134   In 2011, 57 million children of primary school age were not attending school, and by 2015, only 68 out of 122 countries will have achieved universal primary enrollment. UNESCO, *EFA Global Monitoring Report 2013/4*, 52.

CHAPTER 5

Education as a Form of Reparation in Chile

Lorena Escalona González

The human rights violations committed during the military dictatorship that ruled Chile from 1973 to 1990 not only had direct and profound effects on the enjoyment of civil and political rights by the victims and their families; ultimately, their suffering also had consequences for their enjoyment of economic, social, and cultural rights, including the right to education.[1] Moreover, with the dismantling and decentralization of the educative system as part of a broader political reform process aimed at erasing any vestige of Salvador Allende's democratic government, the repressive logic of the dictatorship had profound consequences for the health of the Chilean public sphere.

This chapter will analyze the measures established by the post-dictatorial Chilean state with respect to education reparation, including both the satisfaction and nonrecurrence measures and the compensatory reparations provided directly to the victims and their families.[2] It also examines a little-explored area of reparation in the education field that is directly linked to the history of the dictatorship itself: in opposition to the climate of repression and obscurantism of that time, social movements became protagonists in resistance to the regime and the defense of human rights. They filled a gap created by the dictatorship's prohibition of political parties that had left society devoid of opportunities for participation and association and had facilitated, on the contrary, social fragmentation and the rise of individualism—a situation that, in turn, helped to strengthen the dictatorship's social influence. When thinking about the reparation process, especially in terms of education, it is essential to heed this situation to understand the full scope of the damage the dictatorship caused.

Following a brief explanation of the importance of education within the social movement that opposed the dictatorship, this chapter will analyze the different stages of the truth and reparation process in Chile. In this regard, especially when discussing the work of the Rettig Commission and the National Reparation and Reconciliation Corporation, the text will examine the education proposals made at the time for symbolic reparation and the promotion of guarantees of nonrecurrence.

The chapter will next look at the establishment of the Valech Commission in 2003, followed by a more detailed analysis of the set of education reparation measures that have been adopted and implemented in Chile since 1990. It will conclude by considering human rights education as an element of reparation and the design of public policies. The implementation of the latter developed, one could say experimentally, within the restructuring of the education system during the early 1990s but was suspended and left pending to the present day.

POPULAR EDUCATION AND HUMAN RIGHTS

In September 1973, following a military coup, Chile came under the control of General Augusto Pinochet, whose regime would bring about the imprisonment, torture, and deaths of thousands. Almost immediately, Chilean civil society began to implement a series of initiatives to assist victims of Pinochet's repression. The first to assume this humanitarian welfare role were the churches and religious groups, which together organized themselves into the Pro-Peace Committee. Before long, the work of the committee was taken over by the Vicaría de la Solidaridad (Vicariate of Solidarity) of the Chilean Catholic Church, which continued operating and expanding its mission throughout the dictatorship.[3]

At the same time, as the dictatorial regime was consolidating, a network of more or less formal human rights organizations was woven throughout the country, focusing its activities on the development of human rights complaints, information, promotion, and education. Using the traditional methodological tools of popular education, the network conveyed its message with clarity and simplicity to grassroots groups and organizations which, in turn, built social opposition to the dictatorship, establishing and legitimizing political and moral leadership that was widely recognized in their communities. These groups adopted novel work methodologies to respond to the needs generated by human rights violations, and they were able to coordinate the actions of professionals in the fields of law, education, health, and communications with those of popular organizations, civil society, and the spectrum of political militants, who saw an opportunity for dialogue and protection. Thus, "during the period of the military dictatorship, the practice of defending and promoting human rights constituted an ethical and social reference that acted as a moral reserve and cultural resistance against the authoritarian policy exercised by the State."[4]

Human rights work thus conceived, with this important education function, was fully identified at the end of the 1980s with the struggle for

democracy, and it acquired great significance as an autonomous social movement, especially in the deep and committed citizen mobilization that led to the
triumph of the 1988 plebiscite that put an end to the military dictatorship in
Chile. The movement, which had driven the emergence of human rights education during the dictatorship, also systematized its experience and the lessons
it had learned to apply them to the democracy that had to be reconstructed.
As early as the period immediately before the start of the democratic transition, some of these groups began to develop proposals for education programs
that were incorporated into the government platform of the first democratically elected president, Patricio Aylwin, and later developed in more detail at
the request of the National Truth and Reconciliation Commission.

THE RETTIG COMMISSION: EDUCATION AS REPARATION
AND PREVENTION

With the first democratic transition government recently installed in Chile,
the National Truth and Reconciliation Commission (also known as the Rettig
Commission) was created on May 9, 1990, by order of the president of the
republic, Patricio Aylwin Azócar, and charged with investigating the most
serious human rights violations committed between September 11, 1973, and
March 11, 1990. The most serious violations were understood as

> the situations of the disappeared detainees, the politically executed, and
> those who were tortured to death, in which the moral responsibility of
> the State appears to be compromised because of the acts of its agents
> and persons in its service, as well as the kidnappings and attempts on the
> lives of people committed by private citizens under political pretexts.[5]

In addition, in compliance with its mandate, the commission had to

> establish as complete a picture as possible of the grave events referred
> to and their antecedents and circumstances; gather records that would
> make it possible to identify the victims and to establish their fate or
> whereabouts; recommend the reparation and recovery measures that
> create justice; and recommend the legal and administrative measures
> that, in its judgment, should be adopted to impede or prevent the com-
> mission of the acts referred to in this article.[6]

The Rettig Commission was thus created with the specific objective of

> helping the global illumination of the truth about the most serious
> human rights violations committed in recent years, whether in the
> country or abroad, if the latter were related to the Chilean State or the
> national political life, in order to collaborate in the reconciliation of all
> Chileans, without prejudice to the judicial proceedings to which such
> facts may lead.[7]

The new democratic government harbored the conviction that the search for
the truth would have a rehabilitative effect by providing dignity and honor
to the victims, giving their families an opportunity to honor them properly,
and allowing compensation in some measure for the damage caused, despite
the delay in and inadequacy of justice. The truth was presented as a sine qua
non for beginning to move firmly toward the recovery of the country's lost
democracy, despite the existence of the Amnesty Law, approved in 1978 by
the military government, which prevented the prosecution of those who were
responsible for human rights violations.

Clearly, however, establishing the truth would be only the beginning of
the task to be performed with respect to human rights. While the truth by
itself has a restorative effect for victims of human rights violations and their
families, as well as society in general, the effect is short-lived because once
known, the truth generates demands for more truth, claims for reparations,
and reform. This is exactly what happened in Chile. The knowledge made public about the most serious violations, as defined in the decree that created the
Rettig Commission, was necessarily accompanied by various requirements:
assistance for the families of the recognized victims; an institutional and legal
framework capable of preventing the recurrence of rights violations; and
the adoption of different educational and cultural measures that, in addition
to providing a moral reading of the past, would adopt a preventive purpose,
aimed at manifesting the idea of "never again."

After nine months of work, the commission delivered its final report
to President Aylwin on February 8, 1991, in a solemn ceremony broadcast
throughout the country by the national media. The report responded to the
mandate in its entirety. After conducting interviews with the families of victims and other relevant actors and developing a process for searching records,
files, newspapers, books, and all types of publications, an interdisciplinary
team of professionals—not necessarily from the field of human rights, but
all nationally renowned—reported it had received 3,550 complaints, of which

2,296 were recognized as involving victims of human rights violations or persons who had died as a consequence of the political violence in the country during the period investigated by the commission.[8] Along with a list of victims, the report included a set of recommendations for both reparation measures to do justice by the victims and their families and legal, educational, and cultural measures necessary to prevent repetition of the events. It also included a recommendation we can call "instrumental," in that it referred to the creation of a body that would be responsible for carrying out each and every one of the other recommendations.

The Rettig Commission considered three different areas in its recommendations regarding reparation: symbolic reparation, legal and administrative measures, and social welfare measures (including health, education, and housing). Specifically with respect to education-related reparations, the commission emphasized its concern for those who had "lost educational opportunities" in terms of access to and participation in the different stages of the education system as a consequence of the human rights violations to which their families were subjected.[9] Such lost opportunities had been exacerbated by the deterioration of the economic condition of many of these families and/or by the emotional disorders and learning difficulties suffered by their children.

The commission, therefore, called upon the Ministry of Education to implement a set of measures to benefit the victims or their direct descendants, which included awarding higher education scholarships to the children of the victims able to pursue such studies; studying the possibility of forgiving the student loans of victims' children, spouses, and other direct relatives; and facilitating the free admission to technical training centers for young people and adults (including spouses and direct relatives) who were not able to complete their studies and did not have jobs.[10]

In addition to the strictly reparative measures, the commission made a set of education-related recommendations for preventive and nonrecurrence measures. These recommendations were developed through a participatory process with civil society nongovernmental organizations (NGOs) that formed part of the social movement discussed above, involving the convergence of popular education and human rights work and with the Interdisciplinary Program for Research in Education (Programa Interdisciplinario de Investigaciones en Educación, or PIIE) as the main actor.[11]

Among the recommendations were several directly related to the creation of a suitable cultural environment of respect for human rights. Here the commissioners reflected on the insufficiency of guaranteeing human rights only through legal and institutional reforms. They believed responding to the vulnerability of Chilean society in terms of its democratic stability required more than that, and such institutional measures needed to be complemented by explicit efforts to construct a culture of respect for human rights. The commission thus pointed to education as providing a privileged opportunity for prevention and symbolic reparation, to the extent that, as Mirtha Abraham and Maria T. Rodas have stated, "it falls mainly to education, in its diverse areas, to deploy the efforts necessary to effectively incorporate respect for human rights in the national culture."[12]

In this endeavor, the state would have the task of providing the training and education opportunities necessary to transmit a conception of human rights to all strata of society. For its part, society had to demand that the education system assume, in addition to its traditional functions, a formative, value-based, and moral role in human rights. In this way, the proposals developed by the commission considered the importance of the different levels and modalities of the formal education system (pre-basic, basic, secondary, and higher education; scientific–humanist; technical–professional; professional civil training institutions; professional military training institutions, and so on), as well as the nonformal education system related to community organizations and groups (adult education, popular education, unions, and so on) and informal education, expressed through the mass media (television, the press, radiotelephony, and so on).

Furthermore, according to the report, the development of this education project aimed at prevention must, as with all cultural processes, be a long and consistent process. It was necessary to establish mechanisms that could ensure "the effort to introduce respect for human rights in our culture can be maintained over time."[13] Among the recommendations in the field of formal education were suggestions related to the school curriculum, both explicit and implicit. With regard to nonformal education, and linked to the education potential of grassroots organizations, the Rettig Report referred to methodologies that recognize citizens as subjects of law and peaceful resolvers of conflicts.

Finally, in terms of informal education, the report assigned an important role to the media in the dissemination of information about rights and the formation of a collective consciousness regarding their enjoyment and exercise. It also recognized the importance of professors and teachers in providing this motivation to seek out and get access to human rights education and training, as well as the role of other professionals and social actors, such as media workers, who likewise had to have a deep conviction and proper training to enable them, like teachers, to develop as actors in the field of formal, nonformal, and informal human rights education.

THE NATIONAL REPARATION AND RECONCILIATION CORPORATION: THE EDUCATION AND CULTURAL PROMOTION PROGRAM

Following the work of the Rettig Commission, the National Reparation and Reconciliation Corporation (CNRR, in Spanish) was created in February 1992.[14] The CNRR was meant to implement the commission's recommendations and provide social and legal assistance to the families of victims to enable them to gain access to certain benefits and to help them obtain moral damages for their pain and suffering. It also had to establish, through records and inquiries, the status of victims of human rights violations or political violence in those cases in which the Rettig Commission was unable to form an opinion or did not have sufficient or timely background information.[15] Finally, the CNRR had to formulate a public policy for promoting a strong human rights culture.

The corporation comprised a board of directors, led by a president, Alejandro González Poblete, who was appointed by the president of the republic, and eight elected board members representing different political views in the country. The mission of the board was to formulate proposals for the different public sectors of national life, and its members had to be recognized for their ethics, probity, and public reputation. The corporation was initially to function for a two-year period, but a legal extension granted by the National Congress extended its term until December 31, 1996,[16] after which some of its functions, including the memorialization and education programs, were carried on by the human rights programs of the Ministry of the Interior and the Ministry of Education, respectively.

In accordance with law number 19,123, the CNRR's lines of work covered six areas, each organized in a specific program: the Victims' Qualification Program; the Program for Investigating the Final Fate of the Victims of Forced Disappearance; the Program for Providing Social and Legal Assistance to the Families of the Victims and Support to the Reparation Actions; the Education and Cultural Promotion Program; the Legal Studies and Research Program; and the Program for the Corporation's Documentation and Archives Center.

The Education and Cultural Promotion Program was developed by the Department of Education and Cultural Promotion. Established by the law that created the corporation, this was one of two thematic departments conceived by the legislature to implement the recommendations in the field of education and culture formulated in the Rettig Report. As indicated above, the contribution of this department was to be focused on the nonrecurrence of the events that had occurred. From the outset, it conducted its work with the participation of civil society through NGOs that, as mentioned, had been created during the period of the military dictatorship. To coordinate the work, the department promoted the creation of a Forum of Education and Human Rights Institutions, which brought together the twelve NGOs that had worked in this area during the dictatorship and were now adapting their work to respond to Chile's democratic transition.[17]

The program's development took into consideration the different education opportunities highlighted in the recommendations of the Rettig Report with regard to both formal and informal education. The group of NGOs thus wrote up a set of proposals, plans, and programs to be implemented with different education actors, which, once developed, were evaluated and sanctioned by the corporation's board of directors. The approval process involved a series of thematic sessions in which the board members reviewed an illustrated account of each project, asked questions, and, in many cases, submitted the projects to the scrutiny of their respective sectors to proceed, finally, to their approval. Once approved, the projects received a funding guarantee that would be provided directly under the Budget Law of the Republic annually from 1992 to 1996.

The methodology for the design and execution of the projects conceived in the CNRR's Education and Cultural Promotion Program was also developed with the participation of civil society. This representation included, on the one hand, NGOs from the fields of education and human rights and, on the other, the education actors to whom the projects were addressed. Professors, education supervisors from the Ministry of Education, directors of education institutions, parents, attorneys, and students were consulted for the respective projects aimed at formal education. University academics, intellectuals, writers, and members of the fields of culture and art were important actors in projects aimed at nonformal and informal education.

Furthermore, to contribute to the consolidation of a culture of respect for human rights, the methodology required all of the projects to culminate in publications in the form of texts or pedagogical, didactic, and dissemination instruments. As a result of this process, a set of texts was produced, organized into four different collections—the Proposal Collection, the Essay Collection, Nonserial Publications, and the Basic Library for Human Rights Education—which were distributed to all of the country's libraries and the most vulnerable schools that formed part of the "900 Schools Program."[18]

The corporation's education area linked its operation to the Chilean Ministry of Education, which at the time was beginning to implement postdictatorship education reforms. In particular, these defined minimum curricular objectives and crosscutting fundamentals, including the incorporation of the subject of human rights in formal education. In fact, once the work of the CNRR was completed, the team responsible for the education program was itself incorporated into the Ministry of Education.[19]

THE VALECH COMMISSION: ANOTHER STEP TOWARD CLOSING WOUNDS

In 2003, thirteen years after the Rettig Commission and following the establishment of a negotiation process as part of the so-called Dialogue Roundtable during the administration of President Ricardo Lagos,[20] the government created the National Commission on Political Imprisonment and Torture for the Illumination of the Truth about Human Rights Violations in Chile, or, as it is more commonly known, the Valech Commission.[21] The creation of this commission took into special consideration the fact that, between September 11, 1973, and March 10, 1990, the period investigated by the Rettig Commission, many people suffered unjust and humiliating deprivations of liberty, often accompanied by illegitimate physical duress. In the earlier process, only those who had died in detention or disappeared had been considered victims. The Valech Commission covered a significant omission by acknowledging the many people who had not been recognized as victims of the repression and, therefore, had not received any reparations from the state.

The Valech Commission was created as an advisory body to the president of the republic. Presided over by Monsignor Sergio Valech Aldunate, last head of the Vicariate of Solidarity, it operated between November 11, 2003, and May 31, 2005, with the objective of determining whether people were deprived of liberty and tortured as a result of actions of state agents or persons in the state's service for political reasons, during the same period investigated by the Rettig Commission.

Unlike the Rettig Commission, however, the Valech Commission's work was subject to confidentiality from the outset, provided by its founding decree, with respect to the records it received and the identities of those who provided information or collaborated in its work; those individuals had the option of disclosure. The identities of acknowledged victims, however, were not confidential. By May 10, 2004, the commission had received the testimony of more than 35,000 people who were interviewed at the commission's headquarters in Santiago, the offices of forty-two provincial governments, and 102 remote localities. It also received testimony from forty countries through Chilean consulates and embassies.

The Valech Commission's report contains a list of 27,255 people who were recognized as victims of torture and deprivation of liberty, and it explains the circumstances of these violations.[22] (The list was later expanded to 28,459, after the commission was given an extension to reassess rejected claims.) Several chapters address different aspects of these circumstances, including, in particular, the situations in which the violations occurred, the different periods in which the methods of torture were applied, the places where the victims were detained, the victims' profiles, and the consequences these practices had for the victims.

The report made two kinds of recommendations with regard to reparation: the first pertained to establishing education benefits for victims and their children, as part of a broader set of individual reparations, and the second to a policy for outreach, promotion, and education in human rights. While the individual reparation measures recommended included scholarships for the direct victims of political imprisonment and torture, the commission was able to appreciate the serious impact of torture on survivors' ability to provide education to their children. Additionally, given the survivors' average age of fifty-five years, it recommended establishing a scholarship program, similar to the Rettig Scholarship, for the children of the direct victims.[23]

Among symbolic and collective measures, the commission recommended the creation of a fund for supporting research projects on human rights. Additionally, as the commission received many books and testimonies, most of them self-published by the survivors of victims, it recommended establishing an editorial fund for the publication of testimonies, autobiographies, and other works of nonfiction, as well as another fund for plastic arts. Both funds were aimed to allow expression and acknowledgment of the truth.

With regard to human rights education, the commission assessed the policies implemented by the armed forces and the police on teaching human rights and international humanitarian law and recommended reviewing and improving those programs. It also made recommendations for human rights education and education for democratic participation, appreciation of diversity, critical thinking, and other civic skills.[24]

On December 19, 2009, five years after the publication of the Valech Commission's report, Law 20,405 was published, granting the same benefits—derived from Reparation Laws 19,123 of 1992 and 19,992 of 2004—to the victims of political imprisonment and torture and to the families of the politically executed and disappeared detainees. This new law made it possible for relatives of the victims of human rights violations who were not acknowledged by the Rettig Commission at the time, and the victims of political imprisonment and torture who did not respond to the first call made by the Valech Commission, to receive these benefits by a sort of residual mechanism. This mechanism, in the form of a new commission—called the Valech II Commission—met until August 2011, hearing the testimony of another 32,453 people and qualifying more than 9,795 new victims of political imprisonment and torture and 30 new victims of killing.

EDUCATION-RELATED REPARATION MEASURES

The reparation measures established following the work performed first by the Rettig Commission and the National Reparation and Reconciliation Corporation and then by the Valech I and II Commissions specifically included a set of education-related benefits for the victims and their families, with three different "reparation scholarships" created at different times. In 1992, the Rettig Scholarship was created through Law 19,123.[25] Later, the Valech Beneficiaries Scholarship (Law 19,992)[26] and the Valech Transfer Scholarship (Law 20,405) were created, in 2004 and 2009, respectively. While the Rettig Scholarship was awarded to the relatives of victims of political execution or forced disappearance, the Valech Beneficiaries Scholarship was established to support the basic, secondary, and higher education studies of direct victims of torture or deprivation of liberty, as listed in the Valech Report.

THE RETTIG SCHOLARSHIP

Law 19,123 (the Rettig Law) of February 8, 1992, establishes reparation measures for those recognized as victims of forced disappearance and political execution in the reports of the National Truth and Reconciliation Commission and, later, the National Reparation and Reconciliation Corporation. Among these measures, Title IV of the law specifically establishes a set of "education benefits," which include the Rettig Scholarship for children, up to the age of thirty-five, of persons declared to be victims of human rights violations or political violence, as established by the National Reparation and Reconciliation Corporation.[27] In 2004, this benefit was extended by Law 19,965 to the children of victims of subversive crimes committed during the period 1973–90.[28]

The Rettig Reparation Scholarship (also called the Human Rights Reparation Scholarship) pays the tuition and fees for regular degree programs offered by universities of the Council of Rectors of Chilean Universities (Consejo de Rectores de las Universidades Chilenas, or CRUCH).[29] For other institutions, applications for this scholarship need to be made through the National School Aid and Scholarship Board (Junta Nacional de Auxilio Escolar y Becas, or JUNAEB). The duration of the benefit depends on the duration of the proposed studies: for degree programs of fewer than five semesters, the benefit covers up to one additional semester, and for programs equal to or greater than five semesters, it covers up to two additional semesters. The benefits can be extended for up to one year immediately following graduation from higher education studies when the student is required to take a degree exam or present a thesis for approval.

As established in Article 30 of Law 19,123, the cost of these scholarships is financed by the Scholarship and Higher Education Development Fund of the Ministry of Education. For this reason, since 1992 the awarding of this benefit has been among the general responsibilities of the Ministry of Education, in combination with another set of education aid programs based, for the most part, on socioeconomic criteria.[30] The Department of Student Finance, an office of the Division of Higher Education of the Ministry of Education, is currently in charge of awarding scholarships to students who pursue higher education studies in universities of the Council of Rectors. Article 30 of Law 19,123 also establishes that the cost of the benefit for students of universities, professional institutes, and technical training centers that receive no tax support and are recognized by the Ministry of Education (that is, non-CRUCH institutions) is covered by another scholarship program of the ministry— the President of the Republic Scholarship Program. In 1992, the administration of this benefit was the responsibility of the Ministry of Planning and Cooperation, which in 2005 became the Ministry of Planning and is now the Ministry of Social Development.

Law 19,980, which modified and expanded the education benefits granted under Law 19,123, was enacted in 2004.[31] This law exclusively affects the benefits for relatives of victims of forced disappearance or political executions. Article 1(4) improves benefits for higher education studies by prolonging those provided under the previous law for up to two additional semesters, depending on the duration of the degree program, and for an additional year in the case of a beneficiary graduate who needs to take a degree exam or complete a paperwork requirement for obtaining a degree. The law also makes it possible for a beneficiary to request an additional one-year extension after verifying his or her status as a higher education student, through a certificate issued by the education institution confirming the student had fulfilled the minimum requirements for continuing his or her studies. The benefit granted by this measure consists of the payment of tuition and fees for one degree program, allowing students to change their degree programs once, and it is administered by the President of the Republic Scholarship Program of the Ministry of Education.

THE VALECH BENEFICIARIES SCHOLARSHIP

Following the work of the Valech Commission, Law 19,992 was enacted on December 17, 2004, to provide reparation scholarships and other benefits to those recognized as victims by the National Commission on Political Imprisonment and Torture. The recommendation made by the Valech Commission on granting scholarships to the children of survivors was rejected, though, as the law includes only direct victims, including tortured political prisoners and children born or kept in captivity with their parents. Title III of this law (articles 11 to 14) establishes an education benefit, also known as the Valech Beneficiaries Scholarship. Pursuant to Article 11, "the State guarantees victims recognized by the Valech Commission the free continuation of their studies, at any level of education, which were interrupted by the violation of their fundamental rights" during the military dictatorship.[32] As this involves adults enrolling in basic and secondary education studies in many cases, the law provides that the continuation of studies must comply with adult education regulations, unless, by Supreme Decree of the Ministry of Education, the president of the republic authorizes the pursuit of studies under special modalities.

Finally, the law establishes that beneficiaries who seek to complete their higher education studies may do so in public or private institutions recognized by the state, and they will have their tuition and monthly fees fully covered. As in the case of previous programs, this expense is assumed by the Higher Education Scholarship Fund Program of the Ministry of Education. The application, granting and payment, and expiration of these benefits, and their renewal or extension procedures in qualified cases, are regulated by the president of the republic and the ministers of education and finance. In 2008, in response to longstanding demands of victims concerning the reparation laws, Law 20,232 on the public sector budget established the option for the beneficiaries of Laws 19,123 and 19,992 who had not enjoyed the education benefit to pass it on to their children or grandchildren.[33]

THE VALECH TRANSFER SCHOLARSHIP

On December 10, 2009, five years after the creation of the Valech Beneficiaries Scholarship, Law 20,405 was approved to establish the "Valech Transfer Scholarship," following in part the Valech Commission's recommendation regarding access to education for the children and grandchildren of survivors of torture and the steps already taken by the public sector Budget Law of 2008. This law grants the benefits derived from Law 19,992 to the victims of political imprisonment and torture who were recognized by the Valech I and II Commissions. An important novelty is the ability of people whose names appear on the "List of Persons Recognized as Victims" in the annex "List of Political Prisoners and Torture Victims"[34] and who have not made use of the recognized education benefit to transfer the benefit to a descendant up to the second degree of direct-line consanguinity—that is, to a child or grandchild. In addition, the law provides that in those cases in which the direct victim has died without having made use of this benefit, it will be up to all of the direct descendants of the deceased, together with the surviving spouse, if any, to determine the descendant (child or grandchild) to whom the scholarship will be transferred.

With regard to formal criteria, the benefit can be applied for by students with high school diplomas who were in their first year of higher education during 2014 or by students taking higher education courses. The applicants must be enrolled in degree programs leading to professional or technical degrees recognized in the official curricula.

In addition, the benefit obtained by the students through this transfer is the same as that provided for the higher education scholarship system: for those enrolled in universities of the Council of Rectors, it covers the transfer fee, plus the respective tuition. With regard to private universities and professional degree programs offered by professional institutions, however, the funding is limited to up to 1,150,000 pesos (approximately US$2,500) annually; and for students enrolled in technical degree programs offered by professional institutes and technical training centers, up to 600,000 pesos (approximately US$1,000) is provided annually. These amounts are aimed to limit the possibilities for private universities or professional institutes to offer expensive but low-quality programs, as occurred with the Valech Beneficiaries Scholarship.[35] In the case of first-year students, the benefit will cover the entire duration of the studies defined by the respective academic program. For higher education students, the coverage will correspond to the years that remain, as defined by the academic program.

For a summary of the number of grants that have been awarded under each of the different categories discussed from 1990 to 2013, see appendix 5.3. The benefits administered by the Department of Student Finance as human rights reparations from 1990 to 2013 total 71,675,330,000 Chilean pesos—or about US$102 million (see appendix 5.4 for details). The distribution among regions of the country coincided generally with the distribution of the population. Other characteristics of beneficiaries included the following:

- Socioeconomic status of the scholarship recipients by quintile (arranged from lowest average income to highest): 16 percent corresponded to the first quintile, 11 percent to the second, 13 percent to the third, 15 percent to the fourth, and 7 percent to the fifth. No information was available about the remaining 38 percent.[36]
- Most popular program choices: law, 6.7 percent; social work, 5.3 percent; risk prevention engineering, 4.7 percent; psychology, 4.2 percent; and nursing, 3.7 percent.[37] In 2013, 409 beneficiaries of Reparation Scholarships opted to pursue law degrees.
- Establishments chosen by scholarship recipients (in 2014): private subsidized establishments, 44 percent; municipal establishments, 24 percent; private paid establishments, 11 percent. No information about the remaining 21 percent.[38]
- Types of institutions to which the beneficiaries applied: universities of the Council of Rectors of Chile, 29 percent; private universities, 44 percent; professional institutes, 24 percent; technical training centers, 3 percent.
- Class schedules of scholarship recipients: daytime classes, 78 percent; night classes, 21 percent.
- Students' ages (in 2014): twenty-one to twenty-five years, 46.6 percent; twenty years or younger, 25.6 percent; twenty-six to thirty years, 11.1 percent; over thirty years, 16.7 percent.
- Gender of scholarship recipients: female, 50 percent; male, 50 percent.[39]

CONCLUSION

The need to revise the education-related reparation measures over time arises from recognition of their limitations. The capacity of victims to raise claims for their rights cannot be subject to an expiration date, especially in cases in which previous rights violations impose restrictions on the enjoyment of the economic, social, and cultural rights of the survivors and their families. From this perspective, following the work begun in the 1990s under the efforts of the National Reparation and Reconciliation Corporation, attention has very recently been given again to some of the education proposals made in the early years of the democracy.

Recognizing this need, the electoral platform for Michelle Bachelet's 2012–13 presidential campaign included a commitment to design a National Plan on Citizenship Education, at all education levels, in which human rights would be among the issues covered. In May 2015, her administration presented to Congress for discussion and approval a proposed law to guarantee all primary and secondary schools would implement such a plan.[40] As of this writing, though, the content of the education program and how to present the lessons derived from human rights violations committed in Chile had not yet been defined, as a major education reform process—which has among its most important goals the need to move toward the realization of education as a universal and accessible right for all Chileans—was still underway.

In this new political scenario, a perception exists in Chile today of a political will to provide substance to the issues of human rights and memory in the academic and intellectual fields. Despite the delay in this process, the passage of time has, arguably, allowed the growth of a consensus about its importance and diminished resistance based on fears that it could be politically manipulated. At the same time, new attention is being given to the work of strengthening human rights education in the military and/or the academic schools of the armed forces, police, and investigative police, and to the development of a proposal for an updated curriculum incorporating theoretical normative training that explicitly goes beyond training-in-action protocols.

It cannot be overemphasized that symbolic reparation, as I have argued, generates extended and transcendent social effects for the victims and their families, witnesses, and other actors, reaching all sectors of the population without discrimination, contributing to the national collective consciousness, and ensuring the historical memory of our dictatorial experience.

APPENDIX 5.1. TEXTS PRODUCED FOR 900 SCHOOLS PROGRAM

The four collections of texts listed below were produced under the auspices of the National Reparation and Reconciliation Corporation for distribution to all of Chile's libraries and the schools that formed part of the "900 Schools Program," an education program created by the first democratic government to benefit the nine hundred most vulnerable schools in the country with respect to education quality, infrastructure, teaching staff, and students.

COLLECTION OF PROPOSALS

Prepared in 1994, the collection of proposals constitutes a set of materials for a human rights curriculum.

No. 1: *Educación en derechos humanos: Apuntes para una nueva práctica* [Human Rights Education: Notes for a New Practice].

No. 2: *Unidad de los derechos humanos para la dignidad de la persona: Primer concurso nacional de unidades didácticas para la educación en derechos humanos* [Unit for Human Rights for Human Dignity: First National Competition of Didactic Units for Human Rights Education].

No. 3: *Catálogo de material didáctico para la educación en derechos humanos* [Catalogue of Didactic Material for Human Rights Education].

No. 4: *Para recrear la cultura escolar: Experiencias y proyecciones desde los derechos humanos* [To Recreate School Culture: Experiences and Projections Based on Human Rights].

No. 5: *Manual de capacitación para educadores: La incorporación de los derechos humanos en el aula* [Training Manual for Educators: The Incorporation of Human Rights in the Classroom].

No. 6: *Perfeccionamiento docente: Tarea permanente para la educación en derechos humanos* [Teacher Development: Ongoing Task for Human Rights Education].

No. 7: *Diálogo y juventud: Instrumento para una cultura de derechos humanos* [Dialogue and Youth: Instrument for a Human Rights Culture].

ESSAY COLLECTION

The Jorge Millas Essay Contest that produced the essays below has been held since 1993, and a volume of the prizewinning works is published annually. This contest was transferred to the Ministry of Education upon the closing of the corporation.

Volume I: *Cuatro ensayos sobre derechos humanos*, 1993. Primer concurso nacional de ensayo. Premio anual profesor Jorge Millas [Four Essays on Human Rights, 1993. First National Essay Contest. Annual Professor Jorge Millas Prize].

Volume II: *Ensayos para la reconciliación. Derechos humanos, fundamento de la convivencia*, 1994. Segundo concurso nacional de ensayo. Premio anual profesor Jorge Millas [Essays for Reconciliation. Human Rights, Foundation of Coexistence, 1994. Second National Essay Contest. Annual Professor Jorge Millas Prize].

Volume III: *Nuevos acercamientos a los derechos humanos*, 1995. Tercer concurso nacional de ensayo. Premio anual profesor Jorge Millas [New Approaches to Human Rights, 1995. Third National Essay Contest. Annual Professor Jorge Millas Prize].

Volume IV: *Por una cultura de respeto a los derechos humanos*, 1996. Cuarto concurso nacional de ensayo. Premio anual profesor Jorge Millas [For a Culture of Respect for Human Rights, 1996. Fourth National Essay Contest. Annual Professor Jorge Millas Prize].

NONSERIAL PUBLICATIONS, 1994

Investigación bibliográfica para la educación en derechos humanos [Bibliographic Research for Human Rights Education].

Material educativo para un diagnóstico: ¿Cómo entendemos los derechos humanos [Education Material for a Diagnosis: How Do We Understand Human Rights?].

La convención sobre los derechos del niño [The Convention on the Rights of the Child].

Declaración universal de derechos humanos [Universal Declaration of Human Rights].

Guías de auto aprendizaje en educación en derechos humanos [Self-Teaching Guides on Human Rights].

BASIC LIBRARY FOR HUMAN RIGHTS EDUCATION

Volume I: *Propuestas temáticas para la educación en derechos humanos* [Thematic Proposals for Human Rights Education].

Volume II: *Aportes metodológicos para una educación basada en los derechos humanos* [Methodological Contributions for Education Based on Human Rights].

Volume III: *Contenidos fundamentales de derechos humanos para la educación* [Fundamental Human Rights Contents for Education].

APPENDIX 5.2. EXTRACTS FROM REPARATION LAWS

LAW NO. 19,123 (RETTIG LAW) OF FEBRUARY 8, 1992, TITLE IV: ON EDUCATION BENEFITS

Article 29. The children of the deceased indicated in Article 18 of this law shall have the right to receive the education benefits that are established in this title.

The age limit for obtaining these benefits shall be 35.

Article 30. Students of Universities and Professional Institutes that receive tax support shall have the right to the payment of the tuition and monthly fees. The cost of this benefit shall be assumed by the Scholarship and Higher Education Fund of the Ministry of Education.

Students of Universities, Professional Institutes, and Technical Training Centers that do not receive tax support and are recognized by the Ministry of Education shall have the right to the payment of the tuition and monthly fees of each establishment. The cost of this benefit shall be assumed by the President of the Republic Scholarship Program created by Supreme Decree No. 1,500 of December 18, 1980, of the Ministry of the Interior.

Article 31. Students pursuing secondary education studies, as well as those indicated in both paragraphs of the preceding article, shall have the right to receive a monthly subsidy equal to 1.24 monthly tax units. This subsidy shall be paid for as long as the student verifies his/her status as such, and it shall be paid during the school months of each year.

LAW NO. 19,980, WHICH MODIFIES LAW NO. 19,123, THE REPARATION LAW, EXTENDING OR ESTABLISHING BENEFITS FOR THE PERSONS THAT IT INDICATES. OCTOBER 29, 2004.

Article One. Introduces the following modifications to Law No. 19,123:

[...]

4) Adding, after Article 31, the following Articles 31 *bis* and 31 *ter*:

Article 31 *bis*. The benefits established in this Title may be extended for an additional period of up to one semester with respect to degree programs that have a duration of less than five semesters, and an additional period of up to two semesters with respect to degree programs that have a duration equal to or greater than five semesters.

The abovementioned benefits may be extended for up to one year after the completion of Higher Education studies, when it is necessary for obtaining the corresponding degree, either because a degree or graduate exam must be taken, or a paper must be submitted for approval.

Article 31 *ter*. The benefits indicated in the preceding article shall have an annual duration of ten months, and may be granted again for the following school year if the beneficiary requests their renewal in compliance with the requirements that shall be established by regulation for such purpose.

In order to renew the benefits, Higher Education students shall verify, through a certificate issued by the respective educational establishment, the minimum academic performance that allows them to continue their studies.

The payment of the tuition and monthly fees referred to in Article 30 shall be awarded to finance the expenses corresponding to the studies of a single degree program. The interested party may change his/her degree program only once. The initial or renewal applications of Secondary and Higher Education students shall be made on the dates established in the Annual Process Calendar prepared by the Executive Secretariat of the President of the Republic Scholarship Program.

LAW NO. 19,992 OF DECEMBER 17, 2004, TITLE III: ON EDUCATION BENEFITS

Article 11. The State shall guarantee the free continuity of the studies, whether at a basic, secondary or higher level, of those persons indicated in Articles 1 and 5 of this law, who because of political imprisonment or torture were prevented from pursuing their studies.

Article 12. Beneficiaries who apply to complete their basic and secondary education studies shall do so in accordance with the adult education regulations, and the President of the Republic shall be able, through a supreme decree issued through the Ministry of Education, to authorize special modalities for those cases.

Article 13. Beneficiaries who apply to continue their higher education studies in public or private higher education institutions recognized by the State shall have the right to the payment of the tuition and monthly fees. The cost of this benefit shall be assumed by the Higher Education Scholarship Fund of the Ministry of Education.

Article 14. A regulation issued through the Ministry of Education, which shall also be signed by the Ministry of Finance, shall establish the rules necessary for the effective use of these benefits, their termination, their application and payment procedure, the procedure for renewing or extending them in qualified cases, the conditions for funding the continuity of the studies, and all other rules necessary for the proper application of the provisions of this Title.

LAW NO. 20,405 OF DECEMBER 10, 2009

Transitory Article 6. The descendants to the second degree of consanguinity in direct line of the beneficiaries mentioned by Article 13 of Law No. 19,992, who have not made use of the benefit referred to in that article or at the date of enactment of this Act are deceased, without having use of it, may apply for the Bicentennial, Juan Gómez Millas, New Millennium, or other scholarships established for outstanding students for pedagogy programs, under the form and conditions established by the regulations of those scholarships. The aforementioned regulations shall be approved by supreme decree of the Ministry of Education, which will also be signed by the Minister of Finance.

The benefit established in the preceding paragraph may be granted only in respect of one descendant.

The determination of the descendant who may apply to one of the scholarships mentioned in the first paragraph of this Article shall be made by notarized affidavit, signed by the holder of the benefit of Law No. 19,992, if the person was alive. In case of death, the notarized document shall be signed jointly by the rest of the descendants and surviving spouse, if any.

APPENDIX 5.3. NATIONAL SCHOLARSHIPS AWARDED BY THE VALECH AND RETTIG COMMISSIONS, 1990–2013

Benefit	Rettig Scholarships Law 19,123	Valech Beneficiaries Scholarships Law 19,992	Valech Transfer Scholarships Law 20,405	Total
1990	-	-	-	0
1991	547	-	-	547
1992	864	-	-	864
1993	802	-	-	802
1994	786	-	-	786
1995	632	-	-	632
1996	510	-	-	510
1997	318	-	-	318
1998	207	-	-	207
1999	135	-	-	135
2000	124	-	-	124
2001	110	-	-	110
2002	130	-	-	130
2003	-	-	-	0
2004	-	-	-	0
2005	-	213	-	213
2006	-	1,492	-	1,492
2007	-	2,135	-	2,135
2008	36	2,429	1,386*	3,851
2009	24	2,029	2,810	4,863
2010	11	410	3,563	3,984
2011	10	337	4,115	4,462
2012	3	349	5,075	5,427
2013	2	323	5,534	5,859

Source: Government of Chile, Ministry of Education, Department of Student Finance, Division of Higher Education, July 2014 (report on file with the author).
*Although Law 20,405 was only approved in 2009, the Public Budget Law of 2008 allowed for the first fellowship transfers in 2008.

APPENDIX 5.4. AMOUNTS AWARDED FOR REPARATION SCHOLARSHIPS, 1990–2013 (IN THOUSANDS OF CHILEAN PESOS)

Benefit	Rettig Scholarships Law 19,123	Valech Beneficiaries Scholarships Law 19,992	Valech Transfer Scholarships Law 20,405	Total
1990	0	0	0	0
1991	1,416,477	0	0	1,416,477
1992	1,065,093	0	0	1,065,093
1993	976,156	0	0	976,156
1994	903,465	0	0	903,465
1995	759,926	0	0	759,926
1996	632,532	0	0	632,532
1997	401,248	0	0	401,248
1998	284,033	0	0	284,033
1999	201,630	0	0	201,630
2000	182,555	0	0	182,555
2001	160,135	0	0	160,135
2002	195,769	0	0	195,769
2003	165,247	0	0	165,247
2004	172,861	0	0	172,861
2005	151,615	363,076	0	514,691
2006	124,204	5,639,906	0	5,764,110
2007	85,661	8,112,606	0	8,198,267
2008	43,242	7,989,716	2,031,900	10,064,858
2009	39,635	7,804,757	3,969,940	11,814,332
2010	12,365	737,561	4,916,766	5,666,692
2011	25,487	744,134	5,609,347	6,378,968
2012	10,670	809,493	7,051,761	7,871,924
2013	7,218	743,783	7,133,359	7,884,360

Note: Amounts are in 2013 Chilean pesos. One Chilean peso = 0.00147 2013 US dollars.
Source: Report of the Department of Student Finance, Division of Higher Education, Ministry of Education, July 2014 (document on file with the author).

NOTES

1   This chapter, including material quoted from other sources, was translated into English by Daniel Kaplan. The author wishes to thank Cristián Correa and Clara Ramírez-Barat for commenting on an earlier draft.

2   See, in this regard, United Nations, Office of the High Commissioner for Human Rights, "The Basic Principles and Guidelines on the Right to a Remedy and Reparation for Victims of Gross Violations of International Human Rights Law and Serious Violations of International Humanitarian Law," General Assembly Resolution 60/147 of December 16, 2005, http://www.ohchr.org/EN/ProfessionalInterest/Pages/RemedyAndReparation. aspx.

3   See, for example, Juan Ignacio Gutiérrez, *La Vicaría de la Solidaridad* [The Vicariate of Solidarity] (Madrid: Alianza Editorial, 1986) and Cristián Pretch, *En la huella del Buen Samaritano* [In the Footprint of the Good Samaritan] (Santiago: Editorial Tiberíades, 1998).

4   NOVIB, *Derechos humanos, democracia y desarrollo en América Latina* [Human Rights, Democracy, and Development in Latin America] (Bogotá: NOVIB, 1993), 109.

5   Government of Chile, Ministry of the Interior, Supreme Decree No. 355, May 9, 1990, art. 1.

6   Ibid.

7   Ibid.

8   National Truth and Reconciliation Commission, *Final Report*, 3 vols. (Santiago: CNVR, 1991).

9   Ibid., 2:1263.

10   Ibid., 2:1263–64.

11   The PIIE is a Chilean NGO that has been working for over forty years to foster the construction of policies that promote equity and quality in education with a participatory human rights focus. See http://www.piie.cl.

12   Mirtha Abraham and Maria T. Rodas, "La formación docente y los objetivos transversales" [Teacher Training and Crosscutting Objectives], *Pensamiento educativo: revista de investigación educacional Latinoamericana* [Educational Thought: Latin American Journal of Educational Research] 22, no. 1 (2011): 321–44.

13   National Truth and Reconciliation Commission, *Final Report*, 2:426.

14   Chile, Law No. 19,123, *Official Gazette*, February 8, 1992.

15   The corporation received 2,188 complaints, of which 899 were considered to qualify as human rights violations. Adding the cases considered by the report of the National Truth and Reconciliation Commission brought the total of qualified cases to 3,195. National Reparation and Reconciliation Corporation, *Report on the Qualification of Victims of Human Rights Violations and Political Violence* (Santiago: CNRR, 1996), 28.

16   Chile, Law No. 19,441, *Official Gazette*, January 23, 1996.

17   These NGOs included the Vicariate of Solidarity, the Chilean Human Rights

Commission, the Interdisciplinary Program for Research in Education, the People's Rights Commission, the Chilean Pro-United Nations Association, the Vicariate of the Social Pastoral, and the Human Rights Education Institute.

18   The 900 Schools Program (P900) was an education program created by the first democratic government to benefit the nine hundred most vulnerable schools in the country with respect to education quality, infrastructure, teaching staff, and students. The texts that were distributed to the libraries and the schools in the program are listed in appendix 5.1.

19   Elizabeth Lira, "The Reparations Policy for Human Rights Violations in Chile," in *The Handbook of Reparations*, ed. Pablo de Greiff (Oxford: Oxford University Press, 2006), 61.

20   About this process see Lira, "The Reparations Policy for Human Rights Violations in Chile."

21   Supreme Decree No. 1,040 of September 26, 2003, *Official Gazette*, November 11, 2003.

22   National Commission on Political Imprisonment and Torture, *Report* (Santiago: CNPPT, 2004).

23   Ibid., 525.

24   Ibid., 528–29.

25   With reference to benefits granted by the state, it is important to note that the complementary education aid provided to cover meal and transportation expenses is administered by the National School Aid and Scholarship Board (an office of the Ministry of Education). This specific benefit is associated with the monthly subsidy received by the children of the victims recognized in the Rettig Report.

26   *Translator's note*: The original Spanish formulation would be "*Beca Titulares Valech*." The term *titulares* can be translated as "holders," but the term "beneficiaries" better captures the intention.

27   Chile, Law No. 19,123, Title IV, arts. 29–31.

28   Chile, Law No. 19,965 of August 18, 2004, *Official Gazette*, August 25, 2004.

29   The Council of Rectors of Chilean Universities coordinates the work of universities in the country autonomously. Created in August 1954, it is made up of the rectors of twenty-five public and traditional universities in the country.

30   Currently, more than a dozen types of education aid are managed by the Ministry of Education, including, in addition to the Reparation Scholarship, the Academic Leveling Scholarship, the Bicentennial Scholarship, the Juan Gómez Millas-Chilenos Scholarship, the New Millennium Scholarship, the Technical Excellence Scholarship, the Disability Scholarship, the Coordination Scholarship, the Academic Excellence Scholarship, the PSU [University Selection Test] Score Scholarship, the Scholarship for Children of Education Professionals, the U. del Mar Relocation Scholarship, the Teacher-Pedagogy Vocation Scholarship, and the University Credit Solidarity Fund Scholarship.

31   Chile, Law No. 19,980, which modifies Law No. 19,123, expanding or establishing benefits for the persons whom it indicates, *Official Gazette*, November 9, 2004.

32   Chile, Law No. 19,992, which establishes reparation scholarships and grants other benefits to the persons whom it indicates, *Official Gazette*, December 24, 2004, Title III, art. 11.

33   Directorate of Student Welfare, *Memoria 2010–2014* (Santiago: Universidad de Chile, 2015), 98.

34   In reference to the updated list published in August 2011. See http://www.indh.cl/informacion-comision-valech.

35   See CIPER Team in Investigative Reporting, "Becas Valech: la trama y los protagonistas del fraude," July 28, 2014, http://ciperchile.cl/2014/07/28/becas-valech-la-trama-y-los-protagonistas-del-fraude, accessed July 21, 2015.

36   Division of Higher Education, Ministry of Education, *Student Finance Report*, 2013 (February 2014 ed.), 50 and 51. The quintiles provide a way of classifying families on the basis of their incomes. To determine the quintile to which a family group belongs, the average income must be calculated, considering the number of people who live in the home, with quintile 1 being the lowest and 5 the highest on the scale.

37   Based on the Higher Education Information Service (SIES) classification. See http://www.mifuturo.cl.

38   Division of Higher Education, Ministry of Education, *Student Finance Report*, 50 and 51.

39   Ibid.

40   Chile, Project of Law (Mensaje) 312–63 of May 12, 2015.

CHAPTER 6

Education as Redress in South Africa: Opening the Doors of Learning to All

Teboho Moja

The motto of the United Negro College Fund—"A mind is a terrible thing to waste"[1]—encouraging the provision of education to all, represents the opposite of the apartheid system's approach to the education of African children in South Africa.

Even before apartheid began in 1948, Africans[2] in South Africa were denied a basic right to education by a government that paid little attention to providing it to them. It left this responsibility mainly to various religious groups, which took it upon themselves to provide most of the education Africans received. Under the apartheid system, the government took this deprivation a step further by legislating the closing of even that door to good-quality education. It introduced an education system specifically designed for the African majority population, took over responsibility of it from religious groups, and banned Africans from studying at institutions that provided education to white students.

The African education system, called Bantu education, was formally introduced in 1954, following the recommendations of the Eislen Commission and the passing of the Bantu Education Act in 1953. While the government provided free, compulsory, and good-quality education to the white section of the population, the Bantu Education Act relegated Africans to a system that provided inferior education, limited in scope and underfunded by the government. The education reforms that followed the election of South Africa's first democratic government in 1994, under which segregation became unconstitutional, were intended to ensure these past injustices would be addressed and transitional justice would be embedded in the new system.

In South Africa under the apartheid system, human rights violations were directed toward the majority of the population, with the minority as the beneficiary. The white population was made to believe it was the "chosen and superior race." As a result, the entire nation was denied its rights, especially in terms of freedom of thought and association and interaction with one another, through social engineering and the reorganization of the land into black areas and white areas. Africans experienced further, specific violations of basic rights through exclusion from education and health services and by being stripped of citizenship in their own country. In this sense, policies of redress are rightfully targeted mainly to Africans. The biggest group of beneficiaries consists of poor Africans, based on the understanding that apartheid policies contributed to their poverty.

In December 1995, following the first democratic elections, a Truth and Reconciliation Commission (TRC) was established to address past injustices by revealing the truth regarding human rights violations under the apartheid system and to reconcile a divided nation. Paul van Zyl, former executive secretary of the TRC, suggested the basic obligations of states in addressing past human rights abuses included both the reform of state institutions to ensure abuses did not happen again and the taking of steps to provide victims with reparations for the harm they had suffered.[3]

With regard to education, however, the provision of it by the new government of South Africa would not in itself completely fulfill its responsibility to the victims. Education is a fundamental human right;[4] if people are denied it, their rights are violated. The legacy of apartheid left huge disparities between blacks and whites in terms of available education and the economic benefits and privileges that accrue from its attainment. To rectify those disparities would require extraordinary measures, analogous to the extraordinary measures used to achieve other kinds of justice for victims and a transition from an oppressive and violent society to a peaceful and democratic one.

It is in this light that I interpret the post-apartheid reforms in education in South Africa as mechanisms of redress. Justice was to be served through institutional reform, with the state putting into place an education system that would address past injustices; once this system was in place, increased funding levels would ensure justice was actually delivered. Funding allocations would provide financial assistance, both for access to education and for improving the quality of the education received. These reforms have a reparative element to them, in that they are aimed at repairing some of the harm done through the apartheid system, which is why I interpret them as a type of "redress." At the same time, however, they are distinct from an administrative "reparation" program, which did exist in South Africa, such as would generally be understood to provide material benefits to a (usually) small group of victims of human rights violations, individually or collectively. Education reform in South Africa was not articulated as reparation, but it does function as a form of redress.

This chapter addresses education reform as a measure of redress for the majority of children in South Africa, focusing on access and funding issues in the schools and in higher education. Institutional reform in transitional justice commonly refers to state institutions in the security and justice sectors, but here the concept is extended to include the education sector. The rationale is that institutional reform commonly seeks to prevent the repetition of past injustices and to change culture and structures, often benefiting large numbers of people indirectly but not targeting victims specifically.[5] In South Africa's education sector, these elements of institutional reform are addressed as part of transitional justice. Education has been offered through a reformed education system to the majority of those who were excluded in the past and to their children.

The chapter begins with a discussion of the need for both individual and collective redress through education, followed by a brief overview of the education system in South Africa; a description of the reforms that were implemented as a way of providing programs, benefits, and assistance that are interpreted as redress; an analysis of the implementation of those programs; and, last, an interpretation of what has been achieved, as well as the overall impact on the broader society.

EDUCATION AND REDRESS IN SOUTH AFRICA

South Africa as a transitional justice and education case study has two distinctive features. First, unlike many other countries where justice has focused on individuals, in South Africa it has been pursued as both an individual and a collective response to the masses of people affected. Second, because of how long South Africa took to create a democratic country, the target groups for redress through education have been not only the children who were directly affected, but also their offspring. Policies promoting access to good education have targeted the children of those adults who were deprived of their basic rights.

The rationale for collective redress was that the apartheid system excluded Africans as a group from benefiting from the country's resources. They were offered only limited opportunities for education and were systemically prevented from receiving education of good quality. Often, African children even missed out on those inferior opportunities that did exist, as they rejected the system and spent time out of school in protest. Student organizations that organized the protests adopted the slogan, "Liberation Before Education," and prioritized their political freedom over the poor education that was offered to them. Masses of students, teachers, and academics were arrested, tortured, and harassed, and some left the country to join the liberation movements. Police set up camps on some black university premises, and one, the University of the North (as it was known then; it is currently the University of Limpopo), was occupied by the military, with academics and students under constant surveillance. In addressing human rights violations, reforms had to take these past experiences into consideration.

Generally, individual reparations were offered to the direct victims of gross violations identified by the TRC. The TRC had, by its closing date in 2002, only 18,000 people registered and qualified as victims, identified as those directly affected as well as their relatives and dependents; it later identified an additional 8,000 who had missed the deadline. Registered victims qualified for the Individual Reparation Grant (IRG), which was supposed to consist of a lump sum of money paid out over six years.[6] According to the policy proposed, the IRG was to be paid "to each victim to meet the needs which they have identified, such as medical, education and housing needs."[7] Other proposed benefits for individuals included death certificates; exhumations, reburials, and ceremonies; headstones and tombstones; declarations of death; the clearing of criminal records; and the resolution of outstanding legal matters related to the violations.[8]

In 2003 and 2004, the South African government provided victims with only one-off payments of R30,000.[9] These relatively small individual reparations remain contested. Furthermore, the definition of "victim" in South Africa is debatable because, while many people were affected in the most extreme ways—through death, detention, and torture—many more were affected by human rights abuses that were committed against the nation as a whole. The TRC therefore recommended collective reparations to benefit entire communities and even the nation as a whole. They were symbolic, and divided into, first, community benefits, which took the form of the renaming of streets and facilities, the dedication of memorials and monuments, and the performance of cultural ceremonies; and, second, national benefits, which were similar to community benefits but on a larger scale, including a national day of remembrance and reconciliation.[10]

Education as a form of redress—the main focus of this chapter—preceded the work of the TRC. Redress through education was included in the South African constitution of 1996 in its bill of rights, although it was not referred to as "reparation." The understanding of education reforms as part of an overall approach to redress, however, emerged first from the inclusion of education in the collective reparations recommended by the TRC in addition to other social services, such as health care, mental health services, and housing.[11] The South African government opted to redress the inequalities, adopting policies that were pro-poor, with the poor population largely overlapping with the black majority. In this way, it linked poverty to past apartheid policies that denied the majority population the right to education, jobs, and economic prosperity. In sum, for the democratically elected government to fulfill its obligation to provide education, it needed to address the existing disparities in society.

It is important to note that "redress" was listed as the first of the five norms in the recommendations of the TRC's Reparations and Rehabilitation Committee. It was also a buzzword in policy documents and a key principle in the Reconstruction and Development Program document adopted by government in 1994. Policy research papers, such as those produced by the National Education Coordinating Committee (NECC) and the National Commission on Higher Education (NCHE)—bodies on which this author served—put a lot of emphasis on the need for redress to eliminate past injustices, setting it as a goal whose achievement depended on the provision of adequate funding.[12] Government policy documents, including a white paper on higher education (1997) and the "National Plan for Higher Education" (2001), framed policy around the need for redress.[13] As a result, redress policies were put into place in targeted areas, including education, specifically to address past injustices. In its first five years, for example, the new government redistributed available resources within the Education Department by cutting funding for those who had benefited from the apartheid system and redirecting it to the poorest of the poor.

The apartheid system had implemented Bantu Education as a tool to entrench poverty in the African community. The recognition of the reciprocal power of education to address poverty formed the basis on which the TRC recommended the setting up of institutions to allow those who missed out on education to continue their studies; the building and improvement of schools; and the provision of education support to those who needed it.[14] Again—as indicated above—while these government proposals might be perceived as providing a service that is a basic government responsibility to all citizens, not a form of reparation to be targeted at those who suffered under apartheid, the difference here is that the previous government's divisive and oppressive education system was to be transformed to one that would benefit Africans. I argue, therefore, that the proposed changes to the education system were a necessary form of redress to eliminate inequities imposed by apartheid education and to address the suffering of academics and students who were often detained, had their learning and teaching materials banned and their telephones tapped, and were harassed by the police.[15] The difference between "redress" and "social services" may largely be one of labeling or discourse, but the message it sends in terms of an acknowledgment of past injustice can be important in fostering the trust of citizens in the new system.

Institutional reforms in South Africa included the reform of the entire education system, a process that continues to date and includes a broad range of beneficiaries. The discussion here is limited to two broad categories of beneficiaries, the first of which is society. The literature suggests that the more educated a population is, the more likely it is to participate in a meaningful way in politics and promote democratic governance. South Africa's democracy is hard earned and needs to be sustained. Furthermore, the education system was reformed to address social justice issues and reap the benefits to be accrued in terms of the public good. A well-educated population with the necessary skills, especially at the higher levels, enables the country to become more competitive in a global economy. The higher education system was reformed not only with redress as a goal, but also to position the country advantageously in the broader world and to boost a failing economy.

The second group of beneficiaries—individuals who did not have the benefit of access to good education and those who had access to education loaded with an apartheid ideology—includes both black and white South Africans who are not necessarily poor. As these individuals are now adults, the beneficiaries are their children. The reformed system allows children to learn side by side and get to know their fellow citizens. Schools have been "de-racialized," and the formerly white schools have black students, even though some have experienced "white flight." Despite the reforms, however, formerly black schools remain mainly black because of their geographical locations and lack of basic resources. More people can gain access to good education, and they have had doors of opportunity opened to them for future employment and upward mobility in society; but significant challenges remain, as will be discussed below.

THE EDUCATION SYSTEM IN SOUTH AFRICA

The education system in South Africa has undergone a major transformation since the 1994 democratic elections. The Nationalist Party, elected in 1948 on a ticket of racial segregation and discrimination, had institutionalized racism and passed laws that limited the rights of Africans in South Africa. It set up a "homeland" system of government that divided the black community into different ethnic groups comprising Africans, colored (mixed race) people, and Indians; Africans were divided further into nine tribal groups. The government allocated barren pieces of land to these groups and declared the newly set-up, economically unproductive territories as self-governing, and then declared four of them as "independent countries" that would receive funding from South Africa as "foreign aid." Such actions ended up stripping most people of their natural citizenship, resources, and rights.

In 1954, with the passage of the Bantu Education Act, the government began systematically and progressively to take over schools that had been started by religious organizations for Africans and turn them into government schools. Nineteen separate departments of education were set up along the same lines as the territories. In 1959, the Extension of University Act made provision for the racial segregation of universities. The government claimed its plan to segregate education racially provided a "separate but equal system" for blacks.

Although the 1976 Soweto uprisings are often cited as one of the "epitomic" points in the struggle for education and freedom, we need to remember that systematic exclusions began with the segregation of apartheid when the Bantu Education Act was passed. Teachers and students protested against Bantu Education from the time it was introduced. The defiance campaign included calls to teachers to reject it and offer better education, even if that meant outside classroom times. The Mass Democratic Movement (MDM), begun in 1986, attempted to design and offer a parallel, informal, and alternative education system, referred to as "The People's Education." The idea was to promote people's education for people's power and to provide education to the children who were protesting on the streets because schools had by then become totally dysfunctional. The protest left the school system in desperate need of reform and, in 1994, the government committed to undertaking it.

Post-apartheid transitional justice, therefore, included institutional reform of the education sector, the dismantling of the nineteen racially divided departments of education, and the creation of one national and nine provincial departments of education. Schools were declared nonracial and opened up to all races. Masses of unqualified and underqualified teachers were offered programs to prepare them to offer better education, and the curriculum was reformed, prioritizing the removal of offensive material from textbooks and the creation of new learning materials. Educator to learner ratios were set at one to forty in the primary schools and one to thirty-five in the secondary schools. Surplus teachers, who were largely in the formerly white or well-resourced schools, were redeployed to the poor schools. Below I review the reformed education system, which was transformed to open up access for those who were excluded in the past.

POST-REFORM R–12 EDUCATION

The reformed education system currently is divided into grade reception[16] to grade 6 for primary school, grades 7 to 9 for junior secondary, and grades 10 to 12 for senior secondary. In 1996, education at the elementary and junior secondary schooling levels was made free and compulsory for all children ages seven to fifteen years, or up to the completion of grade 9.[17] Following completion of grade 9 at the age of sixteen years, learners can opt to continue with senior secondary school, which is neither free nor compulsory, for academic preparation for higher education; or they can take an alternative route through Technical and Vocational Education and Training (TVET), which until November 2013 was known as Further Education and Training (FET). TVET is mainly vocational in nature, but it offers options to pursue higher education. It is offered at a range of institutions that include TVET colleges, technical colleges, and community colleges.

The education system is decentralized, with the national Department of Basic Education and the nine provincial departments of education having concurrent powers. The responsibility of the national government is to set policy and maintain norms and standards for all aspects of education, including a common curriculum, the structure of education, and teachers' salaries and qualifications. The provincial governments set provincial priorities but implement national policies.

Since major inequities exist among provinces due to the historical division of the country into the racially and ethnically based homeland system, redress starts with the distribution of national resources to the provinces. Funding allocations, determined through an "equitable shares formula," take into consideration the past injustices and inequities created by apartheid. With respect to education, the inequities are in school enrollment figures, income generated by local governments, and other special considerations that must be taken into account to equalize funding for the entire population of the country.

TECHNICAL AND VOCATIONAL EDUCATION AND TRAINING (PREVIOUSLY KNOWN AS FURTHER EDUCATION AND TRAINING, OR FET)

TVET is the second track (the first being academic) in the post-apartheid public education system, designed to provide education to out-of-school youth and adults. A January 2014 policy paper from the Department of Higher Education and Training (the Department of Education was divided in 2009 into the Department of Basic Education and the Department of Higher Education and Training) listed education and social justice as the department's first objective:

Much remains to be done to rid our country of the injustices of its colonial and apartheid past. Deep-seated inequalities are rooted in our past;
it is not by accident that the remaining disparities of wealth, educational
access and attainment, health status and access to opportunities are still
largely based on race and gender.[18]

In 2012, 657,690 students were enrolled in public FET institutions,[19] and fifty
TVET colleges in the country are following major reforms to consolidate and
merge 150 smaller colleges.

As part of redressing past inequities, the government committed R1.9 billion in 2005 to recapitalizing and refurbishing the colleges and provided a bur-
sary fund in the amount of R1 billion, and it continues to fund them at a cost
of R4 billion per year. It is important to note that the financial aid to this sector
is provided as grants and not loans.[20] The allocation of funds was based on the
historical underfunding of the colleges attended mainly by black students. A
notion of redress underpinned various aspects of the reforms in the sector; for
example, the executive summary of the government paper "Redress in the FET
Sector Focussing on Curriculum"[21] opens with a statement on the damaging
influence of the pre-1994 conditions in politics and education in South Africa.
Furthermore, Naledi Pandor, the minister of education at the time, based the
development of the FET Act of 2006 on redress principles that sought to correct past injustices and stated that public funds should be concentrated on
training for the historically disadvantaged.[22]

Policy and research papers refer to an estimated three million youth as
"persons who are not in education, employment, or training" (NEETs) and
are a concern for social and political reasons. This population so far has not
benefited from the changes that took place post apartheid. Its members are
likely to be children of parents who missed out on education themselves, of
parents who are poor and cannot afford to keep them in the school system,
or of parents who died due to the poor health services provided by the apartheid system. Although the government does not directly apply the concept of
reparation to this group, it recognizes that its members' disadvantaged situation is due to historical inequity and discriminatory practices. It is in this light
that I interpret as redress the reforms that provide them with opportunities
for education and jobs through the TVET sector and through startup funds
allocated by the youth-managed National Youth Development Agency. The
government's goal was to enroll about one million of these youth by 2014,
in the hope of helping to lift them out of poverty and allow for social mobility. Various policy papers on education recognize that vocational education

contributes to social inclusion and poverty reduction and improves chances for employment.

HIGHER EDUCATION

Higher education in South Africa is provided by a national system that has been transformed through mergers and now comprises twenty-five universities, with plans to establish one more. They include eleven traditional universities, eight universities of technology, and six comprehensive universities. Distance learning has also been transformed to open up access to higher education. The system grants a broad range of qualifications, from certificates and diplomas to doctoral degrees.

In 1997, the Department of Education released Education White Paper 3, "A Programme for the Transformation of Higher Education," which articulated a vision for individuals and institutions in higher education, underpinned by the principles of equity and redress. It called for

> a transformed, democratic, non-racial and non-sexist system of higher education that will . . . promote equity of access and fair chances of success to all who are seeking to realise their potential through higher education, while eradicating all forms of unfair discrimination and advancing redress of past inequalities. . . .
>
> The principle of equity requires fair opportunities both to enter higher education programmes and to succeed in them. Applying the principle of equity implies, on the one hand, a critical identification of existing inequalities which are the product of policies, structures and practices based on racial, gender, disability and other forms of discrimination or disadvantage and on the other a programme of transformation with a view to redress. Such transformation involves not only abolishing all existing forms of unjust differentiation, but also measures of empowerment, including financial support to bring about equal opportunity for individuals and institutions.[23]

The goal was to open access to high-quality education to those who historically had been denied their basic rights.

Statistics regarding student enrollment and group participation since that goal was set indicate the degree of progress toward it. In 2010, 892,936 students were enrolled in the higher education system, with staff totaling 127,969, of whom 46,579 were academic staff.[24] The gross enrollment increased from

576,868 in 1996 to 938,204 in 2011. The participation rate of Africans—the percentage of the African population enrolled—increased from 10 percent to 16 percent, while their share of headcount enrollment—the number of students in the system—increased from 53 percent to 69 percent. Although the headcount share of white students decreased from 34 percent to 19 percent, their participation rate remained more or less the same, at 57 percent in 1996 and 56 percent in 2011.[25]

In short, reforms in the higher education sector have increased access for many, opening the doors of learning to students from disadvantaged communities, but more can and should be done.

EDUCATION ACCESS AND FUNDING AS REDRESS

Since the South African TRC recommended reparations for the collective community in areas such as health care, mental health, housing, and education, social services have been provided to the nation as a whole that give more benefits to those who were previously discriminated against and denied those services. Whether the services offered are, in fact, "reparations"—that is, whether they are provided as compensation to victims or not—is contested. The concept of redress in education has assumed shifting meanings, as Teresa Barnes highlights:

> Redress became a blanket code and had different implications at different times for different people in South African higher education. The meanings of this term in use at any one time ranged from "rectifying the wrong" to "reparations" to "restoring equality" to "empowerment."[26]

Given the inclusion of collective reparations among the recommendations made by the TRC, as well as the need expressed in policy documents for the implementation of programs according to the principle of redress, the provision of certain services is interpreted here as a measure of redress for past injustices. These include services previously unavailable to the majority of South Africans, such as adequate housing, social grants, good health services, and education.

Education can, therefore, be seen as a service provided and a sector reformed as part of an effort to address inequities in a system created by apartheid. In South Africa, the entire state budget is directed at redressing the past, with no set period for the redress and equity goals to be achieved due to the mammoth task of implementing those policies for the majority of the nation. This could be seen as a weakness in the strategy because there are neither clear targets nor time frames for achieving the set goals.

The slogan driving education reforms as a form of redress was that "the doors of learning will be opened for all." The goal, as stated in various policy papers, was to address past injustices, to make education accessible, and to fund it at higher levels so good education would be available to all citizens, as a basic right protected by the bill of rights in South Africa's 1996 constitution. To provide it, the country committed to spending more on education. According to the latest available figures, 6.23 percent of gross domestic product (GDP) went to education in 2013,[27] and for 2014–15 about 20 percent of total government spending was allocated to it.[28]

Redress and equity have been cornerstones of education funding policies during the post-apartheid era, in recognition that the less than equal allocations for Africans in the past meant less than equal outcomes in education. In the last education budget of the apartheid system, a white child was allocated per capita expenditure of R5,403, as compared to an African child's allocation of R1,053.[29] Post-apartheid funding was, therefore, allocated on the basis of providing individual redress, which took the form of exemptions from paying tuition fees in the basic education sector and provision of financial aid at higher education levels, and institutional redress, with poor schools allocated more funding than well-resourced ones so they would not have to collect tuition. Redress for formerly African higher education institutions was accomplished through the allocation of additional funds.

As exemption from them implies, the fees schools charge constitute an important issue in access to education. The South African Schools Act of 1996 (SASA) allows school governing bodies (SGBs) to charge fees to supplement government allocations. The SGBs determine the fees for their schools, and the information is often unavailable publicly unless one inquires at each school. A 2012 newspaper report stated that some parent bodies at elite public schools had raised the fees to more than R30,000 per year, to which the minister of education responded that those SGBs were privatizing public education.[30] The fees in such schools are as high as degree fees at universities and only affordable for the middle class (including the African middle class). In the post-apartheid era, however, public education for the first nine years of schooling in South Africa is free to learners whose parents can provide evidence that they cannot afford to pay school fees. In other words, children from poor families are exempt from paying fees. This policy recognizes that the poverty of many black families is due to apartheid, and the government has adopted it among other pro-poor policies to redress those injustices. The policy also exempts from fees orphans, children in foster care, and children of parents who receive social grants. Social grants are offered in six categories—disability, old age, care dependence, foster child, child support, and war veterans—and have been introduced post apartheid as a way to redistribute wealth and create a more equitable society.

The fee exemption policy, though, is very complex, and poor parents often do not understand how the system works and how they can apply for the exemption. Effectively, a family whose combined income is less than thirty times the annual school fees is exempt from paying the fees; but the wording of the policy is confusing, as is its division of exempt families into two not-so-distinct categories. Moreover, the elite public schools have indirect ways of excluding poor students so they can avoid dealing with exemptions from the high fees they charge. This is done discreetly by not admitting those students in the first place, since schools have flexibility on whom to admit.

In 2006, the government introduced a policy of "no-fee schools" for poor neighborhoods after a 2003 review of the financing and resourcing of schools implied that those in poor areas were receiving very little income from fees charged to the families they served.[31] Schools were classified into five quintiles based on the economic situations of their locations. The government increased grants to "no-fee" schools as an incentive to stop them from charging poor families fees.

The criteria for classification as no-fee schools are based on rates of income, unemployment, and illiteracy within the school catchment area. Funding allocation per capita in 2009 ranged from R807 at Quintile 1 schools, which are the poorest, to R134 at Quintile 5 schools, which are the least poor.[32] In 2014, schools in the first three quintiles, classified as no-fee schools, accounted for 60 percent of the classified schools.[33] Although parents are exempt from paying tuition fees, other costs that affect access to good-quality education are not covered, such as costs of uniforms and transportation, registration fees, administration fees, and fees for additional subjects. SGBs are empowered to take legal action against parents who do not qualify for the exemption and fail to pay fees. Another problem is that some corrupt school leaders continue to charge fees at no-fee schools.

For individual redress, funding was given as study grants to TVET (then FET) and higher education students. The National Student Financial Aid Scheme (NSFAS) was introduced in 1995 to provide higher education loans and scholarships to poor students. Starting with a meager R20 million, set aside soon after the new government was constituted in 1994,[34] the scheme had R441 million by the time it was formalized in 1999, and in 2013 it stood at R8.2 billion.[35] The NSFAS is administered jointly with higher education institutions. A provision of the grant is that students who pass and make progress have 40 percent of their loans forgiven and transformed into scholarships. Students can also apply for scholarships in areas of specialization, such as teaching or social work, or based on other criteria, including disability.

Access in itself is insufficient as redress, since poor performance in education was among the effects of apartheid policies. As a result, the government put into place a plan referred to as "Action Plan to 2014" for basic education, which aimed to improve learning by providing a curriculum focused on numeracy and literacy. The government also planned to track progress through standardized assessment tests in grades 3, 6, and 9, ensure access to textbooks, improve school infrastructure and teacher skills, and strengthen school leadership and management. The overall goal was to improve access to basic schooling and its quality, in part as a means of improving access to higher education,[36] and to put the students on a path out of poverty.

Opening the doors to higher education has achieved limited success: as mentioned above, black enrollment has increased overall and, as of 2011, had nearly doubled since 1994, even though the overall participation rate—the percentage of the African population enrolled in higher education—was still very low. Higher Education South Africa (HESA) casts the situation in a more positive light, reporting that African, colored, and Indian students together that year comprised 80 percent of the total student population of 938,200.[37] Despite the reforms, I would argue that the capacity of the higher education system in itself is a major stumbling block to increasing participation of Africans, since the system cannot absorb more students. Ultimately, the gap between white and African participation is still very wide in the country; as of 2012, African participation rates, at 16 percent, lagged behind those of whites at 55 percent and Indians at 47 percent.[38]

Other challenges are emerging, even for those students to whom the doors have been opened, highlighting the mammoth task of redressing past inequalities deliberately created through an apartheid system. Students coming from poor family backgrounds, for example, find themselves dealing with fundamental issues such as hunger even while enrolled in higher education institutions. The NSFAS support covers their tuition and residence fees, plus an allowance for food, books, and transportation, but for students with few or no other resources to fall back on, the allowance may be inadequate.

THE PROCESS OF REFORM AS REDRESS

To redress past injustices, South Africa implemented systemwide institutional reform rather than short-term programmatic reform. Policy reform processes that began during apartheid under the auspices of the Mass Democratic Movement have informed many of the decisions and reforms implemented in the education sector since the transition to democracy. One of these began with the Freedom Charter, adopted on June 25 and 26, 1955, which states,

> The doors of learning and of culture shall be opened!
>
> The government shall discover, develop and encourage national talent for the enhancement of our cultural life; All the cultural treasures of mankind shall be open to all, by free exchange of books, ideas and contact with other lands; The aim of education shall be to teach the youth to love their people and their culture, to honour human brotherhood, liberty and peace; Education shall be free, compulsory, universal and equal for all children; Higher education and technical training shall be opened to all by means of state allowances and scholarships awarded on the basis of merit; Adult illiteracy shall be ended by a mass state education plan; Teachers shall have all the rights of other citizens; The color bar in cultural life, in sport and in education shall be abolished.[39]

Fast-forwarding to the 1990s takes us to the process initiated by the National Education Crisis Committee (NECC), which was formed during the freedom struggle years when children were out of school, protesting in the streets, and burning the schools. NECC set up a project called the National Education Policy Initiative (NEPI), in which a broad range of about three hundred volunteer researchers conducted initial policy research covering all sectors of education. The thirteen reports[40] produced through the Mass Democratic Movement and managed by NECC informed most of the policies that were adopted after 1994. Many activists who were involved, including the author of this chapter, became part of the new government. Other major stakeholders in education reform were consulted in what was a democratic process; they included representatives of students at the high school and higher education levels, faculty and staff associations at universities, and teacher and worker unions. Policy proposals were released to the stakeholders and the general public for comments before the policies were formalized.

The provisions for redressing past inequities and injustices are included in South Africa's 1996 constitution, the most progressive adopted by the

country, and the right to education is articulated in the bill of rights section. The Department of Education released its first white paper, entitled the
"Department of Education White Paper on Education and Training," in March
1995; its main focus was primary and secondary education, although it discussed adult basic education as well. The South African Schools Act of 1996
was then passed to address past inequities in funding and access by setting
up a uniform system of education for all children in the country. The relevant
policy papers listed redress and equity as the first principle informing these
decisions. The higher education process began with the appointment of the
National Commission on Higher Education in 1995; following its recommendations, Education White Paper 3, "A Programme for the Transformation of
Higher Education" (mentioned above), was released in 1997.

Redress through education for past injustices underpinned a lot of thinking
before the transition to democracy and continued to inform most policies formulated soon after. As Barnes stated regarding historically black institutions
(HBIs), "They should receive redress because of the contribution that they had
made to South Africa's liberation struggle. One of the powerful versions of
redress discourse relied heavily on a notion of the HBIs as centers of resistance
to apartheid."[41] Redress was framed in terms of policies to promote access and
equity for all sectors of education. In October 1996, a consultative document
was circulated to the Advisory Committee of Universities and Technikons that
outlined the priorities of basic redress funding, with a proposed amount of
R498 million. Before democracy the need for redress had been debated, and
key stakeholders in higher education reached a consensus on the need to set
aside funds for distribution to the historically black institutions, as long as this
did not reduce the funds that would be allocated to the rest of the institutions
in the system.[42]

As discussed, redress through funding was implemented in two ways: institutional redress for historically black institutions and individual redress in the
form of student financial aid and academic support programs for students
who were ill prepared for higher education. The initial redress monies were
allocated because historically black institutions found themselves in a crisis in
1990 due to high student debt and historical underfunding and were on the
verge of closure. The National Commission on Higher Education (NCHE) recommended that a program of institutional redress should follow a comprehensive institutional audit, and that redress funding should be drawn from an
earmarked portion of the institutional funding. The report further suggested
redress funds be used to modernize fixed assets of the institutions or be added
to their current budgets for other needs.[43]

Policy proposals were adopted in 1997, but only in 2004 did the government finally come up with a new funding formula for higher education that included equity as one of its five main goals. The process for change had been slow for reasons that included lack of capacity and skills to develop new mechanisms, as well as the scope of the problems that had to be addressed. Changes in leadership every five years also led to delays in implementing new policies, as new ministers of education had first to familiarize themselves with the issues in the sector and reaffirm priorities in the system.

The other component addressed by the new formula was quality, which was to be achieved by linking funding to success rates, as compared to the previous approach, which funded the number of students in the system despite their performance levels. Soon after the transition to democracy, however, funding for the school sector was revised, and the government adopted a pro-poor approach to funding schools. The funding mechanism was changed yet again soon thereafter, with block allocations determined by the national government distributed to provinces, which then decided on the further distribution of the funds to different sectors of society. Disparities in fiscal capacity among provinces have led to gaps in the amounts of tax revenue they can generate. To mediate that inequity, the government uses an Equitable Share Formula based on demographic and social criteria to allocate funds to the nine provinces.

SUCCESSES, FAILURES, AND AREAS STILL IN NEED OF ATTENTION

R–12

The outcomes of the reforms in R–12 education discussed in this chapter have been mixed: access to education has improved, but quality and success rates have been low. For example, while access rates have risen, students drop out in large numbers, and there are no clear indicators that learning is taking place.[44] The performance of students in the sector is so poor that, despite their being passed to gain university admission, Ramphele has referred to them as "another generation betrayed."[45] Past inequalities are hard to eradicate within two decades in a system of education apartheid that continues to disadvantage children from disadvantaged groups, the majority of whom are black.[46]

Children from poor families remain disadvantaged due to systemic issues that have not been completely resolved. For many, for example, access to education continues to be limited to schools that do not compare to other schools in terms of resources, both human and nonhuman. Access was promoted through a policy that declared all children were to be educated at schools in their immediate vicinities. For children in poor areas, however, that has meant continued access to schools in very poor condition and in short supply of libraries, laboratories, sports grounds, classrooms, and books. Furthermore, "neighborhood" schools are often located far away from their homes, requiring long commutes. Some children miss school because of the absence from their homes of parents or other adults who work far away, again due to past laws dividing living areas along racial lines, or who die prematurely from AIDS or illnesses related to work in industries that affect their health, such as mining.

FET

The FET sector, established to provide training and skills to the majority of youth whose education is only to grade 9, has recorded very high failure rates. As of 2009, many youth reportedly were not gaining access to the FET colleges, and those who did often failed out.[47]

HIGHER EDUCATION

Access to good education remains a challenge in the entire higher education system. One indication of this is that, despite more students' having access to education opportunities that did not exist before, the formerly black schools and colleges remain predominantly black. The institutions have improved in terms of the resources provided to them, but those resources still do not match what is available at formerly white institutions; because the disparities were so major to begin with, there seems to be no way of truly equalizing. Redress, then, in some ways has only symbolically addressed past discrimination. The formerly white institutions have places for students of all backgrounds and continue to be the standard bearers by default.

Completion rates are also an indicator of success or failure for access policies. The data available for all students, irrespective of race, indicate higher education students are dropping out at a high rate and taking a long time to graduate. For example, according to data based on a cohort admitted in 2000, only 30 percent graduated after five years, and 56 percent left the institution without graduating.[48] Another set of data indicates that, of a cohort admitted in 2006 to pursue three- and four-year qualifications, only 35 percent had graduated at the end of five years.[49] The interpretation of these data leads one to the conclusion that, despite efforts to redress past inequalities, the students are underprepared due to inadequate previous schooling; and it is safe to assume the situation is worse for black students than for their white counterparts.

In short, the government has done well in improving access to education, but quality remains a challenge, as students leave school underprepared for studies at the higher education level.

CONCLUSION: THE CONTRIBUTION OF EDUCATION REFORM TO PEACEBUILDING

Education was used as a weapon for the destruction of the minds of all South Africans under the apartheid system. White children were taught through a curriculum that supported the apartheid ideology of white supremacy, while black children were taught through a curriculum that tried to force them to accept an inferior position in society. It stands to reason that a new and transformed government would want to use education once more as a tool to undo past injustices for the good of all in South Africa and to free the minds of all, both black and white.

It is no longer strange in South Africa to see schools that are de-racialized, particularly those that served the extremely conservative part of the nation. The writer paid a visit to one of those schools recently, and the contrast from the past was stark. For example, seeing black children in a school that still had at its entrance a huge bust of Hendrik Verwoerd was staggering. As the minister of African affairs, Verwoerd was considered the primary architect of apartheid and introduced policies that denied Africans access to good education. He is known for having said, "It is disservice to provide Africans with education—what does he need it for?"[50] Some progress has been made, but a lot more remains to be done.

Inequities in South Africa remain despite efforts by the government to reduce them. South Africa had a high per capita income of US$6,086.45 in 2014,[51] but also a Gini coefficient of 0.63, which indicates the fourth-highest inequity rate in the world.[52] Poverty in rural areas persists, affecting access to good-quality education and access to higher education as a means to employment and upward mobility. Children in rural areas are still underperforming in education, despite government attempts to improve schooling and quality issues. Challenges facing the school sector have been documented and directly relate to students, teachers, resources, leadership, school governance, and problems that spill in from outside the school, such as violence. All these factors contribute to the poor performance of the system. More students attend school, but few learn and succeed so they can continue with education at the tertiary level.

In the 1970s, when schoolchildren were dissatisfied with the low-quality education they were receiving, they walked out of classes and protested in the streets. The unprecedented protests over university fees in South Africa at the end of 2015 are a clear indication of continued dissatisfaction with poor education and with the failure to deliver the promised redress.[53] What we as South Africans acknowledge is a growing gap between the rich and the poor, one that is no longer just between the races. Inequities and dissatisfaction are a recipe for protests and for derailing a peaceful society. Has redress funding fostered greater equity of opportunity in higher education, improved access, and fostered justice? For institutional redress, the efforts made are still not enough to compensate for and to correct the major inequalities created by the education under apartheid. The record for individual redress is much better due to the huge investment the government made in creating a national funding system for poor students to obtain access to higher education.[54] Still, although an improvement over what existed in the past, the individual funding remains inadequate to address past injustices.

The apartheid system created enormous inequities in state expenditures that still pose a major challenge today. Currently, an informal two-tier system of education is in operation—one caters to the wealthy, of whom the majority is white, and the other caters to the poor, of whom the majority is black. Education policies were powerful tools for violating the basic human right to good and meaningful education for the majority of South Africans. It is in this sense that education reform is seen as a means of redress and transitional justice in South Africa. As Barnes argues, "Whether sentimentally or factually based, the concept of redress as 'reparation for the injustices of the past' has had real social power and a hardy life span."[55] The results are a mixed bag of successes and failures, and some, such as Alex Boraine, the former deputy chair of the TRC, argue that more needs to be done to ensure transitional justice is attained in South Africa.

NOTES

1   A slogan developed in 1972 by Forest Young, an executive of the Young and Rubicam advertising agency; see http://www.blackpast.org/aah/united-negro-college-fund-1944.

2   The apartheid classification of blacks in South Africa consisted of Africans, Coloreds (a term used for the mixed-race population), and Indians. Africans were further divided into nine tribal groups. In this chapter, my focus is on Africans, the majority section of the population that suffered the most. I use the term "black" to refer to all three ethnic groups (African, Colored, and Indian).

3   Paul van Zyl, "Dilemmas of Transitional Justice: The Case of South Africa's Truth and Reconciliation Commission," *Journal of International Affairs* 52, no. 2 (1999): 1–21.

4   See United Nations General Assembly, Universal Declaration of Human Rights, A/RES/3/217 A, December 10, 1948, Article 26, http://www.un-documents.net/a3r217a.htm; United Nations General Assembly, International Covenant on Economic Social and Cultural Rights, December 16, 1966, articles 13 and 14, http://www.ohchr.org/Documents/ProfessionalInterest/cescr.pdf; and United Nations General Assembly, Convention on the Rights of the Child, A/RES/44/25, November 20, 1989, articles 28, 29, and 30, http://www.ohchr.org/en/professionalinterest/pages/crc.aspx.

5   Pablo de Greiff, "Reparations and the Role of International Cooperation" (paper presented at Dealing with the Past and Transitional Justice: Creating Conditions for Peace, Human Rights and the Rule of Law, Neuchâtel, Switzerland, October 24–25, 2005, co-organized by the Political Affairs Division IV of the Swiss Federal Department of Foreign Affairs, the Center for Peacebuilding—swisspeace, and the International Center for Transitional Justice), in *Dealing with the Past and Transitional Justice: Creating Conditions for Peace, Human Rights and the Rule of Law*, ed. Mô Bleeker, 2006, 51, http://www.swisspeace.ch/fileadmin/user_upload/Media/Publications/Journals_Articles/Publications_by_staff/Sisson__Jonathan__Dealing_with_the_Past_and_Transitional_Justice.pdf.

6   The number of individuals who qualify for IRGs remains contested, as the Khulumani Support Group counts at least 65,000 victims, based on a broadened definition of victim. International Center for Transitional Justice, "South Africa: New Reparations Plan Embitters Many Victims," June 6, 2011, http://ictj.org/news/south-africa-new-reparations-plan-embitters-many-victims.

7   South African Truth and Reconciliation Commission, *A Summary of Reparation and Rehabilitation Policy, Including Proposals to be Considered by the President*, http://www.justice.gov.za/trc/reparations/summary.htm#who.

8   Ibid.

9   Christopher J. Colvin, "Overview of the Reparations Program in South Africa," in *The Handbook of Reparations*, ed. Pablo de Greiff (Oxford: Oxford University Press, 2006), 209.

10   South African Truth and Reconciliation Commission, *A Summary of Reparation and Rehabilitation Policy.*

11   Truth and Reconciliation Commission, *Truth and Reconciliation Commission of South Africa Report* (Cape Town: Truth and Reconciliation Commission, 1998), vol. 5, 193, http://www.justice.gov.za/trc/report/finalreport/Volume5.pdf.

12   National Education Coordinating Committee (NECC), *National Education Policy Investigation: The Framework Report and Final Report Summaries* (Cape Town: Oxford University Press/NECC, 1993); National Commission on Higher Education (NCHE), *A Framework for Transformation: NCHE Final Report,* January 1996, in particular chapters 5 and 8, http://www.che.ac.za/media_and_publications/other-stakeholder-s-publications/nche-report-framework-transformation-1996.

13   Department of Education, "Education White Paper 3: A Programme for the Transformation of Higher Education," Pretoria, July 1997, http://www.che.ac.za/media_and_publications/legislation/education-white-paper-3-programme-transformation-higher-education; Department of Education, "National Plan for South Africa," Pretoria, February 2001, http://www.cepd.org.za/?q=national_plan_for_higher_education.

14   South African Truth and Reconciliation Commission, *A Summary of Reparation and Rehabilitation Policy.*

15   See Teboho Moja and Nico Cloete, "Transforming Higher Education in South Africa: A New Approach to Governance," *Journal of the Association of African Studies Issue: A Journal of Opinion* 24, no. 1 (1996).

16   Grade reception is the equivalent of kindergarten in the US system.

17   The South African Schools Act (SASA), Act No. 84 of 1996, chapter 2, section 3, no. 1, http://www.education.gov.za/LinkClick.aspx?fileticket=aIolZ6UsZ5U%3D&tabid=185&mid=1828.

18   Department of Higher Education and Training (DHET), "White Paper for Post-School Education and Training," January 2014 (Cabinet approved November 20, 2013), 4, http://www.dhet.gov.za/SiteAssets/Latest%20News/White%20paper%20for%20post-school%20education%20and%20training.pdf.

19   Department of Higher Education and Training, *Statistics on Post-School Education and Training in South Africa: 2012,* 2014, 20, http://www.dhet.gov.za/DHET%20Statistics%20Publication/Statistics%20on%20Post-School%20Education%20and%20Training%20in%20South%20Africa%202012.pdf#search=FET%25202011.

20   Naledi Pandor, "Address by the Minister of Education Naledi Pandor during the South Africa Colleges Principals Organisation Conference," Johannesburg, Department of Education, August 30, 2007.

21   Zaahida Hartley, "Redress in the FET Sector Focussing on Curriculum," Human Capital Planning, Western Cape Education Department, August 2008, 44, http://wced.school.za/home/projects/hcds/strategy/documents/Reflections3_Chapter3.pdf.

22 *Government Gazette*, no. 32010, notice 294, March 16, 2009, 5, 15, http://www.gov.za/sites/
    www.gov.za/files/32010_294.pdf.

23 Department of Education, "Education White Paper 3," sections 1.14, 1.18.

24 Council on Higher Education, "Higher Education in South Africa Data 2010," http://
    www.che.ac.za/media_and_publications/monitoring-and-evaluation/higher-
    education-south-africa-data-2010.

25 Nico Cloete, "A New Look at Demographic Transformation: Comments on Govinder et
    al. (2013)," *South African Journal of Science* 110, no. 1–2 (2014): 2–3, http://www.sajs.co.za/
    sites/default/files/publications/pdf/Cloete_Commentary.pdf.

26 Teresa Barnes, "Changing Discourses and Meanings of Redress in South African Higher
    Education, 1994–2001," *Journal of Asian and African Studies* 41 (2006): 149–70.

27 Trading Economics, "Public Spending on Education—Total (% of GDP) in South Africa,"
    2016, http://www.tradingeconomics.com/south-africa/public-spending-on-education-
    total-percent-of-gdp-wb-data.html.

28 "Lion's Share of the Budget for Education," February 26, 2014, SAnews.gov.za, http://
    www.southafrica.info/business/economy/policies/budget2014c.htm#.VBCc0Evbd4M.
    Unfortunately, no comparable data exist for the apartheid period because data were
    split into separate entities and not well recorded.

29 South Africa Department of Education, provisional 1994 C/S data, DOE 94/95 budget
    estimates. This was actually an improvement over historical funding ratios of ten to one
    in favor of white children.

30 Sipho Masondo, "Public School Fees Shocking," *City Press*, October 28, 2012, http://
    www.news24.com/Archives/City-Press/Public-school-fees-shocking-20150430.

31 The 2003 review noted explicitly that schools in poor areas should not be expected
    to raise funds in lieu of state funding. Department of Education, *Report to the Minister:
    Review of the Financing, Resourcing, and Costs of Education in Public Schools*, March 3, 2003,
    2, 36, http://www.education.gov.za/LinkClick.aspx?fileticket=0AFdXOY5hKo%3D&tabi
    d=452&mid=1038.

32 Shareen Motala and Yusuf Sayed, "'No Fee' Schools in South Africa," Policy Brief No.
    7, Consortium for Research on Education, Access, Transitions, and Equity (CREATE),
    August 2009, 3, http://www.create-rpc.org/pdf_documents/South_Africa_Policy_
    Brief_1.pdf.

33 Western Cape Government, "Background to the National Quintile System," media
    release, October 14, 2013, http://wced.pgwc.gov.za/comms/press/2013/74_14Oct.html.

34 Teboho Moja and Fred M. Hayward, "The Changing Face of Redress in South Africa:
    1990–2005," *Journal of African Higher Education* 3, no. 3 (2005): 12.

35 National Student Financial Aid Scheme Strategic and Annual Performance Plans 2013
    (meeting with deputy minister of higher education in attendance, chairperson D. Rantho,
    ANC, Eastern Cape, acting, May 29, 2013), https://pmg.org.za/committee-meeting/15932.

36   Department of Basic Education, *Action Plan to 2014: Towards the Realization of Schooling 2025*, October 2011, http://www.education.gov.za/Curriculum/ActionPlanto2014/tabid/418/Default.aspx.

37   Council on Higher Education, *Higher Education Participation 2011*, Council on Higher Education, Pretoria, 2013, 2–3, http://www.che.ac.za/sites/default/files/publications/Higher%20Education%20Participation%202011.pdf.

38   Universities South Africa, "Reflections on Higher Education Transformation" (discussion paper prepared for the second national Higher Education Transformation Summit, Durban, KwaZulu-Natal, October 15–17, 2015), annexure 5, 9, http://www.dhet.gov.za/summit/Docs/2015Docs/Annex%205_UnivSA_Reflections%20on%20HE%20Transformation.pdf.

39   The Freedom Charter, adopted at the Congress of the People at Kliptown, Johannesburg, June 25–26, 1955, http://www.historicalpapers.wits.ac.za/inventories/inv_pdfo/AD1137/AD1137-Ea6-1-001-jpeg.pdf.

40   NECC, *National Education Policy Investigation*.

41   Barnes, "Changing Discourses and Meaning of Redress," 214.

42   Moja and Hayward, "The Changing Face of Redress in South Africa."

43   NCHE, *A Framework for Transformation*, 21–22.

44   Nelda Mouton, Gabriel P. Louw, and Gert L. Strydom, "Critical Challenges of the South African School System," *International Business and Economics Research Journal* 12, no. 1 (2013): 31–44.

45   Mamphela Ramphele, "Another Generation Betrayed," *The Times*, January 18, 2009, cited in Mouton, Louw, and Strydom, "Critical Challenges."

46   Mouton, Louw, and Strydom, "Critical Challenges."

47   Monako Dibetle, "FET Sector Is the Class Dunce," *Mail and Guardian*, January 29, 2010, http://mg.co.za/article/2010-01-29-fet-sector-is-the-class-dunce.

48   Ian Scott, Nan Yeld, and Jane Hendry, "A Case for Improving Teaching and Learning in South African Higher Education," *Higher Education Monitor* No. 6, Council on Higher Education, Pretoria, South Africa, October 2007, 12, http://www.che.ac.za/sites/default/files/publications/HE_Monitor_6_ITLS_Oct2007_0.pdf.

49   Council on Higher Education, "A Proposal for Undergraduate Curriculum Reform in South Africa: The Case for a Flexible Curriculum Structure. Report of the Task Team on Undergraduate Curriculum Structure," discussion document, August 2013, 45–46, http://www.che.ac.za/sites/default/files/publications/Full_Report.pdf.

50   Firoz Patel, "A Description of Education System Policy Process: Towards Quality Learning and Teaching in South Africa—A Systems Approach" (presentation to New York University students, Pretoria, South Africa, 2008).

51   Trading Economics, "South Africa GDP Per Capita," 2016, http://www.tradingeconomics.com/south-africa/gdp-per-capita.

52 Human Sciences Research Council, "Income Inequality and Limitations of the Gini Index: The Case of South Africa," http://www.hsrc.ac.za/en/review/hsrc-review-november-2014/limitations-of-gini-index.

53 Elizabeth Redden, "#Fees Must Fall," *Inside Higher Ed*, November 18, 2015, https://www.insidehighered.com/news/2015/11/18/south-africa-push-continues-free-tuition-and-adequate-support.

54 Moja and Hayward, "The Changing Face of Redress in South Africa."

55 Barnes, "Changing Discourses and Meaning of Redress," 216.

PART III

Outreach, Education, and Sustainability

CHAPTER 7

Outreach to Children in the Transitional Justice Process of Sierra Leone

Zoé Dugal

In the past fifteen years, transitional justice mechanisms around the world increasingly have been putting outreach programs in place to ensure public participation in transitional justice processes and to promote local owner-ship of these processes. This recent awareness of the importance of outreach came from the realization that the legitimacy and longer-term sustainability of these processes in societies emerging from conflict heavily depend on how deeply they are accepted and valued by the society.[1] Since children and youth have only lately begun to be directly involved in transitional justice processes, the design and implementation of outreach programming especially geared toward them is an even more recent and novel development that requires strategies specifically targeted to their needs.

In looking at the ways in which children have been included in transitional justice processes, and specifically in outreach programming, Sierra Leone is interesting for several reasons. The situation of children in Sierra Leone in the early 2000s was unique, as the effects of the conflict on them had been par-ticularly profound. For this reason, a truth commission and an international criminal tribunal directly involved children and youth in their proceedings. Lacking comparative experience and international guidelines, both institu-tions had to be creative and courageous in their approaches. The challenges they faced and the impact they had on the involvement of children can serve as lessons to be applied in transitional justice processes elsewhere.

This chapter examines the transitional justice outreach programs targeting children and youth that were carried out by the Truth and Reconciliation Commission and the Special Court for Sierra Leone.[2] The chapter will first briefly discuss the conflict in the country and the specific reasons the involvement of children and youth in transitional justice mea-sures was deemed necessary at the time. This will be followed by a more detailed analysis of the different strategies developed to involve the younger sector of the population, the outreach activities organized and materials produced by both the truth commission and the court, and an examination of their collaboration with civil society and state actors. Finally, the chapter will discuss elements of sustainability with regard to the legacies of such programs and consider some of the challenges and lessons learned from the Sierra Leone example.

BACKGROUND ON SIERRA LEONE

The small West African country of Sierra Leone suffered a devastating civil war from 1991 to 2002. The conflict, in which the opponents were the government of Sierra Leone and the rebel forces of the Revolutionary United Front (RUF), was characterized by extreme brutality, systematic targeting of civilians, and widespread destruction. Other armed groups involved included the Civil Defense Forces (CDF), a civilian militia acting on behalf of the government, and a faction of the armed forces that staged a coup in 1997 and later joined the RUF.[3] All armed groups committed gross human rights violations. Official estimates of casualties amount to 70,000.[4]

The conflict affected Sierra Leonean children especially, as they "were particularly vulnerable to abuse" and "were violated in deep and lasting ways."[5] Besides the obvious loss of opportunities in terms of education and livelihood that come from a long civil war, children's rights were amply and brutally violated by all armed factions. The final report of the Truth and Reconciliation Commission (TRC) notes that "the leaderships of these factions are held responsible for permitting the commission of gross human rights violations against children," and that "perpetrators singled out women and children for some of the most brutal violations of human rights recorded in any conflict."[6]

Children were killed, raped, tortured, maimed, and displaced. An overwhelming number were

> forcibly abducted from their families and held in abominable conditions, mistreated both physically and sexually.... They have been forcibly conscripted into military and paramilitary activities and forced to commit heinous acts against others, often drugged, all the while undergoing brutal treatment by their superiors. Girls have been captured as sex slaves to serve as "wives" to combatants who treated them with the utmost cruelty. Children of all ages have been separated from their families, in many cases never to be reunited.[7]

All the armed factions recruited children. According to the TRC's database, 28 percent of those forcibly recruited were less than twelve years old, and 25 percent of those raped or used as sex slaves were under thirteen.[8] The RUF, which was the main perpetrator in the abduction and forced recruitment of children, created so-called "Small Boys Units" and "Small Girls Units" who were responsible for forcibly recruiting other children during raids on villages. The children in these units were promoted to higher ranks based on their ruthlessness and their ability to commit human rights violations without inhibition.[9] The RUF "branded" children with knives, ensuring their identification as RUF members and discouraging attempts to escape.

According to the National Commission for Demobilization, Disarmament, and Reintegration, operating in Sierra Leone between 1998 and 2002, 6,845 children (92 percent of them boys and 8 percent girls) entered the Demobilization, Disarmament, and Reintegration (DDR) program.[10] This number does not include those who had been forcibly recruited as children but had reached adulthood by the end of the conflict. The United Nations established that the number of children associated with armed forces during the conflict had reached 10,000, of whom around 6,000 would have been conscripted, some as young as five years of age.[11]

The conflict also took a heavy toll on the already problematic education system of the country. Forced displacement, estimated as having affected a total of 2.6 million out of a population of 6 million,[12] disrupted the lives of children and teachers, culminating in the loss of an entire school year in 1997.[13] Overall, the TRC estimated, the lack of education in Sierra Leone had led to the exclusion of the "majority of children and youth from reaching their full potential and enabling them to take their rightful place in society."[14] Other sources have estimated that as many as 70 percent had limited or no access to education during the war years.[15]

In addition, schools, as state infrastructure, were targeted and destroyed by armed groups, who looted furniture and other goods. In 2001, a nationwide survey conducted by the World Bank found only 13 percent of classrooms in usable condition, with the rest in need of significant repairs or reconstruction.[16] By the end of the conflict in 2002, the entire education system was dysfunctional; teachers and university lecturers were rarely paid, at times going for months without receiving salaries, which led to a number of strikes in the following years.

TRANSITIONAL JUSTICE MECHANISMS AND CHILDREN AND YOUTH

The civil war in Sierra Leone was concluded by the signing of the Lomé Peace Agreement in July 1999, which provided all combatants with a blanket amnesty for crimes committed in the context of the armed conflict. This clause was inserted as a concession to the RUF with the intention of securing its compliance in the peace process. The international community was concerned, however, about an amnesty provision that would apply to such brutal and numerous violations of human rights. Civil society in Sierra Leone also put great pressure on the government to address impunity. The amnesty clause came as a great shock, with the RUF portrayed as a legitimate force fighting for the people, even as the atrocities they committed were well known to all in Sierra Leone.[17] The UN representative at the peace conference inserted a written addendum to the agreement saying that, in the view of the UN, the amnesty could not apply to crimes against humanity, war crimes, and other serious violations of international humanitarian law. To counterbalance the clause, the parties to the agreement accepted the creation of a national human rights commission and a truth and reconciliation commission.[18] The abduction of UN peacekeepers by the RUF in May 2000—less than a year after the signing of the peace agreement—forced the government to rethink the amnesty clause and request the assistance of the UN Security Council in the creation of a special tribunal to prosecute international crimes.[19]

The TRC for Sierra Leone and the Special Court for Sierra Leone (SCSL) were both created in 2002,[20] making Sierra Leone the first post-conflict country in which a truth commission and a judicial transitional justice mechanism were operating at the same time. Neither institution, however, had provisions in its mandate to guide how the two should cooperate. This presented major challenges to both in terms of outreach, as many Sierra Leoneans did not understand the difference between the commission and the court. They naturally assumed the TRC was the investigating arm of the court, which made many wary of interacting with the commission for fear of being prosecuted later.

The widespread and systematic targeting of children during the conflict created an unprecedented situation in the history of transitional justice processes. An increased awareness of the specific impact of conflict on the lives of children, especially following the publication of Graça Machel's report in 1996,[21] for the first time made apparent that their involvement in the proceedings of transitional justice measures would be essential, and both the TRC and the court had to reflect on how this could be achieved. The drafters of the TRC Act had already foreseen and stated this need:

The Commission may also implement special procedures to address the needs of such particular victims as children or those who have suffered sexual abuses as well as in working with child perpetrators of abuses or violations.[22]

The main challenge, however, was the lack, both inside Sierra Leone and internationally, of expertise on and experience in involving children in transitional justice measures in safe and meaningful ways, and the reluctance of child protection experts to venture into that field for fear of exposing the children to additional trauma and risk. Indeed, the Sierra Leone TRC was the first truth commission in the world to involve children directly in statement taking and hearings, thus opening the door for their taking a more active role in transitional justice processes elsewhere.

Foreseeing the need for guided support with regard to the involvement of children in both the TRC and the Special Court in Sierra Leone, the United Nations Children's Fund (UNICEF), in collaboration with the Human Rights Section of the United Nations Mission to Sierra Leone (UNAMSIL) and the National Forum for Human Rights (NFHR), convened a consultative meeting of stakeholders in June 2001.[23] The aim was to explore whether and how to involve children in the yet to be created truth commission. The meeting included over forty international and national experts in the areas of child rights, transitional justice, international criminal law, social welfare, counseling, child psychology, and human rights.[24]

Based on the assessment of the major impact of the conflict on children and the numerous ways in which their rights had been violated, the technical meeting concluded that the prospective truth commission had to find ways to ensure their meaningful participation in its proceedings and to address children's issues in its final report. The meeting recommended children be heard by the TRC in a way that would ensure their dignity and safety and avoid retraumatizing them. It further recommended that the TRC design special procedures to ensure confidentiality of their testimonies, including *in camera* hearings, as opposed to public hearings held before an audience.[25] A third recommendation was for the TRC to provide psychosocial support to children participating in its proceedings and to specifically target children in its outreach efforts through radio, religious leaders, child protection agencies, and children's organizations.[26] To facilitate these measures, the meeting recommended a close collaboration between the TRC and child protection agencies throughout the process.

At the time of the technical meeting, a strong fear in Sierra Leone surrounded the possible prosecution of children by the Special Court.[27] The court's purpose was to "prosecute persons who bear the greatest responsibility for serious violations of international humanitarian law and Sierra Leonean law committed in the territory of Sierra Leone since 30 November 1996"[28] (the date the Abidjan peace accord was signed). Article 7 of the court's mandate, however, allowed it to prosecute children above the age of fifteen. Despite the prosecutor's having publicly declared the prosecution of children under eighteen was highly unlikely, stating he was "not interested in prosecuting children" as they could not possibly "bear the greatest responsibility,"[29] child protection experts feared this possibility. Hence, the technical meeting recommended children not be prosecuted by the court, and that the TRC support the court's prosecutorial strategy to address violations of children's rights.[30] The report of the meeting was, however, silent on the involvement of children in the proceedings of the Special Court.

One of the first challenges the TRC had to face when starting its work with children was the dual nature of the involvement of forcibly recruited children in the conflict, as victims and as perpetrators. This dual nature was often seen in individual children in Sierra Leone, who had been compelled to join armed groups and then obliged to commit violations of human rights in the course of the fighting. The TRC explains in its final report, however, what it believed to be the necessity to explore the role of children as perpetrators to capture the entirety of their experiences, to try to understand the causes and motivations behind the abuses committed, and thus to help prevent recurrence.[31]

From a procedural standpoint, this dual identity as victims and perpetrators made it even more crucial for the commission to involve children in its proceedings in a way that would be empowering, instead of treating them as mere passive actors or victims. As children had taken an active role in the conflict, they had also to be involved in transitional justice mechanisms in a way that would recognize that active role when devising solutions for their reintegration into society and in shaping the future of the country.

Early on in the work of the commission, it became obvious that collaboration with child protection experts would be crucial to ensure children participated in meaningful and safe ways. In late 2002, the commission, UNICEF, and the network of Sierra Leonean child protection agencies (CPAs), composed of both local and international nongovernmental organizations (NGOs) and convened by UNICEF, began discussions based on the recommendations of the 2001 technical meeting, especially the necessity of involving children in the truth commission. The commission wanted to involve both child perpetrators and other children who had been victims of or witnesses to atrocities.[32]

One concern of the CPAs in these discussions was that both the TRC and the Special Court involved "inquisitive" and "judgmental" processes that would only retraumatize children. In the case of the Special Court, the CPAs raised additional concerns regarding the physical security of child witnesses and the dangers of self-incrimination, and they recommended the court not use child witnesses at all.[33] The prosecutorial strategy of the Office of the Prosecutor included the use of child witnesses, however, mostly as insiders, and the court became the first international tribunal to prosecute and secure convictions for the crime of recruitment of children into armed forces, creating crucial jurisprudence for this crime and future convictions.

After difficult negotiations, a "Framework for Cooperation between the TRC and the CPAs" was signed in January 2003. Many of the procedures designed under the framework were based on the recommendations of the 2001 technical meeting, including confidentiality of all child testimonies,[34] the provision of psychosocial support, and the appearance of children only during *in camera* hearings.[35] The commission also decided to treat all children equally and did not assign labels to them. When taking statements from children, for example, TRC statement takers were instructed to ignore the categorization used for adults that required the identification of the statement giver as victim, perpetrator, or witness.

Under the framework, a lead CPA was selected in each of the five regions of Sierra Leone. Each was to identify children who were willing to testify before the TRC and provide them with psychosocial support before, during, and after their testimony. Regional staff of the CPAs teamed up with regional TRC coordinators and statement takers to organize the taking of the children's statements. In addition, a vulnerability assessment was to be conducted with each potential child witness, with the decision to refer the child to the TRC statement takers based on that assessment.

In practice, this arrangement worked better in some regions than others, depending on the capacity and enthusiasm of the lead CPAs. In addition, time constraints on the TRC meant statements from children had to be collected in a short time, and the vulnerability assessments were thus not always conducted.[36] Another challenge not foreseen when the framework was designed was that in the course of their regular statement-taking activities in villages, TRC statement takers met children who had not been previously identified by CPAs; often, these children expressed their desire to give statements and could not possibly be turned away. To alleviate the negative effects of children being interviewed without the presence of a social worker, those children were later referred to CPAs for follow-up psychosocial visits.

The TRC also organized a thematic public hearing on children and youth in Freetown on the Day of the African Child (June 26, 2003), with support from the local CPAs, UNAMSIL, UNICEF, and the Children's Forum Network.[37] The hearing was preceded by a children's march through Freetown to raise awareness of their plight. More than 350 children from across Sierra Leone attended the hearing, listening to children testifying and watching videos from TRC child hearings in the districts.[38]

While the operational challenges mentioned above meant the procedures established by the framework were not always followed, UNICEF's overall assessment of the exercise was that the process was child friendly, and no threats to child statement givers were reported.[39] Perhaps more important, the exercise allowed children's participation in the truth commission and for their voices to be heard and considered in the TRC's final report. Although better planning that allowed more time to select and prepare children would have contributed to a smoother process, they were able to tell their stories to the TRC, including the brutal acts they were forced to commit after being abducted by armed groups.

The Special Court entered into negotiations with the CPAs similar to those they conducted with the TRC, with UNICEF again acting as liaison. The resulting "Principles and Procedures for the Protection of Children in the Special Court" included procedures for the identification of child witnesses, vulnerability assessments, and security measures to be taken.[40] In contrast to the collaboration with the TRC, however, this agreement was kept secret, as the CPAs did not wish to be associated publicly with the Special Court. Children participated in its proceedings as witnesses, and their identities were kept secret from the accused through such means as voice distortion and the use of a screen to hide them in the courtroom.[41]

OUTREACH ACTIVITIES FOR CHILDREN AND YOUTH

In the recent past, outreach has come to be viewed as a form of participation for children and youth in transitional justice processes.[42] This involves two broad considerations. First, information about the objectives and operations of transitional mechanisms must be provided to children in a format appropriate to their young ages, with content they will understand. Second, safe environments must be provided for children to participate actively in some of the processes of transitional justice institutions, if they choose to do so.

The reasons to involve children in transitional justice processes are both backward- and forward-looking. Looking at the past, and especially in Sierra

Leone, children have suffered many abuses and are among the most vulnerable groups in the population. Looking to the future, children are crucial stakeholders in the rebuilding of societies based on the rule of law, justice, and democratic institutions.[43]

The TRC began its outreach work during its preparatory phase. In 2002, before starting operations, the commissioners traveled to each district to participate in public information sessions about the mandate of the commission and build relationships with local communities, including chiefs.[44] This initiative was called the "Barray Phase," from a local word meaning public forum. While the Barray Phase in itself was rather successful, operational constraints prevented its being immediately followed up by additional outreach activities; momentum was lost until the TRC started its statement-taking phase several months later and had to restart outreach efforts. The outreach section of the commission had only a small staff, so the bulk of the effort fell on the commission's local staff—regional and district coordinators and even individual statement takers—who had to conduct outreach and explain the role and mandate of the commission to local Sierra Leoneans, many of whom had never heard of it before they were asked to give a statement.[45]

Outreach efforts continued during the statement-taking and public hearing phases of the TRC, although during that period few efforts specifically targeted children and youth. In general, the activities included the design and distribution of posters with TRC messages aimed at explaining the role of the commission to the public, as well as the live broadcasting of some of its public hearings on public television and UNAMSIL radio.[46] Finally, toward the end of its operational phase in late 2003, the TRC launched its National Vision for Sierra Leone initiative, a project that aimed to collect artistic contributions from Sierra Leoneans about their experiences of the war and their vision of the future of the country. In this respect, the work of the TRC was forward-looking in nature.

In looking to the contribution the process could make toward the future of the country, the TRC devised a strategy that "required it to have a sense of the expectations, hopes and aspirations of the people of Sierra Leone." To do so, it needed to invest efforts in "reaching out to individuals and groups with the aim of understanding their unique perspectives on post-conflict Sierra Leone."[47] These contributions, collected by the TRC under its National Vision initiative, would also form part of the legacy of the TRC.

The aim of the National Vision initiative was to provide a public platform for children and adults who preferred to express themselves through art rather than formal testimony, and who wished to express their visions for the future of their country in addition to their own personal stories. The guide-lines offered by the commission for contributions to the initiative included a description of the kind of society the contributor wished to live in, hopes for the future of Sierra Leone, a vision of Sierra Leone in five to ten years, and reflections on the themes of peace, unity, national pride, and so on.[48] The TRC distributed pamphlets around the country, including in education institutions, and issued announcements on the radio to ensure the call for contributions reached as many Sierra Leoneans as possible. The TRC also held a workshop in its offices to inform students and others about the project and provide them with artistic materials to create their contributions.

At the end of the process, the TRC received more than 250 contributions in the form of essays, poems, songs, plays, sculptures, drawings, and paint-ings. The contributions were arranged as an exhibit, which was launched in December 2003 at the National Stadium in Freetown and later moved to the National Museum. There it was viewed by, among others, groups of school-children, who also participated in discussions around the exhibit.[49]

The contributions to the National Vision initiative were overwhelmingly from children and youth, as education institutions had been specifically targeted in the process.[50] The exhibit was meant to be used to create pub-lic dialogue on a vision for the country, prompted in part by the discussion sessions organized around it. The president of Sierra Leone publicly pledged his support for the initiative on national television, and the TRC secured pub-lic endorsements from Archbishop Desmond Tutu and Alex Boraine, former chair and vice chair, respectively, of the South African TRC.

The outreach section of the Special Court was created in March 2003, slightly late in the process, as the first series of indictments had already been issued by the Office of the Prosecutor. The section was staffed with Sierra Leonean officers, both in Freetown and in the districts, to ensure they under-stood the local languages and culture and had entry points with special groups, such as child ex-combatants, women's organizations, and secret societies.[51]

The outreach strategy of the court was developed with special components for children and youth, in recognition of their status as the most vulnerable groups during the war. Indeed, the Special Court saw children as a crucial target group for outreach, not only because of their participation in the war, but also because of their openness to new ideas and eagerness to learn.[52] The opportunity to increase children's knowledge about human rights and the rule of law would provide grounding for the future evolution of a culture of respect for human rights in Sierra Leone.[53] The court's outreach strategy included different approaches devised for different age groups—for example, primary school children were invited to visit its premises, and court officials visited classrooms for question-and-answer sessions,[54] while for the tertiary level, the court created clubs at universities—the so-called ANCs, described below.

The outreach section developed its work in two phases. The first started before the trials, with trainings and other types of activities designed to explain the purpose and mandate of the court, including information on the types of crimes to be covered and discussions on the universality of respect for human rights (as opposed to Western/colonialist values).[55] Groups of children were gathered for outreach sessions during school visits, with participants a mixture of former child soldiers and child victims to avoid stigmatization.[56]

In this first phase, the court staff was forced to address questions on the mandate and operations of the TRC (as TRC staff had to address questions about the court). As mentioned above, this was because the two institutions started their operations almost simultaneously with somewhat related mandates, creating confusion in the minds of many Sierra Leoneans. Among popular misconceptions was the notion that the two institutions were the same, or that the TRC was the investigative arm of the court and would pass on to the court all the information it was gathering to be used as evidence during the trials. This situation was not helped by the refusal of both institutions to engage in any form of collaboration or coordination of their outreach strategies, or by the instructions each gave its staff to ignore the other (because both feared a collaboration would lead to the perception of their not being fully independent of one another).

Clarifying this confusion with children was especially challenging, as it involved explaining complicated legal differences between the TRC and the Special Court. Court staff, for example, had to explain that only those who "bore the greatest responsibility" for the violations of human rights would be prosecuted, but the TRC was another mechanism to address the rest of the cases.[57] TRC staff, on the other hand, had to reach out to former child soldiers who were reluctant to give testimonies to the commission for fear the information would be passed on to the court and used to prosecute them.

In the second phase of the outreach strategy, which the court began at the beginning of the trials, its outreach staff teamed up with Peace Links, a nonprofit organization whose mandate was to empower young Sierra Leoneans, for a second round of visits to schools to explain to children how the trials would go and what procedures they would follow. The outreach section facilitated the participation of other court organs (the Office of the Prosecutor, the defense office, and the Registry section of the court) in school visits.[58] According to the court's annual report, 1,322 school visits were organized in 2009 alone.[59]

In addition to the school visits, the court issued a call for artistic contributions from children, asking them to draw or paint on the subject of their war experiences and what they wished the court would do with convicted perpetrators. In contrast to the TRC's National Vision, the court's initiative was mostly aimed at personal healing for the children involved; the contributions were therefore not made public and were kept in the court's offices.[60] According to Patrick Fatoma, former outreach coordinator at the court, some of the results were shocking in their portrayals of the trauma the children had suffered, and some drawings suggested the court should put the perpetrators in chains and even torture them.[61]

From 2003 to the end of 2013, the court also ran radio call-in programs, beginning at Radio UNAMSIL (the radio station of the United Nations peace-keeping mission) and then expanding to local radio stations in ten districts around the country. Designed in collaboration with the Children's Forum Network, the programs were managed by the court's outreach officers based in the districts, in collaboration with the network and local radio stations.[62] Child callers asked questions about the functioning of the court, the deaths of Foday Sankoh and Sam Bockarie (major RUF commanders who were accused of human rights violations), and the choices made by the Office of the Prosecutor as to whom to prosecute. Children expressed their disappointment that Sierra Leone's president, Tejan Kabbah, had not been indicted along with the minister of interior for his role as commander in chief of the Civil Defense Forces.

In response to such questions, the outreach section acted as a liaison with the Office of the Prosecutor to get answers for child callers. Many children asked why the court had not indicted commanders from the Economic Community of West African States Monitoring Group (ECOMOG), the Nigerian-led regional peacekeeping force that ultimately contributed to ending the war but was accused of committing human rights violations against citizens of Freetown in the process. Court outreach officers took the time to explain that, under international law, countries contributing peacekeepers are responsible for prosecuting any crimes committed by their troops, and the court therefore had no jurisdiction over the Nigerian soldiers.[63] Several children expressed their discontentment with this position.

Finally, looking more toward youth, the court's outreach section created in 2003 the so-called Accountability Now Clubs (ANCs) in universities and institutions of tertiary education in Sierra Leone and later also in Liberia. The objective of these clubs was to involve university and postsecondary students in educating their peers and communities about the Special Court, transitional justice, and human rights.[64] The court partnered with the Sierra Leone

Teachers' Union for this initiative. Club members received training from the court until 2005, when the clubs became independent from the court. For a short period, all the clubs came together in a coalition and received funding from the court to conduct outreach activities with communities outside of schools, taking advantage of the standing of university students in Sierra Leone as educated citizens in a largely illiterate society.[65] In 2010, ANC members who graduated from various universities created a coalition that is currently working as an independent organization on issues relating to human rights and the rule of law. By 2011, there were fourteen ANCs in the country.

As the court approached the end of its mandate, the outreach section worked with some of these ANCs to "institutionalise them and to assist them in applying their experience to institutions in the national system."[66] Whether the coalition will be sustainable in the future, however, is unclear, especially considering that outreach is not a component of the tasks to be carried out by the Residual Mechanism of the Special Court for Sierra Leone, which was created in 2013 to handle the legacy of the Special Court when the latter closed.[67] In addition, the impact of the ANCs has been mostly felt in Freetown, as the location of all the universities in the country; its impact has been very limited in more remote areas.[68]

OUTREACH DOCUMENTS

Both transitional justice institutions in Sierra Leone created outreach documents aimed especially at children and youth. Following a recommendation from the 2001 technical meeting,[69] which was later reinforced in a submission by the Children's Forum Network to the TRC's thematic hearing on children, the TRC decided to produce a child-friendly version of its final report. The commission saw this as a way to ensure Sierra Leonean children could more easily have access and respond to the findings of the report. It was also an important means for emphasizing the stories and voices of children in a separate publication that would specifically reach them.

The child-friendly report project was a collaboration of the TRC, the child protection section of the UNICEF country office, UNAMSIL, and various children's groups, including three nationwide networks: the Children's Forum Network (CFN), the Voice of Children Radio, and the Children's National Assembly. Funding was provided by UNICEF. More than a hundred children participated in the conceptualization of the child-friendly report, and fifteen representatives of the CFN were actively involved in the drafting and designing process.[70]

The child-friendly report includes chapters on the work of the TRC, a summary of the findings of the commission on the conflict, with an emphasis on information relating to children, and a summary of the recommendations contained in the TRC's official final report. It also includes a chapter on children's vision of the future and a plan of action outlining what children intend to do to help disseminate the report—for example, lobbying government on the implementation of the TRC recommendations and organizing discussions around the report in schools and on the radio.[71]

The child-friendly version of the TRC report was officially handed over to President Ahmad Tejan Kabbah during a public ceremony in October 2004, along with the commission's final report. It was the first time a truth commission had produced a children's version of its final report, and the Sierra Leone TRC remains the only one to have done so up till now. The child-friendly report was disseminated in two phases. In 2004, six hundred copies were provided to children's groups, NGOs, the government, and the media. In 2005, an additional four thousand were distributed through UNAMSIL to child advocacy groups, educators, and other civil society organizations. Apparently, however, the materials were not used by teachers, in part because the curriculum reform recommendations of the TRC were never implemented.[72] Several teachers have complained of this situation and of not having received copies of the full TRC report.[73]

The TRC also published a secondary school version of its final report (targeting fifteen- to nineteen-year-olds), using "Sierra Rat" cartoon characters to depict Sierra Leonean youth. The report was produced by the civil society–led Truth and Reconciliation Working Group, with funding from the German government and the active participation of the Ministry of Education of Sierra Leone. The production process also involved secondary school teachers, who participated in an initial brainstorming session.

The secondary school version provides a simplified version of most of the chapters in the TRC's final report.[74] Each contains summarized and simplified text and cartoons illustrating the content. The use of the animal characters from Sierra Rat cartoons was meant to avoid stigmatization by "allow[ing] the story to talk about incidents that happened during the war without referring and seeming to refer to individual persons."[75] The book also includes exercises after each chapter to guide teachers in leading class discussions and debates and to encourage students to develop and express their ideas about the conflict and the truth commission report.[76] Dissemination of this version of the TRC report was done as a one-off, with two hundred copies distributed to secondary schools across the country, reaching about forty thousand students.[77] As with the child-friendly version, however, the resource hasn't been used widely.

Finally, the TRC also produced a video version of its final report entitled "Witness to Truth," in collaboration with WITNESS, a US-based NGO. The video was not meant to target children especially, but rather the vast section of the Sierra Leonean population that is illiterate and unable to read the full report or even the simplified versions. After the TRC closed, WITNESS provided four local NGOs with small grants totaling US$30,000 to organize screenings around the country and provide civil society organizations and schools with copies of the video. Through 2005, a total of eighty-five screenings were organized around the country, with over twenty thousand viewers, including five thousand students.[78]

One of the organizations selected, the National Forum for Human Rights (NFHR), piloted the video in ten secondary schools and five colleges in southern Sierra Leone and the Freetown area. The video formed part of wider sessions with students in which the TRC was discussed, and each screening was followed by a discussion on the themes it addressed.[79] In secondary school screenings, NFHR asked ten questions about the video, and the students who scored the highest in their responses became eligible to take part in a national quiz. In colleges, students were asked to write essays on the themes discussed in the video, with grants awarded for the best. As for the children's reactions to the video, NFHR described them in the WITNESS project internal report as being mostly of "sorrow, disgust, and disbelief."[80]

In 2011, the outreach section of the Special Court published two booklets—*The Court Made Simple* and *International Humanitarian Law Made Simple*[81]—to explain in simplified language the processes of the court and the role of each of its sections (prosecution, defense, and so on), as well as basic notions of international humanitarian law. While these booklets did not specifically target children, they were used in outreach activities with both children and adults and were aimed at an audience with limited education and low levels of literacy. The booklets were published quite late in the process, however, after most of the trials had ended. The court also had difficulties distributing them to remote areas of the country and used some schools and other local institutions as channels for distribution.[82]

FOLLOW-UP AND SUSTAINABILITY

The nature of transitional justice measures is that their lifespans are limited. After they fulfill their mandate, they are usually disbanded, and state institutions, international organizations, and civil society are left to uphold their legacies. In Sierra Leone, the TRC concluded its work in 2004 and the Special Court in 2013. The following explores additional outreach initiatives that were implemented after the work of the two institutions concluded and issues around the sustainability of outreach efforts beyond the life of transitional justice measures.

In 2004, when the TRC finished its work and was closing down, a number of Sierra Leoneans from academia, the diplomatic community, and civil society made an offer to the commission to continue the National Vision initiative discussed above. An NGO was created, and the contributions were exhibited over the following years in the National Museum, the National Library, and the British Council, among other venues. The staff of the National Vision organized guided tours of the exhibit and discussions around the themes of justice, unity, reconciliation, education, peacebuilding, and the conflict, and by 2005, over three thousand visitors had seen the exhibit.[83] In 2007, the National Vision closed down and the exhibit was transferred to the Sierra Leone Human Rights Commission, as recommended by the TRC. In 2011, the Human Rights Commission toured the exhibit to schools to engage students in discussions around themes similar to those addressed previously.[84]

In short, in its various formats, the National Vision offers an interesting example of an initiative that can be used for educational purposes, especially in terms of its capacity to involve children beyond the life of a formal transitional justice mechanism, while also helping establish useful partnerships with local institutions to ensure sustainability with very limited resources.

In 2013, almost ten years after the TRC closed its doors, the Special Court did, as well. It was replaced by a residual mechanism—the Residual Special Court of Sierra Leone—to carry on some of its functions for varying periods of time—up to fifty years, in some cases. These functions do not include outreach, however, which raises questions as to the sustainability of some initiatives, including the Accountability Now Clubs, in a country with limited resources like Sierra Leone.

The residual mechanism, which is much smaller than the court, was the result of an agreement between the government of Sierra Leone and the United Nations, but it depends on voluntary contributions for its survival. Together with it, a Peace Museum was created in 2013 in the former security building of the court in Freetown; it is also meant to host full copies of the archives of both the court and the TRC and to serve as a memorial to the victims of the war, in accordance with a recommendation from the TRC.[85]

The TRC also recommended that the content of its final report be incorporated into curricula in primary, secondary, and tertiary education,[86] and, as explained above, it produced two versions of the report that could serve this purpose. As of this writing, however, the TRC process is not yet taught about in Sierra Leone schools. To be sure, the capacity of the education system was severely damaged by the conflict, and the topics both the court and the TRC dealt with are challenging to introduce into a classroom setting; still, it is possible to consider whether both institutions could have done something more to reach out to the education sector of the country.[87] More recently, the UN has worked with the Ministry of Education to incorporate human rights training into school and university curricula, which opens the door to adding information from the TRC report, as well.[88]

CHALLENGES AND LESSONS LEARNED

Sierra Leone provides the first example of transitional justice measures actively involving children. For this reason, the country's experiences can offer lessons useful for other processes around the world. Below are presented the major challenges it faced, along with some ideas that could be valuable for other times and places.

SEQUENCING OF TRANSITIONAL JUSTICE MECHANISMS AND COLLABORATION

In Sierra Leone, the concurrent operation of the TRC and the Special Court created confusion among the public about their different goals and mandates, especially with regard to children. If similar institutions operate simultaneously in the future, some form of collaboration between them in designing and implementing coordinated outreach strategies would be valuable. This is especially so if the institutions plan to involve children in their activities and need to design outreach measures specifically geared toward explaining complex institutional mandates to them.

INVOLVEMENT OF AND SUPPORT FROM CIVIL SOCIETY GROUPS

At the beginning of the transitional justice process, child protection agencies (CPAs) in Sierra Leone were not convinced of the importance of children's participation. With children becoming increasingly involved in transitional justice processes around the world since then, this challenge has notably diminished; however, a proactive stance is still needed to include CPAs and other organizations that work with children and youth early on in discussions about strategies to involve children in transitional justice, and to get their expertise on ensuring children's meaningful participation while avoiding retraumatization. Transitional justice mechanisms are usually not fully equipped to provide the type of psychosocial support necessary to ensure the safe participation of children and youth, nor do they have expertise regarding how to communicate with them. Often, they must rely on civil society to assist them in these areas.[89] If, however, civil society organizations, and especially those working with children and youth, are not convinced of the value of the transitional justice mechanisms, or if they don't feel a part of the design process, getting them involved in activities such as outreach is challenging.[90]

The TRC and the Special Court for Sierra Leone initially experienced challenges in working with civil society, particularly with the child protection community, for the reasons already explained. Opportunities were lost at the outset to establish strong working relationships, which left strategizing and planning on how to involve children ad hoc. Once collaboration was established, however, both institutions worked closely and rather successfully with civil society and UN agencies on the design of outreach and education materials and the implementation of initiatives.

EXPLAINING COMPLEX LEGAL PROCESSES TO CHILDREN AND YOUTH AND ADDRESSING DIFFICULT ISSUES TRUTHFULLY

Because children and youth are part of the societies emerging from conflict, finding ways to explain to them the complexities of transitional justice processes and engaging with their opinions and objections is crucial. The Sierra Leone example shows conversations with children on the nature of a war and atrocities committed cannot be avoided, yet they are challenging to conduct because they often involve complex legal and moral concepts. Designing creative and safe ways to address children—for example, by creating secure environments for dialogue—where they are allowed to express their reactions to the information presented or ask questions and exchange views on the future of their society is important. Seeking expert advice and help from psychosocial support workers and educators with experience in conveying this sort of information to children and youth is also fundamental, especially considering the delicate nature of the information being conveyed.

DIFFICULTY OF COLLABORATING WITH A DYSFUNCTIONAL EDUCATION SYSTEM AND ALTERNATIVE MEANS OF OUTREACH

Sierra Leone offers insights into the challenges transitional outreach programs will find when trying to work with an education system that has been almost completely destroyed by a conflict. The failures of the education system during the conflict in Sierra Leone and in its immediate aftermath meant children had no safe settings in which to learn and exchange thoughts on the conflict, the transition, and the future of their country. Moreover, in Sierra Leone, where they are seen as figures of social authority who play a key role in mentoring children, the lack of teachers in many parts of the country at the end of the war, due to displacement, killings, and so on, and the trauma suffered by many of those remaining deprived children of an important source of social support.

Both the TRC and the court involved teachers in their outreach activities and in the design of education materials on the transitional justice process in Sierra Leone. Important challenges, however, occurred in this process, mostly because of the state of the education system in the aftermath of the conflict and the slow reconstruction of physical infrastructure and recuperation of human resources. With the need to replace or restore the many teachers who had been killed or displaced and to repair or replace the schools that had been partially or completely destroyed—which was most of them—reconstruction efforts in the education system faced so many challenges that transitional justice issues were not seen as the priority. Despite both transitional justice institutions having produced specific materials to relate to children, follow-up by the education system was very limited, and the materials apparently were not used.

This challenge raises the question of the sustainability of transitional justice initiatives in countries where the education systems are in such disarray post-conflict that they cannot absorb the impact of initiatives after formal transitional justice institutions expire. It also raises a question regarding the importance of devising more comprehensive strategies to ensure the materials produced are finally used in the classroom. The educational quality of these materials and the collaboration with teachers and educators on their design are fundamental in this respect.

In addition, transitional justice mechanisms in countries where children are especially affected by conflict need to find ways to involve those who are out of school. The example of Sierra Leone shows how CPAs and other civil society organizations, as well as children's groups, can be approached to reach out to them. One such initiative that stands out is the work done through radio programs. Sierra Leone has a high illiteracy rate, and the reach of newspapers and television is mostly limited to the Freetown area. The rest of the country relies on radio as the main source of information. The idea to use Radio UNAMSIL during the years after the conflict proved to be a good one, as it was at the time the only station with nationwide coverage. Moreover, as local stations resumed operating as time passed, involving them in outreach programs for transitional justice was also the right strategy; as Radio UNAMSIL phased out, the involvement of those local stations provided at least an opportunity to build sustainability.

FUNDING AND SUSTAINABILITY OF INITIATIVES

The TRC was underfunded throughout its lifespan. This led to the necessity to focus resources on essential operational activities, such as investigations and public hearings, which left funding for outreach activities very limited. Time was also a constraint that led the TRC to start statement-taking activities before proper outreach was conducted. Planning sessions with CPAs and school visits that helped children understand the role of the commission better before the start of the operational phase would have been more effective.

In comparison to the TRC, the Special Court was well funded; however, it had no specific budget for outreach, and the outreach section had constantly to raise funds from bilateral donors to implement its activities.[91] This led to challenges in the timeliness and follow-up of initiatives.

In addition, in a poor country like Sierra Leone, specific challenges are associated with the sustainability of outreach initiatives. Once the transitional justice mechanisms have concluded their work and closed down operations, the risk is strong that the initiatives they designed and funded will stop because of lack of funds and institutional backup. In Sierra Leone, this risk was partially mitigated by working closely with UNICEF, which has an stable presence in the country; UNICEF's mandate in transitional justice is limited, however, and hence it is recommendable in the outreach work to try to establish relationships with other state institutions that will help build sustainability. The education sector is ideally suited for this purpose.

CONCLUSION

The participation of children is crucial to the success of transitional justice processes. Procedures must be designed for them to participate in transitional justice measures in meaningful and safe ways, recognizing the active role they might have played in the conflict but also recognizing their value as citizens who will build the future of the new society.

Since children do not have the same means as adults to gain access to information in the public domain, special efforts are needed to reach them, and these can be made through outreach programs targeting their specific needs, with the content and format of the information adapted to children so they can make informed choices about their participation.

Sierra Leone was the first case in which formal transitional justice institutions used outreach to involve children. Both the TRC and the Special Court made substantial efforts in reaching out to children and youth. This resulted in their meaningful participation in both institutions, as well as a focus on children's issues in the final report of the TRC and groundbreaking convictions by the court. This experience has already inspired other institutions to act similarly, for example, in Liberia and Kenya.

Outreach alone, however, will not ensure the sustainability of initiatives, as transitional justice institutions are, by nature, temporary. Links with the formal education system must be part of outreach efforts to maximize the impact of transitional justice measures and provide chances for such sustainability. Because of the challenges described in this chapter, neither the TRC nor the Special Court succeeded in including or establishing strong links with the education system. This led eventually to outreach efforts phasing out after the two institutions closed down and affected their enduring legacy. Proper linkages with the education system could have helped ensure their longevity, especially with regard to the work done with children and youth. Additional research on how this can be done is needed so practitioners can design better strategies in the future to ensure outreach efforts conducted by transitional justice measures can strategically coordinate with education actors and institutions.

NOTES

1   See, for example, Victor Peskin, "Courting Rwanda: The Promises and Pitfalls of the ICTR Outreach Programme," *Journal of International Criminal Justice* 3, no. 4 (2005): 950–61, and Norman Henry Pentelovitch, "Seeing Justice Done: The Importance of Prioritizing Outreach Efforts at International Criminal Tribunals," *Georgetown Journal of International Law* 39 (2008): 445–94. See also Clara Ramírez-Barat, *Making an Impact: Designing and Implementing Outreach Programs for Transitional Justice Measures* (New York: ICTJ, January 2011).

2   While the definition of "youth" in Sierra Leone includes individuals from fifteen to thirty-five years of age, this chapter will use the term to refer to young adults.

3   A series of external armed groups were also involved, such as the National Patriotic Front of Liberia and ULIMO (the United Liberation Movement of Liberia for Democracy), among others.

4   Mary Kaldor and James Vincent, *Evaluation of UNDP Assistance to Conflict-Affected Countries: Case Study Sierra Leone* (New York: UNDP, 2006), 4.

5   UNICEF, *Submission to the Truth and Reconciliation Commission* (Thematic Hearings on Children, Freetown, June 17, 2004).

6   Sierra Leone Truth and Reconciliation Commission, *Witness to Truth: Final Report of the Truth and Reconciliation Commission for Sierra Leone* (Freetown: TRC, 2004), 2:36, 18.

7   Ibid., 3B:234.

8   Ibid., 3B:264, 268.

9   Ibid., 3B:294.

10 UNICEF, *Disarmament, Demobilization and Reintegration of Children: Lessons Learned in Sierra Leone 1998–2002* (Dakar: UNICEF, 2005).

11 UNICEF, *Submission to the TRC*, 235.

12 Kaldor and Vincent, *Evaluation of UNDP Assistance*, 4.

13 Before the beginning of the war, the education system was already plagued by sporadic teacher strikes due to nonpayment of salaries, teacher absenteeism, and elitist views on education that concentrated most of the schools in the Freetown area, leaving the rest of the country with very limited opportunities for education. Julia Paulson, "The Educational Recommendations of Truth and Reconciliation Commissions: Potential and Practice in Sierra Leone," *Research in Comparative and International Education* 1, no. 4 (2006): 338.

14 Sierra Leone Truth and Reconciliation Commission, *Witness to Truth*, findings chapter, 2:99.

15 Women's Commission for Refugee Women and Children, "Global Survey of Education in Emergencies" (New York: WCRWC, 2004).

16 World Bank, *Project Appraisal Document on a Proposed Grant in the Amount of SDR 15.1 Million (US$20.0 Million Equivalent) to the Republic of Sierra Leone for a Rehabilitation of Basic*

Education (Washington, DC: World Bank, 2003), http://www-wds.worldbank.org/external/default/WDSContentServer/WDSP/IB/2003/02/22/000094946_03021304094462/Rendered/PDF/multiopage.pdf.

17 Arthur Abraham, "The Elusive Quest for Peace: From Abidjan to Lomé," in *Between Democracy and Terror*, ed. Ibrahim Abdullah (Dakar: CODESRIA, 2004), 213.

18 Agreement between the Government of Sierra Leone and the Revolutionary United Front of Sierra Leone (Lomé Peace Agreement), June 1999, arts. XXV and XXVI, http://www.sierra-leone.org/lomeaccord.html.

19 Lansana Gberie, *A Dirty War in West Africa: The RUF and the Destruction of Sierra Leone* (Bloomington: Indiana University Press, 2005), 208.

20 The two institutions were not initially designed to operate simultaneously, but the resumption of hostilities following the Lomé Peace Agreement delayed the creation of the TRC.

21 Graça Machel, *Impact of Armed Conflict on Children* (New York: United Nations, August 26, 1996), UNDoc. A/51/306.

22 Parliament of Sierra Leone, Truth and Reconciliation Act 2000 (Freetown: February 10, 2000), section 7(4). http://www.sierra-leone.org/Laws/2000-4.pdf.

23 The National Forum for Human Rights (NFHR) was an umbrella organization for human rights nongovernmental organizations (NGOs) in Sierra Leone.

24 Natalie Mann and Bert Theuermann, *Children and the Truth and Reconciliation Commission for Sierra Leone: Recommendations for Policies and Procedures for Addressing and Involving Children in the TRC*, compiled for UNICEF, UNAMSIL/Human Rights, and NFHR, 2001, 9, http://www.eldis.org/vfile/upload/1/document/0708/DOC14347.pdf.

25 Ibid., 13, 17.

26 Ibid., 40. This recommendation especially highlighted the need to design proper sensitization messages about the sexual enslavement of children to help communities accept abducted children back and prevent stigmatization.

27 See Ilene Cohn, "The Protection of Children and the Quest for Truth and Justice in Sierra Leone," *Journal of International Affairs* 55, no. 1 (2001): 7–34, and Joshua A. Romero, "The Special Court for Sierra Leone and the Juvenile Soldier Dilemma," *Northwestern University Journal of International Human Rights* 8, no. 2 (2004): 8–78.

28 Agreement between the United Nations and the Government of Sierra Leone and Statute of the Special Court for Sierra Leone, Freetown, January 16, 2002, art. 1.

29 Special Court for Sierra Leone, "Special Court Prosecutor Says He Will Not Prosecute Children," press release, Freetown, November 2, 2002.

30 Mann and Theuermann, *Children and the Truth and Reconciliation Commission for Sierra Leone*, 14.

31 Sierra Leone Truth and Reconciliation Commission, *Witness to Truth*, 3B:286.

32 A positive outcome was that the Sierra Leone experience led subsequent truth

commissions elsewhere to pay attention to children, even where there were no child soldiers. For example, the truth commissions in Liberia (2006–9) and Kenya (2009–12) also involved children.

33   Keith Wright and Donald Robert Shaw, "The Role of CPAS in Supporting Children's Involvement in Transitional Justice Mechanisms, in Particular the SCSL" (UNICEF expert discussion on transitional justice and children, Innocenti Center, Florence, November 10–11, 2005), 1–2.

34   The statement form had a section asking the statement givers whether they wanted to request confidentiality. This meant no information that might lead to their identification would be made public by the commission. Children were not asked this question and were granted confidentiality automatically.

35   Sierra Leone Truth and Reconciliation Commission, *Witness to Truth*, 1:145.

36   Because its mandate was quite brief (with a one-and-a-half-year operational period), the TRC was forced to conclude its statement-taking exercise in four months to allow sufficient time for public hearings and report writing.

37   Sierra Leone Truth and Reconciliation Commission, *Witness to Truth*, 1:181. The Children's Forum Network was launched in June 2001 by the Ministry of Social Welfare, Gender, and Children's Affairs, with support from Plan International and UNICEF. The network has branches all over the country, and its mission is to create linkages and spread knowledge on the rights, responsibilities, and welfare of children in Sierra Leone. See http://cfn-sierraleone.webs.com/.

38   Philip Cook and Cheryl Heykoop, "Child Participation in the Sierra Leone Truth and Reconciliation Commission," in *Children and Transitional Justice: Truth Telling, Accountability and Reconciliation*, ed. Sharanjeet Parma, Mindy Jane Roseman, Saudamini Siegrist, and Theo Sowa (Cambridge: Harvard University Press, 2010), 11.

39   Wright and Shaw, "The Role of CPAs," 6.

40   Ibid, 5.

41   In one instance, a child witness inadvertently disclosed his name while testifying, leading to some criticisms from UNAMSIL and UNICEF of the security measures taken by the Office of the Prosecutor (personal knowledge of the author).

42   Clara Ramírez-Barat, *Engaging Children and Youth in Transitional Justice Processes: Guidance for Outreach Programs* (New York: ICTJ, 2012), 3, http://ictj.org/publication/engaging-children-and-youth-transitional-justice-processes-guidance-outreach-programs.

43   Ibid., 3.

44   Sierra Leone Truth and Reconciliation Commission, *Witness to Truth*, 1:160.

45   Ibid., 1:161.

46   Ibid., 1:161.

47   Sierra Leone Truth and Reconciliation Commission, "National Vision for Sierra Leone," April 5, 2004, http://www.sierraleonetrc.org/index.php/national-vision-for-sl.

48 Sierra Leone Truth and Reconciliation Commission, *Witness to Truth*, 1:163.

49 Cook and Heykoop, "Child Participation in the Sierra Leone Truth and Reconciliation Commission," 13.

50 Anthea Zervos and Sophie Raseman, "The National Vision for Sierra Leone," in *Social Entrepreneurship in the Age of Atrocities: Changing Our World*, ed. Zachary Daniel Kaufman (Northampton: Edward Elgar Publishing, 2012), 23. Unfortunately, no recorded information is available on the number and specific types of institutions targeted in the publicity campaign. The TRC itself did not include that information in its final report.

51 Maya Karwande, "Implementing an Engagement Model: Outreach at the Special Court for Sierra Leone," in *Transitional Justice, Culture and Society: Beyond Outreach*, ed. Clara Ramírez-Barat (New York: Social Science Research Council, 2014), 58.

52 Patrick Fatoma, former outreach coordinator, Outreach Section, Special Court for Sierra Leone, phone interview with the author, October 30, 2013.

53 Ibid.

54 Special Court for Sierra Leone, *Third Annual Report of the President of the Special Court for Sierra Leone* (Freetown: Special Court for Sierra Leone, 2005–6), 38.

55 There was at the time and still is in Africa a heated debate about the enforcement of human rights and the mandates of international tribunals (now the International Criminal Court) being an imposition of Western values on African cultures.

56 Fatoma, interview with the author, November 2013. It is unclear whether mixing the two groups presented any challenges to the outreach team. More information is needed to determine if this is a good practice to be recommended elsewhere.

57 This phrase was coined by the court's first prosecutor, David Crane, in an effort to explain in plain language the prosecution strategy to indict top commanders of each armed group based on command responsibility.

58 Karwande, "Implementing an Engagement Model," 60.

59 Special Court for Sierra Leone, *Sixth Annual Report of the President of the Special Court for Sierra Leone* (Freetown: Special Court for Sierra Leone, 2008–9), 34.

60 Fatoma, interview with the author, October 30, 2013.

61 Ibid.

62 Ibid.

63 Ibid.

64 Special Court for Sierra Leone, *Second Annual Report of the President of the Special Court for Sierra Leone* (Freetown: Special Court for Sierra Leone, 2004–2005), 34.

65 Virginie Ladisch and Clara Ramírez-Barat, "Between Protection and Participation: Involving Children and Youth in Transitional Justice Processes," in *Transitional Justice, Culture, and Society: Beyond Outreach*, ed. Clara Ramírez-Barat (New York: Social Science Research Council, 2014), 190.

66 See Residual Special Court of Sierra Leone, http://www.rscsl.org/legacy.html.

67 Fatoma, interview with the author, October 30, 2013.

68 Karwande "Implementing an Engagement Model," 70.

69 Cook and Heykoop, "Child Participation in the Sierra Leone Truth and Reconciliation Commission," 12.

70 Saudamini Siegrist, interview quoted in ibid., 13.

71 Sierra Leone Truth and Reconciliation Commission, *Truth and Reconciliation Commission Report for the Children of Sierra Leone: Child-Friendly Version*, UNICEF, 2004, http://www.unicef.org/infobycountry/files/TRCCF9SeptFINAL.pdf.

72 Julia Paulson, School of Education, Bath Spa University, email communication, July 3, 2014.

73 Sean Higgins, Governance and Inclusive Development program, University of Amsterdam, email communication, July 10, 2014.

74 Mohamed Sheriff and Elvira M. J. Bobson-Kamara, *TRC Report: a Senior Secondary School Version* (Freetown: Truth and Reconciliation Working Group, 2005), 4.

75 Ibid., 4. Using animals (in this case, rats) instead of humans in drawings was also seen as a way to depict the horrific events of the conflict in a less traumatizing way. When the idea for the cartoon was introduced to TRC staff, the international employees were taken aback, as rats in Western cultures are seen as disease-spreading vermin. Sierra Leonean staff members explained, however, that rats are not subject to these stereotypes in Sierra Leonean culture and can therefore be used as friendly cartoon characters to reach out to youth and tell the story. This was an interesting lesson in cultural differences and the importance of designing programs that work in a local context, especially in situations in which the international community is strongly involved.

76 Ibid., 4. See also Cook and Heykoop, "Child Participation in the Sierra Leone Truth and Reconciliation Commission," 14.

77 Ibid., 14.

78 Gavin Simpson, *Witness to Truth Project Final Report* (Freetown: WITNESS, December 2005), 3 (copy on file with the author).

79 Ibid., 18.

80 Ibid., 18. WITNESS itself provided no comment on these reactions, but future similar projects should seriously consider the traumatic effect such a video can have on children. Psychosocial support should be provided to students before and after the screenings to help them put the information into context.

81 Both booklets can be found at the Residual Court of Sierra Leone website: http://www.rscsl.org/documents.html.

82 Karwande "Implementing an Engagement Model," 62.

83 Zervos and Raseman, "The National Vision for Sierra Leone," 26.

84 Ibid., 27.

85 Residual Special Court for Sierra Leone, "Legacy," http://www.rscsl.org/legacy.html.

86 Sierra Leone Truth and Reconciliation Commission, *Witness to Truth*, 2:204.

87 Cook and Heykoop, "Child Participation in the Sierra Leone Truth and Reconciliation Commission," 14.

88 United Nations Integrated Peacebuilding in Sierra Leone (UNIPSIL) and the Sierra Leone Human Rights Commission, "Matrix on the Status of the Implementation of the TRC Recommendations," November 2007, http://www.sierraleonetrc.org/images/recommendations_matrix/matrix/matrix/matrix/finalmatrix.html.

89 Ladisch and Ramírez-Barat, "Between Protection and Participation," 193.

90 For example, the Truth, Justice, and Reconciliation Commission of Kenya faced a similar challenge with civil society in general and child protection agencies in particular, although they rallied around the process and cooperated with the commission in its final months.

91 Fatoma, interview with the author, October 30, 2013.

CHAPTER 8

Building a Legacy: The Youth Outreach Program at the ICTY

Nerma Jelacic

Two decades after the disintegration of Yugoslavia and the subsequent wars that engulfed Bosnia and Herzegovina (BiH), the Republic of Croatia, Kosovo,[1] the former Yugoslav Republic of Macedonia (FYROM), Montenegro, and the Republic of Serbia, views on the causes and the effects of the split and the conflicts remain divided along national, ethnic, and religious lines. The conflicts, which marked the end of the last century, stretched from 1991 to 2000, cost more than 130,000 lives,[2] resulted in millions of people displaced, and permanently changed the demographic picture of the Western Balkans.[3] With politicians, the media, and historians acting as the main catalysts for the enduring ethnic divisions, deep disagreements about the history and facts of the wars have been exacerbated by academia and education establishments.[4]

Opinion polls carried out in 2013 in Bosnia and Herzegovina, Croatia, and Serbia, the three largest post-Yugoslav countries and those most affected by the war, showed entrenched division about its causes, recognition of the crimes committed by the different ethnic groups, and the requirements to normalize relations in the region. Almost twenty years after the end of the conflict, only 20 percent of people in the Federation of Bosnia and Herzegovina and 6.4 percent in a predominantly Serb Republika Srpska—the two entities into which the country remains divided—believed some progress had been made toward reconciliation and normalization of interethnic relations.[5]

Such disappointing figures take on an even more somber overtone when taking into account an unprecedented focus in the Balkan societies on certain processes of facing the past. In Bosnia and Herzegovina, for example, the number of war crimes trials conducted by international and national bodies surpasses that seen in any other post-conflict country, the money invested in the return of displaced populations and reconstruction dwarfs similar efforts, and the percentages of located and identified missing persons have reached record highs.

It must be noted, however, that for many years, dealing with the past was prioritized and pushed by segments of the international community and not by local governments, which have, by and large, consisted of variations of nationalist parties, often those directly involved in the conflicts of the 1990s. Even political elements not nationalist in their ideology resort to rhetoric that keeps the country in the status quo and state of division that is so profitable to the political elite.[6]

Nowadays, local initiatives and calls to face the past come from civil society groups, which have grown manifold in the aftermath of the wars. These actors have contributed significantly to addressing the legacies of the wars by lobbying and pressuring governments to recognize the importance of transitional justice processes and stop thwarting them. In the domain of truth telling, for example, it was mostly nongovernmental organizations (NGOs) that enabled the voices of victims to be heard in the region and demanded governments make facts about war crimes available to the public. Attempts by some governments to establish truth commissions on the national level have failed, while the RECOM coalition of hundreds of NGOs from all the countries of the former Yugoslavia was, at the time of writing, leading a movement for a regional truth commission for the establishment of facts about victims.[7]

Similarly, in the domain of reparation, none of the regional countries established a comprehensive program, leaving it to victims' associations and NGOs to raise awareness and seek reparations for victims through available administrative and judicial procedures, on a case-by-case basis.[8] Their voices, however, were and continue to be drowned out by predominantly nationalist sentiments in the daily discourse of mainstream media and the public sphere.

Today's young adults in the Western Balkans did not live in the country of Yugoslavia and were born after the end of the wars in Bosnia and Croatia. Exposed to a culture of denial and minimization of crimes, they live in mostly monoethnic communities and have no direct contact with peers of different religious or ethnic backgrounds. Their history books have different takes on the effects of World War I and World War II in their regions and on the fall of Yugoslavia and very little to no information about the violations of human rights and international law that took place in the 1990s.[9] With substantial formal education about the recent past lacking, young people's views are more strongly shaped by the media and dominant narratives among peers and family. As a result, they have very little knowledge about what actually happened during the wars, and especially about the mass, systematic crimes and human rights violations committed. Yet many of them have strong opinions about these issues, often based on popular nationalistic myths.

Efforts were made to introduce common chapters about the recent wars into official history textbooks, but they were few and far between and resulted in failure.[10] NGOs instead turned to alternative programs targeting youth, such as summer schools and evening classes on transitional justice issues; examples include the Human Rights Schools project, implemented regionally by the Youth Initiative for Human Rights,[11] and Open Your Eyes—This Is Your Past, implemented in Bosnia and Herzegovina by the Helsinki Committee for Human Rights in Republika Srpska.[12] But the official education establishments remained out of bounds for most.

Against this backdrop, the Outreach Program of the International Criminal Tribunal for the former Yugoslavia (ICTY) prioritized work with the youth of the former Yugoslavia through education activities in high schools and universities. This chapter looks at how the program evolved into a unique campaign to target the young, as well as their teachers and local authorities; the obstacles and challenges it faced along the way; and the impact it has had thus far. Just as importantly, it surveys the picture that emerges of the views of the region's youth, based on data collected during the life of the project, toward dealing with the past and toward coexistence.

The chapter will first explore the establishment of the ICTY and the mandate given it by the United Nations, as well as the attitudes held by citizens of the countries of the former Yugoslavia toward the institution. It will then explain the background behind the creation of the tribunal's outreach program and how youth emerged as one of the most important target audiences. The second half of the chapter will break down the components of the youth education project and examine the reactions of the authorities, academia, and students to it, as well as their opinions about the recent wars and prospects for reconciliation.

SUMMARY OF ICTY OUTREACH EDUCATION ACTIVITIES

The ICTY has dominated and triggered debate about dealing with the past in the former Yugoslavia for over two decades now. Moreover, as the first court of its kind, it has also been under a constant spotlight as the idea and principles of transitional justice have taken hold globally. Established by UN Security Council Resolution 827, passed on May 25, 1993, the ICTY was the first international criminal court since the post–World War II Nuremberg and Tokyo tribunals, and it has, since its creation, set various precedents for other criminal courts and tribunals, both nationally and internationally. The tribunal has to date indicted 161 suspects, including the high-level politicians and military leaders believed most responsible for crimes committed in the region during the 1990s, of whom 74 have been held criminally accountable.[13]

Yet despite the comparatively high number of trials, the tribunal has neither received the acceptance nor led to the genuine efforts to deal with the legacies of the war in the region that many argued criminal prosecutions would. Throughout its twenty-year existence, the institution has faced an uphill struggle to communicate its aims and achievements to the citizens of the former Yugoslavia. The location of the ICTY in The Hague, in the Netherlands, and therefore far away from those most affected by its work, has constituted a significant challenge. In addition, its latent approach to proactive outreach and communication, partly the result of judicial traditions, has prevented it from effectively addressing the unabating revisionism and debates in the region. Moreover, politically motivated agendas and biased media reporting have made it difficult to provide balanced information about the work of the tribunal and transitional justice processes in general.

As public opinion polls have shown, all this has resulted in predominantly negative perceptions of the ICTY throughout most of the territory of the former Yugoslavia (where views generally mirror the dominant, nationalistic public discourse). Polls have also shown that citizens of the former Yugoslavia know very little about war crimes and human rights violations committed in the 1990s, especially those perpetrated by members of their own ethnic groups.[14]

The formal establishment of an official ICTY outreach program in 1999 constituted a milestone in the tribunal's recognition of the importance of raising public awareness of its work in the former Yugoslavia, but it came six years into the institution's life and was never seen as part of its core mandate.[15] In addition, as a judicial institution, the tribunal was never comfortable with the idea of proactive outreach and so struggled to find a medium of communicating with the public, which narrowed down the type and nature of outreach activities.

Nevertheless, the outreach program implements a number of projects designed to make the tribunal's work more transparent, accessible, and understandable for those most affected by it: the population throughout the territory of the former Yugoslavia. Its representatives in the countries of the region engage daily with local actors and present the work of the tribunal at various public and informal events.[16] Among its activities are the maintaining of a comprehensive social media presence, the production of documentary movies and films, capacity-building initiatives for national judiciaries, and information sharing and direct dialogues with stakeholders and communities in the region. The program frequently organizes information and educational visits to the tribunal, for example, giving journalists, legal professionals, students, and other audiences firsthand opportunities to learn about its work. It also has organized a number of public conferences and debates about the tribunal's work, adjudicated cases, legal achievements, and challenges.

WHY YOUTH?

Like most other institutions of its kind, the ICTY lacks the capacity to gain access to large-scale general audiences through mass media or to public political support that could have an impact on the information available to citizens and on the views they hold. In an effort to secure the biggest effect from its small resources, the outreach program developed specific approaches to addressing different segments of the society, including the media, victims' groups, perpetrators, academics, the national judiciary, and local authorities. But not until 2011 was a first comprehensive attempt made to formalize work with one key group across the region: young people. The Youth Outreach Program was an attempt to reach out to high school and university students in the formal setting of their classrooms while simultaneously securing the support of the local authorities and of school and university faculties.

The trigger for development of the Youth Outreach Program was a single effort that started in 2007 in Kosovo, where outreach representatives gave occasional guest lectures in high schools, with the permission of the Ministry of Education and the schools' leadership. These were at first designed to provide information about the mandate and jurisdiction of the tribunal, its key cases, and the facts it had established. At the time, a number of high-level Kosovo officials, including the prime minister, were on trial before the tribunal, and the security situation in Kosovo was not conducive to implementing the more traditional grassroots activities being conducted by the outreach program in other places. Obtaining access to one part of the population through the support of the favorably inclined ministry allowed the program to get access not only to the youth but also the school leadership and teachers.

The positive feedback collected in Kosovo led the outreach program in 2010 to recognize the value of expanding the project to the rest of the region.[17] The positive response was further supported by public opinion polls, which showed that younger generations, although affected by the distorted picture of the conflicts in the public sphere, were nevertheless open to alternative opinions and sources of information and willing both to learn and challenge the beliefs held by their elders.[18] The outreach program found that young people would be very interested in the past if it were spoken about with facts and supporting evidence and in a manner and language understandable to them—findings in stark contrast to the common wisdom that they were not interested in the wars and the recent past and only wanted to look to the future. Initial research also showed, however, that the level of knowledge about the tribunal, local courts, and transitional justice was very low, particularly among younger generations.[19]

Education activities of the ICTY confirmed the initial presumption that high school students perceived and interpreted recent history, as well as the conflicts, very differently in the different countries of the former Yugoslavia and possessed only a very basic and superficial knowledge about the ICTY, its work, and its achievements. Extensive consultations with students conducted by the outreach program during implementation of the project throughout the region showed their opinions were still shaped by the predominant discourses of victimhood and denial of "our" crimes. Put simply, they were driven by national agendas. This was also evident from a number of inaccurate statements and statistics articulated by the students during outreach sessions about the nature of the crimes and the numbers of the victims, which greatly contributed to the persistent culture of denial. These opinions will be analyzed in more detail below.

The potential for the region's youth to contribute to the normalization of relations, then, was constrained either by a lack of information or by the misinformation embedded in their minds since early childhood, which emanated from sections of the media and political and religious circles through to the very core of their existence—their homes. Concerted and effective action was needed to appeal to the younger generations, engage with them to help them gain a fuller understanding of the tribunal's record and achievements, and speak to them directly without intermediaries, to encourage them to think about how to address in a positive way the issue of crime and punishment, which continues to shape the societies in which they live. It is crucial to note here that the project was never envisaged as a simple public information exercise, "by the tribunal about the tribunal." The aim was to use the ICTY's work, the myriad of facts it had established, and the cases it had adjudicated to encourage youth to reflect on the validity of entrenched public opinion, not only regarding the ICTY, but, more importantly, regarding the conflicts of the past and the views of neighboring nations and ethnicities.

Simply presenting young people with isolated information about the tribunal's mandate and judgments, however, would not have had the desired effect of stimulating critical thought about the predominant, ethnocentric narratives of war and victimhood. If anything, such an approach might have further embedded the view of the ICTY as a foreign institution trying to "rewrite" the history of the conflict, this time by manipulating the young and vulnerable population. In contrast, by bringing the facts to localities through the delivery of tailor-made presentations for each region, rich with audiovisual material and often speaking through the voices of the victims—the tribunal's witnesses—this education exercise attracted the interest of students and often provoked them to reexamine their beliefs.

Furthermore, the exposure of university students to international humanitarian and criminal law and procedure was limited at most universities in the region. Based on the feedback received during the first phase of the project, university students demonstrated only very limited familiarity with the ICTY cases and its jurisprudence, while at the same time indicating willingness and openness to acquire more detailed information. Often students were surprised during lectures upon learning that some information, commonly presented in the mass media as "fact," was, in fact, not true or accurate. They frequently delved into the tribunal's alleged lack of neutrality and its jurisdiction and mandate in general.

COMPONENTS OF THE PROJECT

This section breaks down the components of the youth education project and is followed by a discussion of the reactions to it by authorities, academia, and students, as well as their views on the recent wars and prospects for reconciliation.

METHODOLOGY AND APPROACH OF THE PROJECT

The Youth Outreach Program is aimed at young people in the former Yugoslavia and seeks to promote the work, achievements, and legacy of the ICTY in the overall context of transitional justice processes in the region. The project is focused on the formal education system and, to enhance its legitimacy, can only be conducted with the approval of the respective national education authorities. It offers a unique opportunity for young people to learn in a systematic way about topics related to war crimes, transitional justice, and the ICTY. At the same time, it provides a way to gauge the opinions of younger generations about transitional justice and reconciliation and to use the data collected to shape new approaches and strengthen other organizations' activities in the field. The project targets high school students (sixteen to eighteen years of age) and university students in the Balkans region, focusing on the geographical areas most affected by the crimes, as well as national capitals and other major towns and cities.

In high schools, the project's lectures and discussions are aimed at stimulating the young people's interest in the issues of justice and accountability and the tribunal's contribution to both. Furthermore, the lectures offer an overview of the findings on the crimes committed and the responsibility of the individuals from the cases most relevant to the audience. This involves creating tailormade presentations for pupils in different countries and regions, so the material includes ICTY cases that directly affect their own towns and people. Students are thus able to relate directly to the information and material presented to them, and to reflect on the benefits and limitations of punitive justice and other mechanisms of transitional justice aimed at post-conflict recovery.

The outreach program has also designed guest lectures for university students in countries of the former Yugoslavia. These lectures are more focused than the high school presentations, on single topics related to the work of the ICTY (for example, the prosecution of wartime sexual violence or the concept of joint criminal enterprise), which are analyzed in depth and not exclusively with relation to the former Yugoslavia. In this way, these lectures serve several functions: they introduce the students to the work of the ICTY; they inform students in detail about particular topics in international law; and they provide students with a perspective of the events in the former Yugoslavia with respect to international law and in comparison with other conflicts throughout the world.

The project has been implemented in two phases. The first sought to establish cooperation with local authorities and standardize the project's key activities (that is, the lectures and presentations in high schools and at universities throughout the former Yugoslavia). The second phase, implemented as of mid-2013, aims at transferring ownership of the project to local partners to ensure its sustainability. This is being done by training high school teachers and local NGO activists to deliver the standardized presentations developed by the outreach program, as well as through the production of tailor-made teaching tools and materials to be used in the future education activities.

The requirement of government buy-in to the project was primarily a strategic one and based on four assumptions:

- Involving national and school authorities in the project would sensitize them to the need to include content related to the recent past more prominently in the school's program.
- Placing project activities in the formal school setting would allow for the involvement of teachers, whose contribution would be crucial for any future attempt to introduce more content related to transitional justice into the official curriculum.
- By demonstrating that controversial and sensitive topics can, in fact, be addressed in a constructive and beneficial manner with youth, the project would undermine one of the arguments the authorities most frequently used to justify the status quo in the education system.
- By obtaining the governments' support, the outreach program would be able to start chiseling away at the presumption that the authorities were adamantly "anti-tribunal" and thus show that there was room for

cooperation and the possibility of tolerance—if not full endorsement—of the facts established in the courtrooms.

The phase of the project currently underway (at the time of writing) includes a pilot training activity for high school teachers from Bosnia and Herzegovina, which will equip them with the skills, knowledge, and materials they need to conduct high-quality lectures tackling the issues of dealing with the past, including the role played by the ICTY. In a complementary activity, the ICTY's outreach program is partnering with local NGOs in the region to train their representatives in delivering the same type of presentations, to both high school students and other audiences in various informal education and/ or informational settings. This is a fallback strategy devised by the program to cover for the realistic possibility that the national impetus to change the official curriculum might not be achieved before the project's closure. If that were to happen, civil society partners would be able to continue engaging this important part of the community in the ongoing debate about the legacies of the war. As an additional instrument for conveying knowledge, an informational toolkit that is being developed will serve as the main source of content and material for the newly trained teachers and NGOs, as well as for future educators.

The project has the following goals:

- To increase the knowledge of youth in the former Yugoslavia about the tribunal and stimulate their interest in issues of justice, accountability, and reconciliation, and the ICTY's contribution to these, by delivering presentations and academic lectures in high schools and universities across the region.
- To generate reflection among the students about the crimes committed in the recent past; build an extensive body of data and statistics about their opinions and views of the war and other ethnicities involved in it; and identify ways to prevent such tragic events from happening again by demonstrating that war crimes are deplorable, regardless of the ethnicity of the perpetrator or victim, thereby fostering an environment conducive to durable peace and security in the region.
- To create conditions for the continued and sustainable education of young people in the former Yugoslavia about the work of the ICTY and other issues related to post-conflict justice by producing high-quality informational material about the tribunal's work, as well as by training high school teachers and activists at local NGOs to enable them to continue these activities once the outreach program has closed down.

Overall, the project aims to foster among its beneficiaries a better and deeper understanding of the ICTY and war crimes trials in general. It provides high school students with information and tools for dealing with issues relating to the legacy of the conflicts and atrocities that occurred in the region, while university students benefit from professional development and by learning to approach predominant views critically.

HIGH SCHOOL PRESENTATIONS

The project makes tailor-made presentations across the region about the facts established in the trials before the ICTY to students ages sixteen to eighteen years. Lectures that have, to date, been delivered in more than one hundred high schools and to more than 3,600 students in Bosnia and Herzegovina, Croatia, Kosovo, Montenegro, and parts of Serbia have been designed not only to inform young people about the tribunal, but also to encourage them to think critically about the Balkan Wars and post-conflict efforts to achieve justice. In the ongoing project cycle, an additional thirty schools will be targeted.

Outreach officers mostly visit new schools in each project cycle, but they may also return to some schools to deliver presentations to new groups of pupils. The priority is to reach students in those communities most heavily affected by the conflicts of the 1990s, such as Djakova/Ðakovica, Knin, Konjic, Prijedor, Srebrenica, and Vukovar. The need for impartial information is strongest among the people who have lived through the horrors of war and whose scars from the conflict are deepest. The survivors need to know their suffering is recorded and remembered, while the perpetrators' communities need to face the facts and accept them. Ethnic tensions in these communities, where victims meet their torturers on a daily basis in shops, hospitals, police stations, or elsewhere, are higher than in towns and villages spared such trauma. This is the environment in which new generations of Balkan youth are growing up, and it inevitably affects and shapes their opinions and understanding, not only of the conflict but of other ethnic and religious groups living in their countries.

Presentations in high schools are implemented with the approval of and in cooperation with the ministries of education and other education authorities in target countries. Once both ministry approval and cooperation have been secured, outreach officers approach the directors and teachers of targeted high schools to get their green light and ensure their cooperation for the presentations. This has proved the first major hurdle to overcome. Most governments in the region have not been favorably inclined toward the ICTY and have been skeptical about extending their support beyond what is required of them to aid the core mandate of the tribunal. Furthermore, negotiations with local authorities can often turn into lengthy bureaucratic exercises that eat into the life of the project.

Nevertheless, the outreach program chose this approach over delivering lectures to selected students outside the school environment and without the support or involvement of governments and teachers. It opened doors for other education initiatives by civil society actors, which, in some countries, were previously unable to engage with youth in a formal setting. In Kosovo, for example, the Humanitarian Law Center—a local NGO that partnered with the outreach program at one stage to present details of its "population losses" project—subsequently secured the funding and government approvals to hold standalone lectures in high schools throughout the country. In addition, in the absence of political will to change the curriculum to include teaching of the recent violent past of the region, this approach to the project stands as a viable demonstration that students, teachers, and local governments can be receptive to such an idea and offers valuable data about students' hunger for and need to learn about recent history.

The outreach program had difficulty securing government support in each of the countries targeted. In Bosnia and Herzegovina, for example, implementation was slowed by the cumbersome setup of a system with more than ten ministries of education. In Kosovo, cooperation had to be secured while keeping in mind the neutral position of the United Nations with regard to the status of the territory, which impeded direct communication with the government. In Croatia, agreement was secured only after extensive negotiations, supportive interventions from international actors, and, ultimately, a change of government.

Meanwhile, Serbia remains the only country that has not given a green light to the project. Despite over two years of lengthy negotiations, meetings with representatives of international actors such as the European Union, and the involvement of the highest ranking representatives of the tribunal, the Serbian Ministry of Education has at the time of writing yet to give a formal response to the request. In the interim, the program has managed to secure access to at least one part of the country—the Serbian province of Vojvodina, which has an autonomous Ministry of Education.[20]

Serbia's stance may be seen to undermine the success of the project, given the regional importance of this country's participation in facing the past. That is only the case, however, if the project is evaluated based exclusively on its outcomes in Serbia and by ignoring process and context. The de facto rejection from Serbia to date shows the political reality in which this project operates.

There is no magic wand to change that reality, and the project can only stretch it to an extent. Serbia's lack of political and institutional will to allow the facts about the recent past to be included in the school curriculum exposes the lack of an authentic process of facing that past. While students can, arguably, be reached outside the classroom and school environment, the outreach program has deliberately steered clear of this course, as explained above. The project is envisaged not only to change the perception of youth, but also to engage the local authorities in a dialogue about the reasons for keeping facts about the recent past out of the official curriculum.

The same aim lies behind the project's extensive involvement of school management and teachers. In BiH, for example, the responsible outreach officer would meet with the school principal, senior teachers, and school counselor ahead of an event to explain the project, share the material, and agree on the dates and format of the lecture. Even with the approval of the Ministry of Education, however, making such arrangements with individual schools is not without its challenges. Many teachers have expressed concern about allowing such discussions in their classrooms, citing security fears, reactions of parents, and, most often, their own beliefs about the war. Although security fears and parents' reactions have not materialized as obstacles so far, the extent to which the teaching staff's own experiences in war can influence not only the implementation of the project but also the thought process of pupils is illustrated by two incidents in Bosnia.

The first took place in Rogatica, a town nestled near Bosnia's border with Serbia, whose ethnic makeup was completely changed during the war. There, the school director was reluctant to grant access to the school and premises, citing various reasons. Only after extensive negotiations was access granted. Before the lecture, the director addressed the students, warning them that not everything they would hear would be true. Subsequently, two male students put on tee shirts bearing images of Ratko Mladic, the wartime military leader of Bosnian Serbs who was on trial at the ICTY. The outreach officer dealt with both the director's speech and the students wearing the tee shirts in a non-confrontational manner, offering facts and statistics instead of allowing himself to be drawn into political rhetoric. Tellingly, the rest of the students applauded at the conclusion of the presentation, while looking visibly uncomfortable at the actions of their assertive tee shirt–wearing classmates.

The second incident happened in Foca, another town on the border with Serbia, made infamous by its widespread rape camps and systematic sexual abuse of non-Serb women during the war. One of the teachers attending the lecture interrupted the presentation at the end of the first school hour and, before leaving, expressed her hope that the local population would not react violently to the alleged lies being told to the students. Once again, the students applauded at the end of the presentation rather than following the example of their teacher. Subsequently, it turned out that the teacher was a daughter of a fallen Bosnian Serb soldier who had died in the vicinity of Foca.

Following every presentation in Bosnia, the outreach officer has a debrief meeting with the school director and other teachers in which any incidents, such as the ones above, as well as the outcomes of the presentation and potential subsequent cooperation, are discussed.

In general, presentations entail two-hour meetings with thirty to sixty students. Tailored to each school, they include specific information, facts, and descriptions of cases that are relevant to the respective geographical area or address a particular misconception found to be persistent there. Graphics, photographs, and audiovisual footage from the tribunal's proceedings are used not only to underline the importance of the rule of law, the facts established, and the human suffering involved, but also to address the "dehumanization" of others that had taken root in the region. This helps generate deeper reflection and spark interest and debate among pupils. At least half of the time available is devoted to questions, answers, and discussion. The discussion portion of the event is considered crucial, and the students are encouraged to talk not only about matters related to the presentations, but also wider topics that are important to them.

Outreach officers are trained by youth communications specialists not only to make their presentations interesting to the age groups addressed but also to ensure they are interactive and involve the students as much as possible. Thus, for instance, the outreach officer in some presentations may refer to national literature books that are part of the official syllabus to start a discussion about whether rape is a crime of war. The students keenly debate passages describing acts of sexual violence committed during historical wars, and only after prompting does the presenter offer witness testimonies, documents, and judgments pertaining to similar acts of violence committed in the students' own communities during their lifetimes, drawing them into a discussion closer to home. The benefit of these dynamic classes is recognized by teachers. According to one,

This is an innovative approach compared to the regular curriculum. The students' attention was maintained throughout the presentation, due to the fact that they had an active role in the class, which was quite refreshing compared to a standard lecture format.[21]

273

UNIVERSITY LECTURES

In addition to high school presentations, the ICTY's legal experts regularly give academic lectures as part of the Youth Outreach Program on a variety of tribunal-related topics at various public and private universities across the region. Between 2010 and 2013, they delivered more than seventy lectures to geographically and ethnically diverse groups of young people, comprising some 3,500 students from dozens of universities in BiH, Croatia, Kosovo, Macedonia, Montenegro, and Serbia. Although students in a broad range of disciplines take part in the project, it is targeted toward the law, history, journalism, and political science faculties.

Unlike in the high school part of the project, the national education authorities are not involved in the university-level process. Given the autonomy of universities in designing their curricula, no special government approval is needed for the lectures to be held; arrangements are made directly with the institutions, usually with the deans or professors of relevant faculties and subjects. This has made it possible to include Serbian universities in the project, as well as faculties in Macedonia and Montenegro—places not targeted by the high school segment.

The university segment of the project consists of lectures of a strictly academic nature on specific topics related to students' fields of study. The goal is not only to inform students about the ICTY and some of the facts it established, but also to increase their understanding of international criminal and humanitarian law and its implementation and development by the tribunal and similar institutions. General issues related to justice and accountability, as well as the findings of specific cases, are also discussed following the presentations. Compared to high school pupils, university students are better able to grasp and discuss the more complex issues related to the tribunal, which helps them improve their understanding of the realities in which the trials are conducted, their importance, and their limitations.

Since the lectures are designed to tackle specific legal issues related to the work of the tribunal, they are given by the tribunal's experts from the Chambers, the Office of the Prosecutor, and, in some cases, the Registry.[22] This provides a rare opportunity for the populations affected by the war to hear directly from, for example, the lawyer who prosecuted a case or the legal officer who worked on a judgment. Each lecture lasts for approximately two hours, with half the time allocated to the lecturer's talk and the remainder to questions and discussion. The university is asked to propose a lecture topic relevant to the faculty being approached, or to choose from an extensive list of possible topics one that best suits the interests and backgrounds of their students. Unsurprisingly, topics such as command responsibility and joint criminal enterprise (that is, holding individuals legally responsible for the criminal actions of other individuals within a perpetrating group), which are the two legal concepts most hotly contested by the political establishment, have been extremely popular across the region, reflecting their controversial nature among the many segments of the population who have grown to accept the importance of prosecuting direct perpetrators but remain skeptical about the fairness of prosecuting those higher up in the chain of command.

From Split to Belgrade, the ICTY's experts and outreach officers have delivered lectures on the topics chosen by professors and students, which most of the time have reflected a wider societal concern about the accused individuals from the ethnic group targeted by each specific lecture. While it would be erroneous and overambitious to look for a change of perception after one visit, the program has addressed these issues in detail, not shying away from the controversies and opening the minds of students to a different way of thinking. As a professor in Croatia said,

> I greatly appreciate the ICTY's efforts to explain the work of the Tribunal to my students at the Split Law Faculty. The details of ICTY case law will help the students to understand complex aspects of the Tribunal's jurisprudence, including the issue of joint criminal enterprise.[23]

In Belgrade, another explained that

> a lecture given by an ICTY lawyer is an excellent opportunity for the students of the Union University Law School to become more familiar with the Tribunal's jurisprudence concerning sexual offences, particularly if one bears in mind that the ICTY has contributed to the development of international criminal law most notably by its definition of sexual crimes.[24]

The positive feedback from the students and university professors indicates the need to continue the organized and systematic presence of qualified staff who will bring the ICTY's jurisprudence closer to students. That the students choose their lecture topics is a special quality of this project, one that makes the lectures interesting and useful to their future academic work. Receiving relevant information firsthand, with additional clarification through lively discussion, students can properly understand and recognize the importance of the ICTY's contribution to unveiling the extensive crimes committed during the conflicts. Of course, the debates provoked by the lectures are often heated, with students posing very critical questions about the tribunal and its work and challenging the institution's legitimacy and impartiality. Nevertheless, an overwhelming majority of students and lecturers have given positive feedback.

The format of the lectures is itself a refreshing novelty for students in the Balkans, exposed as they have been to an inherited system of learning theory that does not involve much application of critical thinking. One Sarajevo student made clear that "such presentations are very useful to us because this was our first direct contact with someone who is qualified to provide direct explanations that we usually do not get in our regular classes," while another from Mostar pointed out, "The lecture given by the legal expert was certainly very much different from our everyday lectures. Now, I'm more interested in studying the International Criminal Law."[25]

Unexpected beneficiaries of the project have been the professors and principals who attend the presentations, with many remarking that they, too, had learned new details about the ICTY and were looking forward to incorporating some of them into future lectures. It is important to remember that the professors are citizens of the same countries as the students and thus also affected by the conflicts and the predominant views of their societies. They themselves recognize the wider societal benefit these lectures can have. As one said,

> There is clearly a need for more information and debate about international humanitarian law and the role of the ICTY in the process of dealing with the past. Future generations must recognize the facts about past events as this is the only guarantee that such negative experiences will never happen again. This can only be achieved if we openly speak about crimes committed on all sides and show consideration for the sufferings of others.[26]

BUILDING LOCAL CAPACITY

With the phase-out of the ICTY's outreach program drawing closer at the time of this writing,[27] the youth program is seeking to build the capacity of local actors to continue and extend its activities after the tribunal pulls out from the region. While the ultimate goal of amending the official curriculum of Bosnia and Herzegovina remains unattainable within this time frame, the focus is on creating conditions within some schools and among local partners to continue with the classes. These lectures will form part of the "democracy and human rights" or "civic" education or similar segments of the official curriculum followed by high schools.

The approach here is threefold: training high school teachers from Bosnia and Herzegovina to give effective presentations about transitional justice and dealing with the past, with a focus on criminal prosecutions and the work of the ICTY and domestic judiciary; creating and training a network of NGOs that will implement guest lectures in those areas where teachers are unable or unwilling to be trained; and developing a Digital Education Toolkit, which will aid the trainers but also serve as a repository of tools and information for future initiatives, including the eventuality that an agreement on changing the curriculum is reached.

Regarding the training of high school teachers, as of this writing, a pilot activity has been planned for implementation in Bosnia and Herzegovina in 2014 whose participants will be teachers who have expressed a particular interest in the project, from five or six high schools in the Sarajevo region where the presentations were already delivered during the previous project cycles. Following the training, the teachers will deliver the presentations to pupils in their respective schools, with an ICTY outreach program representative attending to provide feedback and assess the success of the training. The teachers will be invited to continue delivering the presentations in the future to each new generation of pupils. They will also be consulted in the development of the Digital Education Toolkit and involved in its application and the future improvement of its content. If this pilot activity proves successful, the plan at this writing is to extend it in 2015 to other regions of Bosnia and Herzegovina, and perhaps to other countries of the region as well. The goal is to create a pool of teachers able and willing to deliver high-quality presentations about the work of the ICTY and wider issues of transitional justice as a stepping-stone to integration of these topics into the official high school curriculum.

The ICTY's outreach program is also seeking to create an extensive network of NGOs interested in and capable of conducting education activities related to the work of the ICTY and issues of transitional justice, targeted at young people in the region. Primarily, this will involve NGOs whose programs have strong education and/or youth-oriented components. As a first step, the outreach program has invited several such NGOs, with which it has already conducted joint projects or cooperated in the past, to take part in the current or future Youth Outreach Program cycles.

Furthermore, the outreach program is conducting a mapping exercise to identify all organizations and initiatives in the region that implement projects relevant to the ICTY's legacy and transitional justice. Based on the results, the program will contact the organizations identified as having the capacity and experience to take part in the Youth Outreach Program and invite their activists to attend training on delivering effective presentations for teenagers on transitional justice and ICTY-related issues. Like the teachers, the trained NGO activists will be invited to use their new skills to deliver presentations to young people in their respective regions, either through visits to high schools (if approval from the relevant ministry is obtained) or in nonformal education venues.

A long-term aim is to build the capacity and support of local NGO representatives and activists to continue education activities throughout the region. Thus, in the last phase of the project implemented in Kosovo, the ICTY cooperated with the local branch of the Humanitarian Law Center (HLC) to expose the pupils not only to the importance of criminal prosecutions and the rule of law, but also to other mechanisms of transitional justice, such as searching for and identifying the missing and the undertaking of truth-seeking initiatives, in which HLC was involved. HLC subsequently secured additional funding and support to continue these activities with Kosovo youth.

Meanwhile, following the closure of the ICTY's field office in Kosovo, the project team worked with the Youth Initiative for Human Rights, a regional NGO with a strong presence in Kosovo and a strong track record in youth- and education-related activities, to train its representatives to deliver the presentations in schools across Kosovo. The outreach program secured the approval of the Ministry of Education and financing from external funds to cover the costs. Creating similar partnerships in Croatia and other countries will help resolve the issue of lack of personnel in those areas, ensure implementation of the project there, and begin the process of transferring ownership of the activity to local actors.

As an additional step toward ensuring the sustainability of its work, the plan at the time of writing is for the outreach program to standardize fully the existing information tools and materials in the upcoming project cycle and develop new ones to be used to deliver the high school presentations about the tribunal. These will form a Digital Education Toolkit, which will include the following:

- A set of presentations about the work of the ICTY, its cases, case law, and related issues, each of which will be tailored to the interests of the youth in one of the target countries by including examples and materials related to the crimes committed there
- Detailed lecture notes to accompany the presentations
- A set of multimedia materials, including evidence from the trials, photographs, maps, and audiovisual material, such as powerful testimonies given by the victims before the tribunal or statements of guilt by the accused
- A list of questions frequently asked by students and adequate answers

to these questions, based on the extensive experience of the project
team from the previous two cycles of the project

In developing the toolkit, the outreach program will consult with experienced organizations, such as the United Nations Educational, Scientific and
Cultural Organization (UNESCO), as well as local actors, including teachers and activists engaged in the upcoming cycle of the project, to ensure best
practices and approaches are chosen. The toolkit will initially be used by the
teachers and NGO activists trained in the course of the project and then placed
online to make it available to other actors in the region interested in developing presentations or lectures about the work of the ICTY in various formal or
informal education settings. The outreach program will also present the toolkit to its NGO partners and promote its use among other local stakeholders.
This is expected to encourage other educators and NGOs in the region to initiate new awareness-raising and education projects about the work and achievements of the ICTY and to help them do so.

YOUTH REACTIONS AND OPINIONS

From 2011 to 2013, more than 5,500 students from more than 150 high schools
and universities in the region—including from Bosnia and Herzegovina,
Croatia, Kosovo, Macedonia, Montenegro, and Serbia—participated in the
ICTY's Youth Outreach Program. In 2013 alone, in BiH, Croatia, and Kosovo, the
lectures were attended by 1,017 students, of whom 61 percent were male and 39
percent were female. (In the previous year, the gender composition of the 1,500
attendees had been reversed, with 60 percent female and 40 percent male.)
Students were asked to fill out questionnaires at the end of each presentation, which allowed the outreach program to assess the effect of its activities
on the participating students' perception, awareness, level of knowledge, and
opinions about transitional justice in general and the ICTY in particular. In
some cases, this led to the introduction of new forms of presentations. In 2013,
for example, several advanced-level presentations, which included moot court
sessions, were held in those schools that had already been visited in 2012 but
expressed particular interest in the topic. An additional benefit of these questionnaires was the opportunity to poll, for the first time, a large segment of the
youth population on the issues of war crimes, justice, dealing with the past,
and coexistence. What follows is a short overview of their comments regarding the presentations and lectures, as well as these issues.

The great majority (83.6 percent) of participating students assessed the presentations as excellent (53.6 percent) or very good (30 percent). Additionally, three in four (77.5 percent) said they significantly benefited from the lectures and learned new, important facts and information about the ICTY. In Bosnia and Herzegovina in 2013, for example, more than 75 percent of participating students on average claimed to have learned something new, as illustrated in figure 8.1.

Figure 8.1. Large Majorities of Program Participants across BiH Gained Knowledge of Tribunal

Question: Did you learn something new about the ICTY?

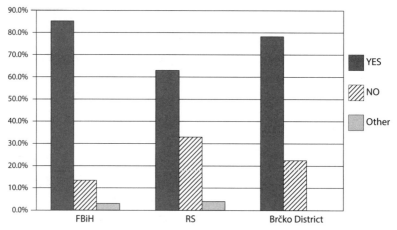

Source: Based on collated data from individual evaluation forms completed by participants in the 2012–13 Youth Education Program from Bosnia and Herzegovina. Questionnaires are on file with the ICTY Outreach Program.
Note: The Federation of Bosnia and Herzegovina (FBiH) and Republika Srpska (RS) are the administrative entities that comprise BiH. Brčko District is a neutral, self-governing administrative unit that is part of both FBiH and RS.

Students' messages of support for this project can be frequently read in their comments; one said, "This kind of presentation should be organized in as many schools [as possible] in the territory of Bosnia and Herzegovina."[28] Some students were very inspired by the lecture given by the ICTY representative, on several occasions saying it influenced their decisions to study criminal law after they finish school. Over 40 percent said their opinion about the tribunal changed for the better after the presentation. Even those who still had a negative opinion about the ICTY or some of its rulings said they were aware that without the ICTY, war crimes trials—or at least impartial trials—would never have taken place.

Nevertheless, data from 2012 and 2013 (that is, from the 2011–12 and 2012–13 programs, respectively) show perceptions of the ICTY overall remained polarized at best. Taking Bosnia and Herzegovina as an example, figures 8.2a and 8.2b show the difficulty of shifting entrenched opinions in communities that have been exposed to decades of denial, and where dealing with the past was never actively encouraged by the authorities. Year to year, both entities—the Federation of Bosnia and Herzegovina (FBiH) and the Republika Srpska—showed minor shifts in opinion, whether positive or negative. In the FBiH, around 40 percent of students in both 2012 and 2013 stated that their opinions of the tribunal had not changed after the lecture, while the proportion in the RS who remained unmoved by the presented facts hovered between 75 percent in 2012 and 65 percent in 2013. On the positive side, the students in both entities whose opinions changed for the better after the presentation should not be disregarded. In the FBiH, that proportion remained above 50 percent in both 2012 and 2013, while in the RS it was at 17 percent and 22 percent, respectively. The negative image of the tribunal reflected by these figures was deeply embedded; it remained the same even when students changed their stance toward criminal and transitional justice processes in general or recognized that crimes were committed within or by their communities.

Figure 8.2a: Participants' Perception of Tribunal Remained Split, 2011–12

Question: Did your opinion of the tribunal change after the presentation?

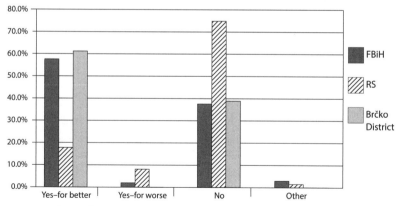

Source: Based on collated data from individual evaluation forms completed by participants in the 2011–12 Youth Education Program from Bosnia and Herzegovina. Questionnaires are on file with the ICTY Outreach Program.
Note: The Federation of Bosnia and Herzegovina (FBiH) and Republika Srpska (RS) are the administrative entities that comprise BiH. Brčko District is a neutral, self-governing administrative unit that is part of both FBiH and RS.

Figure 8.2b: Participants' Perception of Tribunal Remained Split, 2012–13

Question: Did your opinion of the tribunal change after the presentation?

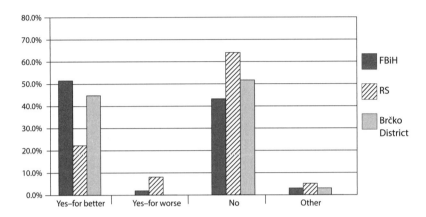

Source: Based on collated data from individual evaluation forms completed by participants in the 2012–13 Youth Education Program from Bosnia and Herzegovina. Questionnaires are on file with the ICTY Outreach Program.
Note: The Federation of Bosnia and Herzegovina (FBiH) and Republika Srpska (RS) are the administrative entities that comprise BiH. Brčko District is a neutral, self-governing administrative unit that is part of both FBiH and RS.

The broader context of this polling must not be forgotten, however. In 2012 and 2013, the ICTY issued a number of decisions and judgments that left the local population deeply dissatisfied. The amount of negative press coverage and commentary from public figures and authorities was enormous and far-reaching. On top of twenty years of consistent efforts to criticize the institution for purposes of local propaganda campaigns and political scoring, these circumstances ensured the ICTY would not receive an overwhelming endorsement by the divided societies in the region. In short, a series of lectures, no matter who gives them, cannot undo a generation of harm caused by a failure to deal with the past. What it can do, though, is help communities begin chiseling away at the presumptions and divisions that have become embedded, and to hold up the mirror to those communities stuck in denial.

With this in mind, the students' responses do give us hope. For example, an overwhelming majority (69 percent) believed the tribunal made a positive contribution by prosecuting war criminals (figure 8.3). Directly related, almost all students (96 percent) held the view that all war criminals should be punished, regardless of their positions and ethnicities (figure 8.4). A total of 66 percent acknowledged that members of their own ethnic groups committed war crimes (figure 8.5). As one of the students put it, "I think that there are criminals in every nation and that they must be held accountable."[29] Another wrote that, "by investigating and punishing perpetrators of war crimes, the tribunal forced people to face the truth and gave families of the victims moral and legal satisfaction."[30]

Figure 8.3. Majority of Students from Bosnia and Herzegovina Feel the Tribunal Contributed to Punishing War Criminals

Question: Do you believe that the tribunal made a positive contribution to punishing war criminals in your country?

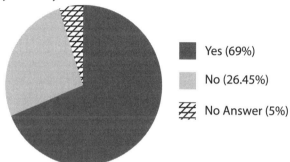

Source: Graphic is based on collated data from individual evaluation forms completed by participants in the 2012–13 Youth Education Program from Bosnia and Herzegovina. Questionnaires are on file with the ICTY Outreach Program.

Figure 8.4. Vast Majority of Students in Bosnia and Herzegovina Believe in Criminal Justice

Question: Do you think all war criminals should be punished, regardless of their position and ethnicity?

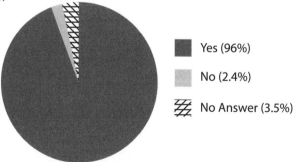

Source: Graphic is based on collated data from individual evaluation forms completed by participants in the 2012–13 Youth Education Program from Bosnia and Herzegovina. Questionnaires are on file with the ICTY Outreach Program.

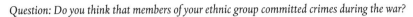

Figure 8.5. Majority of Youth in Bosnia and Herzegovina Recognize Members of Their Own Communities Committed Crimes during the War

Question: Do you think that members of your ethnic group committed crimes during the war?

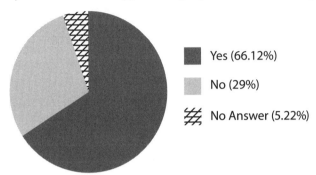

- Yes (66.12%)
- No (29%)
- No Answer (5.22%)

Source: Graphic is based on collated data from individual evaluation forms completed by participants in the 2012–13 Youth Education Program from Bosnia and Herzegovina. Questionnaires are on file with the ICTY Outreach Program.

One of the most significant obstacles to facing the past in the former Yugoslavia is the lack of readiness across ethnic groups to accept responsibility for the war crimes committed in their names and by their compatriots. Therefore, the feedback received from teenagers through the Youth Education Program, which shows around two-thirds are aware and accepting of the fact that violence was perpetrated by people from their own ethnic groups, must be taken as a positive sign. With a more sustained outreach campaign, it suggests, a new generation of decision makers can be raised who will be more willing to take the brave steps necessary to truly move forward the process of normalizing relations among the divided nations.

The lectures and evidence presented often had a deep impact on youth who had previously been exposed to only one side of the story. A high school student from Višegrad, for example, a town on the border with Serbia that saw some of the most heinous crimes committed but where a culture of denial persists, was shocked to hear what took place in her hometown. Following the lecture she wrote, "Ignorance creates a gap between people of different nationalities . . . [and ICTY presentations] contribute to better understanding among people and create the conditions for reconciliation and coexistence."[31]

Yet, in the same school, another female student throughout the discussion asked only about "false witnesses" and how the tribunal identified or punished them. In an informal discussion after the class, the presenter asked this student why she was focused on this issue. She explained that her father had recently been indicted on charges of wartime rape before a local court in BiH, and she was convinced the charges were lies. A girl from the nearby city of Foca was less skeptical of the harrowing testimonies she heard. Following the lecture, she explained that she could not believe her parents and grandparents, who spent the whole war in the city, never told her about the crimes committed and the horrific fate of the town's non-Serb population. She was adamant that she would confront them about this and discuss it at home.

The extent to which official lines adopted by politicians and the media in particular areas had entered deep into society was evident from those students who repeated—many times verbatim—the dominant views in their communities. In the schools in Republika Srpska, for instance, the tribunal was given negative marks for "trying only the Serbs" and "releasing all other nations and convicting only the Serbs." In those areas where a strong sense of victimhood prevailed, particularly among Bosniak students in the federation, students were dissatisfied that "not all war criminals were brought to justice" and with the length of the sentences delivered. In those same communities, although not reluctant to accept that members of their group committed crimes, many sought to clarify and provide justifications in their comments. Crimes were committed "because we were defending ourselves," or they were "fewer than other groups committed." Similarly, in Republika Srpska, the students expressed an overwhelming acceptance of the crimes committed, followed by justifications and counter accusations.[32]

The project opened a dialogue, not only between the students and representatives of the ICTY, but among the students themselves. Although some of the questions and comments reflected widespread bias, in general they participated in the discussion with open minds and asked critical questions. The vast majority of those reached through the Youth Outreach Program showed a readiness to examine war crimes trials and events from the violent past of their communities critically, in a way that belied their young years. Feedback from university lecturers further indicated that the ICTY's jurisprudence, its work, and its achievements were highly relevant topics for university students, especially when presented interactively using a dynamic multimedia approach and in a context to which the young people could relate.

CONCLUSION

Despite the promising results of the ICTY's Youth Outreach Program to date, an urgent need remains for young people in the former Yugoslavia to take a more active role in the transitional justice process that will shape their region for years to come. The program has clearly shown their strong desire to play an important part in the process of dealing with the past. Students who have never before had a chance to hear firsthand accounts of the ICTY's work have greatly appreciated the opportunity to receive such a fresh perspective, hearing arguments of the tribunal that are entirely new to them. Criticism of the tribunal stemming from insufficient knowledge and understanding of the complexity and scope of its work is clearly best addressed through direct engagement with these young people.

The project has lain to rest the assumption that young people are not interested in hearing about the recent past, as the vast majority of students have spoken very passionately about events that took place before they were born. While reconfirming that youth are generally more willing than adults to listen to alternative views and more receptive to changing their opinions, the project has also exposed deeply engrained beliefs about the "other side," formed through years of propaganda and disinformation. This is a dangerous indicator, especially in a society that has permanently changed its ethnic makeup, and whose young people are more and more likely to enter into adulthood without having met people from other ethnicities.

The overwhelmingly positive reception of outreach visits, as well as the students' and teachers' identification of a need for more regular activities of this nature in their schools, shows that projects targeting the young should not only concentrate on those who are willing or able to secure space in out-of-school extracurricular activities. Space for a more permanent approach to teaching transitional justice could be carved out; but this is not and cannot be the job of international organizations, including the tribunal. Changes of that magnitude and impact in a society have to be made from within.

Most of the high school students included in this project were born near the end of the war, so their opinions about the recent conflict could not be formed from their own experiences, but rather on the basis of transgeneration memory, things taught in schools, stories heard from their relatives, or accounts by the mass media, heavily influenced by politicians. Yet, somehow, the youth and the key institutions shaping their opinions in childhood have largely been left out of the bigger transitional justice process of dealing with the past events in the region. Their basic right to be able to form their own opinions based on untainted information would be supported by access to a variety of sources of information, including that which has come firsthand from the ICTY.

Through its Youth Outreach Program, the ICTY has had a modest impact on some of the current generation of high school and university students. In light of the strong influence of various political actors, and therefore the different political interests, on the processes of transitional justice in the former Yugoslavia, providing balanced information and education is crucial for the success of these processes and their wider aims.

The evaluation and assessment of the ICTY's Youth Outreach Program show that educating youth about the conflicts, as well as wider transitional justice processes and responses, is instrumental in achieving a successful transition from a (post-)conflict situation to sustainable peace, democracy, security, and reconciliation. This cannot be achieved, however, through ad hoc projects and programs, no matter how positive their immediate impact may appear. The cooperation of local authorities and a political will to tackle the inadequacy of the official curriculum are essential if the affected countries wish to ensure new generations learn from the mistakes of the past. At this writing, Bosnia and Herzegovina, the country in the region that suffered the biggest losses, was nearing the twentieth anniversary of the end of the conflict. Yet another push to introduce the facts about the war and its legacies is needed, and it should come from the local actors, teachers' associations, local authorities, civil society, and international partners from European and UN institutions.

NOTES

1   All references to Kosovo in this chapter should be understood to be in the context of United Nations Security Council Resolution 1244 (1999).

2   No official figures exist for the human losses across the former Yugoslavia. Different international and national initiatives have attempted to establish a register of violent deaths during the Yugoslav conflicts, and the cited figure here is arrived at by using demographic studies produced by the International Criminal Tribunal for the former Yugoslavia, the Bosnian nongovernmental organization (NGO) Research and Documentation Center, and Serbia's Humanitarian Law Center.

3   Ewa Tabeau, ed., *Conflict in Numbers: Casualties of the 1990s Wars in the Former Yugoslavia (1991–1999)* (Belgrade: Zagorec, 2009).

4   See, for example, Sanja Kutnjak Ivkovic and John Hagan, *Reclaiming Justice: The International Criminal Tribunal for the Former Yugoslavia and Local Courts* (Oxford and New York: Oxford University Press, 2011).

5   Office of the UN Resident Coordinator in Bosnia and Herzegovina, *Public Opinion Poll Results—Analytical Report*, June 2013, http://www.un.ba/upload/documents/Prism%20 Research%20for%20UN%20RCO_Statistical%20report.pdf.

6   See Bodo Weber and Kurt Bassuener, *EU Policies Boomerang: Bosnia and Herzegovina's Social Unrest* (Sarajevo and Berlin: Democratization Policy Council, February 2014), 6–7.

7   RECOM is the acronym for the Regional Commission for Truth-Seeking and Truth-Telling about War Crimes and Other Serious Violations of Human Rights in the Former Yugoslavia.

8   See, for example, Peter Van der Auweraert, *Reparations for Wartime Victims in the Former Yugoslavia: In Search of the Way Forward* (Geneva: International Organization for Migration, June 2013).

9   See Nemanja Stojanovic, *History Schoolbooks and Reconciliation* (available in Serbian only), Youth Education Committee, December 2013, http://ooo.org.rs/en/2013/12/06/ udzenici-istorije-i-pomirenje/.

10   Alternative education materials for teaching history have been developed and are available throughout the former Yugoslavia; most prominent are those developed and distributed by the Center for Democracy and Reconciliation in South-East Europe. They tend to be little used in everyday classrooms across the Balkans, however. See more at http://www.cdsee.org/projects/jhp.

11   See Insight on Conflict, "Youth Initiative for Human Rights (YIHR)," http://www. insightonconflict.org/conflicts/western-balkans/peacebuilding-organisations/youth-initiative-for-human-rights-yihr/.

12   See http://bhstring.net/tuzlauslikama/tuzlarije/viewnewnews.php?id=49716 (not available in English).

13   International Criminal Tribunal for the former Yugoslavia (ICTY), "Key Figures of the Cases," http://www.icty.org/sid/24.

14   These are the findings from a series of public opinion polls conducted by the Organization for Security and Co-operation in Europe (OSCE) and the Belgrade Centre for Human Rights in BiH, Croatia, and Serbia, http://www.bgcentar.org.rs/istrazivanje-javnog-mnenja.

15   ICTY, "Outreach Programme," http://www.icty.org/sections/Outreach/ OutreachProgramme.

16   In 2012, in line with the tribunal's completion strategy, the outreach offices in Croatia and Kosovo were closed, but the offices in Bosnia and Herzegovina and Serbia continue to work and implement activities in the field.

17   See ICTY, *Report of the President on the Conference Assessing the Legacy of the ICTY*, April 27, 2010, http://www.icty.org/x/file/Press/Events/100427_legacyconference_pdt_report.pdf.

18 Strategic Marketing Research, *Stavovi prema ratnim zlocinima za OEBS* [*Opinions about War Crimes for OSCE*] (Belgrade, June 2009; full unpublished version on file with the author).

19 Ibid.

20 The official name of the institution is the Provincial Secretariat for Education, Administration, and National Communities.

21 ICTY, "Students React Well to 'Refreshing' and 'Innovative' Presentation," Tuzla, June 14, 2012, http://icty.org/sid/11011.

22 For an explanation of the tribunal's three organs—the Chambers, the Office of the Prosecutor, and the Registry—see http://www.icty.org/sections/AbouttheICTY/Chambers.

23 ICTY, "Outreach Programme Launches Series of Lectures in Croatian Universities," press release, March 21, 2012, http://www.icty.org/sid/10940.

24 ICTY, "Outreach Programme Launches Series of Lectures in Universities in Serbia," press release, May 9, 2012, http://www.icty.org/sid/10964.

25 Extensive feedback and commentary provided by students are available from the ICTY's outreach program and online at http://www.icty.org/en/outreach/youth-outreach, but the actual questionnaires on which the students offered their comments are not provided on its website.

26 ICTY, "Tribunal's Outreach Programme Launches Second Phase of Its Youth Education Project," February 5, 2013, http://www.icty.org/sid/11196.

27 The outreach program was set to close in 2015, unless further funding was secured or its staff and activities incorporated into the core budget of the ICTY or its inheriting institution, the Mechanism for International Criminal Tribunals (MICT). At the time of writing, indications were that donations had been pledged sufficient to secure its existence to 2017, but no formal announcement had been made.

28 ICTY, evaluation questionnaires, Bosnia and Herzegovina, batch 2013, not available online.

29 Ibid.

30 Ibid.

31 ICTY, "Outreach Programme's Youth Education Project Concludes amid Praise from Participants," press release, October 19, 2012, http://www.icty.org/en/press/outreach-programme's-youth-education-project-concludes-amid-praise-participants.

32 ICTY, evaluation questionnaires, Bosnia and Herzegovina, batches 2011, 2012, and 2013, not available online.

CHAPTER 9

Outreach and Education at the Liberation War Museum in Bangladesh

Mofidul Hoque

In 2010, students from various high schools in Freetown were taken on a tour of the Special Court for Sierra Leone, and, as part of a Sites of Conscience education program, they engaged in dialogue on questions of justice, forgiveness, and reconciliation. When asked how the violence of the past affected their lives today, however, the students were stumped. After much consideration, a teenage girl noted that they were part of the generation born toward the end of the country's bloody civil war. While they were too young actually to remember the war, she observed, the violence had inevitably affected her generation, as many of her peers were themselves violent, engaging in acts of bullying and the use of weapons in school. After further discussion within the group, the young people decided to form their own "coalition" to address the problem of violence in schools. This is but one example of how Sites of Conscience programs can address legacies of the past and their contemporary ramifications; across the globe, they have facilitated historical perspectives of places in which they work, with public dialogue and education programs to inspire change among young people and the broader public.

The International Coalition of Sites of Conscience is a worldwide network of more than 190 historical sites, museums, and memory initiatives in fifty-four countries, specifically dedicated to remembering past struggles for justice and addressing their contemporary legacies through the use of places of memory—such as historic sites, place-based museums, or memorials—to confront both the history of what happened there and its contemporary implications.[1] The coalition was founded in 1999, when nine museums from four continents came together with a common commitment: to foster civil engagement by using their powerful places of memory as catalysts for new dialogue on contemporary issues. It advocates for every community's right to preserve sites where struggles for human rights and democracy have taken place, to talk openly about what happened there, and to confront their contemporary legacies.

In the aftermath of mass atrocity, such places of memory—or Sites of Conscience—serve as safe places that continue to engage communities beyond the limited time frames of formal and informal truth and justice mechanisms. In South Africa, for example, the District Six Museum in Cape Town continues, long after the closure of the truth and reconciliation process there, to work with the local community to lobby for land restitution for victims who were forcibly removed from their land during the apartheid years.

Sites of Conscience also go beyond the limited scope of victim/perpetrator dichotomies to engage the broader public on issues related to justice, accountability, and reconciliation. One such undertaking is in Cambodia, where members work with local youth and elders, facilitating intergenerational dialogues that seek to explore the larger patterns of cause and effect related to the genocide there and focus on questions related to individual responsibility in building an active citizenship and fostering cultures of peace and tolerance.

The Liberation War Museum (LWM) in Bangladesh, a founding member of the coalition, reflects one of the roles of Sites of Conscience in preserving the memory of war and building a culture of human rights and social justice in post-conflict societies. This chapter presents the education outreach work of LWM as a memory museum and a Site of Conscience, established twenty-five years after the massive human rights violations that accompanied the 1971 war for independence.

The advent of a post-liberation generation made it imperative that the museum address young students in an effective and inspiring way. How to link the past with the present and imbue the new generation with the core values of the liberation war was a challenge that led to the formulation of a project that aims to inspire and activate students with the power of memory as they collect eyewitness accounts of the events of 1971 from older members of their families or communities. The chapter attempts to convey the significance of this oral history project of LWM.

ESTABLISHMENT OF THE LIBERATION WAR MUSEUM

In 1996, Bangladesh approached its twenty-fifth anniversary of independence. As nothing had been done by the state to preserve the memory of the nine-month bloody war that took place in 1971, after which the country gained independence from Pakistan, civil society activists stepped in, putting forth the concept of a museum of memory that would serve as a place for the community to remember and learn from those events.[2] To be established as a citizen's initiative, the museum was promoted by an eight-member board of trustees, who understood that such a museum could be established only with support from the people. Initial funding was, however, collected from friends and sympathizers close to the trustees, with no public call for funding at the beginning; the aim was to start the work to make the project visible and earn the trust of the people. An old, two-story colonial house was rented to host the museum, and only when that was ready did the trustees appeal widely for donations of articles, memorabilia, photos, documents, news clippings, old publications, and so on, as well as for funding.

The community support the new Liberation War Museum received was overwhelming, and LWM opened its doors on March 22, 1996. People continued their strong support by enriching its collection in many different ways. Over the years, the museum became recognized as an institution of national importance, and it earned prestige for the services it rendered to society. Fortunately, during this period, Bangladesh started its journey from dictatorship to democracy, and the government gradually came forward to support the initiative, which continued with the subsequent change of regime.

In 1999, believing it was important to reach out to the younger generation, LWM initiated a program in Dhaka to bring students to the museum in groups by providing them with transportation—a program that continues today. The visiting students are shown a documentary film, produced by LWM and directed by an award-winning Bangladeshi filmmaker, on the history of the freedom struggle, using actual footage of the historic events. The students are guided through the galleries and finally sit for a quiz competition. At the end of the program, they are addressed by the museum staff or trustees, and prizes are given to the winners of the quiz competition.

Also in 1999, LWM and eight similar museums around the world joined hands to preserve the past together and to link it with present-day humanitarian issues; this was the launch of the International Coalition of Sites of Conscience. The coalition helped LWM broaden the concept of museum activities, as well as its focus, and the museum decided to depict the history of the war until December 16, 1971, when the Pakistan Army surrendered to the joint command of Bangladesh and India and the new state was born.

This cutoff enabled LWM to address a broader audience across the political divide. Dealing with the past conflict was complicated, with different political parties promoting different versions of history; debate on which leader contributed what often became heated, and the focus on the core values of liberation was lost. LWM tried to address the audience irrespective of its political positions, depicting history through documents, artifacts, and memorabilia and refraining from imposing a particular point of view of historical events. It placed the documents and facts before visitors and allowed them to formulate their own positions. At the same time, LWM highlighted the liberal syncretistic culture and tradition of Bengal, which was reflected in the liberation struggle of the people, who were upholding secular democratic values to ensure the rights of all religions.

The establishment of LWM had a significant impact on society. Its collection continued to be enriched over the years with contributions from many quarters, as victims' family members, former freedom fighters, victims of sexual violence, and others donated many touching pieces of memorabilia. Political posters, newspaper clippings, and rare photographs all helped to portray the past in a powerful way. The museum organized concerts, art camps, and theatre and film festivals to raise funds, while national days and commemorative events also attracted people to it. LWM thus became an active museum, a hub of memorialization linked to society in many different ways.

In 2001, with donor support, LWM launched a "Mobile Museum," a bus with displays mounted inside that began taking the museum to people far outside Dhaka, where it was enthusiastically received. The Mobile Museum made a special appeal to the younger generation, and its experiences with such activities led LWM to formulate a more focused program addressing the children and youth who were born after the events of 1971. It was important for the younger generation to learn about the country's history and, at the same time, be imbued with the core values of the struggle to establish a secular liberal democratic society. In 2004, LWM developed a new program specifically aimed at students, entitled "Introducing the History of the Liberation War in the Light of the Universal Declaration of Human Rights and Concept of Peace and Tolerance," which aimed to connect the new generation with the past to give them a vision for the future. The new program received support from Manusher Jonno, a national offshoot of the program funded by the United Kingdom's Department for International Development and its partners.

OUTREACH PROGRAM

The impact LWM had on young people and the commitment they showed to carrying forward the ideals of the liberation war inspired the museum to take further steps in this direction. Under the new program, the Mobile Museum visits education institutions in various parts of the country, where representatives implement a multicomponent program and appeal to the students to collect eyewitness accounts of 1971 from their elders. The aim of the program is to establish an interactive relationship with the students that does not end with the daylong event but opens new possibilities for developing mutually beneficial contacts.

The target population of the program is students from the post-primary to university levels, although secondary-level students respond more enthusiastically than those from higher levels and thus form the core target group. The members of the Mobile Museum team make advance visits to each institution, in which they brief the head of the institution and teachers about the program and arrange a date for the official visit. When the bus travels to a district, it usually spends a month in the locality, and the team formulates the schedule to include all subdistricts in an attempt to be as inclusive as possible, reaching out to the education institutions of towns as well as deeper rural areas and marginalized communities. Once the month-long schedule is fixed, the Mobile Museum starts its journey from Dhaka. The exhibition includes the following components:

- A mini-museum with a display of historical documents and artifacts, mounted inside the bus.
- A projector and screen to show the twenty-two-minute documentary film "History of the Liberation Struggle: 1947–1971." A generator is included for screenings in case of power failure or lack of electricity in the locality.
- A display on the Universal Declaration of Human Rights (UDHR), in which various articles of this document are presented through posters created by an eminent Bangladeshi artist.
- A poster display on the concept of peace and tolerance, designed by a leading Bangladeshi cartoonist. The display, "The World as a Village," scales down the world into a village with one hundred people, showing how many of them belong to each religion, nationality, language, and so on. It also highlights how many children the village has and their access to food and education, as well as the importance of respecting diversity and ensuring social justice. The idea is to enable the students to contextualize the violent past of the war period with the UDHR and learn not only about their own rights, but also the rights of other people.
- A comment book for the students to write down their reactions.

ORAL HISTORY PROJECT WITH A DIFFERENCE

In response to the enthusiasm of the young students who take part in its program, LWM has given them the task of oral history collection. As mentioned, an appeal is made to the students, who have been given a glimpse of history and may feel inspired by it, to gather eyewitness accounts. Although they were born long after the war, they may have senior members in their families or communities who witnessed the events of those days.

The students are encouraged to select and ask any one of the eyewitnesses about his or her experiences of 1971, and write down what they hear from the person. The process has been made simple and manageable. There is no set of questions to ask or instruction manual to be followed, just a leaflet that is distributed among the students explaining the process. The students are told not to bother about their handwriting or spelling mistakes; the important thing is to be authentic in doing the write-up. Each student records his or her name, class, and institution and the name and age of the person interviewed, with the written version of the oral interview following. Each institute nominates a network teacher who collects the oral accounts and sends them to LWM.

To encourage the students to do the exercise, LWM promises that all who submit oral testimonies will receive personal letters of thanks, reflecting that somebody in the museum read their write-ups. LWM also publishes a quarterly booklet with the basic information about each interview, which is sent to the institutions so the students can see their names in print, maybe for the first time in their lives. The booklet also includes a few of the testimonies. The museum pledges that each and every piece of oral testimony will be preserved in the museum, thereby creating an "Archives of Memory." If the students come to the museum years later, they will be able to see their write-ups from their student days.

At this writing, LWM has received more than twenty thousand oral accounts collected by the students. Since 2004, the Mobile Museum has traveled to forty-four of sixty-four districts of the country and has brought 530,525 students into the program. More than 50 percent of the participants are girls, and the oral accounts received contain testimonies from slightly more women than men, as girls usually go to their grandmothers to learn about their experiences of those unforgettable days. The number of eyewitness accounts overall is increasing as more and more students come into contact with the LWM outreach program.

This kind of oral history, which is neither formal nor structured, produces fascinating results. LWM addresses various strata of society through its outreach program, with the Mobile Museum connecting with a diverse range of institutions, from urban, elite schools to those in slums, from institutions in towns to those in deep rural areas, and from schools for the general population to those for small ethnic groups. Such diversity and wide reach is reflected in the oral accounts the students collect.

Furthermore, as Bangladesh expands its education system, increasing numbers of boys and girls are enrolling in school. In many cases, the students are from the first generation in their families to go to school, and their parents or grandparents are mostly illiterate—people who never had a chance to register their voices or write down their experiences. This initiative, then, may represent the first time somebody has asked about their pasts and recorded what they witnessed in 1971. As the students submit the eyewitness accounts to LWM, the opportunity opens up for the broader society to share these experiences. What remained private for so long can now become public.

It is difficult to convey in short the historical and social significance of the eyewitness accounts collected by the students. With their great diversity, the narratives can serve as source material for understanding people's views of history, as the accounts are about not only the past itself but also how the participants look at the past. The testimonies represent human stories, narrated mostly by common people. In most cases, the interviews are conducted in intimate surroundings of family or the community, which is reflected in the feeling of spontaneity in the write-ups. In a formal oral interview process, a person will often become stiff when faced with a microphone or other recording instrument and an interviewer with a set of well-prepared questions. In the LWM program, the interviewer and interviewee know each other very well, and when a member of the third generation wants to learn about experiences of 1971 from an elderly person in the family or community, it can make for a special encounter. The whole process has a very human dimension, which is difficult to attain in a more formal setting. In many respects, then, the collection of oral histories created by the students is very different from most such projects.

Initially, LWM was apprehensive about the truthfulness of oral accounts collected through such an informal process since, as mentioned, the museum provides no guidelines to the students on how to approach the person to be interviewed or conduct the interview. LWM has not provided any set questionnaire, as is usually done in oral history collection. But the concerns disappeared as the accounts started to reach the museum. The feeling of authenticity in the oral accounts was not difficult to identify. Some of the accounts may have contained minor factual mistakes, but in some ways these were a reflection of how the narrator looked at history. The statements collected by the students are not historical documents; rather, they demonstrate how history is perceived by common people.

The collection of such eyewitness accounts has significance in many ways beyond their historical value. The process of collecting them by the students plays an educational role by, for example, helping them develop their writing skills and creativity and giving them confidence in undertaking individual projects. Furthermore, against the backdrop of distortion and debate regarding the history of the liberation war and the tinkering with the textbooks by subsequent government authorities, students get confused about the past events. Through LWM's education outreach activity, they come to understand that history is not only what is written in the textbooks; it is also present around oneself. The students collecting testimonies gain an understanding of the past beyond the official version provided in the textbooks, which comes as a blessing to those teachers committed to upholding the truth in history.

The testimonies have also proved of great educational benefit for LWM by constituting a rich storehouse of historical knowledge. A significant number of eyewitness accounts put together from a particular area provides a depiction of local history. As the students collect and send the accounts individually to LWM, they do not know what other students have done. LWM therefore makes printouts, binds them in spiral volumes, and sends them back to the schools so the students can share the accounts they themselves delivered. This collection contributes to the creation of a new kind of synergy in the community, as students and teachers see what they have done collectively. They are also encouraged to organize events based on the oral testimonies—for instance, inviting persons selected from those whose oral accounts have been collected to join various national events held at the institution and share their narratives in more detail.

Finally, LWM plans to put more than twenty thousand testimonies on the Internet with a search option so people everywhere can have access to this treasure. The testimonies have opened up many other opportunities for researchers and educators. They have created greater opportunities for the sharing of personal experiences of the days of 1971.

A significant product of the outreach program has been the network of more than 1,200 teachers who have volunteered to work with LWM in promoting the ideals of the liberation war. The network teachers form the core group that oversees the follow-up activities of the program. Their primary task is to collect the eyewitness accounts from the students and send them to LWM. They also ensure the exhibition materials provided by LWM are used properly on various occasions. They form the bridge between the students and the museum.

So far, LWM has organized eighteen regional meetings of the network teachers to discuss the collection of oral accounts and relevant issues. In addition, one important meeting of teachers was held in Cox's Bazar, where an attack on the minority Buddhist community was carried out and Buddhist monasteries burned in 2012. The attack was instigated by the spread of false news on Facebook that a Buddhist youth had trampled on the Holy Quran. LWM conducted its outreach program in the locality, which was followed by a special meeting of the network teachers, joined by academics and activists from Dhaka. The discussion focused on promoting religious tolerance and harmony. At the end, a musical program conveyed the spirit of harmony in traditional culture.

LWM has not organized many such meetings, as the number of network teachers is quite large, and organizational expenses are high. Nevertheless, the teachers keep contact with LWM and are eager to cooperate in whatever way they can. Importantly, they also try to involve local communities in various follow-up activities using the oral testimonies. The network teachers also form a group that can be engaged in further research based on local history, as reflected in the testimonies.

EDUCATION MATERIALS AND FOLLOW-UP ACTIVITIES

As part of the Mobile Museum program, LWM provides institutions with materials that can be used in celebrating various national days. These include a DVD copy of the documentary film shown to the students and two sets of posters on the UDHR and the concepts of peace and tolerance. Besides these, LWM has also published a set of 101 posters with photographs depicting the history of the liberation struggle and its links with the history of Bengal from ancient times. How different waves of civilization and religion mixed together in Bengal is highlighted in historical perspective. LWM provides this set of posters to the education institutions so they can organize visual displays on various occasions.

LWM has also made efforts to present the eyewitness accounts to the wider public. It has so far published two anthologies of selected accounts, with a third volume forthcoming as of this writing. LWM considers each account significant, reflecting a human experience. It makes clear in the introduction to the anthologies that the included accounts are not necessarily the best write-ups of those experiences, but rather a selection meant to capture the diversity of the participating institutions.

LWM has also produced two short documentaries based on the eyewitness accounts, and, each quarter, it distributes to education institutions a publication with news and information about the ongoing program. Annually, LWM organizes a Freedom Festival, in which the students and network teachers of Dhaka who have visited the museum during the past year participate.

It is held at a large sports ground, usually with approximately ten thousand students attending.

As LWM constructs a new and permanent museum, it has organized a nationwide fundraising drive, which students and network teachers are enthusiastically joining. In many schools, the students have collectively raised funds and contributed to the building effort. LWM believes the students' slogan, "This museum of ours will be built by us," will provide them with a sense of ownership. LWM has found good partners in the students, their guardians, the network teachers, and the management committee members of the institutions. Together they form a source of strength for the museum, always ready to cooperate and implement joint programs.

While the oral history project has provided a rich dividend to the museum and opened up opportunities to promote the ideals of harmony and contribute to educating the new generation, it should be kept in mind that part of its value is symbolic. Since the program has only one bus to travel to the schools and address students, it has no other option than to be highly selective. Most of the country's institutions remain outside the domain of the program.

Moreover, LWM does not have the means or resources to run elaborate follow-up activities, nor has it created any manuals or education materials to be used in the classroom. As a memory museum, its education strategy is to play a supportive role in strengthening students' understanding of history and promoting peace and human rights education. LWM's input can enrich the mainstream education system as an informal contribution from outside, through the synergy the program has generated and the enthusiasm it has created among various stakeholders. But the museum is also aware of its limitations and knows what it can and cannot do. It works in parallel to other government and civil society initiatives, including large nongovernmental organizations (NGOs) such as the Bangladesh Rural Advancement Centre (BRAC), which runs its own community schools for girls, as well as many local NGOs working in the education sector.

Nevertheless, the changing reality of education in Bangladesh and the growing recognition of LWM's work in the field have made it an important stakeholder. This author, for example, a trustee of LWM and director of the education program, was appointed a member of the committee formed by the National Curriculum and Textbook Board in 2000 to study and recommend how the history of the liberation war can be properly incorporated into textbooks. The recommendations of the committee have contributed to improving the textbooks' quality.

One major achievement of the network teachers was changing the practice of keeping schools and colleges closed on government-approved holidays commemorating days of national importance. Bangladesh observes February 21 as Language Martyrs Day, March 26 as Independence Day, and December 16 as Victory Day. These are important occasions that the nation celebrates, but education institutions remained closed, with no activity on their campuses. A memorandum drawing attention to this problem was submitted to the Education Ministry on behalf of the network teachers, and many other civil society organizations also raised their voices on the matter. Subsequently, the government decided classes would remain suspended on national days, but students could go to the institutions to celebrate. Thus, education institutions are now more vibrant and engage in collective action on days of historical significance, which has created opportunities to connect the new generation with history by planning effective ways to celebrate.

Another positive development is the national education policy adopted in 2010 after elaborate discussion and exchange of opinions. LWM organized a special meeting of network teachers and submitted to the ministry a proposal highlighting the importance of having textbooks that reflect secular liberal values, and it recommended including a section on the UDHR in a textbook used in secondary schools, *History of Bangladesh and World Civilization*.[3] Although the UDHR was not specifically mentioned in the new textbooks, a section on the United Nations and its accomplishments was added to the curriculum. The social science textbook also has a chapter on children's rights.

Moreover, the 2010 national education policy stated that one aim of education, among others, would be "to inspire students with the spirit of liberation war (*Muktijuddher Cheteona*) and foster in them patriotism, nationalism, and human qualities."[4] It thus created the scope and opportunity to redesign LWM's education outreach program in light of the revised curriculum and new methods of teaching. The education reform aimed to promote creativity among the students, and the textbooks and examination system were changed accordingly. This is a new reality, to which LWM has to respond effectively. It is important, for example, to target secondary school students to ensure the program is in accordance with the new curriculum and with *History of Bangladesh and World Civilization*.

THE NEED FOR BROADER EDUCATION REFORM

The LWM outreach program was designed to create a synergy in its interaction with the new generation, which is why the program was made open ended. While the program presented by the Mobile Museum at individual institutions is only for a day, the connection remains ongoing, kept alive by the collection of oral history accounts and the role played by network teachers. Follow-up is a big challenge, however, with LWM lacking the staff to look after such activities. LWM also feels it must engage researchers and academics to evaluate the eyewitness accounts. There are many other ways to develop and make the program more effective, but LWM requires more human resources to undertake them. Hopefully, with the new museum being built, LWM will be more effective in future.

A major challenge, however, stems from the country's education sector, which has two other systems in addition to the widespread national system— one of theological learning and one of Western education. This has created a chaotic situation in the sector, with a mixture of different education trends and focal points. The total numbers of schools, colleges, and *madrashas* (theological institutions) in 2012 were 19,208, 3,547, and 9,441, respectively, and the numbers of students in these institutions were 7,937,235, 3,044,320, and 2,247,983. The gross enrollment rate at the secondary level was 64 percent, with a very high dropout rate of 44.7 percent for both males and females.[5]

Within the network of theological education institutions, some—known as *alia madrasha*—follow the government rules and curriculum, while many others—*quami madrasha*—are independent and externally well funded. The latter provide food and lodging to students free of cost and attract children from the poorer sector of society.

Government theological schools, in contrast, operate under the Madrasha Education Board, and after completion of their theological education, students have the option to enter into the mainstream national education system. Nevertheless, LWM has not been successful so far in bringing the *madrashas* into its program. The number of students at *madrashas* is quite large; according to the Ministry of Education, their total enrollment in 2012 was around 2.2 million, of whom 53 percent were women.

The other system of education in the country is the English system, offering degrees approved by the UK or US authorities. With education becoming increasingly privatized, attending these schools has became a strong trend, but in their pursuit of an international-standard education, students are finding it "de-linked" from their own nation's culture and history.

A major challenge for Bangladesh in regard to these three distinct education systems is to streamline the state of national education by bringing them under a common program. LWM's education outreach activities are an opportunity for the museum to play a more effective role in education reform, but, again, as a museum, it can only play the role of a facilitator, not a lead agency.

TRANSITIONAL JUSTICE IN BANGLADESH

In recent years, Bangladesh has experienced significant political change. The shift began in the run up to the December 2008 national election, when the trial of 1971 war criminals became a major electoral issue, and the voters went on to support overwhelmingly the alliance committed to pursuing justice for international crimes. This was partly the result of the support expressed by young voters, who are in the majority, for justice and secular liberal values, which was in turn a reflection of how the experiences of the 1971 liberation war had become intergenerational and of the power of memory and the contributions of many to keeping it alive.

In 2010, the International Crimes Tribunal of Bangladesh, popularly known as ICT-BD, was formed; the ICT Act was updated; rules and procedures were formulated; and, finally, the trials started, signifying the end of impunity for the perpetrators after four long decades. At the time of writing, nine trials had been completed, and six more were nearing completion.

The trials have opened up discussion in the country about transitional justice, restitution, reparation, healing, reconciliation, posttraumatic stress disorder, and many other related issues. The nation, engaged in a long and hard struggle to establish justice, is gradually learning about the role society can play in justice processes, and that the trials are meant not solely to ensure punishment but also to serve the broader interests of truth and humanity.

The initiation of the criminal justice process for crimes committed during the war period has made a strong impact, both nationally and internationally. As a major domestic tribunal established to address international crimes, the ICT-BD has attracted the attention of relevant international organizations. The accused have also organized well-funded lobbyists to plead their cases. A lot of confusion and misunderstanding surround the nature of the tribunal, which has enhanced the responsibility of LWM to promote the cause of justice and strengthen the trial process. The tribunal is operating under many constraints and is, of course, not free of mistakes and missteps. But the judges are committed to following due process of law, a commitment that has been expressed in various ways, including the rights accorded the defense. The tribunal does not have sufficient funds or expertise to run an outreach program, which means civil society actors will come to play a more proactive role. The initiation of discussions about transitional justice and the organization of support for the victims of sexual violence reflect the role civil society and LWM are playing.

CONCLUSION

LWM began its journey as a memory museum in 1996, during a difficult period in the history of Bangladesh. Religious fundamentalist forces were gaining strength, and the major perpetrators of crimes during the war in 1971 not only enjoyed impunity but had gradually become members of the ruling coterie. At the same time, though, the struggle for justice continued and was strengthened by various processes of memorialization, including artistic rendition of the past through cinema, theater, paintings, poems, fiction, and, most importantly, heartrending personal memoirs, all of which helped to make the past an intergenerational issue. LWM has since played its role in this memorialization.

Established as a private, small museum of memory, LWM has grown over the years and gained strength to become a people's museum in the true sense. In 2008, with the cooperation of the government, LWM acquired a piece of land at a prime site in Dhaka, and the construction of a permanent museum is now underway. As of this writing, the new museum was expected to open its doors in the second half of 2015, giving new strength to the various activities of LWM, including its education outreach.

The LWM education outreach program has provided a valuable—and valued—experience to all the stakeholders. At the same time, the transformation of Bangladeshi society and the beginning of the criminal trials have created new opportunities to move forward with the concept of justice to create a peaceful society. How to make use of these opportunities is the challenge of this time. LWM is ready to offer its best efforts to open a new chapter in the nation's life with the cooperation of the global community.

NOTES

1   See www.sitesofconscience.org for more information. The author wishes to thank Ereshnee Naidu for her support in the writing of this chapter.

2   For more information on the Bangladesh war of independence, see International Commission of Jurists, *The Events in East Pakistan, 1971: A Legal Study* (Geneva: International

Commission of Jurists, 1972), http://icj.wpengine.netdna-cdn.com/wp-content/uploads/1972/06/Bangladesh-events-East-Pakistan-1971-thematic-report-1972-eng.pdf.

3   Bangladesh National Curriculum and Textbook Board, *History of Bangladesh and World Civilization* (Dhaka, Bangladesh: National Curriculum and Textbook Board, 2012), https://bangladeshresults.files.wordpress.com/2013/03/9-10-28_history-of-bd-eng.pdf.

4   Government of the People's Republic of Bangladesh, Ministry of Education, *National Education Policy 2010*, 2011, 3, http://planipolis.iiep.unesco.org/upload/Bangladesh/Bangladesh_National_Education_Policy_2010.pdf.

5   Bangladesh Bureau of Educational Information and Statistics (BANBEIS), *Bangladesh Education Statistics 2012* (Dhaka: BANBEIS, 2012), 21.

CHAPTER 10

Historical Commissions and Education Outreach: Challenges and Lessons for Transitional Justice

Alexander Karn

As transitional justice scholars and practitioners have come to understand,[1] one of the principal difficulties of "reckoning with the past" is accounting for and managing what Doreen Massey has called history's "multi-vocality."[2] Competing claims about the past, Massey writes, "seek to stabilize and establish as dominant"[3] the meaning of events and places, which are crucial to the development and maintenance of specific group identities. Owing to this multiplicity of perspectives, the past can be a serious impediment to peace, particularly where it has entailed large-scale violence and/or severe political repression. Even where historical facts are not in dispute, rival groups often imbue them with divergent meanings, adding yet another layer to the conflict. For peacebuilders and conflict mediators, this makes the past a dangerous minefield of contested memories, but also a potentially useful tool for cultivating intergroup dialogue.

Since the mid-1990s, historical commissions (HCs) have become an increasingly prevalent mechanism for confronting past injustices and sorting through the contested memories attached to them. Defined broadly, HCs are investigative bodies whose charge is to develop new understandings of the past based on fresh archival research. In general, these commissions have appeared where "difficult" and shameful episodes have been suppressed in the public discourse, or where the specific details surrounding these events have become the focal point for destabilizing political debates. While most HCs have arisen through official (that is, governmental) channels, some have been sponsored by nonprofit and nongovernmental organizations (NGOs) based in civil society. And while most have been local or national initiatives, important examples of bilateral and international commissions must be considered as well.

The multiparty commissions, generally speaking, have pursued intergroup reconciliation more overtly than the local and national ones, but many of the latter have also engaged with divisive histories that give fuel to conflicts. Some historical commissions have devoted themselves explicitly to public education and the promotion of "democratic values," while others have been little more than window dressing for governments eager to give the appearance of moral rectitude without having to absorb the costs required for actually achieving justice. In any case, while the commissions' specific aims and rationales have differed from place to place, the HC "model" has shown significant potential for linking truth telling and historical clarification to the goals of transitional justice—accountability, redress, reconciliation, democratization, and so on.[4]

This chapter focuses on a subset of HCs that were convened in Europe beginning in the mid-1990s to deal with unresolved issues related to World War II, and the Holocaust in particular.[5] While these commissions have a great deal to teach about the potential of history to promote democratic values and human rights, here I address the lessons they provide for transitional justice experts seeking new approaches to public outreach and education. More specifically, I deal with the efforts of HCs to make their work resonate in communities where the past has been suppressed and to engage with, especially, the younger generations in societies where the history of the Holocaust has been either misrepresented or contested.

The Holocaust commissions have employed a variety of strategies for this purpose, ranging from the relatively banal (such as publishing reports that rehearse or reiterate the commission's findings) to more innovative schemes rooted in experiential learning (such as oral history projects and cultural exchange programs) and the digital humanities (websites designed to support and enhance in-school learning). For reasons I will discuss further on, assessing the effectiveness of individual initiatives is difficult. This chapter aims to identify some of the key criteria according to which such judgments might be made.

While education would seem to be fundamental to the work performed by HCs—why clarify details from the past except to encourage serious reflection on their meaning(s) among society's stakeholders?—they have not always attended to the challenges of education and outreach in the energetic and thoughtful ways one might expect. Thus far, the literature on HCs remains somewhat underdeveloped, particularly compared to the scholarship on truth commissions. Interest is growing, however, in comparing the work of the two types of commissions and refining the techniques of each by borrowing from the other.[6]

One interesting feature of the HCs is their ability to produce and circulate *mediating narratives* in societies where historical injustices have not been fully acknowledged. "Mediating" refers to the recontextualization of past events to ensure they are presented in a nuanced, explanatory framework, rather than in a caustic, accusatory one. While it has not always been possible—nor would it be desirable—for HCs to bridge the most intensely partisan histories of the Holocaust (such as those reflecting the determination of certain ethno-national majorities and governments to understate or minimize the scope and scale of their collaboration with the Nazi regime), their ability to unpack the ideological baggage that burdens misleading and exculpatory Holocaust narratives makes them a potentially important tool for using history to support peacebuilding. HCs, as we shall see, do not solve the problem of history's vulnerability to politics so much as they present the politicization of the past openly, in the best of cases, to promote a dialogue aimed at mutual understanding. Whether this understanding penetrates the thinking of ordinary people is, of course, a different matter. For this reason, we need to consider and evaluate carefully the efforts HCs have made to connect with the communities where they perform their work and ensure the dialogue they seek to inspire is one that members of the public, especially youth and students, will actually want to participate in.

In the next sections, I will present four historical commissions, two that were government sponsored (in Switzerland and France) and two that arose from civil society (in France and Germany and Poland and Ukraine). Of the several dozen Holocaust commissions convened in Europe, I have selected these four examples for the variety they display in their basic approaches to outreach and education, the degree of innovation these entailed, and their overall contribution to historical reconciliation in societies divided over the past.

REACHING OUT TO YOUTH IN THE CLASSROOM

Unsurprisingly, the most traditional form of education outreach takes place in school. The following describes two different efforts—one government sponsored and one emerging from civil society—that took different approaches to creating textbooks as tools for teaching young people about the Holocaust.

SWITZERLAND: THE NATIONAL HISTORY TEXTBOOK INITIATIVE

A recurrent criticism of truth commissions' public outreach and strategies for disseminating their findings relates to the reports they normally publish at the conclusion of their work. Besides ignoring the high illiteracy rates and language differences common among victim populations, these reports tend to be long, dry, and unadventurous, both in their prose style and their hesitancy to make strong moral judgments concerning the past that might be educational. Many reports incorporate statistical data and technical terms that put off casual readers. While there are important exceptions (from, for example, Argentina, Timor-Leste, and Sierra Leone), truth commissions at times have seemed to go out of their way to bury or diminish the impact of their findings.

With a few notable exceptions, the same criticisms can apply to the reports written by Holocaust commissions. In their size and accessibility for general readers, most have ranged from long and arid to gargantuan and impenetrable. Switzerland's Independent Commission of Experts (ICE), for example, published the results of its research in twenty-five individual volumes, totaling more than eleven thousand pages. Created in 1996 through a joint decree of the legislature and executive, the ICE emerged at a time when Switzerland faced a foreign relations crisis stemming from accusations that Swiss banks had profited from the Holocaust by retaining and absorbing so-called "dormant accounts" belonging to Jewish victims. While the ICE probed weighty moral questions concerning Switzerland's refugee policy, the relationship of Swiss industry to the Nazi economy, and the intricacies of Jewish property restitution in the postwar era, much of its work dealt with technical topics of little interest outside a small circle of specialists. For example, volume five, *Swiss Electricity and the Third Reich*, consisted largely of recounting energy transfers (tabulated in kilowatt hours) and the industrial benefits derived from these by Germany. While no data have been published on sales or distribution for individual volumes, it is safe to assume sales have been modest.

In a press release that accompanied the final report, Jean-François Bergier, the commission's chairman, explained that the ICE had tried to "shed light upon certain controversial or insufficiently analyzed aspects of [Swiss] history" to stimulate a public discussion regarding how Swiss authorities "had perhaps been derelict in assuming their responsibilities."[7] The final report helped rekindle a debate, which stretched back to the 1970s, regarding Swiss conduct during the war and the widely held belief, particularly among older Swiss who lived through the period, that Switzerland had vigorously asserted and defended its neutrality throughout the Nazi era.

Although the Swiss government endorsed the commission's final report, it was strongly criticized by politicians and media figures on the right, who felt the ICE had given a one-sided account of the Swiss record by emphasizing a few failings rather than the many honorable aspects of the country's actions. By contrast, relatively little debate took place among Swiss historians regarding the merits of the commission's work or the validity of its findings. Unfortunately, the ICE never developed a coherent strategy for disseminating its work beyond the final report, which was released in 2002. In an interview he gave in 2003, Bergier ventured that "a shorter version [of the report] is necessary if we're to make the findings accessible to young people,"[8] but by that time the ICE had already dissolved.

Ultimately, it was the Ministry of Education in the canton of Zürich[9] that took responsibility for disseminating the ICE's work to Swiss youth. In 2003, the ministry began working on a new history textbook for secondary school students, which it prepared specifically to present the findings of the ICE, while also rehearsing some of the debates that emerged from the commission's work.[10] This was, in part, a political response to shifting power relations within Switzerland, and it reflected the reemergence of a conservative, nationalist ideology. At the same time, the new textbook project reflected a more general shift in global public memory, which brought the Holocaust to the fore in historical accounts of the Second World War and focused on the "shared responsibility" of other European states, besides Germany, for enabling the genocide in which six million Jews perished.

Coauthored by two professors in the field of history education and two historians who conducted research for the ICE, *Hinschauen und Nachfragen: Die Schweiz und die Zeit des Nationalsozialismus im Licht aktueller Fragen* [Looking Closely and Inquiring: Switzerland in the Period of National Socialism in Light of Current Questions] was published in 2006 and approved for use in the canton of Zürich, although teachers there were not required to adopt it.[11] To defuse some of the criticisms coming from the right, the ministry created an advisory board to oversee the writing process. This was a five-person committee composed of four trained historians and one former member of the Swiss Parliament, a staunch conservative born in 1923, whose presence was intended to represent "the generation that lived through the war."[12] The inclusion of a nonspecialist, and, moreover, one whose views were in sharp contrast with the ICE's overall framework, was important to the initiative, insofar as it signaled a desire to give a balanced account of Switzerland's past rather than indoctrinate students through the assertion of a single and potentially narrow perspective. While this gesture did not satisfy all of the textbook's critics, the ministry could at least claim that the writing reflected different political viewpoints, which it did, albeit in a limited manner.

The authors of *Hinschauen und Nachfragen* deliberately sought to engage Swiss students on a moral level. This objective can be detected in the preface, where the authors explain that the textbook was created to lead students through a specific set of questions: "How did people in Switzerland behave after a friendly neighboring state turned into a dictatorship, suppressed its political opposition, and discriminated against, expelled, and eventually murdered Jews and other minorities? *Could or should government, businesses, or private individuals have acted differently than they did? Who carries which responsibilities, and why did decision makers act as they did?*"[13] The authors insist their textbook provides no "ready-made answers" to these questions, although the ICE's interpretations, in the end, are presented as authoritative.[14] Although it touts itself as an open-ended tool intended to teach critical thinking and historical methodology, the textbook is built around a narrative that mirrors the views of the ICE and the Swiss politicians, primarily from the left-center, who endorsed the commission's report. It gives a nod to the perspective of the conservative opposition by insisting that students must evaluate the evidence and reach their own conclusions, but, finally, *Hinschauen und Nachfragen* instills "a version of collective memory, values, and national identity that is shared by the majority within state power."[15]

It is important to ask whether a textbook that proclaims the truth of the current political majority and fails to engage the perspective of the minority seriously (while pretending to do so) is really capable of mediating the past, promoting reconciliation, or reinforcing the values inherent to human rights and international law. For transitional justice practitioners interested in building a *positive peace*, one that nurtures cooperation and reconciliation between rivals, it is crucial that one side's outreach and education policies not be received as propaganda by the other side. This does not mean the authors of *Hinschauen und Nachfragen* are wrong about Switzerland's past failings, or that historians cannot present an authoritative version of the past in cases where doing so is likely to provoke a strong political backlash. Rather, it is a reminder that transitional justice practitioners will always deploy their education and outreach initiatives within the sphere of politics. To run roughshod over contravening viewpoints, as if this entailed no political costs, is to accept and settle for the negative peace scenarios that arise where rivals agree to halt their conflict, but cooperation and democratic state-building are limited by fractured understandings of the past and conflicting visions for the future.

While there is no need to include or validate the egregious distortions that partisan hardliners have at times tried to promote, in Switzerland, moderate perspectives on the right pose challenging and important questions that merit consideration—for example, how do we balance the positive aspects of the country's past with the moral failures of its government and citizens? To put this slightly differently: how can historians and historical commissions encourage a dialogue on the politics of memory that assumes responsibility for past injustices without imposing collective guilt on those who played no part in those events and wish to nurture a positive self-image?

When thinking about history textbooks as a form of youth outreach or as education products, a great deal hinges on how the text is presented in the classroom. As we know, teachers can develop lesson plans with or against the grain of a particular pedagogical resource. Unfortunately, there are no published data that reveal how *Hinschauen und Nachfragen* is actually used by Zürich's secondary school teachers; we have no way of knowing, for example, whether the teachers who have adopted it reinforce or challenge the book's basic framework and premises. The approach taken will obviously have important implications for students' conceptions of the responsibilities of citizenship. It is now widely accepted within the field of history education that textbooks should strive to develop critical thinking skills, which are necessary to "overcome narrow national and nationalistic approaches to historical inter-pretations and geopolitical visions of the world."[16] Less clear is whether doing so enables students to transcend partisan discourse, or whether it does not simply swap out a conservative worldview for a liberal one.

Of course, liberal democracy is built on certain core commitments, so this comment should not be taken as an endorsement for a postmodern "any-thing goes" perspective. At some point, a historical commission must plant its flag beside a specific worldview, which may be incommensurate with the one that inspires conservative nationalist thinkers. Education and outreach cannot devolve into an endless, relativistic exchange of viewpoints. It is unrealistic to expect historical commissions to bring all contending viewpoints into perfect harmony, but if their pedagogical initiatives merely reverse, or invert, existing political polarities, their achievements are unlikely to endure beyond the next electoral reshuffling. Preparing students to handle and analyze political differ-ences would be productive for fostering support for fundamental liberal dem-ocratic values; but if these programs entail mostly disingenuous exercises that mimic critical thinking without encouraging serious dialogue between compet-ing perspectives, there is no reason to expect their impact to be entirely positive.

To overcome this problem, transitional justice practitioners and textbook authors might elect to "teach the debate"—that is, elucidate without any attempt at adjudication how the same historical facts can be used to support divergent, and even contradictory, interpretations of the past. This strategy poses a problem of its own, however, if transitional justice aims to serve as a foundation for liberal democratic norms, which are understood to be non-negotiable. In the case of Switzerland's policies regarding Jewish refugees, for example, if we want to assert that the right of asylum is universal, we cannot also entertain a narrative that validates the decision of Swiss officials to turn Jews away at the border (sometimes using rifle butts to discourage entry), even if that policy can be partly explained through the sort of contextualization historians normally value. What the ICE's research reveals, and what *Hinschauen und Nachfragen* reiterates, is that Switzerland's "boat" was *not* full in 1938 (when Swiss border officials asked Berlin to begin marking the passports of German Jews with a special "J" stamp) and should not have appeared that way to informed officials if they were committed to objective and thoroughgoing analysis.[17] In this case, asking educators to "teach the debate" puts political appeasement ahead of social scientific imperatives, and critical questioning becomes an end in itself, rather than a means to truth and understanding.

FRANCE AND GERMANY: THE BILATERAL TEXTBOOK INITIATIVE

The issues raised by *Hinschauen und Nachfragen*, which are partly methodological and partly epistemological, become even more complicated in bilateral textbook initiatives. As difficult as navigating the politics of history in the domestic setting can be, the challenge is even greater when mediating international debates concerning the "proper" interpretation of the past. Of the various bilateral textbook initiatives that have dealt with World War II and the Holocaust, the one that best illustrates these difficulties is the Franco-German textbook *Histoire/Geschichte*, which was published in three volumes between 2006 and 2011. Unlike the Swiss example described above, in which the textbook project piggybacked on the official report of a government-sponsored HC, the concept for *Histoire/Geschichte* originated in civil society, and only afterward did the governments of France and Germany get involved to facilitate the work.

The idea for *Histoire/Geschichte* first emerged in 2003 from a Youth Congress, which was convened in Berlin to celebrate the fortieth anniversary of the Élysée Treaty.[18] Sponsored by the Franco-German Youth Office (FGYO), this meeting assembled more than five hundred high school students (ages fifteen to nineteen) to draft a set of resolutions aimed at deepening reconciliation between the two countries. Among their recommendations, the students proposed a jointly written history textbook, which would appear in both languages but would otherwise include the same content.[19] The aim was to produce a new education resource that would cover the history of the two nations, from antiquity to the present, and be written specifically, as the students put it, "to reduce bias caused by mutual ignorance."[20] Eager to highlight the results of their programs (and presumably to protect their funding), the FGYO sent the students' proposal to the two heads of state, Jacques Chirac and Gerhard Schröder, who both endorsed it enthusiastically. Within six months, a ten-person team (five French, five German), consisting of secondary school teachers and "prep" instructors for university applicants, was assembled to begin working on an outline. Responsibility for coordinating the project was split between France's Ministry of Education and Germany's Office of Franco-German Cultural Cooperation.

Working in five binational teams of two, the writers started with the most recent history first (1945–present), which they published as a separate volume in 2006. According to Ila Koerner-Wellerhaus, the editorial coordinator for the German side, the authors agreed from the outset that their project would focus on the history of "inter-relationships and interactions,"[21] rather than juxtapose two distinct nationalist narratives, as other bilateral textbooks had sometimes done.[22]

After completing work on the most recent period, the authors next tackled what they all agreed was the most challenging material: the period from 1815 to 1945. Published in 2008, this volume covered not only the two world wars, but also the Franco-Prussian War (1870–71), which previous textbooks had treated as a stepping-stone to the Great War in 1914, and the aftermath of the Napoleonic Wars, which had been described as a catalyst for the rise of aggressive—that is, modern—nationalism. The authors concluded their work in 2011 in a volume on Europe from antiquity to 1814, a long interval they viewed as less controversial than the two time periods covered previously.

Described by one reviewer as "the world's most adventurous history textbook project" and credited for shifting students' thinking "from nation-centered history education to international understanding and reconciliation,"[23] Histoire/Geschichte received significant media attention.[24] In an interview in 2011, Koerner-Wellerhaus described sales of the textbooks as brisk and judged the project to be "a real success."[25] Volume III (2006), the first in print, was greeted with high praise by both the French and German governments, whose leaders hailed the work as "symbolically sealing Franco-German reconciliation."[26]

Queried by journalists about the mechanics of the writing process, the authors described a series of free-flowing conversations and negotiations in which individual word choices sometimes triggered lively, but also civil, debate. At the end of these discussions, the two sides had usually arrived at what the authors called a "common view" and a "shared narrative." In a few cases where they were unable to do this, the authors agreed to highlight their differences and discuss them directly in the text. In their coverage of the role of the United States in postwar Europe, for example, the German authors found their French counterparts to be unjustifiably "anti-American," while the French writers saw too much enthusiasm for American culture and uncritical acceptance of American policies on the German side.

Again, these disagreements are presented openly in both editions of the textbook, without any attempt at forcing a resolution.[27] Instead, these topics are used to foster debate and expose the prejudices and assumptions of students in the two respective countries. In other words, the authors of *Histoire/Geschichte* appear to have capitalized on the same strategy (that is, to teach the debate) that the authors of *Hinschauen und Nachfragen* toyed with before ultimately committing themselves to the side of the ICE.

Despite the original intention of the youth delegates in Berlin that the French and German editions should be identical, some discrepancies occur between the two. For example, where the textbook deals with the Holocaust, the German edition cites six million Jewish victims and five hundred thousand Roma victims. The French version offers significantly lower figures: five million Jewish victims and two hundred thousand Roma victims.[28] Unlike other differences, which the authors highlight for the purpose of promoting debate and discussion, this significant discrepancy with respect to "the numbers" and the delicate political issues they raise receives no comment or special attention in either of the two versions of the text. The authors do not expand on the difficulties of making precise estimates of victims based on what are sometimes ambiguous or insufficient source materials or on the strong political pressure Germany faces to accept the highest credible numbers.

Despite these incongruities, the authors have spoken enthusiastically about the potential of their work for promoting a shared vision of the past. Government officials in both countries have also praised the work. At the jointly sponsored release party for volume III, France's education minister emphasized the project's potential for transforming international relations by contemplating the past through a shared lens: "The great lesson of this story is that nothing is set in stone; antagonisms that we believe are inscribed in marble are not eternal."[29]

Significantly, the publishers elected to hold the launch event for volume III at the Museum of the Great War near the Somme battlefield, where Europe's history had already been presented in transnational and comparative terms.[30] As Peter Geiss, the head writer for the German side, explained,

You always have two views, at least two views, and that allows pupils to develop their own standpoint, their own image of history. . . . That's very useful within democratic and liberal teaching of history. One needs to know others' points of view and think of the history of one's nation in that way.[31]

On the French side, one writer added, "It is only when each national side has the courage to reveal the dark sides of its own national history . . . that work on the joint history textbook becomes possible."[32] Both these comments reflect a similar belief that good history depends on a willingness not just to weigh the perspectives of rival parties, but to actually work to internalize them, even (or especially) if this requires confrontation with shameful episodes from the past.

While there is no guarantee instructors who adopt this resource will implement a pedagogical approach that supports this perspective, it is difficult to imagine any mature secondary school student missing the textbook's implicit message. On the other hand, no hard data exist, to this point, that can tell us how French and German students respond to this notion—that is, whether they internalize the future-oriented and pan-European message the authors have tried to promote, or whether they push back against the idea of a common past. In any case, the hope is that these textbooks will jumpstart a process of reconciliation where populations have resisted it or deepen reconciliation where other initiatives have already paved the way. Obviously, the joint textbook reflects the extraordinary progress that has been made toward Franco-German reconciliation since 1945, but what we see with some of the historical commissions is that they can also help to create a shared vision of the future, in settings where finding common ground has been a challenge.

Histoire/Geschichte has also received some negative attention, which warrants consideration here. While some have touted the textbook as a revolutionary tool for promoting liberal democratic values, others have attacked it for undermining the epistemological framework of the social sciences and encouraging relativism. The second volume in particular, which covers the long nineteenth century and the two world wars, elicited criticism from some readers, who felt excessive attention to methodological questions would lead students into a nihilistic black hole, where the authority of well-vetted evidence is never fully accepted and reasoned argument is seen as merely one "opinion" among others. In a withering review written for the European Association of History Educators, Wojciech Roszkowski, formerly the director of the Institute of Political Studies at the Polish Academy of Sciences and a member of the European Parliament from 2004 until 2009, criticized the authors of *Histoire/ Geschichte* for "mak[ing] students think that reaching the truth is harder than it really is."[33] According to Roszkowski, *Histoire/Geschichte* is marked by a "leftist ideological tone," which improperly suppresses national feelings and discourages what he calls "natural and valuable attachment to one's own . . . community."[34] Instead of giving an objective account grounded in empirical evidence, Roszkowski laments, "The intention of creating common Franco-German memory has become all the world to the authors."[35] Claiming to have transcended the ideological perspective of nationalist histories, the authors of *Histoire/Geschichte*, according to Roszkowski, have merely imposed their own ideological agendas.

Indeed, this may be unavoidable for textbooks that emphasize a supranational or a post-national identity. In France, for example, where the (extreme right) National Front made significant gains in the 2014 elections and where the 2005 referendum to adopt the European Constitution failed by a substantial margin, there is clearly resistance to the pan-European narrative that *Histoire/Geschichte* constructs. While this problem is not unique to textbooks written by historical commissions or those that incorporate their research, it speaks to one of the inherent challenges for outreach and education initiatives that aim to promote intergroup reconciliation. Even if there exists a history of interrelationship from which to draw, it cannot be taken for granted that all readers will understand this as good news or as inspiration for building a common consciousness. On the one hand, a textbook that provokes debate and disagreement may be viewed as a good sign that liberal democratic values and principles of citizenship are being taught in the classroom. From a pragmatic perspective, however, we also need to be concerned with any pedagogical tool that incites a political backlash from the partisan groups that have consistently stood in the way of intergroup cooperation. History in the service of peace must mediate between rival perspectives, not impose the political agenda of the current majority.

NEW APPROACHES: COMMISSIONED HISTORY BEYOND THE CLASSROOM

While the history of textbook initiatives like the ones discussed above stretch back to the years immediately after World War I,[36] more recent HCs have spawned some novel tools for education and youth engagement.

FRANCE: THE MATTÉOLI COMMISSION

Convened by French prime minister Alain Juppé in 1997, the Mattéoli Commission was charged with investigating the facts related to Jewish despoliation in France from 1940 to 1944, as well as gauging the extent of postwar restitution, and its report was the most critical and far-reaching of any

Holocaust HC. Members of the commission understood their primary task to be historical, but from the beginning, they also saw their work as having moral and pedagogical dimensions. The commission's vice president, Ady Steg, put it this way:

> We have an obligation to consider the human circumstances and consequences of despoliation. This means taking into consideration the sum of the anguish, humiliation, suffering, and death that resulted from being despoiled.[37]

In its final report in 2000, the Mattéoli Commission described the extent of Jewish despoliation under the Vichy regime as "stunning." More than mere plunder, despoliation was judged to be a deliberate program to demean and dehumanize the victims and to prepare them for the more coercive measures—arrest and deportation—that led directly to the Final Solution. For the commission, this meant France's debt to the victims was not only material; it was also, at its core, moral. The members of the commission described this moral dimension as a "crushing responsibility," understood to be both eternal and infinite. It could only be managed (though never discharged) through what one member called "a doctrine of action."

Given this conception of French guilt, an understanding always existed within the Mattéoli Commission and in the government that justice required more than monetary compensation for the victims. To get at the deep, moral failures of the Vichy period, payback would have to encompass further work geared toward public education and a specific commitment to disseminating the findings of the commission through state-funded school curricula. To accomplish this, the French government provided major funding for a new public resource devoted to Holocaust education and remembrance. The Shoah Memorial Museum and Documentation Center opened in Paris in January of 2005. As part of its core mission, this self-described "museum of vigilance" has invested heavily in curricular revision and the creation of new teaching materials to heighten public understanding of the Holocaust, in particular among students and youth. These programs reflect the conviction of the Mattéoli historians that "nothing enduring [is] established without public recognition of facts."[38]

Since 2002, Holocaust education in France has been compulsory at the primary, secondary, and high school levels. In 2008, the Shoah Museum published new lesson plans for teaching the Holocaust to primary school students (ages eight to twelve), which it linked to an interactive website. Called "Sarah's

Attic," the website invites users to "witness the daily life of Jews during the war" by following nine "itineraries" based on the real-life experiences of children whose lives (and deaths) are documented in the museum's archives.[39] It includes video presentations, seven to eight minutes long, that aim to bring these stories to life through the display of various artifacts, such as passports and other official documents, as well as first-person narration of key life events described in the diaries and letters penned by some of the children. Another section of the website, "Once Upon a Time," is designed "to give a glimpse of the diversity of Jewish cultures,"[40] while the "Words to My Ear" exhibit is intended to "open a window on the pluralism of Judaism" by letting students hear "traditional" idiomatic expressions recorded in Hebrew, Yiddish, Judeo-Spanish, and Judeo-Arabic.

According to its creators, "Sarah's Attic" was designed to anticipate and respond to actual questions posed by elementary school students in the classroom. Its introduction explains that the site can be used in the classroom or for extracurricular exploration. In either case, it recommends that adults be available to "create a dialogue and answer questions." Although the site offers worksheets, maps, and timelines for teachers who want to help with this, parents (and others) without any official institutional affiliation are not given access to these supplementary materials.

A more interesting initiative connected to the Mattéoli Commission's work is the "Just Memories" program, which the France-Israel Foundation has sponsored since 2010.[41] One of several strategies developed by the foundation to promote mutual understanding and closer ties between the two countries, "Just Memories" provides travel stipends for the grandchildren of French rescuers (that is, "Righteous Gentiles" who risked their lives to assist Jews during the Vichy period) to visit Yad Vashem in Jerusalem and meet Holocaust survivors, whose lives, in some cases, were saved by these visitors' own relatives. The trip provides additional opportunities for the French visitors—most of whom are mature adolescents or young adults—to meet with Israeli youth, students, soldiers, and kibbutzim face to face.[42]

While exchanges like this take place a long way from the diplomatic circles where policies governing bi-state relations are determined, the foundation has consciously attempted to utilize the past as a tool for fostering mutual understanding and intergenerational reconciliation. Although information on the costs of the program is not provided in any of the foundation's literature, an impressive array of sponsors (governmental, corporate, and nonprofit) has lined up behind the organization.[43]

POLAND-UKRAINE: COMMON GROUND

Another notable example of innovative outreach involves Poland and Ukraine and the borderland conflicts that unfolded in and around Volyn from 1943 to 1947.[44] While official relations between the two countries have been stable since the end of the Cold War, tension at the grassroots level, fed by unfortunate stereotypes, has persisted for decades, and the Volyn conflict, which, according to some estimates, claimed between fifty thousand and a hundred thousand lives and displaced 1.5 million, has been an ongoing source of unease and controversy.[45] Much of this history was silenced in the Communist era, when political constraints made free-range analysis of the past and dialogue aimed at reconciliation (which presumed estrangement between Socialist republics) virtually impossible. Following the events of 1989 and 1991, ordinary citizens and mainstream politicians in both Poland and Ukraine attempted to reconstruct the history of the conflict and commemorate the victims, which helped open new channels of communication between the two countries. Nevertheless, when President Aleksander Kwaśniewski of Poland and President Leonid Kuchma of Ukraine issued a conciliatory joint statement in 2003 to mark the sixtieth anniversary of the conflict, not all of their constituents were eager to go along with the program. Internal political conditions in both countries had, by this time, complicated the matter in ways that diminished hopes for a shared understanding of the conflict. In Poland, some complained that Ukrainians still refused to accept full responsibility for the killings and expulsions their side perpetrated during the war. In response, some Ukrainians countered that Kwaśniewski's statement did not admit guilt for Poland's postwar reprisals to the same extent as Kuchma's.

Fearful that a new cycle of recrimination would have dangerous economic consequences, Yulia Tymoshehko, the erstwhile leader of Ukraine's Fatherland Party, spoke out strongly against Kuchma's official statement of regret: "Today, when relations between [the] Ukrainian and Polish nations are so friendly and there is such a partnership, I cannot imagine who got the idea in their head to propose a declaration that seriously breaks our nations apart."[46]

Taking the opposite tack, religious leaders sought to facilitate reconciliation by exposing past injustices to the light of day. Pope John Paul II, the former archbishop of Kraków, urged Catholic and Orthodox Christians to "consider the events of the past in a new perspective and [take] responsibility for building a better future for all."[47] In Kiev, Ukraine's Orthodox archbishop, Ihor Isichenko, lamented the "bloody nights . . . where common Christian love was missing." Isichenko also warned against conjuring the past as a way to advance narrow interests: "The speculation about painful memories . . . is a heinous way to gain political benefits through irritating the aching wounds of alienated people."[48]

Despite such calls for brotherhood and neighborly relations based on reciprocal forgiveness, the "double memories" surrounding Volyn have proved resistant to historical mediation. Poles, to a large extent, have insisted that Volyn was guaranteed to them in the international treaties negotiated at the Paris Peace Conference of 1919 that ended World War I. In Ukraine, others have maintained that these settlements did not reflect the situation in Volyn, where Ukrainians outnumbered Poles by a margin of two to one. Timothy Snyder writes that in 1939, following the signing of the Hitler-Stalin pact, "the invasion and occupation by foreign troops seemed to open historical possibilities (for Ukrainians) or threaten the end of historical eras (for Poles)."[49] In 1943, this combination of hopes and worries unleashed an alternating current of violence and terror, first by the Ukrainians and then by the Poles. Ethnic atrocities that began against the chaotic backdrop of foreign occupation and were undertaken, for the most part, by paramilitary "irregulars" evolved into official state policy at the end of the war when Polish statehood was restored. With sufficient guilt to go around and a tendency to shift blame to their more powerful neighbors, Germany and Russia, partisans on both sides of the conflict locked themselves within an accusatory framework, which they continue to bolster through a selective reading of the evidence.

Among efforts to mediate the conflict over Volyn, one of the most impressive education initiatives to emerge was the Common Ground project, which the Karta Center, a nongovernmental organization headquartered in Warsaw, sponsored from 1996 to 2008.[50] Although Common Ground was not an official historical commission, it worked in a similar way, by assembling historians from both countries for a series of public seminars devoted to exploring the Volyn conflict and the competing memories surrounding it. Each of the seminars, which moved between Warsaw and Lutsk, featured one Polish and one Ukrainian historian, who delivered papers on the same topic related to Volyn, after which members of the audience were invited to ask questions and contribute to the discussion. While these events were open to all members of the public, Karta actively sought the participation of war veterans' groups and cultural heritage associations, who were deeply involved in the debates over which side absorbed greater losses and who was at fault. The seminar papers were compiled and published in both languages, together with a summary report, in eleven volumes under the title *Poland-Ukraine: Difficult Questions*.

Unlike most official HC reports, which resemble extended monologues, *Difficult Questions* strove to incorporate multiple perspectives and voices by reprinting the transcripts from the question-and-answer portion of each seminar. The organizers endeavored in this way to bring divergent memories of Volyn into contact, while still allowing for differences of interpretation (the more pointed term, "disagreement," was avoided in all official materials).[51] To add empirical depth to the project and to ensure individual stories were not sacrificed for the sake of general understanding, Karta created a victims' database, which pooled biographical information from more than fifty archives scattered between the two countries. Hennadiy Boriak, the chairman of Ukraine's State Archive Committee, characterized the database as a joint effort to "repay our moral debt to the thousands of innocent victims."[52] While there have been efforts to maintain this academic dialogue in spite of the generally unfavorable political conditions that have arisen, the mediating approach to this historical chapter has once again been overtaken by nonnegotiable narratives, which some have characterized as "parallel monologues."[53]

Besides Common Ground and the victims' database, Karta pursued several other projects geared toward achieving historical justice and democratization, including two aimed specifically at students and youth. One of these, developed by Karta in conjunction with Germany's Remembrance, Responsibility, and the Future Foundation and the Russian civil society organization Memorial, is a network of Internet portals created to promote history education and an approach to teaching the past "that contributes to a society based on . . . human rights and democracy." Dubbed "Learning from History," these websites employ uniform standards to foster the international exchange of expertise in the field of history education and promote "open-minded and critical attitudes toward history/histories in schools and other educational settings."[54] Designed to "take into account national characteristics and prerequisites," while still drawing on mutual experiences that respect "the supranational values of human rights and democracy," each affiliated website has content areas designed specifically for educators and students, with all materials developed to support high school–level coursework. The portals focus on methods and models that encourage students to undertake team-based research projects outside of the traditional (that is, classroom-based) curricula. While each site is tailored to meet the education standards for a particular country, a set of core principles is evident across the network. These include the following:

- An open and critical approach to historical sources and subjects
- A view of history from multiple perspectives, taking into account the perspectives of different groups within a nation, as well as differences

across national boundaries
- A commitment to "disarming" history from hatred and prejudice
- A readiness to tell one's own story, along with a willingness to listen to the stories of others, without a sense of superiority and without judgment
- Respect for human and civil rights
- Attention to the role of history in shaping the self-understanding(s) of contemporary societies[55]

Among the specific teaching and learning units available through the portals are projects dealing with National Socialism and the War Youth Generation; archival digitization (for example, digitized issues of *Aufbau*, the journal of German Jewish émigrés published from 1951 to 2004); the fostering of connections between history and human rights (for example, by using local libraries to promote human rights education); guidelines for collecting and using survivor testimonies in classroom-based learning; the history of deportations in Poland and Russia; teaching with audio podcasts; and the contributions of archaeology to history (for example, the project "Dig Where You Stand," which put tenth-grade students to work at a dig site inside the Ravensbrück concentration camp).[56]

Beginning in 1996, Karta also sponsored "History at Hand," a series of annual history competitions for schoolchildren and gymnasium students.[57] Responding to different themes and topics each year, students were asked to devise and carry out their own local history projects. Upon completing their research, they presented their findings at a public event, where a panel of judges provided feedback and handed out awards for the best projects. As of 2008, Karta had reviewed more than 6,700 projects, with contributions from approximately 11,700 students.

The theme of the last competition, in 2013, was "Poles and Their Neighbors After World War II: Against Each Other, Side by Side, and Together." Participants, who for the first time included international teams, were asked to solicit oral histories from family, friends, and acquaintances to learn how World War II and subsequent events transformed relationships among neighbors, including both co-nationals and individuals living in neighboring countries. Students were encouraged to focus on the history of "everyday life" and to approach the subject at a local level (village, town, precinct, and so on). They were also encouraged, whenever possible, to include supporting documentation, such as photographs and newspapers, collated into a record of "daily memory." While Karta allowed students to present their work in whatever format they chose, the judges placed special emphasis on presentations that utilized technology, including DVDs, podcasts, and "multimedia exhibitions."

At the end of the competition, awards for the best work were presented in Warsaw's Royal Castle, where students nominated for special honors and distinction were given an opportunity to compare their projects with those submitted by their peers. Projects were displayed in a temporary exhibition space inside the castle, and journalists were invited to view the submissions and interview the competitors for local and national news stories. Among the projects that received awards, several dealt with longstanding intergroup conflicts—one, for instance, tracked the appearance of Polish and Lithuanian "mutual stereotypes" in public discourse—and prospects for building trust and cooperation between historically estranged groups, such as a study of the first German mayor elected in Poland after 1945.[58]

Unfortunately, History at Hand was discontinued in 2014 due to financial constraints, although Karta's website notes that the competition might resume in the future.

CONCLUSION: EXPERIENTIAL LEARNING AND IMPACT ASSESSMENT

Like other tools for transitional justice, HCs have not always approached outreach and education in a thoughtful or coherent manner. While some commissions have regarded them as essential obligations within their overarching moral missions, others seem to have stumbled into this territory almost as an afterthought. There are also cases, which I have not explored here, in which governments stymied all efforts at translating the commissions' findings into serious programs for public education, either out of a concern that doing so would increase pressure to pay additional restitution to the victims of previous wrongs, or because the commissions' findings simply posed too much of a threat to the myths and amnesiac misperceptions that perfused the national identity. And, to be sure, the work of some HCs has been principally academic, a word I use here, unfortunately, in its pejorative sense.

On the other hand, examples also exist of HCs that have made serious attempts to establish channels of communication with the general population, and with children and youth in particular. While some have been rather clumsy in these attempts, others have developed innovative approaches to public education and outreach worthy of further study. Textbook projects, while still unproven in terms of efficacy, have ranged from unhelpful and intellectually dishonest to well intended and innovative.

More interesting and compelling, I would argue, are the projects that seek to take education and outreach beyond traditional "book learning." While I am skeptical about the application of technological solutions to longstanding pedagogical challenges, the public history initiatives that seek to move students into a practitioner role by giving them access to, or by encouraging them to experiment with, new media open interesting and admirable possibilities. With the proper guidance, even a relatively simple oral history project, which does not require the use of digital technology, has an important leg up on pedagogy that conceives of students as the passive recipients of vetted knowledge.

Of course, it also must be said that there is no substitute for gifted and skilled teachers. The published reports HCs produce, which I have denigrated as mostly dry and unreadable, need not remain so in the hands of an inspired (and inspirational) instructor. On the other hand, we should not expect (or require) a middle-school civics instructor to plow through eleven thousand pages of Holocaust history.

One of the great strengths of initiatives like the Just Memories travel program, which builds on the work of France's Mattéoli Commission, or like Karta's History at Hand competition for high school students is their potential for fostering intergenerational connections. Perhaps this will seem just as outmoded and hierarchical as the "book learning" disparaged here (a bit unfairly), but the idea of adolescents collecting oral histories from their elders who have lived through the events they are attempting to understand is, I would say, naturally appealing and intuitively worthwhile. I do not pretend oral history methodologies are entirely unproblematic, given what we know about the vagaries and malleability of memory, and I understand good oral history entails pushback from informed interviewers, who already have some sense of the historical landscape; but, again, it seems to me that the truly open-ended and instructive debates about the past are the ones that concern newly recovered source materials and point toward what we might call "micro-historical" insights. Naturally, these will have to be compared to and fitted within what we have already gathered in terms of general historical knowledge, but as a starting point for sustained engagement with difficult history, these oral accounts represent an important complement to more traditional—that is, reading-oriented—approaches.

What I am advocating is an approach to education and outreach that privileges experiential learning—that is to say, it emphasizes "doing" history rather than simply reading and discussing it. Since I do not wish to be ensnared in the debates over the potential benefits and drawbacks of this mode of pedagogy, I will simply mention here that a good deal of research points to its being valuable, both for understanding the past and for overall intellectual development.[59]

The experiential model is particularly salient when the past entails traumatic episodes characterized by large-scale injustices, not because students who practice it will be able to overcome fully all of the various obstacles to comprehension, but because contact with witnesses, victims, survivors, perpetrators, and bystanders will be invaluable for understanding the "multi-vocal" quality of the past, and because real social interactions transmit the emotional and personal stakes these histories entail in a way the vast majority of textbooks do not.

Finally, although it is not really the purview of this chapter, I want to add a few comments about the importance of developing a pragmatic standard and critical framework for impact assessment. Advocates for HCs (of whom I am one) are frequently told their interest in using history as a tool for promoting peace and reconciliation is overly idealistic. I fully accept we are still a long way from knowing whether the practices and initiatives described above really deliver what we want from them. There is still no rigorous empirical instrument for measuring whether HCs help realize the principles they espouse or whether they reliably effect the changes they seek to make in historical understanding, acceptance, and acknowledgment.

In any post-conflict society, one has to be careful about managing expectations. The rhetoric around HCs and other tools for promoting transitional justice can be seductive. "Facing up to the past" and "giving voice to the voiceless" are easy notions to embrace before we know how they will play themselves out in a particular society. If we wish to move beyond the rhetoric and cement a real (that is, measurable) connection between truth telling and social transformation, we will need to pin down with greater precision the meaning(s) of social healing and intergroup reconciliation. If, through education, we aim to cultivate in children and youth exposed to large-scale conflict and mass violence the commonly invoked indicators of democratic citizenship, such as empathy, compassion, tolerance, and critical thinking, we must also consider the relationships these core values have to justice (and also injustice) and prosperity (and also poverty). To do this requires that we think through—all the way through—the problems and difficulties of assessment and evaluation. What counts as impact? What counts as conflict mediation? Where and how is democratic citizenship most clearly expressed in the children and young people whom we now recognize as key agents of social change?

These are the questions that need to be answered before we can convincingly assert the value of historical commissions and history education, more generally, to the broader aims of transitional justice.

NOTES

1   The author would like to thank Clara Ramírez-Barat and Elizabeth A. Cole for their feedback on an earlier draft of this chapter.

2   Doreen Massey, "Places and Their Pasts," *History Workshop Journal* 39 (1995): 187.

3   Ibid., 188.

4   For further discussion of historical commissions and "the desire to address the legacy of historical wrongs from a contemporary perspective," see Elazar Barkan, "Historians and Historical Reconciliation," *American Historical Review* 114, no. 4 (October 2009): 899–913.

5   This chapter draws on a recently completed monograph that compares and analyzes the work of fourteen Holocaust commissions. See Alexander Karn, *Amending the Past: Europe's Holocaust Commissions and the Right to History* (Madison, WI: University of Wisconsin Press, 2015).

6   Attention to historical commissions is increasing. The *Journal of International Affairs* published a collection of essays on "Historical Reconciliation" in 2006 (vol. 60, no. 1). The *American Historical Review* also devoted a special issue to the topic of "Truth and Reconciliation in History" in 2009. Historical commissions were also the subject of a two-day workshop held at Columbia University in 2010. Video for all panels and discussions can be accessed online at http://hrcolumbia.org/historical/.

7   See Jean-François Bergier, "Introductory Speech by Prof. Jean-François Bergier at the Press Conference of 22 March 2002," http://www.uek.ch/en/presse/pressemitteilungen/220302redebergier.htm.

8   See "Bergier Report Heading for the Classroom," http://www.swissinfo.ch/eng/bergier-report-heading-for-the-classroom/3537838.

9   In Switzerland, jurisdiction over education belongs to the cantons.

10 Bernhard C. Schär and Vera Sperisen, "Switzerland and the Holocaust: Teaching Contested History," *Journal of Curriculum Studies* 42, no. 5 (2010): 653.

11 Barbara Bonhage, Peter Gautschi, Jan Hodel, and Gregor Spuhler, *Hinschauen und Nachfragen: Die Schweiz und die Zeit des Nationalsozialismus im Licht aktueller Fragen* [Looking Closely and Inquiring: Switzerland in the Period of National Socialism in Light of Current Questions] (Zurich: Lehrmittelverlag Zürich, 2006).

12 Schär and Sperisen, 654.

13 Ibid., 655. Emphasis mine.

14 Schär and Sperisen write that the textbook "pretends to help readers grapple with supposedly open, uninterpreted history . . . while surreptitiously delivering a diluted version of the experts' interpretation of this history." Ibid., 657.

15 Ibid., 658.

16 See, for example, Falk Pingel, "Can Truth Be Negotiated? History Textbook Revision as a Means to Reconciliation," *Annals of the American Association of Political and Social Science*

617 (May 2008): 181–98.

17 This is a reference to Alfred Häsler's widely read book, *Das Boot ist voll* (1967), which gives a critical perspective on Switzerland's restrictive wartime policies relating to Jewish refugees.

18 A symbol of Franco-German reconciliation, the Élysée Treaty was signed in 1963 following direct negotiations between Charles de Gaulle and Konrad Adenauer. Under it, the two countries agreed to hold regular bilateral summits for the purposes of bolstering joint security and fostering economic and cultural development.

19 Other proposals included additional funding for existing youth exchange programs and a statement of support for the creation of an official "Franco-German Day" on January 22 (the anniversary date of the Élysée Treaty).

20 See Éduscol, "Manuel d'histoire franco-allemand," http://eduscol.education.fr/cid45744/manuel-franco-allemand.html.

21 See Bildungs Klick, "Das Buch ist ein echter Erfolg: Interview mit Projektleiter Dr. Ilas Körner-Wellershaus," September 29, 2011, http://bildungsklick.de/a/80619/das-buch-ist-ein-echter-erfolg/.

22 In an essay prepared for the Georg Eckert Institute (Braunschweig, Germany), Corine Defrance, Reiner Marcowitz, and Ulrich Pfeil describe an Israeli-Palestinian project in which two markedly different national narratives face each other on opposite pages of a joint history textbook. Defrance and colleagues call this technique "a first step along the road to recognising and accepting difference." See Georg Eckert Institute, "Europe and the World," http://www.gei.de/de/publikationen/eckert-dossiers/europa-und-die-welt/europe-and-the-world.html.

23 Kim Seungryeol, "International History Textbook Work from a Global Perspective: The Joint Franco-German History Textbook and Its Implications for Northeast Asia," *Journal of Northeast Asian History* 6, no. 2 (December 2009): 78.

24 French and international press coverage is summarized online in "Une couverture média importante au niveau national et international," http://www.nathan.fr/manuelfrancoallemand/ressources/Revue_de_presse_mfa.pdf.

25 See Bildungs Klick, "Das Buch ist ein echter Erfolg."

26 Alain Auffray, "Le Manuel d'histoire, noveau symbole franco-allemand," *Libération*, May 4, 2006.

27 See volume 3, 127.

28 Cited in Seungryeol, "International History Textbook Work," 88–89.

29 BBC News, "Franco-German Textbook Launched," May 5, 2006, http://news.bbc.co.uk/2/hi/europe/4972922.stm.

30 The Battle of the Somme was one of the largest and bloodiest of World War I. For many, it came to symbolize the horrors of that war and of modern warfare in general.

31 *Deutsche Welle*, July 10, 2006.

32 Etienne François, quoted in Seungryeol, "International History Textbook Work," 82.

33 Wojciech Roszkowski, "Opinion on French-German Secondary School History Textbook," http://www.euroclio.eu/download/2009/Wojciech%20Roszkowski%20-%20Criticism%20of%20New%20History%20Textbook.pdf.

34 Ibid., 3.

35 Ibid., 15.

36 For a good look at the early history (that is, pre–World War II), see Mona Siegel and Kirsten Harjes, "Disarming Hatred: History Education, National Memories, and Franco-German Reconciliation from World War I to the Cold War," *History of Education Quarterly* 52, no. 3 (2012): 370–402.

37 Ady Steg, "Statement to the U.S. House of Representatives on the Work of the Mattéoli Commission," http://democrats.financialservices.house.gov/banking/91499ste.shtml.

38 Ibid.

39 See http://www.grenierdesarah.org/index.php/en/.

40 It should be noted that all of these stories appear to feature an Orthodox Jewish peasant, a bearded rabbi character, or some tidbit of Talmudic folk wisdom.

41 Program details can be accessed at http://www.fondationfranceisrael.org/actions/education/item/109-m%C3%A9moire-justes.

42 Video testimonies for the 2010 trip can be viewed online at https://www.youtube.com/watch?v=lcMUUo6YsNY.

43 The foundation's 2012–13 annual report, with information on program sponsorship, can be accessed at http://issuu.com/fondationfranceisrael/docs/rapport_d_activit___201 3?e=3682664/8314944.

44 National self-determination and the right to sovereignty were the focus of the conflict, which affected approximately eight million people living in the Polish-Ukrainian borderlands.

45 For an overview of the Volyn conflict, see Timothy Snyder, "To Resolve the Ukrainian Problem Once and for All: The Ethnic Cleansing of Ukrainians in Poland," *Journal of Cold War Studies* 1, no. 2 (1999): 86–120.

46 *Eastern Economist Daily*, "After Much Soul Searching, Ukrainian PR Passes Volyn Declaration," July 11, 2003.

47 Ibid.

48 Religious Information Service of Ukraine, "Autocephalous Orthodox Archbishop Addresses Volyn Tragedy at Conference in Kyiv," July 11, 2003.

49 Snyder, "To Resolve the Ukrainian Problem Once and for All," 90.

50 Following a period of financial instability, the Karta Center was partially absorbed by the Institute for National Remembrance (IPN) in 2013.

51 For more information on Karta and the Common Ground initiative, see Waldemar Rezmer, "Ethnic Changes in Volhynia and Eastern Galicia during the Second World

War in the Light of the Work of the 'Poland-Ukraine: Difficult Questions' International Historical Seminar," in *Divided Eastern Europe: Borders and Population Transfer, 1938–1947*, ed. Aleksandr Dyukov and Olesya Orlenko (Newcastle: Cambridge Scholars Publishing, 2012), 121–31.

52 *The Warsaw Voice*, "Opening the Archives," July 24, 2003.

53 Volodymyr Viatrovych, "The Polish-Ukrainian Memory Monologue," *Kyiv Post*, July 11, 2013, http://www.kyivpost.com/opinion/op-ed/the-polish-ukrainian-memory-mono-logue-326886.html.

54 The German portal can be accessed at http://learning-from-history.de/.

55 These are adapted from the network's published document on quality standards and procedures. See Karta; the Remembrance, Responsibility, and the Future Foundation; and Memorial, "International Network *Learning from History*: Quality Standards and Procedures for Web Portals," http://lernen-aus-der-geschichte.de/sites/default/files/attach/quality_standards_and_procedures_for_web_portals_-_karta_memorial_lernen_aus_der_geschichte.pdf.

56 A detailed list of projects is available at Learning from History, "Current Postings," http://learning-from-history.de/International.

57 More information on this program, including an archive of past competitions, is available at Learning from History, "History at Hand," http://hsqjxtt.karta.org.pl/en/history-at-hand.

58 A full list of jury prizes for the 2013 competition (in Polish) is available at http://historiabliska.pl/wp-content/uploads/2013/06/Komunikat-Jury-HB17_do-druku1.pdf.

59 See, for example, Linda S. Levsik and Keith C. Barton, *Doing History: Investigating with Children in Elementary and Middle Schools*, 4th ed. (New York: Routledge, 2011).

PART IV

Civil Society, Education, and Transitional Justice

Facing the Past—Transforming Our Future: A Professional Development Program for History Teachers in South Africa

Dylan Wray

With all of us facing our past, according to our own experiences, it brought a new sense of being together as South Africans.

— Participant in a Facing the Past introductory seminar

In 1996, South Africa, and much of the world, listened to and watched the past unfold as the Truth and Reconciliation Commission (TRC) began the process of telling and unraveling the country's apartheid past. The hearings told of pain, humiliation, retribution, reconciliation, forgiveness, and shame. Seven years later, South African history teachers were required to teach about this apartheid past, lessons that included some of the more painful stories from the TRC hearings that echoed through community halls, headphones, radios, and televisions sets all over the country. But while the education system that emerged post-apartheid gradually came to see the teaching of South Africa's apartheid past as a crucial step in nation healing and nation building, little official support was provided to help teachers take on this role and teach a past they lived through, as beneficiaries, bystanders, perpetrators, or victims.

The past each teacher brings into the classroom can be one of pain, anger, guilt, indifference, or shame or, most likely, a combination of bits of each. Not much attention has been given to what this means for those teaching this past, however, or, importantly, for their students attempting to construct a picture of it from their teachings. With this omission in mind, Facing the Past—Transforming Our Future was formed in 2003 with the aim of supporting South African teachers in the use of historical case studies—associated, for instance, with apartheid and the TRC—to help their students connect the past to the ethical decisions they make today as young South Africans. Crucial to this effort has been helping the teachers face their own past and understand how it shows up in their classrooms and in their teaching.

This chapter is an account of this project.[1] The first part explores some of the curriculum processes that have placed a particular importance on the subject of history in schools and brought the teaching of apartheid and the TRC into South African classrooms. The second part looks at what it has meant for history teachers to teach the past they lived through, which, with many, still sits uncomfortably. The third part explores the Facing the Past program, and the fourth details the model of professional development that has been offered to South African history teachers through this intervention. A short conclusion closes the chapter.

PLACING THE PAST INTO THE SCHOOL CURRICULUM

Since the end of apartheid in 1994, South Africa has engaged in a curriculum reform process that has been underway almost the entire twenty years. During all this time, a constant thread in the writing and rewriting of the curriculum was the recognition by its designers that classrooms could and should help transform and create a better society in which moral values and human rights are upheld. In 1998, the Truth and Reconciliation Commission (TRC), set up in 1995 to reveal past human rights violations committed by the apartheid system, recognized in its final report that reconciliation, as much as healing, forgiveness, and nation building, was a process that needed to continue beyond the formal term of the commission.[2] The TRC hearings were just one step in that process, and education represented another way in which it could and would continue.

Mindful of this, the new democratically elected government realized the education system in South Africa needed to be reformed, if not transformed, to redress the damage caused by forty years of apartheid. Not only did issues of education quality and equality need to be addressed, but in some subjects— such as history—years of indoctrination, mistruths, and silences had to be fixed and filled.[3] A whole new school curriculum was therefore recognized early on as a tool for reconciliation, nation building, and renewal, and, as it began to be rewritten, the teaching of South Africa's past in particular came to be recognized as a crucial step in the country's transition from conflict, division, and authoritarianism to peace, reconciliation, and democracy.

In 1997, as the TRC was doing its work, the Department of Education started the first of these major curriculum reforms, referred to as Curriculum 2005. As South Africans came to tell their stories, and other South Africans found themselves unable to escape listening, a radically new school curriculum was constructed that stressed learning skills over content.

Furthermore, the teaching of history only appeared in Curriculum 2005 in combination with geography, as a new subject called social studies. In practical terms, this meant less teaching time for history. Combined with an absence of any clearly assigned historical content, South African teachers would be able to avoid teaching the apartheid past if it were too painful for them or they saw it as harmful or, perhaps, if it carried with it too much guilt. Ironically, this meant that while South Africans across the country were busy uncovering and learning their history through the TRC hearings, the architects of the new school curriculum were, in fact, "advocating collective amnesia."[4]

Gail Weldon, the former head of history in the Western Cape Education Department who led the history curriculum revisions, has argued that, just as it was reasonable to expect the TRC hearings to have influenced the formal curriculum being constructed, it was equally understandable for the architects of the first post-apartheid curriculum to choose to leave the question of what history teachers would teach in their classrooms for a later stage. For many who were hearing the TRC testimonies, it was perhaps too soon to understand how these painful recent accounts could be told and heard about in South African classrooms in ways that would benefit the students and not leave them damaged. The past, at that time at least, seemed still too present.

While the TRC hearings seemed to have little direct influence on the curriculum writing process that was underway at the same time, according to Weldon, "The extended curriculum, represented by the testimonies of the TRC, was being shaped into the core of a new official memory."[5] It was this new official memory that would come to influence the second major curriculum reform, where history found a better place to fit.

Curriculum 2005 was never fully realized or implemented. In 1999, Kader Asmal was appointed minister of education, a role he would hold until 2004. During his term in office, Asmal launched the second curriculum revision process, the Revised National Curriculum Statement (RNCS) of 2000 (later known as the National Curriculum Statement, or NCS). Unlike the developers of Curriculum 2005, the creators of the RNCS saw history, and apartheid history in particular, as crucial to the building of a new South Africa. That the new minister of education was one of the early advocates and designers of the TRC process was not a coincidence.[6] Far from being content to let the past lie quietly, he felt history had an important and valuable place in the school curriculum. In fact, his curriculum reform singled out history as vital to building a values-based, democratic society.

One of Asmal's first major initiatives was to create a working group, comprising ten South Africans appointed by the ministry and selected for their expertise and personal records, to explore how values could better show up in the curriculum revision process and in schools in general. As a result, in 2000, the Department of Education released the *Values, Education and Democracy* report, which became an important foundational document for the curriculum being revised under Asmal's leadership. Published with the hope of beginning "a national debate on the appropriate values South Africa ought to embrace in its primary and secondary educational institutions,"[7] the report recognized South Africa as a country damaged by apartheid which, after the TRC, would still be in transition, requiring deliberate efforts to promote reconciliation and healing:

> It would be foolish to expect that the severe corrosion of our human dignity [during apartheid] would heal quickly and without purposeful effort, active reconciliation and focused attention to developing the values necessary to underpin our democracy.[8]

The report also cited the need for South African schools undergoing transition to recognize and have their programs based upon the value of tolerance:

> By tolerance we do not mean the shallow notion of putting up with people who are different, but a deeper and more meaningful concept of mutual understanding, reciprocal altruism and the active appreciation of the value of human difference.[9]

Crucially, the authors recognized the important role history and "truthfulness about the failures and successes of the human past" had to play in this process:

> More than any other discipline, good history put to good use taught by imaginative teachers can promote reconciliation and reciprocal respect of a meaningful kind, because it encourages a knowledge of the other, the unknown, and the different.[10]

Finally, the report identified teaching about the TRC in particular as an important preventive measure to keep the mistakes of the past from being repeated:

> A history of past abuses of human rights does not by itself prevent but can serve as a powerful reminder of the folly of repetition. About this matter we must not be naive. Human beings have the remarkable capacity to repeat the mistakes of the past. It is the combination of memory and democratic politics that minimize the risk of repeating past mistakes. But the memory base must be there. This is why it is so important to recognize the importance of the record left by the work of the Truth and Reconciliation Commission.[11]

Values, Education and Democracy helped to guide the writing of the Revised National Curriculum Statement, which began to be rolled out in schools across the country in 2003. The NCS (as it was later known) was very clear about the role of schools in transforming society and the kind of student who would emerge from classrooms at the end of grade 12, as this extract shows:

> The National Curriculum Statement Grades 10–12 (General) seeks to promote human rights, inclusivity, environmental and social justice. All newly developed Subject Statements are infused with the principles and practices of social and environmental justice and human rights as defined in the Constitution of the Republic of South Africa. The kind of learner envisaged would be imbued with the values and act in the interests of a society based on respect for democracy, equality, human dignity, and social justice, as promoted in the constitution.[12]

Unlike Curriculum 2005, the NCS identified history as particularly important to transforming society and prescribed a history syllabus that now covered apartheid and other difficult episodes of South African and world history, as well as the TRC. The curriculum writers viewed the study of these particular histories as a "vehicle of personal empowerment."[13] "History," they wrote into the History Learning Program Guidelines, "engenders in learners an understanding of human agency. This brings with it the knowledge that, as human beings, learners have choices, and that they can make the choice to change the world for the better."[14]

As had been suggested in the *Values, Education and Democracy* report, the TRC was now included in the content outline of the history syllabus under the heading "Dealing with the Past and Facing the Future." Unlike with the previous curriculum revision, the architects of this one were not doing their work while the TRC was still in place, and, perhaps, distance made it easier to think about the role this history could play in schools. Far from turning away from it, these curriculum designers—led by Gail Weldon—were now asking teachers and students to face the past. In doing so, they declared, young people should "explore issues of race, gender, class, xenophobia, and genocide and the impact that these have had in the past and present. These are critical issues that need to be challenged."[15] Furthermore, if history is taught well, they argued, "it should promote non-discrimination, raise debates, confront issues and address current social and environmental concerns."[16]

Reflecting on this process in her later study on the construction of memory and identity in the curricula of societies emerging from conflict, Weldon cites Guillermo O'Donnell and Phillipp Schmitter, who emphasize the need for countries to address the most painful parts of their past before moving on. According to them,

> It is difficult to imagine how a society can return to some degree of func-
> tioning which would provide social and ideological support for political
> democracy without somehow coming to terms with the most painful
> elements of its own past. By refusing to confront and to purge itself of its
> worst fears and resentments, such a society would be burying not just its
> past but the very ethical values it needs to make its future livable.[17]

The NCS did not allow the past to be buried. By prescribing the teaching of apartheid and, specifically, the TRC, the curriculum writers asserted that learning about the past was a first step in ensuring young people in history classrooms would be able to develop the values South Africa needed to pros-per. Quite clearly, the study of history was presented in the NCS as a support to democracy by "engendering an appreciation and an understanding of the democratic values of the Constitution; encouraging civic responsibility and responsible leadership; and promoting human rights, peace, and democracy education."[18] That this past must not be forgotten was clear. But, as we will discuss in more detail below, it is one thing to say the record left by the TRC should be taught and quite another to understand what actually teaching this difficult past means for teachers.

THE PAST SITS WITH US

Unfortunately, throughout the twenty years of education reform, the South African Department of Education (now the Department of Basic Education) has, for the most part, not engaged in any meaningful way with what it means for teachers to teach a history that is complex, difficult, and possibly painful, while still achieving the curriculum aim of creating value-laden critical thinking and producing active and compassionate democratic citizens. Moreover, most history teachers in the country have not been helped by the national education department in systematic and deliberate ways to understand how their pasts affect them, what they teach, and how they teach it. They have not been given room to reflect on their pasts, share their stories, hear from the "other," and, crucially, think deeply about what their students might be hearing from them when they teach. This last point is illustrated best by the remarks of a teacher who, in contrast, was given the room and support to reflect on these issues:

I know how indoctrinated I was, so people who are [older] are much more so than me and that has to influence their teaching, irrespective of what race they are. And if we're not critically looking at how it is that who we are influences how we teach then we're just perpetuating either hatred, maybe indifference towards the other, whoever they are, and then how do we possibly create a new way of being?[19]

If O'Donnell and Schmitter are correct, teachers who do not seriously engage with their pasts will have difficulty nurturing the ethical values needed to bring about a livable future in their classrooms. In 1996, South Africa, as a country, needed the TRC to tell the story of its past; similarly, teachers, as a very distinct community, also needed—and still need today—to tell their stories to begin this process. Unfortunately, most history teachers have not been asked to speak or invited to listen.

To understand why it is so important to give history teachers the room and support to engage with their own pasts—especially pasts that contain so much conflict, division, suffering, and humiliation—it is worthwhile to part from the intellect briefly and look at the emotional impact apartheid has had on some South African teachers. Allowing parts of their stories to be told helps explain the need for many more stories to be faced by history teachers who cannot but bring this past in some way into their classrooms.

Nkululeko Ngada teaches history at a school in Cape Town. The neighborhood where the school is situated was created as a township for black South Africans during apartheid, to separate them from white and coloured (mixed-race) residents of Cape Town. Nkululeko, whose name means freedom or independence, was born in 1959. His parents were hoping South Africans would soon finally also gain their freedom, as was occurring across the African continent. In his words, "My parents were wrong by thirty-five years!" Nkululeko was born into a family deeply involved in the resistance to apartheid, and his father, a leader in the resistance movement, was imprisoned on Robben Island along with Nelson Mandela and others who fought against the apartheid government.

Nkululeko left school in 1976. Soon afterward, he was arrested during the student uprisings against apartheid that overwhelmed the country that same year. He was arrested and detained a number of times after that. Eventually, he was approached by members of the African National Congress (ANC) resistance movement and recruited into their military wing to fight the apartheid government. In attempting to flee South Africa to receive military training in the ANC military camps in neighboring countries, he was once more arrested. He described his detention in an interview:

What would happen: you would sit in the cell. There is nothing in the cell. There is a bucket there. There are some blankets here. Then, you would sit here. Next door, there is another cell. You would hear the cries of that guy being interrogated. I mean, you are a human being. Then, oh god, you'd think, they are coming to me. They wouldn't come to you. The whole day, you've been sitting alone. Now, this was working in your mind. To an extent, you would end up counting the blocks in the ceiling. You've got nothing to do . . . Then, you would sleep.

Then, at two o'clock, they would come to interrogate you. Two in the morning! . . . They will take you out to an interrogation room. They will ask you questions. Some of them, you really, truthfully, don't know the answers. They would hit you. Then you would go unconscious . . .

When I hear other stories, I feel like my story was much smaller. When I hear other stories, I will never forget that. A tire tube. They tighten it around your neck. If that thing they say, they ask you questions and you beat around the bush. They take that thing, put it around your neck. Let me tell you. There's a moment whereby you feel that you are about to die. You hit the table and say, "Ok! I want to tell the truth."[20]

At this point, one needs to pause for a moment and remember this is a person who is required to stand in front of a room full of young people and teach the very history he has described. On a personal level, what must it do to him as he teaches this history? What does it do to him, that every year he has to consciously revisit his traumatic past? What does he do if remembering and telling brings him pain and anger? When so much of teaching revolves around the confidence one has as a teacher, how does telling this history not leave him vulnerable before his students? What message do his students receive from his history?

One can deduce some of Nkululeko's answers to these questions from the way in which he ends this interview:

You as a person, you need to forgive. Some want to take revenge. It won't help. Revenge won't help. My next door neighbor, he's white—Mr. Ricks. My kids say—ah, Mr. Ricks, you should get him! I say no. It won't help. Really. It won't help. Because if I kill Mr. Ricks, I've got to go to jail. Who is going to feed you? Another thing—it was not Mr. Ricks. It was his cousin or whatever. But not Mr. Ricks. That's the thing that we must teach our kids. Forgiveness.[21]

There are thousands of other stories like Nkululeko's that can be told by the history teachers who lived them. These same questions can be asked of them, as well as of those history teachers who, unlike Nkululeko and other victims, benefited from apartheid or even perpetrated acts to uphold the system. Their answers would, no doubt, all be different.

Janine Kaptein, for instance, who teaches with Nkululeko at the same school, is acutely aware of the ongoing difficulty in teaching apartheid. She was classified as coloured under apartheid laws and says, "I think every time that I teach apartheid it's always like a first time."

> When you talk about many of the very bad things, well, apartheid was bad, but when you really talk about a lot of the bad things . . . There are many times when you actually stop, when you're teaching and you realize you just said something, not something wrong, but you think about what you just said. Then, I actually stop to think over that again.
>
> So if I can just make an example . . . there was an incident in Athlone in the 1980s which was called the Trojan Horse incident [in which the police hid inside crates on a truck and deliberately drove into an area where they knew they would be met with resistance. Once in the middle of the protest, the armed police emerged and opened fire, killing three young people]. So, and this is just an example. Then, I talk about it, because I was a high school student during the time, and then when I explain what happened . . . I would think about this horrible incident and think over it again, and actually stop talking.
>
> So, that's the kind of impact that it has. It doesn't happen a lot, I mean, teachers can keep themselves together. So that's one of the things that happens, that because we are witnesses and we lived through apartheid and resistance. As teachers or as adults, it's difficult to sum it up.[22]

Finally, for Susan (not her real name), who grew up classified as a white South African under apartheid, it is teaching about the TRC that brings up the hurt and pain of apartheid. During a workshop that explored what it means to teach the TRC, which she attended with other South African history teachers, Susan broke down. Crying, she said, "We worry about our learners, but we should be worrying about ourselves." She added, "What is teaching this doing to us?"[23] She later reflected on her reaction to the TRC content:

> I have been thinking about the TRC and our response to it—and the difficulties I find in dealing with our past. I must admit, I didn't sleep so

well last night . . . partly because I felt the need to reflect on our session . . . I realized that what we are attempting to do is to teach our own nation's trauma while still in a period of mourning—especially for those of us who experienced apartheid. I don't have a psyc [sic] background but I suspect that this may not be the wisest course of action. However, the curriculum is the curriculum and teach it we must, but I have a suspicion that some "shrinks" would question our intention to examine our trauma in a formal pass or fail exam.[24]

For these teachers and the tens of thousands of others across South Africa, what must it mean to have to relive the past every year? At what point does the telling become numbing and damaging, and at what point does it present the possibility of healing?

FACING THE PAST—TRANSFORMING OUR FUTURE

With answers to these questions lacking, the new curriculum presented an urgent need for South African history teachers to begin engaging deeply with what it would mean for them to teach about the divided, violent, and traumatic past they had lived through. By 2002, however, no professional development support program was in place to help them teach the new history curriculum. That changed in 2003, when the Facing the Past—Transforming Our Future program was set up as a partnership of the Western Cape Education Department (WCED) with the US-based teacher professional development organization Facing History and Ourselves and the Cape Town Holocaust Centre, the first Holocaust memorial center in Africa. In 2005, Shikaya, a South African nonprofit organization working for education for human rights and democracy, took over the management of the program, and it has run it since then with the WCED and Facing History.[25]

In its early days, the Facing the Past partnership aimed to use the pedagogical resources and methodologies of Facing History and Ourselves to support the rollout of the National Curriculum Statement across South Africa.[26] Both Facing History and the WCED saw synergies in the approach to history teaching, and the founding partners of Facing the Past saw the possibility of specifically adapting them for South Africa.

Like Facing History's approach, the approach to history outlined in the NCS required students to move from simple factual recall to engagement with issues of historical interpretation, cause and consequence, and similarity and difference. Teachers in South Africa were now required to teach about Nazi Germany, eugenics, and the US civil rights movement, all key historical case studies explored in Facing History's education work. Furthermore, like Facing History, the NCS saw history as a means to engender in learners an understanding of human agency. Facing the Past was, therefore, formed to support teachers in their use of such historical case studies, along with the history of apartheid South Africa, to help young people learn to become active, tolerant, and responsible democratic citizens who value diversity, human rights, and peace. In doing so, the program would also support them in dealing with their own pasts as South Africans and their role as South African history teachers.

Since 2003, Facing the Past has offered teachers an ongoing program of professional development. It includes intensive introductory seminars, follow-up workshops and events, a free resource lending library, and one-on-one support. So far, over five hundred teachers have come through the program, and a few thousand more have engaged with and used the program's resources. These teachers represent the diverse range of schools in South Africa and include both under- and well-resourced schools. Many of these teachers, of all races, continue to receive support in a variety of ways.

Most of the teachers involved in Facing the Past have begun this professional development journey through an intensive introductory seminar focused on historical case studies that include apartheid, Nazi Germany, eugenics, and the US civil rights movement. In the early years, these seminars were four to five days long. More recently, given the increasing burdens on teachers' time, with much already taken up by official departmental curriculum training, these seminars have been held over two sessions of two days each. Following their participation in the seminars, the teachers are offered at least four follow-up workshops where they are able to share their practice, explore new content and methodologies, and continue an ongoing personal reflection on their teaching.

Besides the resources and lesson plans they receive, community-building events have been central to the support offered to teachers. These events have brought Facing the Past teachers into conversation with historians, anti-apartheid stalwarts, such as Ahmed Kathrada and Denis Goldberg, journalists, authors, and politicians. In addition to providing them with opportunities to enrich their teaching by learning from a wide variety of viewpoints and experiences, bringing teachers together with influential South Africans has been a way to value them and to show the work they do is important. Through all of these events and activities, though, the teachers are continually supported in reflecting on their pasts and how their pasts show up in what and how they teach.

LESSONS IN FACING THE PAST

Facing the Past has been guided by five main principles that emerged from Facing History's thirty years of experience and the past twelve years of building the program in South Africa. Elaborating on these five guiding principles can be helpful in understanding the procedures and strategies the program has put into place to help South African teachers teach difficult histories, including their own, in ways that allow the young people in their classrooms not only to learn about history, but also to develop the critical thinking skills they need to make good choices as democratic citizens. The five principles are as follows:

1. Teachers teach best what they experience.
2. The learning journey is guided by the *Scope and Sequence*.
3. Learning happens in the head and the heart.
4. To explore the past, one must first slowly turn to face it.
5. Then, one can tell one's stories.

The following briefly explores these principles.

TEACHERS TEACH BEST WHAT THEY EXPERIENCE

An ongoing presupposition of Facing the Past is that teachers learn best when they do what their students will be doing in class. Too much of the formal professional development undergone by teachers in South Africa does not reflect the classroom environment we hope most will eventually create—one in which learners are engaged, discussing, reflecting, thinking, and being challenged. Many educators teaching in South Africa did not themselves have these kinds of classroom and learning environments when they were schooled during apartheid. Across the divide of racially segregated schools, engaged, critical thinking environments were not encouraged or nurtured.

It is essential, therefore, that South African teachers today know how these methodologies are experienced by learners, what the conversations entail, and what it means to be engaged in the process of reflection and learning. Without this experiential learning engagement, teachers cannot see what is possible. It is also through this engagement that they are able to develop themselves personally. Facing the Past workshops have always provided opportunities for teachers to discover or hone new methodologies and content, and equally, to experience their own personal growth.

During the introductory seminars, it has been important for teachers to have as much time as possible to go deeply into the content and methods as learners, but they have also needed time to pull back and reflect on the experiences as teachers. Participants in Facing the Past workshops, consequently, find themselves wearing two hats at any given point. At times they are asked to engage with the content or methods for their own development; for instance, to ensure all voices are heard and everyone has had a chance to reflect and voice their opinions, Facing the Past commonly uses a technique called *Think-Pair-Share*. The method, used extensively by Facing History and Ourselves, asks the teachers or learners first of all to reflect on a specific prompt, resource, or moment in writing by themselves. They then pair up and discuss some of what they personally reflected on. Finally, those who are willing share their thoughts with the larger group. At other times, they are asked to think about the implications of what they are learning for their own teaching. So the discussion after a Think-Pair-Share activity could revolve around the use of the methodology to engage quieter learners or around the suitability or relevance of the content for a teacher's particular environment.

THE LEARNING JOURNEY IS GUIDED BY THE *SCOPE AND SEQUENCE*

Central to the program is a methodology and approach to history teaching developed by Facing History and Ourselves and used in different settings that revolves around what is termed the *Scope and Sequence*—a journey of discovery about oneself and others.[27] Through a very specific series of steps, the Scope and Sequence guides the learning process. It frames the exploration into the past and allows teachers, and eventually students, to investigate very difficult, complex, and emotional histories in ways that do not leave them with hate, anger, guilt, or indifference and that allow them to connect to their own ethical decision making today.

The Scope and Sequence is a five-step process that begins with *The Individual and Society*. The focus is on how both individual and national identities are formed, as well as how these identities influence behavior and decision making.

The second step, *We and They*, focuses on the processes of national and collective identity that help people connect with one another but also contribute to misunderstanding, stereotyping, and conflict. Teachers and students learn that the way a nation defines itself affects the choices it makes, including the choice to exclude those who do not fit the nation's concept of itself. They see that membership can be a tool for both constructive and destructive purposes.

347

Students move on to *History and Human Behavior*, where they explore issues of personal choice and ethical decision making within the context of historical case studies. Whether the history is that of apartheid or Nazi Germany, a key focus is on exploring the small steps that led to these difficult periods so students can grasp the complexities of the past, while also connecting it to their lives today. A fundamental component of the Scope and Sequence methodology is precisely that it guides teachers and students to connect the history with which they engage to their own behavior and choices today.

Crucially, the journey next moves to looking at *Judgment, Memory, and Legacy*, the fourth step. As teachers and students confront these historical case studies of terrible atrocities, they explore the meaning of concepts such as guilt, responsibility, and judgment—and what those concepts mean in our world today. They also discover that one way of taking responsibility for the past is to preserve its memory. They explore the importance of monuments and memorials as communal gestures of remembering, of acknowledging injustice, and of honoring individuals and groups who have suffered.

The last stage in the Scope and Sequence learning journey is *Choosing to Participate*. Here participants focus on how understanding the past can connect not just with their own lives, but with the issues of today. Contemporary stories show how history is made every day by ordinary human beings. Students begin to understand they, too, have the power to change the course of history through their own individual actions. They explore what it means to be a citizen in a democracy—to exercise one's rights and responsibilities in the service of a more humane and compassionate world. Crucially, ending the journey with Choosing to Participate allows a sense of hope and possibility to rest in the classroom. Students need to leave a Facing the Past classroom knowing there are things they can do to fix the wrongs they encounter. They need to be inspired to action and need to be given the opportunity to develop the habits of active democratic citizenship.

LEARNING HAPPENS IN THE HEAD AND THE HEART

For a South African teacher, facing a past like that of apartheid is not only an intellectual engagement; having the room and opportunity for an emotional engagement with it is equally important. Interviewed for a United Nations Educational, Scientific and Cultural Organization (UNESCO) journal article on Facing the Past, Karen Murphy, international director for Facing History and cofounder of Facing the Past, summed up why a Facing the Past seminar or workshop creates an emotional and intellectual engagement for teachers:

Head and heart matter. They are tied, inseparable, compatible, and sometimes they even collide. You must be able to "touch" someone in these settings, I think. These are not sanitized academic environments where we analyze and hold each other at a distance. We can't.[28]

The emotional side of the program was a key feature for Gail Weldon, senior official in charge of history in the WCED and a cofounder of Facing the Past. It was, indeed, Weldon who saw an opportunity in the partnership built around the work of Facing History and Ourselves for South African teachers to begin to engage with their pasts on a personal level so they would be able to teach difficult histories in more reflective, understanding, and compassionate ways. The recognition implicit in Facing History that teachers need personal as much as professional support was what Weldon saw as lacking in the national education department's own official countrywide training of history teachers, which focused mainly on traditional historical skills and assessment.

Using the Facing History methodologies and approaches, Facing the Past frequently creates moments for emotional and intellectual engagement. One strategy is the use of journals. Reflection, both on what is in the head and what is in the heart, is a constant of the training seminars. Sometimes teachers are asked to turn to their journals and spend a few minutes in intellectual reflection—for example, on issues surrounding the fragility of democracy during Weimar Germany. At other times, especially those moments when the content is painful or disturbing, they may be invited to write a few words describing their emotions at that particular time. Here the focus is not on offering explanations or even writing in full sentences but, rather, on expressing the emotions they are feeling. The exercise is then taken further by asking each teacher to read just one of the words captured in his or her journal. The mind is not at work here; the teachers are not asked to analyze why those feelings are present in the room. Rather, the purpose is just to hear the emotions that the written content has brought to the surface in the group. This becomes a way of gently voicing the emotions in the room and hearing reflections from every participant.

At other times, the teachers are asked to juggle the emotional and the intellectual at the same time. When watching a video, for instance, the teachers are often asked to create "double entries" in their journals. A line is drawn down the middle of a page, with one side for writing how they feel about what they are watching and the other for what they are learning about history—the content, facts, and questions that arise from the video resource. Using the journals in this way not only provides another experiential learning example for the teachers—in this case, how they might create an engaged viewing experience for students—it gives them their own space in which to learn from and reflect on what they are watching and how they feel about it as people, not necessarily as teachers.

Since Facing the Past is as much about personal growth as professional development, these moments of emotional engagement are as vital as the intellectual ones. Of course, teachers need to have a continually improving understanding of the history and the issues present within the case studies they are asked to consider. But they also need to be allowed to respond as human beings with feelings, however that response may manifest. If teachers can emerge from Facing the Past seminars and workshops better equipped intellectually but also more aware of their own feelings and emotional responses to these difficult histories, they are more likely to be able to recognize these reactions in their students and, ideally, even be prepared for those that may arise in their classrooms. Healthier people, if only emotionally, become better teachers.

In an interview with two teachers conducted a few years after they attended their first Facing the Past seminar, they specifically emphasized the importance of emotionally and intellectually engaging with the past as they reflected on their teaching of apartheid back in the classroom. Said one,

> I think it was difficult preparing myself for that type of lesson . . . because I needed to search my own heart for my own prejudices and my own thoughts and be confronted with my own inadequacies . . . Just thinking through where I was at the time. How the laws that I wasn't even aware of at the time as a child impacted on me. [This] was actually harder than understanding what the law meant.[29]

The other commented,

> I think that having done the Facing the Past course, it forced me . . . to interpret my place in apartheid, so when I taught apartheid it was no longer the facts of what happened, you know the laws, but the impact that had on different people in society at the time. But it has also forced me to pose the question to the learners how it has impacted them, their families, and how also to look out for the dangers that take place in terms of our democracy. Not only the political impact on the lives of people, and not only those that were disadvantaged, but also those who were advantaged.[30]

TO EXPLORE THE PAST, ONE MUST FIRST SLOWLY TURN TO FACE IT

As already discussed, teachers at the introductory seminars follow the Scope and Sequence, which guides their learning together and the lessons they take back to their classrooms with the support of the program. In the seminars, as in the classroom, when they begin to move into the history stage of the Scope and Sequence, the starting point is Nazi Germany and the Holocaust, eugenics, or the US civil rights movement. It is through these more distant case studies that South African teachers (and students back in the classroom later) first wrestle with issues of personal choice and ethical decision making, begin to reflect on and talk about perpetrator and bystander behavior, and explore how the issues of identity that were introduced at the start of the learning journey influenced decision making at the time.

The journey led by the Scope and Sequence allows teachers to start conversations and reflect on broad issues first—issues of difference, otherness, inclusion, and exclusion—and slowly begin to explore them in a case study from a history that is not their own. In doing so, they are able to explore issues that are at the heart of their own past but in a way that does not immediately speak of it. They explore perpetrator behavior in Nazi Germany, for instance, by looking at the work of the historian Christopher Browning, who studied interrogations conducted in the 1960s and early 1970s with 210 men from Reserve Police Battalion 101. The battalion was originally formed from the German equivalent of city policemen and county sheriffs, who were asked to participate in the early murder of Jews. Members of this particular battalion were given the choice to participate in the killings or not. Some chose not to take part.

The conversation the teachers have in response to this reading begins by looking at the factors that influenced the interviewed members of Police Battalion 101 in their choices to take part or not. But the conversation ends by looking at human behavior in general and what we can learn from this specific moment about ourselves and each other. The issues of identity, difference, and otherness with which the teachers' journey began come up again in the discussion of this specific moment. In this way, a case study that is distant from the direct experience of South African teachers is used to open a conversation among them about perpetrator behavior, without referring from the outset to apartheid perpetrators. This allows for the conversations to begin more gently and slowly than they would with a more direct approach. The teachers are given the space to explore these issues in some depth in a different historical context before turning to their own past.

Sharing our own past—our own choices and actions in the past—is very difficult, especially when the past is one of division, conflict, and trauma. Allowing teachers to make connections between the issues they are engaging with and other histories they teach, between the present times and, occasionally, their own past, provides an easier entry point into exploring that past than having them dive straight into apartheid.

THEN, ONE CAN TELL ONE'S STORIES

Storytelling is an important tool in Facing the Past. From the outset of the program, its developers understood that the introductory seminars, in particular, needed to create a space for teachers to tell their stories of the past. The experience South Africans already had of the TRC meant the developers in many ways expected that history teachers coming together to explore Nazi Germany and the Holocaust and apartheid would need, and possibly want, to tell their own stories of the past.

While the TRC process primarily unearthed the stories of gross human rights abuses, for many South Africans, themselves not victims of these extreme abuses, it mainly provided a moment to listen, to hear, and to no longer deny or be denied a place in the past. What the TRC did not (and possibly was unable to) do was create a space for ordinary South Africans to share their stories of the everyday experience of apartheid and the everyday humiliation most, including teachers, faced. Despite the silences the TRC process failed to fill, though, it would have been more difficult to get teachers to talk about their own pasts in the Facing the Past seminars if the country had not already watched, listened to, and read such stories.

Not until midway through the introductory seminars do the teachers begin to speak about their pasts to each other and tell their own stories. These conversations, while not avoided, are until that point generally confined to the pages of their journals and moments of personal reflection. From the start of the seminar, however, the teachers have been supported through deliberate and attentive facilitation to begin conversations about issues of prejudice and discrimination and, equally, of care and compassion. By allowing all voices to be heard, creating moments for connections of intellect and emotion, and engaging in this process using the lens of specific historical case studies that highlight human behavior, choices, and decisions, the process has created that safe space for the teachers to open up.

With that safe, open, and compassionate environment in place, the teachers are now able to begin to tell their stories. Many are doing so for the first time in their lives. Workshop notes from one of the first Facing the Past introductory seminars, held in December 2006, show how storytelling was used to deliberately begin the engagement with the apartheid past at that midpoint of the seminar when the historical focus moved to South Africa's past:

> On the morning of the third day a Holocaust survivor told her story to the teachers. This was followed by Themba Lonzi performing a dramatic and musical piece about the impact that apartheid had on all South Africans. Afterwards, Themba shared his story of how apartheid impacted on him personally. The teachers then went into small groups and began a silent reading activity, Silent Conversations, in which they read and respond to personal accounts of the impact of apartheid on people of various races. They were allowed to respond initially only in writing and were asked to write down their own feelings, reflections, and thoughts on the large sheets of paper surrounding the stories. They could respond in any way and to anything in the story, but they had to respond silently. After nearly an hour, before moving back into the large group, the smaller groups talked amongst themselves about what they had read and written. The teachers then sat around in a large circle to talk about what they had read. Initially the conversation centered around the accounts that they read. Gradually, however, teachers began to talk about their own experiences. For some, it was the first time that they were talking about the past. Teachers opened up, told their stories and supported others when doing the same.[31]

This "silent conversations" technique (as it is called in the program) has been particularly effective in beginning the process of storytelling for teachers. Because the stories they respond to when communicating in silence with their groups represent the diversity of apartheid experience, most are able to find one that resonates with their own experience in some way. These are not the stories of Mandela and Hitler, the extremeness of which distance them from the rest of us; these are stories of everyday South Africans living out what apartheid meant for them. It is in the "normality of experience" that teachers are able to find some connections to their past.

The invitation to read in silence allows for an atmosphere of reflection, and it honors both the stories shared on the pages the teachers are reading and those they themselves begin to share on the sheets of paper surrounding the readings. To be asked to respond to their peers only in writing also makes it easier for softer voices to join the conversation. Writing at first rather than speaking is a less threatening way to share for those teachers who might not initially wish to do so. They can respond in words, phrases, questions, sentences, and even drawings. In essence, after the hour is up, the teachers have had a very intimate conversation with and about their past together, without ever speaking.

When the silent conversations are over, the reflections written on the sheets of paper provide a starting point for teachers to share their stories aloud. In the same way that turning to a historical case study from somewhere other than South Africa to begin this bigger conversation was a useful starting point for the seminar, turning to the stories of the South Africans on these pages allows the bigger conversation about and sharing of their own pasts to begin. Initially, the teachers talk about what they read, what stood out for them, what reflections written by their peers stuck with them; but it doesn't take long before someone makes a connection to his or her own past.

In one silent conversation activity, a teacher responded to one of the apartheid texts by writing an account of what had happened to her:

My father was lighter skinned than the rest of us. People thought he was white. My father once took us to a "Whites Only" beach. The whole family drove to the beach. We got there and the police were standing at the turn-off. They stopped the car. They said they would allow my father to go in but not "the maid and her kids." He turned the car around and drove home. All of us, including my father, cried all the way home.

In response to this recollection, another teacher wrote, "I left my footprints and realize I have always been allowed to leave them. Where I place my feet, my smelly, sweaty feet, has never been legislated against. I have never had to tread lightly."

In over twelve years of running these seminars, with over three hundred teachers having gone through this silent conversation, never has one taken place in which the teachers' personal stories of the past have not been shared and heard.

Hearing the stories and learning with and from "the other" in this way can test the assumptions many teachers hold. According to one participant,

The stories of the "white" teachers especially were significant. I think there are many generalizations that this group had no need to complain and that they all benefited from the old system. I think there is also a stereotype that those who did suffer must just get on with it, move on. What the Facing the Past workshops have done is to give us space and acknowledgment that our stories are powerful, too. This of course is mirrored in what we then do in our classrooms.[32]

A second participant in a previous workshop commented,

> I had to look in the mirror and had to face, yet again, the atrocities committed by my people to my people. It made me realize again how important my role is to be an agent for human rights—not only in my classroom but also my community.[33]

And a third said,

> I needed to search my own heart for my own prejudices and my own thoughts and be confronted with my own inadequacies . . . Just thinking through where I was at the time.[34]

For many teachers, this process of storytelling, understanding, and reflecting on their past is a journey that continues beyond and between Facing the Past seminars. Some have found that over time, and after conscious reflection on their pasts from a storytelling perspective, they have been able to bring their own stories into the classroom in a way that has made the history more personal for their students. Roy Hellenberg, interviewed some years after he attended his first Facing the Past seminar as a teacher, openly spoke about the need for his story to be told, if only initially to himself:

> I actually found, until two years ago, I taught apartheid very dispassionately, kind of at arm's length. And that maybe that was my, it probably was my way of dealing with it. Until one of the boys said to me, "Sir, you lived through it. How did you feel?"
>
> And then I started reflecting on some of my experiences and in fact, all those emotional memories come back, and you have to deal with that. What I try to do here is that even though I may be provocative and biased, you don't want the emotion to turn to anger and for that to be unleashed, because that's destructive. So, I'm kind of, very careful about it, maybe too careful, I very seldom relate my personal experiences of it. Which, I think, the boys find strange. Because I can be so open about a lot of other things. Unless they ask very specific questions, I don't normally speak about it. I suppose that's part of the baggage that I still carry. I'm busy unpacking the suitcase, but there's still lots of clothing items in there.[35]

REACHING WIDER

Facing the Past is now in its twelfth year and has reached over five hundred teachers and, through them, tens of thousands of students. The majority of teachers have volunteered to attend the workshops. Initially, invitations went to a wide selection of schools in the Western Cape that reflected the diversity of the province. Over the years, teachers already participating in the program have invited their colleagues to attend. Considering the growth over time of the Facing the Past program, an ongoing challenge has been to balance the need to scale up with the ever-increasing realization that the kind of work that offers personal and professional support emerges best in small groups of teachers who get to know each other and form relationships over time and are able to learn together. Also an increasing realization, however, is that this work is important for all teachers across South Africa.

Taking this into account, the program has developed a number of blended model interventions that have allowed it to reach more teachers to introduce them to a reflective and engaging way to teach the past that emphasizes ethical and moral decision making. Throughout the twelve years in which the program has been implemented, Shikaya has run larger history teaching conferences and events that have brought together more than the twenty or thirty teachers who generally attend the seminars and workshops.

So far, almost another thousand teachers in addition to those who have participated in the program have been reached through these events. While it is difficult to recreate the "introductory seminar" experience of the original project for one hundred teachers, these events, which generally run over several days, have infused Facing the Past methodologies and principles into their proceedings. In 2011, for instance, Shikaya hosted a Teaching the TRC conference that took around a hundred teachers from the Cape Town area on a three-day journey in understanding the TRC that centered mostly on storytelling. The teachers heard from survivors, TRC translators, and musicians and artists who had interpreted the TRC through music, art, and photography. While the emphasis on teachers sharing their own stories was less than in a Facing the Past introductory seminar, teachers were supported in reflecting on the TRC and apartheid in deep ways through the use of journals, paired discussions, and graffiti walls, on which they could write any thoughts, comments, or feelings as their journey proceeded.

The evaluations from this conference show that even in the absence of very specific moments for teachers to talk about their own experiences, the Facing the Past Scope and Sequence, methodologies, and resources still create an environment of deep reflection and learning. As the forms collected after the conference show, for some teachers it began a slow process of healing:

> I am left in awe of the proceedings of this conference. Learning and hearing from survivors was incredible. As a survivor who has never had the opportunity of appearing before the TRC, I've found it very difficult to relate to the whole issue of reconciliation. But after today, I've come to terms with it and have forgiven, even though I still find it difficult to forget.[36]

For some, the opportunity they were given to engage with this history on a very personal level gave them the confidence to teach it. According to one teacher,

> I feel emotionally attached with the subject matter now, which will enhance my ability to teach it. It has sensitized me to how complex and emotionally challenging teaching about the TRC can be. I now know that I have to approach the TRC in a special way. I believe engagement and bridging gaps to discuss different perspectives is key, so linking schools that are from different contexts would be an option.[37]

Similarly, another said,

> This conference has made me to fully understand that for genuine reconciliation victims and perpetrators must be able to love and find one another. Although I have taught the theme for the grades for the past three years, I feel more confident and empowered to teach it now.[38]

As in the Facing the Past workshops and seminars, the opportunity to learn with a diverse group of teachers and to listen and talk to each other was of particular value for some of the South African teacher attendees:

> This conference truly made the TRC come alive for me, in a way I have never previously experienced. It was incredible, and it is conferences such as these that our country needs. As difficult as it is to accept our past, I really felt that through this conference and through individual and collective engagement across numerous boundaries, there is a sense of how to create a better future. You should be proud of the seeds of change you are helping to plant. Interaction amongst teachers from radically different backgrounds, and different schools, the sharing of personal narratives, the open honesty, all strike me as incredibly valuable.[39]

These kinds of interventions that bring more teachers together are increasingly needed for Facing the Past to move forward. While giving smaller groups the space and support to reflect deeply and connect through these explorations of their past is worthwhile, and even important, the reality is that more teachers need to be reached. The Teaching the TRC conference, as well as other, larger interventions through which Facing the Past has reached more educators at once, has shown it is still possible even when a great many are present to create a space for teachers that is guided by a learning journey, that is experiential, that allows for the head to meet the heart, and that, through other histories, allows South African teachers to turn slowly to their past and tell their stories to each other.

CONCLUSION

As we have seen, the post-apartheid curriculum architects saw a very particular role teachers must play to ensure active, democratic citizens emerge from South Africa's classrooms. That role has not gone away. Twenty years after apartheid ended, South Africa is still dealing with the legacy of the past. Racism and prejudice still infiltrate a deeply divided society. Poverty still divides along racial lines. While many South African children attend mixed schools, most go to school with children who look like them. For many, change still needs to come. As a nation, South Africans are also still learning what it means to live in a democratic country and show up as active citizens. Two generations have not necessarily emerged from the new school system equipped to be critically thinking, engaged citizens.

Now more than ever, teachers, and especially history teachers, need to use their teaching to help students think more deeply about their choices, the country in which they live, and the fellow citizens with whom they share it. But without support that allows them to be recognized as people affected as much as any others by their country's past, and without providing them with strategies for personal and professional growth, teachers cannot be expected to live up to the task we as a country have set for them. As long as history is taught in schools, teachers need to be supported to engage with it in ways that are personal, challenging, and, in the end, empowering and uplifting. Without this, the past can easily return to being the mere recollection and memorization of facts. It is very difficult to become an active and democratic citizen if all one can do is remember names, places, and dates.

NOTES

1   Dylan Wray, cofounder and executive director of Shikaya, is a cofounder of Facing the
    Past—Transforming Our Future and has led the management of the program since 2003.

2   Truth and Reconciliation Commission in South Africa, *Truth and Reconciliation of South
    Africa Report*, 5 vols. (Cape Town: Truth and Reconciliation Commission, 1998).

3   See, for example, Peter Kallaway, ed., *The History of Education under Apartheid, 1948–1994:
    The Doors of Learning and Culture Shall Be Opened* (New York: Peter Lang, 2002). See also
    June Bam, *A New History for a New South Africa* (Cape Town: Kagiso Publishers, 1996).

4   Gail Weldon, "A Comparative Study of the Construction of Memory and Identity in the
    Curriculum in Societies Emerging from Conflict: Rwanda and South Africa" (PhD diss.,
    University of Pretoria, 2009), 150.

5   Ibid., 149.

6   Professor Kader Asmal was South Africa's second education minister. He was one of the
    architects of the TRC and an influential leader of the African National Congress (ANC) in
    exile during the apartheid years.

7   South African Department of Education, *Values, Education and Democracy*, (Pretoria:
    Department of Education of South Africa, 2000), 12, http://www.education.gov.za/Link-
    Click.aspx?fileticket=pB0c8Qg4LmQ%3D&tabid=92&mid=495.

8   Ibid., 3.

9   Ibid., 22.

10 Ibid., 24.

11 Ibid.

12 South African Department of Education, "The Revised National Curriculum Statement
    Grades R–9" (Pretoria: Department of Education of South Africa, 2002), 8, http://www.
    education.gov.za/LinkClick.aspx?fileticket=JU1Y7NGqqmk%3D&tabid=390&mid=1125.

13 South African Department of Education, "National Curriculum Statement Grades
    10–12 (General): Learning Program Guidelines, History" (Pretoria: Department
    of Education of South Africa, 2008), 7, http://www.education.gov.za/LinkClick.
    aspx?fileticket=x8iXsnJdqNU=.

14 Ibid., 7.

15 Ibid.

16 Ibid.

17 Guillermo O'Donnell and Philipp C. Schmitter, *Transitions from Authoritarian Rule: Tenta-
    tive Conclusions about Uncertain Democracies* (Baltimore: Johns Hopkins University Press,
    1986), 30, quoted in A. Sparks, *Beyond the Miracle: Inside the New South Africa* (Jeppestown:
    Jonathan Ball, 2003), 160.

18 South African Department of Education, "National Curriculum Statement Grades 10–12
    (General)," 7.

19 Teacher response from post-seminar evaluation questionnaire (Facing the Past introductory seminar, Cape Town, January 2006), copy on file with author. Name withheld to protect teacher's confidentiality.

20 Jocelyn Stanton, *Oral History Interviews* (internal document, Cape Town, 2010), 81. Copy on file with author.

21 Ibid., 83.

22 Ibid., 42.

23 Teacher comment recorded in author's notes (Facing the Past workshop, Cape Town, August 25, 2008), copy on file with author. Name withheld to protect teacher's confidentiality.

24 Teacher comment in personal correspondence with author, August 26, 2008. Copy on file with author. Name withheld to protect teacher's confidentiality.

25 The WCED is one of the nine provincial arms of the national Education Department of South Africa. Facing History and Ourselves is an international education and teacher training organization run from Boston, Massachusetts. Facing History has regional offices in the United States, as well as an office in London. Finally, Shikaya supports teachers to help ensure students leave their classrooms thinking more critically and acting more compassionately as responsible democratic citizens than they did when they arrived. Beyond its involvement with Facing the Past, Shikaya has initiated numerous education conferences and support programs and created resources that have reached thousands of teachers across South Africa. See www.shikaya.org.

26 With over thirty years of experience, Facing History provides ideas, methods, and tools that support the practical needs, and the spirits, of educators worldwide who share the goal of creating a better, more informed, and more thoughtful society. Specifically, Facing History uses historical case studies, such as the histories of Nazi Germany and the Holocaust, to help young people engage in explorations of ethical decision making and human behavior. For more information, see www.facinghistory.org.

27 For more information about the Scope and Sequence, see Facing History and Ourselves, "Scope and Sequence," https://www.facinghistory.org/for-educators/educator-resources/our-pedagogy/scope-and-sequence, accessed April 20, 2015.

28 Felissa Tibbitts, "Learning from the Past: Supporting Teaching through the Facing the Past History Project in South Africa," *Prospects* 36, no. 3 (2006), 13.

29 Interview with author (Cape Town, January 2006), copy on file with author. Names withheld to protect teachers' confidentiality.

30 Ibid.

31 Author's notes (Facing the Past workshop, Cape Town, January 2006), copy on file with author.

32 Teacher response from post-seminar evaluation questionnaire (Facing the Past introductory seminar, Cape Town, December 2009), copy on file with author. Name withheld to

protect teacher's confidentiality.

33   Ibid., December 2008.

34   Ibid., December 2005.

35   Roy Hellenberg (Facing the Past teacher), interview with the author, Cape Town, April 2010.

36   Teacher response from post-conference evaluation form (Teaching the TRC conference, Cape Town, 2011), copy on file with author. Name withheld to protect teacher's confidentiality.

37   Ibid.

38   Ibid.

39   Ibid.

CHAPTER 12

Addressing the Recent Past in Schools: Reflections from Côte d'Ivoire

Virginie Ladisch and Joanna Rice

Oh li o li oh, la guerre a commencé, mais ce n'est plus un jeux, il y a bien trop d'enjeux, je suis un soldat, un enfant soldat, qui veux tout arrêter.

—"Petit Soldat"[1]

In 2010, after ten years of intermittent conflict in which youth and the education sector were used to advance political ends of the elites in power, often through violent mobilization, the post-conflict government of Côte d'Ivoire (CDI) called for the creation of several transitional justice measures.[2] Starting in 2013, the Children and Youth Program of the International Center for Transitional Justice (ICTJ) and the United Nations Children's Fund (UNICEF) undertook a joint program to engage children and youth in Côte d'Ivoire in their country's process of reckoning with its violent past and help them become responsible and valued political actors in their own right.[3] Young people played a highly visible role in the horrors of the war, provoking a social tendency to characterize Ivorian youth as reckless thrillseekers taking out their frustration with life on the society around them by destroying it.[4]

Now, however, after two years of working with Ivorian youth on questions of peacebuilding and transitional justice, the nature of their widespread participation in the conflict appears much more complex than the common narrative would suggest. A transitional justice approach—understood as efforts to examine past human rights violations with an eye toward preventing their recurrence—opened possibilities for a group of young people to begin explaining the complexities surrounding their mass involvement as primary victims and perpetrators and, based on that reflection, to put forward their vision for a new role for youth in CDI based on *politique positive*," a term coined by the youth leaders involved in the ICTJ-UNICEF project, as a call to their peers to become engaged citizens through positive and nonviolent means.

In 2011, as part of CDI's efforts to address past violations, the government established a truth commission, the Commission for Dialogue, Truth and Reconciliation (CDVR), with a mandate to identify the root causes of the conflict, reveal acts and patterns of violations, and find ways for the country to overcome its legacy of violence through reconciliation and the recognition of victims.[5] At the time ICTJ and UNICEF's partnership in CDI was formed in early 2013, the CDVR was just getting underway. Building on previous efforts worldwide to engage children in truth commissions, this provided a unique opportunity early in the CDI commission's process to advocate for the involvement of children and youth in its work.[6] For ICTJ and UNICEF, it was also an important opportunity to explore the possibility of establishing links between the commission and the education sector. ICTJ's efforts to engage youth in truth seeking elsewhere had suggested that early interaction with the education sector could facilitate more youth engagement and build buy-in, with the result that at the end of the truth-seeking process, key people within the education sector could carry on the truth commission's legacy (by, for example, applying its findings to education materials for children and youth).

A deeper assessment of the political situation in CDI, however, soon made clear that this plan would not work. The idea that a truth commission's early engagement with the education sector would enhance its objectives was predicated on the assumption that the commission would be part of a legitimate and genuine effort to acknowledge recent human rights violations and seek redress for victims. Yet in CDI, as in several other places emerging from recent conflicts, transitional justice measures lacked legitimacy and genuine political will. Taking a formulaic, data-focused approach, the CDVR gathered over sixty thousand statements in less than one year. Analyzing so many statements posed significant challenges. The final report was handed over to the president in 2015, but it had not yet been made public as of this writing.[7]

In the fall of 2013, when the CDVR stalled for several months partly because of the contested political situation, ICTJ and UNICEF reassessed their initial objectives and refocused the project on three goals: facilitating truth-seeking opportunities for youth, adapted to their needs; opening communication between youth and authorities; and engaging youth in reflections on their future, in light of the past.

Thus, the project adapted to the realities and challenges facing transitional justice measures in CDI and turned to working with youth leaders outside the formal education sector. Under the new framework, the group of youth leaders, who were initially mobilized to engage with the formal truth-seeking process (led by the CDVR), instead held their own dialogues and gathered youth perspectives on CDI's past. This parallel project between the youth leaders and the ICTJ-UNICEF partnership resulted in a youth-produced audio report about the violent past and its consequences. The youth leaders involved in this project formed a new association of youth, Réseau Action Justice et Paix (RAJP), to pursue accountability and reconciliation in CDI. As of this writing, that organization is in conversations with representatives from the Ministry of Education about working with national extracurricular "peace clubs"[8] set up by government decree in all primary and secondary schools to foster students' engagement in peacebuilding at the school and community levels, and with the Ministry of Youth to support initiatives that allow for the meaningful civic engagement of youth.

This chapter seeks to share some of the challenges and questions that emerged in the implementation of this joint project that can help guide other such efforts. The first section provides historical background for the antagonistic relationship maintained by children and youth with the state authorities in Côte d'Ivoire and the way the education sector was used by the latter for political purposes. This history is important to document, as it tells the larger story behind the common narrative in CDI of criminal or manipulated youth. The broader view shows youth involvement in the Ivorian civil war as part of a larger intergenerational conflict, one that reached a boiling point after decades of institutionalized violence against the younger generation, in a social environment that normalized acts of repression.

The second section discusses the ICTJ and UNICEF project, highlighting the challenges it faced in trying to build a bridge between the truth commission and the education sector—in a situation where the latter was a site of both resistance and repression that played midwife to a history of violence—and the various efforts to overcome these challenges. As this particular experience shows, in post-conflict situations where, as in Côte d'Ivoire, a genuine transition in power structures is lacking and the narratives of the past are still very politically contested, it is very difficult, if not impossible, for a truth commission to introduce issues of accountability and democracy into the education system at the official level. Rather than trying to influence the education sector from the top down, it proved more effective in CDI (in what is inevitably a very long-term process) to build momentum from the bottom up, in the hope that eventually some of these discussions would find their way into schools as complementary teaching and learning materials or as materials for extracurricular teaching, such as the peace clubs.

HISTORICAL BACKGROUND: YOUTH, EDUCATION, AND CONFLICT IN CÔTE D'IVOIRE

The politicization of schools and universities in Côte d'Ivoire began in the 1980s, just after the world economic crash. Suddenly, the so-called "Ivorian model" of rapid development appeared more a chimera than a miracle. For decades, modernization-development theorists had lauded Côte d'Ivoire as a model of economic progress for the African continent.[9] Yet, in hindsight, the relationship of wealth, violence, and political power maintained under the leadership of independence-era president Félix Houphouët-Boigny (in power from independence in 1960 until his death in 1993) was not dissimilar to that in other regimes in West and Central Africa grappling with natural resource wars as the price for rapidly accumulating wealth in the upper strata of the state.[10]

For almost thirty years, the Ivorian leadership enjoyed the profits of at least one-quarter of the world's total cocoa consumption. There was a lot of money to go around. Through state-controlled marketing boards, the government kept the pay of plantation laborers in the cocoa sector low but consistent, stifling the threat of mass discontent by nulling the possibility that price fluctuations would touch the workers themselves. The tactic also ensured that the regime kept at its disposal the huge sums of cocoa wealth left after paying the farmers.[11]

A portion of this wealth was distributed broadly, but it largely benefited Houphouët-Boigny and the ruling elite.[12] Houphouët-Boigny's control of cocoa wealth also allowed the president to manage every aspect of economic and social life in Côte d'Ivoire through an elaborate and well-funded system of patronage networks that controlled industry, unions, security services, and markets. The surest road to success under the Houphouët-Boigny regime was to win a high-ranking place in the ruling (and only) political party, the Parti Démocratique de Côte d'Ivoire (Democratic Party of Côte d'Ivoire, or PDCI).[13] In the short term, the Houphouët-era development model worked well: during this period, Côte d'Ivoire enjoyed a level of economic success that fast outpaced its neighbors in the region.[14]

With global cocoa prices high, the economy grew quickly, allowing average Ivorians to gain a better living, even if most of the profits ended up in the hands of the elite. Education and urban migration started to appeal to Ivorians much more than the agricultural life of their grandfathers. With an eye to positions in the lucrative public sector, a generation left their plantations for the cities, creating a labor void on the cocoa and coffee plantations.To fill the ever-growing need for labor, Houphouët-Boigny adopted a policy of open borders to immigration from West Africa under the mantle of a pan-Africanist *fraternité* and welcomed anyone willing to work in the cocoa and coffee sectors, promising that "the land belongs to whomever works it."[15]

While Houphouët-Boigny's pan-Africanism gained Côte d'Ivoire an international reputation as a cosmopolitan paradise within West Africa, at home the policy was in direct contradiction to customary law that considered land possession the inalienable right of its traditional owners. As elites in Abidjan amassed huge personal fortunes thanks to abundant cheap labor in the cocoa sector, the seeds were sown for a bloody land conflict between the original inhabitants and a new class of regional immigrants in rural areas.[16] Forty years later, the policy would become the basis for the xenophobic violence of President Henri Konan Bédié's "*Ivoirité*" doctrine.[17]

The economic prosperity that followed independence in Côte d'Ivoire included a major investment in education, with 40 percent of the national budget going to the sector until structural adjustment programs took hold in the 1980s.[18] In part, this investment was in response to teachers' syndicates. Teachers received generous salaries and extensive benefits compared to standard practice in postcolonial and developmental states at that time. These benefits included state-subsidized housing in otherwise unaffordable city centers—a situation they were happy to maintain.[19]

Teachers' syndicates had played a crucial role in Houphouët-Boigny's approach to statecraft. For social cohesion to be maintained, teachers had to hold the frontline of the Ivorian nation-building project.[20] At the same time, the president's major investment in education transformed the children of agriculture laborers into a generation of state functionaries and urban professionals. Ultimately, though, the model built an educated middle class that began questioning the legitimacy of one-party rule.

One beneficiary of Houphouët-Boigny's education policy was Laurent Gbagbo. A history professor at the National University in Abidjan (UNCI) during the early eighties and president from 2000 to 2010, Gbabgo was detained in 2011 at the International Criminal Court (ICC) for alleged war crimes. Along with other likeminded colleagues and students, he led a new class of leftist intellectuals, determined to claim their constitutionally protected civil and political rights. The movement transformed Ivorian high schools and universities into the epicenter of resistance against the one-party state. From this period onward, the leaders of the PDCI would find it increasingly difficult to control the teacher syndicates they themselves had created.

After the crash in cocoa prices in the late 1970s, international donors—frantic to recover their significant investments in Côte d'Ivoire's cocoa sector—imposed strict structural adjustment schemes ill-suited to the political and economic realities in the country. The schemes hit the education sector first and hardest,[21] leading Laurent Gbagbo to accuse the regime of using austerity measures to punish the teachers for demanding multiparty elections. After the teachers' syndicates officially broke with the PDCI and launched a series of strikes and political standoffs, they were disbanded, and a number of their leaders were submitted to torture and imprisonment. The result of this repression was not, however, what Houphouët-Boigny expected. Rather than shying away from future action, the teachers continued their resistance, now joined by police, firefighters, and even the security sector. With his grip on the armed forces loosening, Houphouët-Boigny agreed to meet the public sector at the negotiating table.[22] The outcome was that in April 1990, multiparty elections were declared; and although Houphouët-Boigny won the first of them in a landslide, the teachers' strikes had directly contributed to the end of the one-party state.

A day after Houphouët-Boigny agreed to the elections, on April 21, 1990, the student movement Federations des Etudiants et Scolaires de Côte d'Ivoire (Students and Scholars Federation of Côte d'Ivoire, or FESCI) was officially formed in the Sainte-Famille Church in Cocody Riviera—just a few blocks away from the presidential palace, where many of its members would later lose their lives defending Gbabgo's presidency. The FESCI soon took a lead role in mobilizing opposition, organizing mass rallies in support of their teachers' leftist politics, and distributing pamphlets that openly criticized the regime. The most volatile student response of the period came after policemen found guilty of assaulting and raping students in the Yopougon University housing complex were cleared of all charges by a decree from Houphouët-Boigny himself.[23] Although this was only one of many instances of police violence against students and teachers during the 1990s, the symbol of "Yopougon, the martyr" has shaped the FESCI's relationship with the PDCI (and later the Rassemblement des Républicains, or RDR) ever since. To paraphrase Eric Lanoue, the state responded to student activism with repressive force, creating a relationship between political power and student and youth movements characterized by violence and repression rather than dialogue. In many respects, this dynamic persists even today.[24]

Following the death of Houphouët-Boigny in 1993, his successor Henri Konan Bédié took over the PDCI and the presidency. Although he was a protégé of Houphouët-Boigny, he lacked the personal appeal of his independence-era predecessor, and the cracks already visible in the PDCI's unchallenged domination would soon burst open and unleash a rapid series of events culminating in civil war and partition.

Bédié was displaced from power in 1999 by a military coup lead by General Robert Guéï. Guéï, who had promised to hand over power to a democratically elected ruler immediately after ousting the president, soon became comfortable holding the reins of the state and through various maneuvers tried—unsuccessfully—to win the 2000 presidential election against the Front Populaire Ivorien (Ivorian Popular Front, or FPI) candidate, Laurent Gbabgo.

Under Gbabgo, the leftist intellectual-come-president, murders of so-called "strangers" suddenly became commonplace. Although heated debate persists regarding whether or not Gbabgo personally ordered the violence, it is clear that under the banner of protecting "*Ivoirité*," xenophobic violence was perpetrated by "autochthones" with ambitions to reclaim their "native" lands from the immigrants brought to Côte d'Ivoire under Houphouët-Boigny's open border policy.

Under Gbabgo, political space finally opened up for youth to begin expressing their political views and desire for change. They would prove themselves a ready and willing pool of recruits on both sides of the conflict, and the violence committed by them, together with the mystique Gbabgo held for the younger generation, were to become central dynamics of the ten-year protracted conflict.

To understand the role of youth in the conflict in Côte d'Ivoire, it is helpful to look more closely at the FESCI and its leadership. On September 19, 2002, a familiar voice would come on the radio under the pseudonym Dr. Koumba, announcing that Côte d'Ivoire was henceforth partitioned. A northern rebellion had formed, intent on ousting Laurent Gbagbo and restoring liberal, democratic values to the country. The voice was instantly recognized by his former classmates and FESCI compatriots as that of Guillaume Soro, the recently exiled ex-general secretary of the FESCI.

Soro's story leading up to this turn of events and afterward provides important insight into the attitudes and actions of Ivorian youth throughout the civil war and electoral crisis. Over a twenty-year period, Soro fought on both sides of a long and protracted conflict and, at least in this one respect, his story is not unique. Testimony of child and youth combatants recounts tragic and sometimes strange circumstances that resulted in participation on both sides at different stages of the conflict.[25]

Being from modest origins, Soro worked hard in school to earn a much-coveted study grant at the Law School of the National University. Having met the necessary requirements, he arrived in Abidjan only to discover that at school and in the job market, the best posts were reserved exclusively for those who could pay their way into them.[26] Soro saw this structural violence as being deeply connected to the rampant physical violence against children, students, and youth so common in the patronistic style of education, politics, and social life dominant in Côte d'Ivoire. Outraged by the harsh reality facing young Ivorians, he became a prominent student activist, eventually assuming the leadership of the FESCI.[27]

Years later, when he made his radio announcement, the former head of Gbabgo's main support base had become an unlikely rebel leader. In his own words, Soro had been an adoptive son to Gbabgo during his time in college.[28] In his 2005 autobiography, *Why I Became a Rebel*, he explained his choice to lead the rebellion as "nothing less than an effort to prevent an impending genocide—of the scale of Rwanda in 1994"—which Gbabgo and his young armed followers were allegedly preparing to unleash.[29]

The student movement Soro left behind was weakened by his defection but not broken. Highly organized and staunchly supportive of Gbabgo's regime, the FESCI operated on campus like a mafia, ensuring one political perspective dominated university life. The organization used its vast numbers to hold the education system hostage with a credible threat that it could shut down any school or university within a moment's notice.[30] Many sources accuse FESCI members of moonlighting as Jeunes Patriots, a paramilitary group that allegedly assisted gendarmes in attacks against so-called foreigners. Their victims were often guilty of nothing more than holding an identity card with a northern- or Muslim-sounding name on it.[31]

In their own version of events, only a minority of FESCI members participated in the violent crimes of the Jeunes Patriots, as evidenced by their frequent marching slogan "*Aux Mains Nues*" (with empty hands). In this account, those who did take arms were acting in self-defense squads whose aim was to protect the elected president after the police and military had largely abandoned their posts. From the perspective of Gbabgo's supporters, their country was under attack from a rebel force orchestrated and financed by international elites, desperate to win back control of the vast economic potential of Côte d'Ivoire.

The youth manning the northern rebellion behind Soro, on the other hand, were there to destroy President Gbabgo's fascist dictatorship. They maintained that Gbabgo's rule centered on the xenophobic concept of *Ivoirité*, a political ploy now morphed into a widespread ideology justifying indiscriminate violence against immigrants, Muslims, and northerners. In reality, the rebels' Forces Nouvelles (New Forces) did not always fit the image of virtuous antigenocidal fighters described in Guillaume Soro's account. The conflict resulted in an unknown number of massacres in villages,[32] as local conflicts were played out within the chaos of a civil war.[33]

On both sides, many youth found economic opportunities and status they could never get access to in times of peace. This was true across Côte d'Ivoire, but particularly in the occupied region. Many contented themselves with extortion at roadblocks and other forms of small-scale looting, while others amassed small fortunes through such activities as covert mining operations, notably involving child labor.[34] It is also documented that both sides recruited child soldiers during the conflict.[35]

On both sides of the partition, youth leaders adopted a discourse that appealed to the frustrations and moral outrage of their peers. In the North, second-, third-, and even fourth-generation immigrants saw their lands, families, and lives under immediate threat from the Gbabgo regime and its Jeunes Patriots. In the South, youth responded to a sense that those in power had sold the wealth and heritage of Côte d'Ivoire to immigrant laymen and foreign business tycoons. On both sides of the front line, these discourses radicalized a youth population already at boiling point after a decade of crisis and the systematic attacks on students and youth that had accompanied it. In addition to making moral claims, both sides promised monetary rewards and perhaps even a steady job to anyone who joined (but only once the battle was won, of course).

In the climate of daily violence and fear, presidential elections were delayed for nearly a decade, until the patience of international onlookers finally wore out. Following the 2010 elections, international observers concluded that the opposition candidate and leader of the rebellion, Alassane Ouattara, had won a clear victory. But in a dramatic scene on live national television, Gbagbo's party leaders prevented the results from being officially read, and the Constitutional Council declared Gbagbo the winner after invalidating nearly half a million votes due to claims of fraud. This moment heralded the darkest period of Ivorian modern history, as Ouattara and Gbagbo set up parallel governments within Abidjan, with both sides committing terrible atrocities in a vicious scramble for power. Considered the legitimate winner in the elections by the United Nations and international community, Ouattara, and the forces loyal to Ouattara, were supported by French and UN military forces, which allowed them to take the capital of Abidjan and arrest Gbagbo.

Upon assuming office, President Ouattara established the Cellule Spéciale d'Enquête, or Special Investigative Unit, under the Ministry of Justice to investigate crimes punishable under national law, including economic crimes, violent crimes, and crimes against the state. A UN Commission of Inquiry was instituted in March 2011 to investigate the violence and recommend possible ways to redress its consequences. Later that year, Ouattara established the Commission for Dialogue, Truth and Reconciliation, a truth commission to investigate violations at the national level, as was called for in the peace accord. Born in the absence of a real transition in power structures while Ouattara maintained a tenuous hold on power, the CDVR faced conditions hardly ideal for an equitable and inclusive examination of the past and the pursuit of accountability.

TRANSITIONAL JUSTICE, YOUTH, AND EDUCATION IN CÔTE D'IVOIRE: THE ICTJ-UNICEF PROJECT

As this series of transitional justice measures began to be implemented in spring 2013—in large part in response to international pressure—to build democracy and peace in Côte d'Ivoire, the Children and Youth Program of ICTJ and UNICEF initiated a two-year project to include young people in the process. The project focused its efforts on truth seeking, targeting specifically the CDVR, both because it was timely, with the CDVR just beginning its operations, and because a truth commission lent itself well to various forms of participation and possible connections to the education sector. The project included a two-pronged and phased approach: first, to support the CDVR in its efforts to engage children and youth and, second, to make the products of the commission more accessible to young people all over the country by integrating them into the curriculum. The overall strategy was to help the CDVR take statements from children and youth, to include their perspectives in the final report, and then to incorporate the report's findings into the education sector through the creation of education materials based on its findings.

Beginning in March 2013, ICTJ and UNICEF met with the commissioners in charge of statement taking for the CDVR, who agreed it was important to gather statements from children and young people, and that a special form and methodology would be necessary to do so safely and effectively. Yet efforts to involve the education sector with the work of the CDVR, both as a potential partner for outreach activities addressed to children and youth and as a stakeholder with an eye to incorporating the commission's findings into the curriculum, soon made apparent several internal challenges the CDVR faced. The commission's decentralized structure, for instance, which divided tasks into independent mini-commissions that often competed for influence, made it difficult to situate work with children appropriately and more challenging still to establish clear links between the commission and the education sector.

Despite these challenges, ICTJ and UNICEF continued to support the work of the CDVR and prepared a statement-taking manual, including guidance, methodology, and tools, to gather testimonies specifically from children. At the same time, they worked on facilitating conversations with representatives from the Ministry of Education about a possible role for the CDVR and the adoption of a transitional justice approach in the national curriculum. Although in the initial conversations the ministry representatives expressed general interest in the idea, it soon become clear that any project aimed to influence the national curriculum would need several years to be implemented and would need first to go through many layers of approval as part of the standard required process for revising curricula.

In contrast to this realization, the ICTJ-UNICEF team found a surprising amount of latitude for more immediate work at the civil society level, especially among youth, to foster learning about the past. In August 2013, following a training workshop for CDVR statement takers who would be interacting with children, ICTJ organized a workshop with youth organizations and child protection agencies to discuss ways to engage children and youth in the transitional justice process. The emphasis for youth organizations was on how to lobby the CDVR to consider their views and how to influence the official truth-seeking process. The participants were very receptive and eager to take part in the transitional justice processes going on in their country, and they requested further training and information on how to play a more active role.

That fall, however, the revised project faced a major obstacle, when delayed funding and a political stalemate between the commission's president and President Ouattara over its future direction brought the CDVR process to a halt. At that point, it was unclear whether the CDVR would resume its work. With the official process stalled, the ICTJ-UNICEF project shifted strategies, searching as broadly as possible for local partners and entry points into the education sector, regardless of whether that involved formal schooling or extracurricular projects in the arts, music, literature, and sports. Free of the constraints of trying to fit into or interact with an official truth-seeking process, the team saw opportunities for young people to develop their own ideas. If the CDVR were to resume its operations, this youth work could eventually be realized as a civil society submission for consideration by the commission.

This new approach led ICTJ and UNICEF to hold regular discussions with the leadership of fifteen nonpartisan student- and youth-run local nongovernmental organizations (NGOs), which, for more than a decade, had coordinated in a loose alliance of young activists promoting human rights and peacebuilding in Côte d'Ivoire. These organizations represent the full spectrum of

Ivorian society, including high school student and university student groups, Muslim and Catholic student groups, a child and youth workers' association, two young women's organizations, and an association of young conflict victims and jurists. Among them, they appear in every corner of the country, with more than five thousand active members, and they vary broadly across religious, ethnic, language, gender, and regional lines. Given their wide reach, working with a core group of twenty to thirty youth leaders from in and around Abidjan would, in the long term, lead to the mobilization of networks far beyond the capital area.

The engagement with youth leaders started off with a three-day retreat outside Abidjan that introduced them to the main concepts of transitional justice. The goal was to help them articulate their own thoughts and recommendations on how the past could be dealt with from the perspective of children and youth. Afterward, they continued the conversation within their organizations and began a project of collecting youth experiences during and after the conflict. To help them, ICTJ-UNICEF gave each group a small amount of seed money to organize peer truth-telling events within their existing networks. The first meetings took place within the groups, but the leaders soon expressed interest in linking these dialogue sessions. Muslim and Christian student organizations began sharing their respective experiences during the war that pitted these communities against each other.

In response to the groups' demand for broader dialogue, ICTJ and UNICEF organized another, larger retreat to provide a discussion forum for the youth to present their findings and decide collectively what they would like to do with the stories and perspectives they gathered. There, they learned about examples of transitional justice involving children and youth, ranging from small-scale, independent projects to major national truth commissions. The workshop also highlighted the way transitional justice initiatives tend to build momentum and transform over time, encouraging the attendees to look for avenues for productive, nonpartisan dialogue that could serve as platforms for larger, far-reaching initiatives in the future.

In the brainstorming sessions of this second retreat, the young people came up with the idea of creating a radio report that would feature stories, testimonies, music, and debate about the conflict and its aftermath from the perspective of Ivorian children and youth. While the use of music and radio as a peacebuilding education tool was not new, the conception of this approach by the youth themselves as a strategy for achieving their goals was. The choice was especially interesting given the important role played by public media, music, and radio in Ivorian conflict dynamics. At the peak of crisis, two official television and radio channels had broadcast their respective accounts of events from Abidjan's luxury hotel, the Golf, and the presidential residence where Gbagbo and Ouattara were waiting out the war. Musicians also had their allegiances. Indeed, one of the fieriest debates among youth leaders was about the extent to which local musicians were responsible for inciting violence among the youth.

A year later, the youth leaders completed a four-part radio program based on the testimonies and dialogues they had documented from peers across the country. The appeal of radio was its potential to be an interactive learning tool for telling a living history, adapting it over time, and incorporating new stories or perspectives. In this sense, the young people created a powerful and broad-reaching transitional justice education tool that added their voices to a national debate about the role of youth in the recent conflict and its enduring impact today.

The radio program chronicled a very different history than the one told in official circles, setting aside the notion that youth violence was a form of mass hysteria and instead exploring the idea that the Ivorian conflict was the boiling point in a longstanding intergenerational conflict. The testimonies shifted the focus from the violent acts themselves to the social and political apparatus at work behind child and youth militias. The report looked at the root causes of youth mobilization during the recent crises and included a discussion of politicization in schools and through media and music. It also addressed the difficult choices of individual young people and recognized that, while in many cases youth were perpetrators, they were also victims of a larger system that violated their rights. Through this audio report, the youth began to put forward their ideas for what could be done to redress past violations and their enduring consequences, as well as how to prevent their recurrence.

According to its producers, the radio report was not about the past as something only to look back on;[36] it was about the past as it related to the current situation of youth and their hopes for an improved future. Recognizing the negative role youth had played in the past and the desire to break from that dynamic, the commentator Amandine summed up a roundtable debate held in the first section of the report with these remarks:

> Youth have been involved in violence during the Ivorian conflict for various reasons. But we think youth still have a key role to play in preserving peace, social cohesion, and respect for human rights. By advancing solutions to the social difficulties facing youth we can help establish a certain level of social peace. But you have also highlighted [in the

debate] the importance of raising awareness among youth themselves so that they individually and collectively can become actors for peace.

Actors we have been. Perpetrators, too, in the recent history of CDI. But what type of actors will we be? What role do we want to play in the future of our beautiful nation, our beautiful country? What do we need to do to avoid the return of massive human rights violations and the unnecessary suffering of the population?[37]

These are the questions the youth now planned to take to the communities as they held discussions at the local level, with the goal of starting dialogues among other children and youth; of exploring alternatives to violence that emphasized their idea of *"politique positive"* (a term coined by the youth leaders to encourage their peers to become active, engaged citizens through nonviolent means and to refuse the call to violent mobilization); and of proposing strategies or reforms that would, they hoped, help prevent the return of violence in the October 2015 elections and beyond.

Earnest about their work and committed to maintaining their momentum, the youth decided to form their own official independent association: the Réseau Action Justice et Paix (RAJP). Unlike other instances in which ICTJ has needed a lot of persistence to engage and keep engaged with youth and a lot of prodding to get them to participate, the youth leaders in Côte d'Ivoire who received basic training on transitional justice and peacebuilding issues responded enthusiastically, eager for more information and opportunities to drive the process. The in-country organizers from ICTJ and UNICEF would receive calls from them, for example, asking about upcoming meetings or reminding them of their commitments, in a sense keeping the program organizers on task rather than the other way around. One major result has been that, under the leadership of the coalition, the members of RAJP have continued to build on initial efforts. The dedication and enthusiasm they bring to this work is encouraging, signaling the likelihood that it will carry on past the end of the ICTJ-UNICEF project.

That said, it is important not to idealize youth, and to recognize they are also a product of their society. While they advanced the notion of *"politique positive"* in their elections to become an independent association, for example, the process was riddled with many of the same problems for which they criticized adult politicians at the national level, demonstrating the extent to which the often nefarious nature of Ivorian national politics was ingrained in their way of thinking about democracy. In the end, leadership roles were chosen through nomination, followed by group debate until unanimous decisions could be made. Interestingly, none of the original presidential candidates won key roles through this process, and the top leadership role was given to a woman, although no women held decision-making power in the original model.

As the work with youth really gained momentum, the CDVR resumed its operations and launched the statement-taking phase. Following lobbying and support from UNICEF and ICTJ, the commission included a focus on children, using the form and methodology designed specifically for taking statements from children and youth. Its records show that in July 2014, it gathered statements from 757 children.

To date, however, the CDVR has not publicly released its final report (the mandate calls for one to be delivered to the president, leaving it to his discretion to make it public or not). Based on a leaked version, the chapter on children includes only tables and statistics, with no analysis or contextualization of the testimony they provided to the commission. In interviews with statement takers who worked with them, their sense was that the children came to testify mostly to get their names on the reparations list, not so much as to be part of a wider truth-seeking process.[38] Due to very poor and minimal outreach, this process was not well explained or understood.

While in one sense having the CDVR gather statements from children with a specific methodology was a significant accomplishment, upon reflection, and in light of the larger challenges the commission faced in terms of legitimacy and effectiveness, the impact of the children's involvement on its findings or on themselves is unclear. Some of those who testified expected to receive reparations, but whether that will happen or not remains to be seen. Without a public report or other output from the CDVR, there is nothing that can be adapted for or incorporated into the education system.

Within the realm of transitional justice work, there is a tendency to prioritize engagements at the official level and work with formal institutions, based in part on the belief that change comes from the state. In CDI, however, engagement with official institutions has yielded very mixed results, and the impact of this investment is not clear. Meanwhile, the work with youth continues, building even more momentum. What started as a disparate group of youth leaders, each with his or her own constituency, has become one organization, RAJP, committed to carrying on the dialogue begun as part of this project.

At this writing, with the radio report now complete, the youth leaders are engaged in the next phase of the project, which focuses on taking the report to different communities across the country, using it as a tool to initiate discussions about the past, and gathering ideas and perspectives from other young people on how to redress past violations and what reforms to undertake to prevent their recurrence. The leaders are mobilizing their national network to promote the radio program as an informal education project, using peer-to-peer learning strategies at the local level.

In addition to working through their civil society networks outside the school system, their engaging final product may give the youth a chance to work with the education sector as well. In March 2015, a Ministry of Education official from the pedagogical service unit attended a workshop with the youth leaders in which they were designing a dissemination strategy and a methodology for starting dialogues with other youth. Whereas in earlier meetings with the ICTJ-UNICEF project leaders, representatives from the Ministry of Education were reluctant to take on transitional justice work in school, in large part because it is a new and unknown domain as well as being politically contentious, the ministry official present at the workshop became much more enthusiastic once he saw the youth at work and the product they had created. While schools in CDI do have a curriculum on human rights—Human Rights and Citizenship Education (EDHC)—he acknowledged that students do not find it very engaging. In his view, the audio report, exhibiting the voice, creativity, and energy of the youth, would resonate much more with their peers. The representative from the ministry left the retreat very enthusiastic about this work and eager for the youth to use it as a discussion tool with students through the peace clubs.

In practice, establishing direct links between the formal education sector and the CDVR was not possible in Côte d'Ivoire, in large part due to the way the CDVR process unfolded. Instead, ICTJ and UNICEF worked with organized youth and supported them as they developed their own truth-seeking exercise which, in turn, grew into a peer-based informal education project with the potential for national reach. One of the youth leaders involved in the RAJP reflected on the value of an informal approach:

> The formal education system here is bureaucratic and slow. Talking to youth across the country, we see that many of us realize we were manipulated and suffer from the war, but we don't understand. There are so many young people searching to understand and to talk about what they did and saw. The formal system will never move fast enough, and it doesn't even reach the youth who were most involved in the war; these are people outside schools. These youth already have political parties at their doors asking for so-called "youth support" in the next elections. They need to talk now, and we were able to do that.[39]

In short, rather than waiting for a final report from an official truth-seeking process to feed into the formal education sector at the highest level and then trickle down to all schools and students, it seems more realistic in some instances where transitional justice measures are in place to start working on some of these ideas on a smaller scale through the informal sector. Once there is a clear product and a method by which to share it (for example, a youth-produced audio report as a discussion piece), opportunities may arise to work with the Ministry of Education to bring it into afterschool programs and into the EDHC. In this way, those working on transitional justice can serve as catalysts for change to build momentum and demand, which may in turn be taken up by youth leaders and/or representatives of the state.

CONCLUSION

While Côte d'Ivoire may be unique, given the central role of the education sector in conflict dynamics, education will likely be a pressure point in any post-conflict situation, as it is the vehicle by means of which a state shapes the values and opinions of the next generation. For this reason, extreme sensitivity to local dynamics will be necessary for any progress at all in this sector. Yet, if an objective of transitional justice is to include younger citizens in a national effort to shape the public sphere by means of dialogue around peace, justice, and civic trust, the education sector will need to be central to this project.

This reflection on ICTJ-UNICEF's work with youth around issues of transitional justice and the education sector in CDI does not yield a set of best practices that can be directly applied elsewhere. It does, however, reveal key themes or questions we hope will be helpful in guiding similar work. The experience in CDI highlights the importance of undertaking an in-depth analysis of the situation, through a child-and-youth lens in this case, and evaluating on the basis of that analysis the capacity of proposed approaches to address effectively the grievances, needs, and demands of youth before starting any project or activity.

If the assessment of the current situation is, as it was in CDI, that established transitional justice measures and the education sector are not in a position to address the youth's grievances, needs, and demands, it is important to explore and devise alternative strategies with the youth. In an environment where the relationship between political power and students and youth was characterized by violence and repression rather than dialogue, the groups of youth we worked with jumped at the chance to engage in dialogue among themselves. The ICTJ-UNICEF team at first assumed the ideal place to initiate that dialogue would be within the formal school sector, but the analysis of the situation revealed that envisioning that sector as an ally in this work was premature. The difficulties faced by the CDVR pushed the project team further to seek alternative, nonofficial channels to develop its work.

What turned out to be much more effective was working through informal channels and providing a platform for youth to come together around a shared need and common goal. For the youth, the experience of gathering narratives from their peers and having discussions among themselves seemed to have more impact, even to be transformative, and perhaps more important than having their views recorded by an elite-led truth commission. More than just being part of the process, the young people were agents driving it, which proved very empowering.

In many ways, the catalytic effect of this project—helping launch a group of youth leaders working toward peace and justice—mattered more than any final product. Instead of going straight to the crux of the conflict in CDI by tackling the education sector directly, the dialogue process begun among youth leaders resulted in the creation of a powerful tool, produced by youth for youth. Perhaps more importantly, it created momentum for what is and will be a long-term process of awareness raising, advocacy, and, eventually, reform.

NOTES

1   Refrain from the song "Petit Soldat," written by the youth hip-hop group Impact Positif, with the help of famous hip hop artists Kajeem and Nash. Impact Positif consists of young artists Peggy Octavie, Aziz Adams, and Martialo. They are a human rights–promoting group within the Réseau Action Justice et Paix, a youth association supported by UNICEF and ICTJ in Côte d'Ivoire.

2   Virginie Ladisch heads ICTJ's work on children and youth. Joanna Rice is currently pursuing her PhD on transitional justice and was a consultant for UNICEF on this project from July 2013 to October 2014. The authors would like to acknowledge and thank Didier Gbery, ICTJ program officer in Abidjan, an essential member of the project leadership team, as well as Carolin Waldchen, who oversaw this project within UNICEF under the direction of Aby Mze-Boina.

3   This project was part of UNICEF's global Peacebuilding, Education, and Advocacy in Conflict-Affected Contexts Programme (PBEA), funded by the Government of the Netherlands. See http://learningforpeace.unicef.org/category/pbea/ for more information about the global program.

4   See Mike McGovern, *Making War in Côte d'Ivoire* (Chicago: University of Chicago Press, 2011), 135.

5   Ordonnance No. 2011-167 du 13 Juillet 2011 Portant Creation, Attributions, Organisation et Fonctionnement de la Commission Dialogue, Verite et Reconciliation, Abidjan, July 13, 2011, http://www.abidjan.net/gouv/p.asp?Id=11, accessed July 27, 2015.

6   See UNICEF Innocenti Research Centre and International Center for Transitional Justice, *Children and Truth Commissions* (Florence: United Nations Children's Fund, 2010).

7   As a point of comparison, the TRC that operated for five years from 2009 to 2014 to investigate the legacy of the Indian Residential School system in Canada gathered over 6,750 statements, which are included in a final report. See Truth and Reconciliation Commission of Canada, *Honouring the Truth, Reconciling for the Future: Summary of the Final Report of the Truth and Reconciliation Commission of Canada*, 2015, http://www.trc.ca/websites/trcinstitution/File/2015/Exec_Summary_2015_06_25_web_0.pdf). To carry on its work, the newly established National Centre for Truth and Reconciliation (NCTR) has become the permanent home for all statements, documents, and other materials gathered by the commission. See http://umanitoba.ca/centres/nctr/mandate.html.

8   A Ministry of Education (MoE) decree institutionalizes the peace club model in schools. UNICEF is supporting the MoE in its operationalization of the peace club model in selected primary and secondary schools, with the understanding that children can play a crucial role in preventing and mitigating violence, in bridging divisions, and in resolving conflict. Training sessions on conflict mediation and constructive dialogue, along with dialogue, participatory theatre, child-led radio programs, and sports activities, enable

children to engage on peacebuilding issues and build the foundations for becoming constructive, proactive citizens.

9   On the Ivorian miracle, see Abbott A. Brayton, "Stability and Modernization: The Ivory Coast Model," *World Affairs* 141, no. 3 (1979): 235–49.

10 McGovern, *Making War in Côte d'Ivoire*, 140–56.

11 Ibid., 138.

12 Ibid., 16, 140.

13 Anonymous interview by Joanna Rice with the heir of one of Côte d'Ivoire's wealthiest plantation-owning families, who reports her father was arrested and tortured by Houphouët-Boigny personally over a period of months (Abidjan, September 14, 2014).

14 McGovern, *Making War in Côte d'Ivoire*, 144.

15 Declaration made by Houphouët in 1963 following a 1962 failure to pass a land reform act that would have made his land policy law. Even today, the conflict between his decree and customary law remains the central debate of land reform and, according to some interpretations, the Ivorian conflict in its totality. See Ruth Marshall-Frantani, "War of Who's Who," *African Studies Review* 47, no. 2 (2006): 20.

16 Ibid., 20. See McGovern's *Making War in Côte d'Ivoire* on the matter of elite wealth generated from the cocoa sector.

17 "*Ivoirité*" was a term coined by the intellectual Pierre Niava as a pan-African, anticolonial call to value African music, philosophy, and *griot* (oral history) traditions. Under Houphouët-Boigny's heir to power, President Bédié, *Ivoirité* became a justification for excluding those from the North—namely, Alassane Outtara—from participating in the 2000 presidential elections. When Laurent Gbabgo took power in 2000, this political culture tolerant of prejudice and, at times, overt violence against northerners and Muslims grew ever more entrenched in Ivorian civil and political life. See Thémélé Ramsés Boa, *L'ivorité et l'unité de la Côte d'Ivoire* (Abdijan: Editions CERAP, 2015), 40.

18 Dwayne Woods, "The Politicization of Teachers' Associations in the Côte d'Ivoire," *African Studies Review* 39, no. 3 (1996): 115.

19 Cyril Kofie Daddieh, "The Management of Educational Crises in Côte d'Ivoire," *Journal of Modern African Studies* 26, no. 4 (1992): 655.

20 For example, Côte d'Ivoire was never permitted to have a political science program or any schooling that included the teaching of politics.

21 Cyril Kofie Daddieh, "Universities and Political Protest in Africa: The Case of Côte d'Ivoire," *African Studies Association: A Journal of Opinion* 24, no. 1 (1996): 60.

22 Daddieh, "The Management of Educational Crises in Côte d'Ivoire," 658.

23 Éric Lanoue, "L'école à l'épreuve de la guerre: vers une territorialisation des politiques d'éducation en Côte d'Ivoire," *Politique Africaine* 92 (2003): 132.

24 Ibid.

25 Jean-Pierre Chauveau, "Question foncière et construction nationale en Côte d'Ivoire: Les

enjeux silencieux d'un coup d'état," *Politique Africaine* 78 (2000): 96.

26 Guillame Soro, *Pourquoi je suis devenu un rebelle* (Paris: Hachette Littératures).

27 Ibid., 45. In his autobiography, Soro describes extensively the use of strapping and other forms of violent punishment within schools, particularly against primary students. He also seems to observe a continuum between violence within schools and the rampant state violence against student activism. Whether or not he exaggerates these claims, violence against students remains a very salient issue among student activists in Côte d'Ivoire.

28 Soro, *Pourquoi je suis devenu un rebelle*, 49.

29 Ibid., 9–16. Despite these noble words, many of his critics believe Soro was not motivated to defect by ideological self-sacrifice, but rather by cynical self-interest. Even today, his close friends from his FESCI days cannot make sense of his true motives, recalling a confusing string of messages sent back and forth across the partition line in the weeks after his radio announcement. FESCI members, interview with author Joanna Rice, October 3, 2014. Individuals must remain anonymous for their protection and that of the author.

30 FESCI members, interview with author Joanna Rice, October 8, 2014. Individuals and place must remain anonymous for their protection and that of the author.

31 The Jeunes Patriots are accused of looting, building roadblocks to terrorize civilians, and, in some cases, adopting the horrific "Article 125" and other forms of torture and execution for those deemed traitors to the regime. (Article 125 refers to execution by burning. It signifies one hundred francs for gasoline and twenty-five for matches.) See Gnangadjomon Koné, *Les Jeunes Patriots ou la revanche des porteurs de chaises en Côte d'Ivoire* (Abdijan: Les Classiques Ivoiriens, 2014).

32 Accounts of these were given in more than eighty testimonies given to the CDVR. Victim groups' lawyer, confidential interview with author Joanna Rice, San Pedro, July 18, 2014.

33 Stathis Kalyvas gives a compelling description of war as a multilayered social experience with individual, local, regional, and national logics and motivations that function simultaneously. See Stathis Kalyvas, *The Logic of Civil War* (Cambridge: Cambridge University Press, 2006).

34 McGovern, *Making War in Côte d'Ivoire*, 182.

35 Evidence indicates child trafficking networks set up during the war remain embedded in Côte d'Ivoire today, following the ultimate success of the northern rebellion in May 2011, as the use of children as mine laborers and drug traffickers remains an ongoing problem in the country. See Human Rights Council, "Report of the Independent Expert on the Situation of Human Rights in Côte d'Ivoire, Doudou Diène," UN Doc. A/HRC/25/73, January 13, 2014, http://www.ohchr.org/EN/HRBodies/HRC/RegularSessions/Session25/Pages/ListReports.aspx. Information confirming these allegations also appeared in multiple testimonies from child conflict victims given to the CDVR, particularly in the western region of Côte d'Ivoire.

36   As a clear example of this, the youth who participated in the ICTJ-UNICEF project
      agreed the report resulting from their work needed to emphasize the current "microbe
      phenomenon." During the civil war many children were orphaned or abandoned, or
      they ran away in response to violence, family deaths and disappearances, or economic
      hardship. Although the last official study on street children was written before the war,
      the problem clearly has reached unmanageable proportions, with the formation among
      street children in Abidjan's ghettos of gangs known as "microbes," many of whose mem-
      bers are former child militants. The resulting national hysteria has brought about the
      creation of a new special police task force instructed to "eradicate" the microbes. In a
      video available online denouncing the state for its tracking and incarceration of gang
      members, the "brigade for the eradication of microbes" is accused of using extreme
      violence in their operations and, recently, of leaving the bodies of children who die in
      these operations at the side of the road as an example to others. See "Lutte contre 'les
      Microbes,'" YouTube video, 5:36, posted by Armée de Côte d'Ivoire, September 12, 2014,
      https://www.youtube.com/watch?v=bf6opidM5rA.

37   Réseau Action Justice et Paix (RAJP), Youth Audio Report, part 1, Abidjan, October 10,
      2014, copy on file with the authors.

38   Statement takers, personal conversations with author Virginie Ladisch, Abidjan, Octo-
      ber 2014.

39   Youth leader, interview with Joanna Rice, Abidjan, June 2, 2015. Interviewee prefers to
      remain anonymous.

CHAPTER 13

Grappling with Lebanon's Enduring Violence: Badna Naaref, an Intergenerational Oral History Project

Lynn Maalouf and Christalla Yakinthou

As this is being written, Lebanon's capital city streets—normally clogged by traffic and drowning in a deafening racket of unleashed horns and construction work—stand eerily empty. And yet, the holiday season is over, schools have reopened their doors, and people have gone back to work. Two car bombs less than a week apart, framing the 2014 New Year, partly account for this unusual scene—and for the overriding sense of gloom and doom shared by most Lebanese.

The gloom is the product of a year fraught with incidents of violence, including targeted assassinations, car bombs, and armed clashes erupting in different parts of the country. The resulting tension sits alongside a debilitating economic crisis, an unprecedented humanitarian crisis with an estimated one million Syrian refugees, the absence of a government since March 2013, and a Parliament that has autoprorogated its mandate, in effect canceling expected parliamentary elections. Moreover, Lebanese parties are directly involved in the war in neighboring Syria, and the domestic repercussions are gaining ground.

The doom comes from an overriding sense of fatigue derived from the awareness that Lebanon's short-lived existence as a state has mostly been marred by political conflict and violence. Fear of war's resurgence has become the norm among the Lebanese across generations, confirmed every few years by an outbreak of real armed conflict. In the past year alone, a period supposedly of "peace," or at least cold conflict, 229 people were killed and more than 4,000 wounded in various clashes and explosions across the country.[1]

Today's fear derives mostly from the current regional political dynamics, with Lebanon again becoming a platform on which regional and international interests are played out. But the farther-reaching fear, tinted by this fatigue, derives from persistent structural, political, economic, and societal factors: twenty-five years after the signing of the Ta'if National Reconciliation Accord, which ended a fifteen-year-long succession of conflicts that erupted in the mid-1970s, few domestic safeguards have been put into place to eliminate, or at least minimize, the country's vulnerability to recurring conflict, let alone to address the causes of the persistent violence. Recently published reports have highlighted the enduring aspect of politically motivated violence, well beyond the official "end" in 1990, as well as the impact of impunity and how it shapes society today.[2]

The Ta'if Accord, also known as the National Agreement Accord, that formally ended the 1975–90 war was, in essence, a power-sharing agreement between the protagonists of the conflict, implemented under the tutelage of Lebanon's neighbor, Syria. Two decades later, it is quite clear this agreement fell short of providing the basis for establishing a sustainable political system in the country, for reinstating the rule of law, or for rebuilding state institutions.[3]

Despite its shortcomings, however, the agreement did seek to address decisively issues that had been contentious before the war, such as the Arab identity of Lebanon and national unity. With this in mind, it called for developing a unified history curriculum, which was seen as essential to fostering national unity:

> The curricula shall be reviewed and developed in a manner that strengthens national belonging, fusion, spiritual and cultural openness, and that unifies textbooks on the subjects of history and national education.[4]

The former head of the Center for Educational Research and Development (CERD),[5] Nemer Frayha, explains that "the intention of the Parliament members at that time was to have all students learn about their country from one book in order to avoid different interpretations of the same event, as had been the case."[6] This intention, however, was never realized. The repeated failed attempts to develop a history curriculum is emblematic of both the state's inability to implement constructive and sustainable policies overall and of civil society's active role in palliating that inability.

Officials continue to mention sporadically the need for a unified history curriculum,[7] although the latest effort, in 2012, was brought to a halt. The very failure to construct a common narrative within the confines of state institutions has taken the debate to the wider public arena, involving a more diverse profile of actors and expanding the limits of discussion. Projects led by nongovernmental organizations (NGOs) are proliferating, as are partnerships between the Ministry of Education and various other stakeholders. Beyond the projects per se, the field is also widening to include a number of questions related to the relevance of a common historical narrative, best methodological practices, the function of education, and the role and limits of the state in the sphere of education.[8] Interestingly, the discussion includes questions about the interconnectivity of education reform in a post-conflict society with processes of reconciliation.

This chapter seeks to take a closer look at civil society's engagement with education and, more specifically, at one particular project, "Badna Naaref" (We Want to Know), which was conducted between 2010 and 2012.[9] Framed as an oral history project, Badna Naaref sought to raise awareness among the younger generation of the implications of living through a war and foster greater empathy with the experience of their elders, while simultaneously providing a platform for a truth-telling exercise on behalf of the persons interviewed.

As it examines how the project's concept, design, and implementation were shaped by the real and perceived threat of renewed violence within a deeply fragmented society, the chapter also reflects on the difficulties of upholding the relevance of such initiatives in such an environment.[10] Badna Naaref took place during a period of relative calm that facilitated its implementation and clearly tapped into a demand among the youth—namely, for a better understanding of the war and its consequences. At the same time, the continuing instability and consequent rise in violence in the country, and the confines inherent to the nature of nonofficial initiatives, accounted for the project's limited scope and lack of subsequent momentum.

LEBANON'S ONGOING CONFLICTS

In February 1975, Maarouf Saad, a member of Parliament representing the southern city of Sidon, was shot and killed while leading a fishermen's protest. Although the source of the shots remained anonymous, the assassination of a man who represented the pan-Arab nationalist movement in the country came to expose the deep divides running through Lebanese society, notably between a leftist, Arab nationalist, pro-Palestinian, largely Muslim community and the Christian Maronite community, which to a large extent exerted control over the state's institutions and was eying with growing concern the rapid militarization and empowerment of Palestinian groups based in Lebanon.

Barely two months later, on April 13, what became known as the Lebanese "civil war" erupted. The conflict in great part resulted from the collapse of a fragile consensus among the various religious groups, as well as the failure of the Lebanese power-sharing system to accommodate the rapidly evolving social and demographic changes of the 1960s and '70s. The Palestinian armed struggle against Israel, which found its base in Lebanon after being evicted from Jordan in 1970, deepened already existing divisions within the Lebanese society between those who supported the struggle from Lebanon, and indeed joined forces with them, and those who viewed this struggle as impinging on Lebanese sovereignty and putting at risk Lebanese civilians, who had already suffered from regular bouts of Israeli retaliatory air raids before the full-fledged escalation in 1975.

The different rounds of confrontations throughout the war years saw scores of mass killings; wide-scale population displacements, including forced evictions; thousands of persons "disappeared"; multiple sieges of cities, camps, and villages; and car bombings, assassinations, and intensive bombardments.[11] The series of sieges, mass killings, and population displacements homogenized entire regions along sectarian lines, in effect creating geographical divides that endure to a large extent to this day. The capital city itself was divided between a Muslim-dominated West and a Christian-dominated East Beirut, and civilians were frequently victims of snipers or mobile militia checkpoints that carried out waves of religion-based abductions, often ending in forced disappearances.

At the same time, the war was not just internal; besides the direct participation of Palestinian armed groups since the beginning of the conflict, the Lebanese warring parties sought foreign support to strengthen their domestic positions against local rivals, and foreign players exploited the country's sectarian divisions to enhance their regional roles. The various militias played off existing communal fears, deepening the sectarian divisions within Lebanese society but also compartmentalizing these communities in geographical areas that remained isolated from each other over the duration of the conflict. Schools, reflecting this configuration, also lost a lot of their mixed student representation, thus, in effect, isolating the communities' younger generations from each another.[12] Meanwhile, as a result of the indiscriminate pattern of bombings, 156 public schools and 272 private schools were destroyed, as well as a great deal of public infrastructure.[13]

In October 1989, the Parliament members headed to the city of Ta'if in Saudi Arabia to ratify a "Document of National Understanding" as part of an Arab League initiative. Commonly known as the Ta'if Accord, it was meant to put an end to the war and lay the political groundwork for a new power-sharing agreement among the major religious sects.[14] But the war did not end until a year later, when the Syrian army conducted an air and land attack that ousted the last pockets of opposition to Syrian control.

In May 1991, Lebanon and Syria signed the Treaty of Brotherhood, Cooperation, and Coordination and, four months later, the Defense and

Security Agreement, thus setting the stage for what many called the *Pax Syriana*, a system under which Syria had effective control over Lebanon's military, security, economic, and political decision making. In August, a law passed by Parliament in effect granted amnesty for crimes committed before the previous March. But, rather than conferring a blanket amnesty, this law was shaped in such a manner that prosecutions were kept in the hands of the pro-Syrian elite who were in power and facilitated by a politicized judiciary. In parallel, Israel retained control over South Lebanon, directly and via a proxy militia—the South Lebanon Army (SLA)—cutting off that region from the central authorities and the rest of the country. In 2000, the Israeli forces withdrew from Lebanese territory, and the SLA disintegrated immediately. Five more years passed before the Syrian army and security forces also left, following wide-scale protests in Lebanon that erupted following the assassination of the former prime minister, Rafik Hariri.[15]

The multiplicity of Lebanese actors involved in the war, with almost all sects and political parties having created their own militias at one time or another, supported the commonly heard sayings that "we were all victims and guilty at the same time" and that there was "no victor and no vanquished." Such arguments, repeated to this day, have contributed to an exculpatory feeling among Lebanese that has helped mute any subsequent considerations of accountability, redress, or truth seeking. Under the judicial, political, and societal conditions described here, reconciliation and amnesty were both presented and accepted as deeply interdependent and necessary. Many surviving leaders of the war held ministerial portfolios or parliamentary status, thus enjoying immunity from prosecution. As also happened in post-conflict Spain and Cyprus, conflict-related, society-wide "amnesia" became the norm, upon which only the intellectual and artistic spheres infringed from time to time.

THE TRANSITIONAL JUSTICE LANDSCAPE IN LEBANON

Between 1990 and 2005, Lebanon had little room to set up sustainable and effective mechanisms that could have fallen along the spectrum of "transitional justice" tools—indeed, the situation was marked by the amnesty law, the two parallel occupations and an accompanying repression of opposition voices, and the continuation of the perpetrators' rule into peacetime, not to mention a judiciary that was to a large extent politicized. A number of initiatives did see the light of day, but these were flawed and far from being part of a comprehensive approach to dealing with the past.

With regard to criminal justice, the amnesty law was promulgated so as to whitewash all perpetrators but keep the threat and use of prosecution very much alive as a means of silencing voices opposed to Syria's stranglehold over the country. The most emblematic case was that of Samir Geagea, head of the Lebanese Forces, a Christian political party. Accused of a crime that took place in 1994 of which he was found innocent, Geagea was thereafter convicted of four assassinations that took place between 1975 and 1990 and sentenced to life imprisonment.[16] In any case, the judiciary's lack of both independence and resources mooted any real effort at criminal prosecutions.

In 1993, the government created a Ministry for the Displaced and a Central Fund for the Displaced to manage and fund the return of the almost one-third of Lebanon's population that had been displaced during the war. The program focused on restitution and compensation, but the process was marred by corruption, political nepotism, and selectivity.[17]

Concerning demilitarization and demobilization, the government called upon all armed groups to surrender their weapons to the state, although it allowed Hezbollah, which it deemed a legitimate armed group fighting against the Israeli occupation, to maintain its arms. Hezbollah was permitted to keep its weapons even after Israel's withdrawal, as were Palestinian armed groups based in camps falling outside of Lebanon's control.

With regard to truth seeking, the government created a fact-finding commission in 2000, following pressure from victims' groups, to help clarify the fate of thousands of persons who had gone missing during the war. At the time of writing, three such commissions had been formed, none of them yielding any information to the families.[18] Sites of mass graves remain unprotected, and relatives are still grappling with a host of administrative, legal, and financial issues, along with an unending wait for answers about the fate of their loved ones. Victims' groups have been able to develop a draft bill to set up an institutional, legal, and technical framework to conduct a fact-finding process with the necessary investigative powers to yield effective results. The draft bill was presented to Parliament in May 2014 and, as of this writing, was awaiting discussion.

Following Syria's withdrawal from Lebanon, the country found itself freed from the shackles of the twin foreign hegemony (of Syria and Israel) that had clamped down on any effort to set the ground for addressing the past. But the lack of meaningful political, institutional, and judicial reforms has meant the same ruling class remains in power, with no incentive to begin making any such efforts. At the same time, an extremely volatile security situation, heightened by the ongoing war in Syria and continuing violence, makes the relevance of transitional justice–related work very difficult to highlight.

EDUCATION UNDER CONDITIONS OF STATE-IMPOSED AMNESIA

As mentioned above, the development of a national history curriculum was initially set as a priority in the Ta'if Agreement. In November 1993, the government approved a comprehensive Educational Development Plan, which covered the physical rehabilitation of more than 1,200 public schools, as part of its larger postwar reconstruction plan.[19] In October 1998, a new curriculum began to be produced for all subjects taught in public schools, to replace one that had not been updated since the 1970s because of the war. It included the introduction of a new subject, civic education, which was meant to help foster social cohesion, along with a unified history curriculum.

The process of developing the history curriculum stalled, however; CERD produced history textbooks for grades 2 and 3 (primary school), but these were shelved.[20] Two more committees were since formed, but no curriculum made its way through to classrooms. The last official textbooks to have been published date back to 1970. They are only for the primary and intermediate levels, and they stop at 1943, the date of Lebanon's independence from the French mandate. According to one study, "All secondary schools, public and private, use privately published textbooks at the secondary level because there is no official textbook, and in reality many public schools do not use the outdated CERD textbooks at the primary and intermediate levels."[21]

In light of the generally silent environment about their country's history, young people are growing up with scant knowledge of the topic. Students have repeatedly voiced their dismay at this,[22] and teachers have had to forge their own paths to respond to students' curiosity and questions. One history teacher in a private school, who was also a member of one of the commissions, spoke of organizing seminars as a way to respond to these questions: "It's essential if we want to educate them so as to become entirely Lebanese citizens. They need to understand what happened to prevent it from recurring."[23] Frayha has also pointed out the role fragmented history education can play in undermining peace and societal cohesion:

> In Lebanon, a fragile country struggling to create its national identity, teaching conflicting versions of identity in history can present a threat to peace and coexistence. Hence, developing a national history textbook which emphasizes a unified and shared identity is crucial.[24]

CIVIL SOCIETY STEPPING IN

The end of Syria's armed presence in the country paved the way for a plethora of NGOs, including several international ones, that set up offices in Lebanon. They were supported by a diplomatic community that had been largely absent under Syria's hegemonic rule but had moved its presence to Beirut after the withdrawal. New projects dealing with memories of the war began to see the light of day, with civil society groups organizing several public events to commemorate the beginning of the war, as well as workshops to discuss approaches to addressing it. New advocacy strategies were also developed to push for the right to know for relatives of persons who went missing during the war.

On a broader level, however, this was all happening amid continuing political polarization, institutional paralysis, and ongoing violence marked by a string of car bombings; a particularly brutal war with Israel in July 2006; a three-month conflict between the Lebanese army and armed groups; and sporadic armed clashes in various parts of the country. Lebanon's newfound sovereignty helped loosen the noose that had muted any discussion about the war, but its limits quickly emerged as the lack of an effective change in leadership and structural reforms made this new dynamic fall short of translating into public policies or reforms that sought to address the war in any form.

Paradoxically, however, the absence of an overarching curriculum created an opening to explore new methods of addressing the country's history in classrooms and, especially, to promote different perspectives in education. Several nonofficial initiatives have responded to the absence of any discussion about the war in classrooms. The Permanent Peace Movement (PPM), for example, an NGO created during the war, has been organizing youth summer camps, workshops, and trainings in schools on issues such as peacebuilding, conflict resolution, and memory and reconciliation. The Sustainable Democracy Center (SDC), another NGO that works on issues of conflict resolution, is in the process of conducting teacher trainings and recently finalized a kit to help teachers address the issue of the war with their students through questionnaires, film references and scenes, specific terminology, and biographies of artists, activists, and intellectuals who made positive contributions to the country during that time.[25] The Canadian Bureau for International Education (CBIE), in partnership with CERD,[26] carried out a conflict resolution program that included teacher training sessions in Canada and the production of a guide for teachers and parents entitled "Education for Conflict Resolution," which benefited the twelve private and public schools that participated on a voluntary basis.

More recently, in November 2012, in response to the still stalled process of producing a history textbook, a group of history teachers from public and private schools came together to create the Lebanese Association for History, with a view to involving individuals from other disciplines and NGOs in the teaching of history. To date it has held several meetings to reach consensus on the objectives and activities of the association, but the main purpose is to focus on teaching methodology and the training of students by means of a multi-dimensional approach and exposure to multiple narratives, rather than the traditional top-down, unified history approach. In June 2013, the association organized a two-day workshop at the American University of Beirut entitled "Teaching and Learning the Civil War," which brought together teachers and NGOs active on the issues of war memory, reconciliation, and peacebuilding to discuss practical ways of teaching the war to students. Participants were divided into groups, each of which was asked to identify the root causes of the fifteen-year war and to agree on the order of their importance. Most groups identified the same causes, but their prioritization varied.

Maha Shuayb, who cofounded the association and is a visiting fellow on the education faculty at the University of Cambridge and the University of Oxford,[27] has argued that the process of addressing the past in classrooms must be led by educators, not historians, with the objective of developing students' historical analysis skills. She maintains that the process can be "killed . . . by saying you want a unified history textbook." Scholars such as Shuayb draw on the emerging literature surrounding multidimensional approaches that emphasize the development of skills allowing for critical analysis, debate, and interpretation. The building of these skills through the focus on pedagogy, together with the nurturing of historical and intercultural empathy, offer one way out of the current impasse regarding the history textbook.[28]

BADNA NAAREF: A "SUBVERSIVE" PROJECT

With successive conflicts spilling over generations, Lebanon carries a significant legacy of human rights and humanitarian law violations that are not being addressed in any meaningful way. Very little transparency surrounds those violations, and perpetrators continue to hold positions of power today. Moreover, the society itself remains fractured and even more polarized with each renewed wave of violence. This directly influences the enduring taboo on talking about the past. The dominant narratives either glorify or normalize the war and what life was like during it.

In 2009, as part of a wider project to encourage discussion about the war in the public sphere, "Badna Naaref" (We Want to Know) was conceived and conducted by the International Center for Transitional Justice (ICTJ), in partnership with the Lebanese nongovernmental organization UMAM Documentation and Research[29] and Saint Joseph University's Center for Modern Arab World Studies[30] (USJ/CEMAM). The project was designed to bring into focus the consequences of the conflict on people's everyday lives, as well as its impact on their understanding of the past and how it would continue to shape narratives in the future. It was designed as both an oral history and truth-seeking project for the students and a truth-telling process for the people being interviewed. For many, it represented the first time they talked about their experiences during the war.

The idea materialized during a workshop organized the previous year by UMAM,[31] during which representatives of the South African Historical Archive (SAHA) discussed an oral history project entitled "Meeting History Face to Face," which had brought students to collect stories from elders in their communities as a way to share their experience of living under apartheid.[32] The idea of engaging secondary school students as active participants in such a project to address the issue of conflict seemed particularly relevant to Lebanon, despite its dissimilarities from South Africa.

The name Badna Naaref purposely hints at a rebelliousness, expressing the notion of youth raising their voices to demand their right to know what happened in their country, and to have it take place in their households if it was not happening in their classrooms. Badna Naaref was by no means the first project to focus on youth, education, and the war in Lebanon, but it was the first actually to encourage young people to talk to their elders directly about the war—to start an intergenerational dialogue of sorts between those who experienced the war and the impact of it and those who live with its consequences but have little or no comprehension of how life today is linked to the broader legacy of the conflict and its violence.

A second key component of the project was to address the conflict in a way that exposed themes relevant across communities, regions, and religions— that is, to explore aspects of daily life during the war with which anyone who had lived in Lebanon at the time would be able to identify, or would at least recognize. This was important, because very few commonalities are perceived among communities in Lebanon today. Instead, a culture of deep "other-ization" prevails, alongside a strong feeling that only one's own community has suffered.

The project, then—activist in its framework and pedagogical in its methodology—sought to build bridges both between generations and between groups. Relevant issues that cut across communities included mobility between the divided parts of the city, crossing checkpoints, how to deal with the rationing of water and food, living in shelters, and communicating with family and loved ones. These themes were chosen by the organizers, the project advisory board, and the teachers who attended the teachers' training because they would not only increase the participants' insight into what it meant to be living in a state of war but would also increase their knowledge of their parents' and grandparents' experiences.

The project had five key objectives: to increase the participants' understanding of political violence, its consequences, and its long-term effects; to raise awareness of the impact of the conflict on their parents' generation; to generate an intergenerational discussion in a safe environment; to train students to use oral history methodology as a frame for reflection about a volatile present and future; and to create an archive of narratives focused on individual experiences of the conflict that could be used as part of future teaching curricula. In addition to their own elders, students also interviewed families of the missing and disappeared.[33] Ultimately, the project was broadly cross-sectarian and included segments of the Palestinian community living in Lebanon.

Difficult questions of an ethical nature arose beyond the logistical or content-based aspects: Who were "we" (as organizations) to "force" this discussion, if it were not taking place naturally? How would we be able to "protect" the young participants from issues or details that could be traumatizing to them? But, mostly, how could we make sure what we were doing was justified? The organizers decided to set up an advisory committee that would try to respond to such questions, inviting select individuals from diverse professional backgrounds to discuss the project. Among those invited were the director-general of the Ministry of Education, representatives of NGOs active on youth-focused projects, history teachers, a psychiatrist, a psychoanalyst working mainly with teenagers, a sociologist, an anthropologist, and a victims' group representative.

"Subversive" is how the psychiatrist described the project—subversive in a positive way. Instead of prompting the usual parent to child transmission, it would engage the children as actors in a sharing of knowledge:

A discussion of the past was absolutely necessary to overcome any trauma; and tackling it in this way, by encouraging the children to assume a responsible role in this process, having them start the discussion with their peers rather than the other way around was a way to also empower these students.[34]

During this meeting, attendees agreed that students would only participate voluntarily; they would be asked to interview only people they knew well and with whom they felt safe; and focus group discussions would be organized to get them together and allow them to share their concerns, questions, and thoughts as they proceeded with the project.[35]

SETTING UP BADNA NAAREF

Given the intense debates around history education, students are clearly aware that what they learn is part of a contested history. Badna Naaref appeared to have tapped into a vein of genuine interest among secondary school students in learning more about what happened during the conflict. When asked at the outset why they wanted to participate in the project, many spoke about a desire to gain a better understanding of the more historical, political, and military narratives of the war or of the reasons for it. A number felt they lacked knowledge about the past and talked about the consequences of this in terms of tolerance. Many students also spoke about the need to understand the conflict and its roots to prevent its being repeated. A commonly expressed fear was that Lebanon was driving toward another intercommunal conflict.

Despite a great deal of interest among students in learning about Lebanon's recent past, however, teachers involved in the project also identified a lack of resources and tools to teach it. One related the current attitude to a "head-in-the-sand philosophy":

> At schools, we play ostrich. We should open the wounds, because they are open anyway. Not pretend it never happened. All this collective memory, the students don't know it. Unfortunately, in Lebanon, our history repeats itself.[36]

With the advisory group, the project team identified a list of schools to be approached, all based in the capital city, Beirut, and selected with an eye toward ensuring representation by the different ethnic groups (Armenian, Palestinian, and Lebanese), religious groups, and private and public schools.[37] The team approached the directors of the private schools to explain the purpose and methodology of the project, which the school boards then put up for approval. While these discussions went relatively smoothly, some schools subsequently refused to participate, expressing their concern about the possible repercussions of engaging in such a project in the midst of a highly tense political situation. Others declined because they were already engaged in other extracurricular projects, or their history teachers did not have time to attend the sessions and oversee their students' work on the project. The project team separately approached the Ministry of Education, which then sent a memorandum to Beirut's public schools asking them to participate.

This stage of approaching the schools, explaining the project in detail, and waiting for their responses turned out to be one of the most crucial and sensitive, sometimes necessitating several visits to the same school. Those who were willing to have their schools participate approved the project and provided their feedback to the project team. Each school then assigned a teacher who functioned as a liaison. The liaisons attended a one-day teacher training and provided feedback to the project team. Teachers then discussed the project with their students and enlisted those who voiced interest in participating. Initially, each school was to send two students, but in some cases more than two wanted to participate. Once all the students were selected, they were divided into small groups to attend a two-day training, in the presence of their teachers. As the students went on to collect the interviews, the teachers' role included making sure they continuously received the necessary support, advice, and monitoring.

The trainings for (primarily second-year) high school students and their teachers were conducted over the first half of 2011. Participating students were between fifteen and sixteen years old, selected because children of that age are not as politicized as university students and not under as much academic pressure as third-year high school students with end-of-year official exams. The trainers conducting the sessions, who were drawn from the partner organizations, were key members of the project team, with experience in oral history techniques, including talking about sensitive histories, as well as in teaching and journalism. They underwent their own week-long training with a member of SAHA who had a background in oral history collection.

In total, forty-four students representing twelve schools participated in the project under the supervision of their teachers, who were drawn predominantly from the disciplines of history, geography, sociology, and civics. Their training sessions focused on clarifying the function of oral history and teaching the students oral history techniques, after which they were trained to prepare and conduct interviews and collect oral testimonies on sensitive topics. Each was asked to conduct two interviews with someone in the student's close circle who was his or her age during a portion of the conflict and with whom the student felt completely safe. The various questions to be addressed during the interviews were discussed, the methodology for preparing the questionnaire and how to conduct an interview were explained, and the students were shown how to use the digital audio recorder and to archive the recording.

The questionnaire consisted of open questions bearing on similar themes related to daily life issues during civil war in a place with fragmented geography. Students could use it as a tool to help them, but they were also encouraged to prepare their own questions as they saw fit before the interviews, in accordance with the profiles of the persons they chose to interview and their own curiosity. While they prepared for their interviews in class, they conducted them at home or in the homes of their interviewees.

The trainers emphasized to the students and teachers that the goal was to collect the "human" stories—stories about situations their subjects had lived through but did not necessarily talk about at home. Students would be responsible for creating something entirely new: an archive of lived histories during the conflicts in Lebanon. While a number of the people interviewed would talk extensively about injustice and violence they witnessed or experienced during the conflict, the topic was not one the students would directly ask about.

Finally, the students were encouraged to start thinking about ways to use the material they would be creating, beyond the process of developing the archive—that is, how also to become an end user of it. Teachers were encouraged to do the same and to start thinking of ways in which the project could be shared with more students in their institutions.

COLLECTING THE TESTIMONIES

The students collected their testimonies over the course of 2011. Ultimately, 150 audio testimonies were recorded in a combination of French and Arabic and developed into the oral history archive, which houses an unprecedented pool of material drawing on "stories from below"—that is, on the daily life experiences of people in Lebanon during the war.

Once the interview sound files were received, the recordings from interviews conducted in Arabic were given to UMAM and those in French to the Francophone partner CEMAM for transcription. All were then translated from the original language so that each interview had an Arabic, French, and English transcript. In addition, concise summaries of the testimonies were extracted, together with representative quotes, in preparation for the archive and the production of material for broader public engagement. The transcripts and summaries were made fully anonymous to protect the individuals who shared their stories through this process.

When the material was ready, a website was built to showcase the project and increase public awareness.[38] At the launching party held at the exhibition space adjacent to UMAM's documentation center in Beirut's southern suburbs to which the students, their families, and their teachers were invited, students from across the confessional spectrum had the opportunity to meet. In the presence of religious and political figures, the media, and their families, several gave speeches about interviewing family members and learning about the war. They were also taken through the website and its functions and watched short interviews in which they themselves reflected on their experiences as oral historians.

As an element of the project, the launching party had its own didactic dimension, as it constituted a platform to bring together children from across sectarian boundaries. For many students (and some project staff), their trip to south Beirut became its own forum for exchange and learning. It was, for a brief period, a "safe" zone, where students who would not normally interact were able to meet and swap stories. Thus, the event itself was designed to build on the core purpose of the activity: to demystify the "other," to share experiences of other people in Lebanon, and to build relationships across borders so that youth in the country are less inclined to be drawn into sectarian violence.

In writing, the students reflected at length on their experiences and how they saw the initiative. Comments such as the following from participant Christine Bekarian highlighted both the difficulty some family members had talking about the project and the students' new understanding of their parents' experiences:

> This project allowed me to go back in time and discover the hardships that my parents have passed through during the Civil War. However, I had to ask a lot of questions during the interviews because the interviewees were reluctant to share their war stories.[39]

During their trainings, students had been prepared to deal with potentially difficult moments in the interview; for instance, if a painful personal trauma were recounted—of loss, displacement, or fear—students were told to respect the interviewee's wishes at all times, not to press on if the person wished not to continue, and to respect the silence and the time needed to return to the story. Trainers insisted on the value of silence and body language as part of the narrative, even for oral interviews, and students were encouraged to write down their own notes and feelings if they felt the need for it afterward.

For many students, this was the first time their families had spoken to them about their experiences of the war. For Nour Hajjar, the project gave insight into her own history, as well as allowing her to "communicate with my family circle about the war." She went on, "I also discovered the 'hidden' part of my personal history and that of my country. Finally, this project has taught me to treat my elders with more respect."[40]

DEVELOPING SUSTAINABLE PLATFORMS: THE WEBSITE AND DOCUMENTARY

The wider application and sustainability of the concept behind Badna Naaref depend in large part on making the project and the oral histories it produced known and accessible to others beyond its participants. At the time of the website launch, both the project and the students received significant press coverage, including from television talk shows,[41] and broadly supportive responses. The archive itself is based both at UMAM and USJ/CEMAM, with the capacity to be stored at international institutions as part of a broader pool of oral history narratives in conflict and post-conflict societies. The website, designed by the project's partner organizations as the narratives were being collected and collated, is intended to showcase the work and make sure a blueprint of the initiative is easily accessible for others who might want to replicate it. Its purpose is to serve as an interactive platform for people to discuss both the content of the testimonies and the legacy of the conflict in Lebanon.

The creation of the website turned out to be one of the more difficult aspects of the project, from a logistical perspective. The data themselves were complicated, comprising 150 interview summaries, each with a number of component parts, as well as details about the project and the participating schools and students. Everything existed in three languages, and the goal was essentially to create a site that was identical and fully populated in all three languages.

Furthermore, the website had to be designed so it could be added to over time, and it needed to have interactive forums, such as a blog and a discussion group, to which students could directly contribute. The idea was that, as the initiative gathered steam and moved around the country, the website could slowly be expanded. This would also allow for the addition of testimonies regarding the missing. To these ends, the website was perceived not just as a blueprint or concept that could be franchised, but as something that could evolve. It was agreed that UMAM would host the site after the project ended.

As Badna Naaref was drawing to a close, documentary filmmaker Carol Mansour was brought on board to create a film about the concept and the students' experiences. Although in the project's planning phase the documentary was designed to be pedagogical—a tool of instruction to go out to all schools in Lebanon, showing them how to replicate the project with their own students—Mansour's inclusion brought to it an artistic component. In addition to being a pedagogical tool, the documentary would both reflect on student and teacher experiences of the project and tell stories of the broader conflict.

An excerpt from the documentary was shown at the website's launch and distributed to the media, while the film itself was launched separately.[42] It told the story of daily life during the war in Lebanon through the eyes of four middle-aged characters who lived through the period, most of them sharing their experiences of the conflict for the first time. Interspersed between interviews with the characters was archival footage of the conflict and short interviews with a number of the students and teachers, who spoke of what they learned, how it affected them, and what they thought about Lebanon's future. The documentary was to be screened on national television, and then kits would be sent out to all schools, explaining the project and welcoming the schools to replicate it. The kits, which would include the documentary, would be prefaced with a letter of support from the Minister of Education.

The idea, then, was for this unofficial education project to create impetus for the development of similar ideas in the formal school system. Despite the expression of support from the Ministry of Education, however, a lack of resources on the part of the lead partner to follow through, together with changing political dynamics in Lebanon, has left the project on the sidelines.

REFLECTIONS: ACHIEVEMENTS AND SHORTCOMINGS

Projects such as Badna Naaref highlight some of the benefits gained and challenges faced when engaging with transitional justice and education in societies still overcoming conflict. The initiative provided secondary school students with an opportunity to inquire, in the unfamiliar terms of personal experience and loss, about a past that is not spoken of in schools, and it gave them tools to begin questioning conflicting versions of the war. Many spoke of how, after the interviews with their families, they began to see the world through the eyes of their interviewees and to understand why they held particular fears or perspectives. In many households, a new, more open, narrative began as a result of the interviews. Some students started to see themselves as early researchers and historians. Others, for the first time, started thinking about the consequences of conflict that the country is facing again.

The project faced specific logistical and substantive challenges, however, as well as a number of unknowns. While students had ongoing, open discussion with their teachers and feedback loops about what it was like to begin talking about the past with their loved ones, the project did not measure long-term effects of these conversations, and any hidden trauma or increased tension within families was, by its nature, invisible to the project team. Post-project interviews with all participants—interviewers and interviewees—as well as focus groups guided by the advisory group's trauma experts would have been useful as both a feedback tool and a way of ensuring the participants had access to ongoing sources of support.

Logistical challenges to Badna Naaref included significant underresourcing on the part of the lead project team and all of the partner organizations. Staff had to manage multiple processes simultaneously, while significant internal administrative burdens and staffing shortfalls meant project work was juggled instead of prioritized. In addition, many schools approached did not want to participate because they considered the effort too sensitive or without merit in encouraging dialogue about the war.

From a broader perspective, the project touched on a significant issue of debate both in the literature and among practitioners about whether transitional justice is a relevant concept in societies that are not clearly in transition—that is, if a conflict has not come to a clearly defined "end," or a society is still deeply unstable, what value is there in approaches or projects designed to unpack legacies of conflict-related violence? Badna Naaref's shortcomings emphasized a number of vulnerabilities in the "practice" of transitional justice, especially in countries that are still politically fragile. Talking about what happened during the war carries a high cost when trauma has not been dealt with, when perpetrators of violence are still in positions of power, and when people are worried about new conflicts bringing back old instabilities. Unpacking the past is complicated enough in stable societies and those clearly post conflict. It is far more fraught when no clear transition has taken place.

In addition, elite support can often be transient, and it is easily lost. While all relevant parties recognized the importance of the Badna Naaref initiative and its capacity to stimulate discussion about the conflict both within homes and in schools, there are no immediate prospects for its continuation. Each of the three partner organizations has embarked on other projects with different priorities; and although the Ministry of Education supported the initiative, its endorsement of a package to be sent to schools across the country has not been forthcoming.

To a certain extent, such problems with regard to sustainability and strategy are in the nature of NGO work. Badna Naaref remains one among several projects on reconciliation and education being carried out by NGOs in Lebanon. The project's failure to gather the momentum hoped for is largely a reflection of a difficult political and social environment; between the launch of Badna Naaref and the time of writing, polarization had increased significantly, and it was becoming increasingly difficult to justify the relevance of such projects when the country was going through a dramatic rise in the number of bombings and armed clashes, as well as the humanitarian Syrian refugee crisis. The lack of momentum also has to do with the inherent nature of projects carried out by multiple partners, as in this case, where each of the organizations, local and international, has shifted to different projects and priorities and lacks the resources and capacity to sustain or geographically expand the original project.

Badna Naaref's underlying principle represents a crossroads well known among transitional justice practitioners: the closer a society gets to cascading into violence, the more important it becomes to examine the way past conflict influences current attitudes. In a striking end to Carol Mansour's documentary, every one of the students interviewed expressed his or her fear and certainty that Lebanon was heading toward another war. The students also said the past needed to be talked about and its impact understood, otherwise it would be repeated. The closer the conflict appears, the greater the perceived cost of talking about potentially divisive issues, such as who did what to whom and why in the various wars.

People are currently seeing all the markers of another war, and the fear of rocking the boat by reliving the past is at its greatest. Given this fear, Badna Naaref is unlikely to be replicated in the near future.[43] An internally paralyzed political leadership sees itself as having bigger considerations than encouraging critical thinking among students.

It is the present, however, that provides the richest opportunity for children to learn about their families' experience of the conflict, both because memories are closest to the surface and because the fear of reliving the experience is proving well founded. Projects such as Badna Naaref highlight a society's need to address its ongoing conflicts, particularly in response to the younger generation's demand to understand why their lives are jeopardized by a multigenerational cycle of violence. In the absence of official will to do so, and in a country in the grip of enduring violence and instability, it is civil society (including the education sector, intellectuals and artists, and NGOs) that continues to tap into such work, within the limits inherent to any unofficial effort.

But what Badna Naaref also highlights is the different direction transitional justice processes can and should take when young people are involved. Their needs in relation to justice processes are different from those of older generations, as is the way they interact with "transitional justice." Multimedia projects and social media are more natural avenues than public assemblies and newspapers for young people to engage with the principles underpinning transitional justice, and Badna Naaref has highlighted one avenue for this kind of exploration.

NOTES

1   Lebanese minister of health in phone call-in to *al-Fasad* political program on Al Jadeed TV, January 8, 2014.

2   International Center for Transitional Justice (ICTJ), *Lebanon's Legacy of Political Violence: A Mapping of Serious Violations of International Human Rights and Humanitarian Law in Lebanon, 1975–2008*, ICTJ, New York, September 2013, http://ictj.org/publication/lebanon-legacy-political-violence, and Dima Smaira and Roxane Cassehgari, *Failing to Deal with the Past: What Cost to Lebanon?* ICTJ, New York, January 2014, http://ictj.org/publication/failing-deal-past-what-cost-lebanon.

3   In fact, the post-conflict phase has been marked by "selective justice and marginalization of victims, minimal truth-seeking efforts, partial reparation tainted by corruption, and incomplete institutional reform leading to weak guarantees of non-repetition. The amnesty laws and subsequent failures to prosecute individuals involved in waves of violence have reinforced and normalized the culture of impunity in Lebanon." Smaira and Cassehgari, *Failing to Deal with the Past*, 31.

4   Ta'if Agreement, Ta'if, Saudi Arabia, September 1989, http://www.al-bab.com/arab/docs/lebanon/taif.htm.

5   CERD is a semiofficial institution, affiliated with the Ministry of Education and responsible for developing and producing textbooks and curricula in Lebanon. See http://www.crdp.org/CRDP/default.htm. Nemer Frayha headed CERD between 1999 and 2002.

6   Nemer Frayha, "Education as a Way of Building Social Cohesion in Lebanon: An Unfin-ished Task," in *Rethinking Education for Social Cohesion: International Case Studies*, ed. Maha Shuayb (Houndmills, Basingstoke: Palgrave Macmillan, 2012), 105.

7   *The Daily Star*, "Mikati: History Curriculum No Place for Narrow Interests," February 28, 2013, http://www.dailystar.com.lb/News/Local-News/2012/Feb-28/164870-mikati-history-curriculum-no-place-for-narrow-interests.ashx#axzz2r6tuoida.

8   See, generally, Shuayb, *Rethinking Education for Social Cohesion*.

9   The authors offer a firsthand account of the project, as they were directly involved in its design and implementation.

10   It is important to note that although several initiatives in Lebanon have dealt and con-tinue dealing with the issue of education and memory of war, this chapter focuses on Badna Naaref because the authors were directly involved in the project.

11   See, generally, ICTJ, *Lebanon's Legacy of Political Violence*.

12   See, generally, ibid.; Samir Kassir, *La Guerre du Liban, de la dissension nationale au conflit régional* (Paris: Karthala-Cermoc, 1994); Elisabeth Picard, *Lebanon: A Shattered Country: Myths and Realities of the Wars in Lebanon*, rev. ed. (New York: Holmes & Meier Publish-ers, 2002); Kamal Salibi, *Crossroads to Civil War: Lebanon 1958–1976* (New York: Caravan, 1976).

13   Franck Mermier and Christophe Varin, eds., *Mémoires de Guerres au Liban (1975–1990)* (Paris: Actes Sud/Sindbad, 2010), 344, 349.

14   Lebanon has eighteen officially recognized religious sects.

15   The Special Tribunal for Lebanon (STL) was set up in The Hague, by UN Security Council resolution, to try those responsible for Hariri's assassination and possibly other assas-sinations and attempted assassinations that took place between October 2004 and December 2005.

16   The amnesty covered crimes that took place prior to 1991; if, however, a crime took place after that date, it would be subject to investigation and prosecution and the persons sus-pected of committing it would no longer be protected by the amnesty law, and therefore liable to prosecution for crimes that occurred before 1991. The amnesty law, moreover, included exceptions with relation to assassination of politicians, religious dignitaries, and foreign diplomats, another loophole that could be used by the political-judicial establishment to silence any unwanted voices. Geagea was released from jail in 2005, as per another amnesty law.

17   For more in-depth information and analysis on Lebanon's post-conflict initiatives, see Smaira and Cassehgari, *Failing to Deal with the Past*.

18   For more information, see Lynn Maalouf, "Enforced Disappearances in Lebanon: A Nation's Unyielding Legacy," in Mermier and Varin, *Mémoires de Guerres au Liban*, Eng-lish translation available at http://www.actforthedisappeared.com/assets/documents/Report/Article_LynnMaalouf_ENG.pdf.

19   Mark Farha, "The Historical Legacy and Political Implications of State and Sectarian
      Schools in Lebanon," in Shuayb, *Rethinking Education for Social Cohesion*, 72; Council for
      Development and Reconstruction (CDR), *Progress Report*, October 2013, 42, http://www.
      cdr.gov.lb/eng/progress_reports/pr102013/Eeduc.pdf.

20   According to CERD's director at the time, the minister of education stopped the process
      because of disagreement over the formulation of Lebanon's identity (see Frayha, "Educa-
      tion as a Way of Building Social Cohesion in Lebanon," 107).

21   Gregor Nazarian, "A Common Vision: Contesting History and Education in Postwar
      Lebanon" (MA thesis, Center for Contemporary Arab Studies, Georgetown University,
      Washington, DC, April 2013), https://repository.library.georgetown.edu/bitstream/han-
      dle/10822/558224/Nazarian_georgetown_0076M_12283.pdf?sequence=1.

22   Minutes of student training conducted in framework of Badna Naaref project, February–
      March 2011.

23   Joelle Touma, "Liban: Les trous de mémoire dans les manuels scolaires," *Libération*, Janu-
      ary 7, 2003, http://www.liberation.fr/monde/2003/01/07/liban-les-trous-de-memoire-
      des-manuels-scolaires_427027 (author's translation).

24   Frayha, "Education as a Way of Building Social Cohesion in Lebanon," 104.

25   See http://www.sdclebanon.org/.

26   Frayha, "Education as a Way of Building Social Cohesion in Lebanon," 104.

27   Also senior fellow at the Center for Lebanese Studies, affiliated with Oxford University.
      Interview with author, Beirut, January 10, 2014.

28   Andrew Chapman, Lukas Perikleous, Christalla Yakinthou, and Rana Zincir Celal, *Think-
      ing Historically about Missing Persons: A Guide for Teachers* (Nicosia: UNDP-ACT, 2011).

29   See www.umam-dr.org.

30   See http://www.cemam.usj.edu.lb.

31   Held in collaboration with ICTJ in 2008, the workshop featured projects from Iraq,
      Lebanon, Palestine, and South Africa focusing on issues of historical memory and
      memorialization.

32   See http://www.saha.org.za/publications/meeting_history_face_to_face.htm.

33   In phase one of the project, stories of the missing and disappeared came up incidentally.
      In phase two, students who had missing relatives and loved ones were specifically asked
      if they wanted to participate.

34   Chawki Azouri, citation found in the project midterm evaluation report, ICTJ, 2011.

35   Another decision made at the meeting was to change the initial plan from producing
      audiovisual interview recordings to making purely audio recordings to simplify setup
      procedures for students.

36   Comment of teacher in teacher training workshops, March 2011.

37   After consultation with the advisory group, the project shifted from a Lebanon-wide
      initiative to focus only on Beirut, which provided the necessary wide array of class and

sectarian diversity. It was felt that the smaller geographical base, as well as simpler logistical considerations, would allow the group to hone its methodology and focus on student responses to their interviews. A follow-up project could then develop the pilot into something that could be implemented across the country.

38   See http://www.badnanaaref.org/.

39   From written reflections. Excerpt available at http://www.badnanaaref.org/index.php/testimonies-student/2.

40   Ibid.

41   See http://www.badnanaaref.org/index.php/press/1.

42   See Forward Film Productions, "Badna Naaref Trailer," 1:00, posted c. 2013, http://vimeo.com/61187388#.

43   The Lebanese NGO Act for the Disappeared found in Badna Naaref a suitable platform to create empathy among youth about the issue of missing persons and to help students understand why it remains relevant to this day. With ICTJ's agreement, Act used the same team as Badna Naaref but decided to target older students in their first and second years of university, since the interviews would require more maturity and less emotional vulnerability. A new questionnaire was drafted, and the students' trainings were focused on the psychological, legal, social, financial, and administrative repercussions on relatives of the disappearance of their loved ones. Act for the Disappeared conducted the project over two years, the first with a group of thirty students from two universities, as well as a group of young Palestinian activists, and the second with forty-eight students from three other universities. The age difference, however, proved to have its own set of challenges. With no teachers' trainings and the students participating outside of their academic curricula, keeping their momentum going through the training, the interviews, and the transcription was difficult. What proved even more challenging was finding people to interview, as relatives of missing persons would not automatically agree to talk (Justine di Mayo, interview with author, Beirut, January 17, 2014). Indeed, in the absence of an official truth-seeking process to clarify the fate of their loved ones, relatives of missing persons are not necessarily amenable to discussing what is an ongoing source of suffering to them. But those who did agree to share their stories were content with the opportunity to do so, perhaps for the first time.

CONTRIBUTORS

Cristián Correa is a senior associate in the Reparative Justice Program at the International Center for Transitional Justice (ICTJ). An expert in the definition and implementation of reparation programs for mass human rights violations, he provides advice and technical assistance to victims' organizations, civil society groups, and governments in Colombia, Liberia, Nepal, Peru, Sierra Leone, Timor-Leste, and other countries. Correa was legal advisor for a commission of the presidency of Chile responsible for identifying the disappeared and defining a human rights policy. Previously, he was the legal secretary of Chile's National Commission on Political Imprisonment and Torture (known as the Valech Commission) and then worked for the government to implement reparations recommended by the commission. His publications include "Making Concrete a Message of Inclusion: Reparations for Victims of Massive Crimes," in *Victimological Approaches to International Crimes*, ed. Rianne Letschert et al. (Tilburg University, 2011), as well as articles on comparative experiences of reparation programs, the jurisprudence of the Inter-American Court of Human Rights with regard to reparations, and the evolution of jurisprudence in Chile regarding the amnesty law. A lawyer from the Pontifical Catholic University of Santiago (1993), Correa holds an MA in international peace studies from the University of Notre Dame (1992).

Roger Duthie is a senior associate in the research unit at ICTJ, where he has managed or comanaged multiyear research projects examining how transitional justice relates to education, forced displacement, and development. He has also contributed to projects on the reintegration of ex-combatants and institutional reform. Duthie's publications include *Transitional Justice and Displacement* (SSRC, 2012) and *Transitional Justice and Development* (SSRC, 2009), which he coedited with Pablo de Greiff, as well as "Transitional Justice and Displacement" and "Toward a Development-Sensitive Approach to Transitional Justice," both published in the *International Journal of Transitional Justice* (2008 and 2011, respectively). He also coedited with Megan Bradley a special issue of the *Journal of Refugee Studies* on "Accountability and Redress for the Injustices of Displacement" (2014). He previously worked for KMPG, the Carnegie Council on Ethics and International Affairs, and Oxford University Press. Duthie has a BA in history from Cornell University and an MA in international relations from Yale University.

Zoé Dugal is currently the project manager for Afghanistan for the International Bureau for Children's Rights, having served as the international advisor on transitional processes for the GIZ Social Justice, Reconciliation, and National Cohesion project in Kenya from 2011 to 2014. From 2002 to 2004, Dugal was a research and operations officer with the Truth and Reconciliation Commission in Sierra Leone, after which she further deepened her engagement in the country as the capacity-building and information officer for the community disarmament program of the United Nations Development Programme (UNDP), Sierra Leone. Returning to Canada in 2006, she worked for CANADEM (the Canadian government roster and deployment mechanism) and, from 2007 to 2011, for the Pearson Peacekeeping Centre as project manager for a capacity-building project with ten police services in West and Southern Africa. Dugal holds a master's degree in political science and international relations from McGill University in Canada.

Lorena Escalona González is currently a prosecution attorney in the juridical section of the Ministry of Justice in Chile. In 2010 and 2011, she was a member of the Juridical Team set to preclassify cases for the National Commission on Political Imprisonment and Torture (the Valech Commission). With long professional experience with issues of education in values and human rights, González has researched the situation on human rights education among adults in Latin America for the Centro Estudios Estratégicos de América Latina (Center for Strategic Studies of Latin America, or CEEAL). She also coordinated two research projects for the National Corporation of Reparation and Reconciliation on Fundamental Content of Human Rights for Education (1992–96) and on Methodological Contribution to Human Rights Education. González obtained her BA in social and juridical sciences from the Catholic University of Chile, and she holds a master's degree in public policy and management from the University Adolfo Ibáñez and one in law from the University of Chile.

Mofidul Hoque cofounded the Liberation War Museum in Bangladesh, which came to be known as the people's museum of Bangladesh history, in 1996. He is currently a trustee of the museum and the director of its education project. A publisher by profession, Hoque is also one of the founders of the Combined Cultural Alliance, an apex body of national cultural organizations, as well as immediate past president of the Communication Committee of the International Theatre Institute (ITI) and the coeditor of ITI's biannual publication, *The World of Theatre*. He is the author of ten books on the history and culture of Bengal and received the Bangla Academy Literary Prize in 2014. A member of the International Association of Genocide Scholars (IAGS), Hoque holds an MA in sociology from Dhaka University.

Nerma Jelacic is head of external relations for the Commission for International Justice and Accountability (CIJA), a pioneering organization that takes an innovative approach to investigating and documenting atrocities in Syria and other places in conflict. From 2008 to 2014, she was the spokesperson and head of outreach and communications for the International Criminal Tribunal for the former Yugoslavia. Since 2011, Jelacic has had extensive engagements in Egypt, Iraq, Lebanon, Syria, Tunisia, and Yemen, working with local judiciaries, investigators, police, civil society, and media on issues concerning transitional justice and rule of law programs. Jelacic is one of the founders of the Balkan Investigative Reporting Network (BIRN), a regional nongovernmental organization (NGO) promoting public interest journalism and media development. In addition, she established a series of award-winning media outlets dedicated to investigating and reporting on the legacies of the Yugoslav wars while continuing to promote the principles of dealing with the past. Jelacic is a seasoned investigative reporter, specializing in the subjects of war crimes and organized crime. A UK-based journalist in the 1990s, she worked most notably for the *Observer*, the *Telegraph*, and the *Financial Times*, for which she covered post-conflict situations and the developing world.

Alexander Karn is an assistant professor of history and a faculty member in the Peace and Conflict Studies Program at Colgate University. His research interests include the politics of history in contemporary societies, historical justice in transitional regimes, and the role of historical commissions in conflict mediation and reconciliation. He has published several works on these topics, including *Amending the Past: Holocaust Commissions and the Right to History* (University of Wisconsin Press, 2015); a coedited volume (with Elazar Barkan), *Taking Wrongs Seriously: Apologies and Reconciliation* (Stanford University Press, 2006); and "Depolarizing the Past: The Role of Historical Commissions in Conflict Mediation and Reconciliation," in the *Journal of International Affairs* (2006). Karn graduated from the University of California, Los Angeles, in

1993 and holds MA degrees in nationalism studies and history from Central European University and Claremont Graduate University, respectively. In 2006, he obtained his PhD in history from Claremont Graduate University.

Virginie Ladisch leads ICTJ's work on children and youth. In that capacity she has provided technical support to efforts to engage children and youth in transitional justice processes in Canada, Colombia, Côte d'Ivoire, Kenya, Liberia, Myanmar, Nepal, and Tunisia. From the time she joined ICTJ in 2006 until 2009, Ladisch worked as part of the the organization's reparation program and headed the country programs for Cyprus and Turkey. Before that, she was awarded a Thomas J. Watson Fellowship for independent research, for which she carried out extensive fieldwork on truth commissions and reconciliation in Guatemala and South Africa. Results of her research on the challenges of reconciliation were published in the *Journal of Public and International Affairs* and the *Cyprus Review*. More recently, her reflections on engaging children and youth in transitional justice have been published in the *Journal of the History of Childhood and Youth*. Ladisch holds a BA in political science from Haverford College and an MA in international affairs from the School of International and Public Affairs (SIPA) at Columbia University.

Lynn Maalouf is a Beirut-based writer, researcher, and trainer whose work has mainly focused on the issue of missing and disappeared persons and transitional justice in Lebanon. She headed the Lebanon program of ICTJ from 2007 to 2011. In 2010, she cofounded Act for the Disappeared, an NGO that works on engaging youth with the issue of the disappeared in Lebanon, and she is currently overseeing Act's research program on possible sites of graves. She is the main author of *Lebanon's Legacy of Political Violence: A Mapping of Serious Violations of International Human Rights and Humanitarian Law in Lebanon, 1975–2008* (ICTJ, 2013), and she developed the draft for a set of policy recommendations released in the ICTJ publication, "Confronting the Legacy of Political Violence in Lebanon: An Agenda for Change," following the input of a consortium of civil society representatives. Before working with ICTJ, Maalouf was a freelance journalist, reporting mainly for the English-language service of Radio France Internationale (RFI) and the *Washington Post*. She also scripted *Blue Line*, a twenty-minute award-winning fiction film. In 2014, Maalouf was fellow of the Alliance for Historical Dialogue and Accountability Program at Columbia University. She holds a BA in international affairs from the Lebanese American University (1996), and she completed her MBA at the École Supérieure des Affaires (2000) and her MA at the Center for Contemporary Arab Studies at Georgetown University (1998).

Teboho Moja is a professor in the Higher Education Program at New York University and holds the appointment of extraordinary professor at the University of the Western Cape. She has authored articles on higher education reform issues in areas such as the governance of higher education, policy processes, and the impact of globalization on higher education. She is also a co-author of *National Policy and a Regional Response in South African Higher Education* (James Curry, 2004), a book on education change in South Africa since the first democratic elections in 1994. Moja has held key positions at several South African universities, including having been appointed chair of the Council of the University of South Africa. In 2010, she was appointed visiting professor at the University of Oslo (Norway) and University of Tampere (Finland). She was instrumental in setting up the Center for Higher Education Transformation (CHET) in South Africa to monitor and stimulate debates on change issues. Moja served on the boards of such international bodies as the UNESCO Institute for International Education Planning and the World Education Market. A policy researcher and policy analyst for higher education in South Africa, she was appointed by President Nelson Mandela as the executive director and commissioner of the National Commission on Higher Education, which produced a national report that provided a framework for higher education reform in the country. Before her appointment at NYU, Moja served as a special advisor to the first and third post-1994 ministers of education.

Karen Murphy is the international director for Facing History and Ourselves, an international education and professional development NGO. Murphy oversees Facing History's partnerships and the development and implementation of its programs in countries outside the United States and Canada. She has a particular interest in divided societies with identity-based conflicts and countries emerging from mass violence and/or in transition. She has done work within and regarding several countries, including Bosnia, Colombia, Kenya, Mexico, Northern Ireland, Rwanda, and South Africa. She is particularly interested in the role of education interventions in the development of stability and peaceful coexistence. Murphy has also published journal articles, presented papers, and lectured on the (often neglected) role of education in transitional justice processes. She is on the boards of New Haven Academy, a Connecticut-based public school; Shikaya, a human rights NGO in South Africa; and the Human Dignity and Humiliation Studies Network. Murphy is also on the editorial boards of *Intercultural Education* and the Change Handbook Project, focused on history and human rights. Murphy codirects a multiyear research project funded by the Spencer Foundation that is studying adolescents and civic development in Northern Ireland, South Africa, and the United States, and she is the proud coauthor of *Learning from the Past: An Exploration of Truth, Justice, and Reconciliation in Kenya* (ICTJ and NCIC, 2015). Murphy obtained her PhD in American Studies from the University of Minnesota in 1996.

Gustavo Palma Murga is a researcher at the Asociación para el Avance de las Ciencias Sociales en Guatemala (AVANCSO). Before joining AVANCSO, Palma Murga taught at several private universities in Guatemala and at the University of San Carlos, where he was also director of the Institute for Political and Social Research of the Political Science School. His research and publications have focused on different topics related to economic and agrarian history in Guatemala, the development of Guatemalan historiography, the formation of the nation, the Guatemalan national identity, and the contemporary educative question in Guatemala. Palma Murga holds a BA in history from the University of San Carlos in Guatemala and a PhD from the École des Hautes Études en Sciences Sociales (EHESS) in Paris.

Clara Ramírez-Barat is the director of the Educational Policies Program at the Auschwitz Institute for Peace and Reconciliation (AIPR). The recipient of several grants during her graduate studies, Ramírez-Barat did research and fieldwork in Oxford, Cape Town, and New York. She also worked on a study about the politics of memory in European Union countries, developed at the Spanish High Council of Research (CSIC). Before working for AIPR, Ramírez-Barat was a senior research associate at ICTJ, an organization she joined in May 2009 as a Fulbright Research Fellow. At ICTJ her research primarily concerned outreach programs for transitional justice measures, as well as the relationship between transitional justice and the sociocultural sphere. Most recently, her work focused on the intersection between transitional justice and education, both with regard to ICTJ's Children and Youth Program and as part of a broader two-year research project on transitional justice, education, and peacebuilding conducted in collaboration with the United Nations Children's Fund (UNICEF). Ramírez-Barat holds a BA in humanities from the University Carlos III of Madrid and an MA in philosophy from Columbia University. She obtained her PhD from the University Carlos III of Madrid in 2007, with a thesis on transitional justice.

Joanna Rice is a doctoral candidate in political science at the University of Toronto. Her research focuses on critical perspectives in transitional justice, peacebuilding, and victims' rights. She was previously transitional justice specialist for the UNICEF office in Côte d'Ivoire, working there from July 2013 to October 2014. Before joining UNICEF, Rice provided technical support to the National Coalition of Victims Associations in Nepal, and she worked as a program associate in the Truth and Memory Program at ICTJ from 2009 to 2011. In this capacity she coordinated a global program on indigenous rights and truth seeking. During this period she also provided technical assistance on indigenous approaches to transitional justice to the Canadian Truth and Reconciliation Commission, in collaboration with ICTJ's Children's Program. Rice holds a BA from the University of Toronto's Trudeau Center for Peace and Conflict Studies and a master's degree in political science from the New School for Social Research.

Ana María Rodino is a professor at the Universities of La Plata and Buenos Aires in Argentina. She was coordinator of the Pedagogical Unit of the Inter-American Institute of Human Rights in San Jose, Costa Rica, from 2000 to 2009 and has authored specialized materials on human rights aimed at both the informal and formal education sectors for children and teachers in all of Latin America. She has also consulted for government and nongovernment-based institutions in Latin American countries, as well as the Organization of American States (OAS), UNICEF, and the United Nations Educational, Scientific, and Cultural Organization (UNESCO). Rodino is the author of several books, including *Hallazgos sobre democracia y derechos humanos en la educación media en Costa Rica y Panamá* (Instituto Interamericano de Derechos Humanos y Autoridad Noruega para el Desarrollo Internacional, 2000) and *Educación en derechos humanos para una ciudadanía democrática* (EUNED, 2015), and of a great many scientific articles on education and human rights, language development, and the production of education media and materials. Rodino has studied linguistics in Argentina and Costa Rica and holds a PhD in education from Harvard University.

Dylan Wray is the cofounder and executive director of Shikaya, a South African nonprofit organization that supports teachers in creating responsible, caring, and active democratic citizens. Shikaya has assisted over five thousand teachers and affected over twenty thousand young South Africans. Wray, a former history teacher and visiting lecturer at the University of Cape Town, has written numerous school textbooks and created a wide range of education resources teachers can use to help young people grapple with ethical and moral decision making. One resource, Truth, Justice, and Memory, is used in over five hundred South African schools to help young people engage with the

Truth and Reconciliation Commission, which is covered in the South African school curriculum. Dylan sits on boards of the Centre for Early Childhood Development in South Africa and Routes2Peace in the United Kingdom.

Christalla Yakinthou is a member of the Institute for Conflict, Co-operation and Security in the University of Birmingham's Department of Political Science and International Studies (POLSIS), where she holds a Birmingham Research Fellowship. Yakinthou's work focuses on transitional justice and conflict transformation, political design for conflict societies, power sharing, and the role of ethnic conflict and historical memory in society. She is actively interested in the politics of the Middle East and North Africa (MENA) and Mediterranean regions and the author of several works about these areas. Yakinthou is firmly committed to bridging the divide between academia and practice. Before her appointment at Birmingham, she worked extensively in transitional justice and conflict transformation, establishing and managing ICTJ's Cyprus Program between 2009 and 2011 and moving in 2011 to ICTJ's MENA headquarters in Beirut, where she primarily managed projects on memory and conflict in Lebanon. Yakinthou has provided policy advice for international organizations, large NGOs, and a number of governments. She is cofounder of the Bluestocking Institute for Global Peace and Justice, an Australia-based NGO fostering dialogue on issues of global importance, including peacebuilding, sustainable development, and social movements. Yakinthou received her PhD at the University of Western Australia.